Homesick Blues

**MUSIC AND
PERFORMING
ARTS** OF ASIA
AND THE PACIFIC

SERIES EDITOR: FREDERICK LAU

Homesick Blues

POLITICS, PROTEST, AND MUSICAL
STORYTELLING IN MODERN JAPAN

SCOTT W. AALGAARD

University of Hawai'i Press
Honolulu

First printed, 2023

Library of Congress Cataloging-in-Publication Data

Names: Aalgaard, Scott W., author.
Title: Homesick blues : politics, protest, and musical storytelling in
    modern Japan / Scott W. Aalgaard.
Other titles: Music and performing arts of Asia and the Pacific.
Description: Honolulu : University of Hawai'i Press, [2023] | Series: Music
    and performing arts of Asia and the Pacific | Includes bibliographical
    references and index.
Identifiers: LCCN 2023009887 (print) | LCCN 2023009888 (ebook) | ISBN
    9780824895587 (hardback) | ISBN 9780824896669 (kindle edition) | ISBN
    9780824896652 (epub) | ISBN 9780824896645 (pdf)
Subjects: LCSH: Popular music—Political aspects—Japan. | Popular
    music—Japan—History and criticism. | Narrative in music.
Classification: LCC ML3917.J3 A17 2023 (print) | LCC ML3917.J3 (ebook) |
    DDC 781.630952--dc23/eng/20230310
LC record available at https://lccn.loc.gov/2023009887
LC ebook record available at https://lccn.loc.gov/2023009888

Cover art: Strumming an acoustic guitar. Photograph by Yoshimura Teruyuki.

For Masako and Yuki, loving companions on what has been a long and occasionally arduous journey. I could not have told this story without you.

CONTENTS

ACKNOWLEDGMENTS

Book writing, it seems to me, is at once the most solitary and the most collective of tasks. I could never have told the story I tell in these pages without the guidance, support, and love of many. My parents, Al and the late Trudy Aalgaard, encouraged and supported my very early travel to Japan—without that support, none of this work would have been possible. I'm grateful to my teachers, and especially to Michael Bourdaghs, Hoyt Long, Travis Jackson, Katsuhiko Mariano Endo, Cody Poulton, Richard King, Joe Moore, and Leslie Butt, each of whom has played a pivotal role in guiding this project, in different ways. The research at the core of this book was generously supported by funding from the Social Sciences and Humanities Research Council of Canada, the Japan Foundation, and the Center for East Asian Studies at the University of Chicago, and I'm grateful to Mouri Yoshitaka and Tokyo University of the Arts for hosting me during a year of Japan-based fieldwork in 2014 and 2015. I've also benefited from the support and guidance of Cameron Penwell and the Library of Congress in tracking down a good deal of the material that I take up herein. My colleagues at Wesleyan University have been a constant source of support and inspiration, and I'm particularly grateful to Stephen Angle, Hyejoo Back, Joan Cho, Lisa Dombrowski, Mary Alice Haddad, Miyuki Hatano-Cohen, Yu-ting Huang, Masami Imai, William Johnston, Mengjun Liu, Naho Maruta, Keiji Shinohara, Ying Jia Tan, Ao Wang, and Takeshi Watanabe for sharing their wisdom, expertise, and friendship throughout this process. My students at Wesleyan have kept me on my toes, and I'm thankful for their earnest, enthusiastic engagement with this material in classroom settings as I worked to compile it into its present form. My friend and colleague Alex Murphy selflessly shared his time and expertise as a first reader and insightful critic of most of these pages; I'm grateful to him and to the subsequent anonymous readers who provided helpful suggestions and feedback on multiple versions of the manuscript.

Masako Ikeda, Gianna Marsella, and the publishing and copyediting professionals at University of Hawai‘i Press, meanwhile, have been steadfast and patient guides in the process of transforming that manuscript into what you, dear reader, now hold in your hands (or see on your screen). The true heart of this book, though, lies among the people with whom it engages. So many artists, fans, industry stakeholders and friends in Japan have played pivotal roles in the development of this project, and while they are simply too numerous to list exhaustively here, I'm particularly grateful to Takada Ren, Itokawa Yōji, Kosai Fujiko, Kobayashi Naokazu, Kitagawa Yoshio, Hirata Noriko, Sakamoto Masayoshi, Yoshimura Teruyuki, Makuta Junko and the staff of the Fukushima International Association, the International Affairs Division of the Fukushima Prefectural Government, the staff of the Nihon Amachua Kayō Renmei (Japan Amateur Popular Song Federation, NAK) and the membership of its Fukushima Branch, the leaders and membership of the Nagabuchi Tsuyoshi fan society Ougoukai, Iwamoto Taichi of the publishing company Kawade Shobo Shinsha Ltd., Nagabuchi Etsuko of Office Ren, Nagabuchi Tsuyoshi, and especially Kagawa Ryō for all they have shared and taught me over these past years. There are so many others who have had a hand—a voice—in the development of this book, and I regret not being able to thank them all here. It is these individuals, named and unnamed, to whom I owe any success that this book may enjoy. Any shortcomings that may remain in these pages are attributable to me, and me alone.

Homesick Blues

Liner Notes

O<small>N</small> August 22, 2015—as widespread public discontent over then prime minister Abe Shinzō's (1954–2022) strong-armed "reinterpretation" of Article 9 of Japan's constitution (its so-called pacifist, war-renouncing clause) continued to reverberate—more than two thousand buses from various places around Japan converged on Fumotoppara, a rugged camping area in Shizuoka Prefecture that sits at the foot of Japan's iconic Mount Fuji. Once there, they disgorged tens of thousands of music fans—myself among them—who then set off on a mile-long hike through the Shizuoka woodlands to a vast field surrounded by foot-hills, where legendary Japanese rocker Nagabuchi Tsuyoshi (b. 1956) was set to mount a massive, all-night outdoor concert for an audience of one hundred thousand. People poured in from across the country and around the world, traveling for hours and often overnight to take part in a multihour marathon of music by one of modern Japan's most insightful and acidic musical minds, an event that—as the site selected for the concert made abundantly clear—was oriented toward a critical interrogation of what it meant to live in Japan, to "be Japanese." Over a span of more than nine hours, until shortly after sunrise the following morning, Nagabuchi used his music and the contexts (historical, political, and economic, as well as geographical) of the performance itself to tell intersecting, critical stories of everyday life in modern Japan—and out of these wove a new story of how Japanese life might be conceived of, *lived,* differently.

The concert opened with Nagabuchi's 1991 rock ballad "JAPAN," a bitingly critical work composed in the wake of the first Gulf War—a "transformation[al]" (Yamaguchi 1992) moment that helped propel Japan's repositioning as a "normal" country more amenable to warfare. Its English-language opening lyrics erupted out of the summer darkness without introduction or instrumental preamble: "Oh JAPAN! Where are you going? Oh JAPAN! What are you doing?" The historical links between the Gulf War and Abe's 2015 "reinterpretation" were unmistakable, and "JAPAN" provided a fitting way to set the stage for the event: "Opening the show with that song was entirely intentional," the concert's producer told me three years later. As the night deepened, Nagabuchi went on to spin up harsh musical denunciations of contemporary politics in Japan—articulated through a blisteringly critical collaborative performance of his "*Kazoku* [Family]" (1996), which saw the artist share the stage with Zainichi Korean rapper Han'ya, Okinawan singer Maico, and hip-hop artist Yūnyūdō—and sang songs critiquing life under the U.S. nuclear umbrella ("*Ashita wo Kudasee* [Gimme a Tomorrow]," 2012), condemning nuclear power ("*Kamome* [Seagulls]," 2012), and confronting the sacrifice of Japanese lives by the state during the Pacific War ("CLOSE YOUR EYES," 2005). Musically, the entire show seemed propelled by a sense of urgency, as Nagabuchi's characteristic rock and shuffle beats carried the event through the night and toward sunrise the following morning (with occasional respite given through ballads and short breaks). Visually, too, the event was striking, even provocative: concertgoers were furnished with creatively desecrated (Welch 2000) Japanese flags emblazoned with the artist's romanized signature, for example, which they thrust toward the stage in sweaty, clenched fists as the beat rolled on; Nagabuchi's performing body itself was clothed in the red and white of the rising sun. And the whole thing unfolded, of course, beneath the looming presence of Mount Fuji. Nagabuchi growled and howled his way through the night, embodying his role as the consummate "Japanese" rock star for hours on end. But what he was really singing was one particularly powerful rendition of what this book calls the Homesick Blues. I'll explain what I mean by that later, in the section "Singing the Homesick Blues."

Students with whom I've shared video records of the Mount Fuji concert have said, memorably, that the event looked like a "fascist's dream." But while there were undoubtedly nationalists on that field, maybe even fascists, who found affirmation of their own desires in the performance regardless of the artist's intent (as "folk" singer Takada Wataru insists later in this book, "[J]ust like shit and piss, once [music's] out in the world there's not a goddamned thing you can do about it"), the story being told wasn't a simple reflection of something called "Japanese nationalism." Even as Nagabuchi's performance orbited tightly around questions of "Japan," the musical stories told at Fumotoppara afforded precious little space for sinking into an ahistorical, nationalist sort of reverie or escape. Rather, they seemed intended to do precisely the opposite, closing off all avenues of flight and propelling attendees along new paths, like bumpers on a pinball machine. By deploying his own music and lyrics in telling stories of some of the crises of everyday "Japanese" life, Nagabuchi seemed intent on rewriting stories of "Japan" itself, subjecting it to critique from within and challenging the authority of a key narrative anchor that, for better or for worse, framed and informed a great many lives in the audience. None of this was about making "Japan" great again; rather, it was about prying the concept open by bringing the fight to Japan's conceptual center (Washburn 2007), forcing it to accommodate heterogeneous, scrambled potentials and changing it from a closed-ended question to an open one.

As the concert hurtled toward its climax and a new day began to dawn over Fumotoppara—not so subtly, the event was always oriented toward the rising of the sun the following morning—Nagabuchi and his multinational band tore into "*Fuji-no-Kuni* [The Fuji Nation]" (2015), a rousing rock number with a thumping shuffle beat that was written specifically for this occasion. It's a very long work, especially in live performance (so long, in fact, that Nagabuchi's exhausted drummer came perilously close to being unable to finish it), and one that intersected with its own moments of composition and performance in a range of ways. It seemed to directly call out the aforementioned efforts at constitutional "reinterpretation" that were ongoing in this moment, for instance— "[t]here is no nation that can stand on a foundation of violence"—and referenced Japan's own "histories of war," just two among a litany of rhetorical moves too extensive to list here. Its chorus, however, is particularly revealing in terms of the story that Nagabuchi wanted to tell. It seemed to repeat almost endlessly, sometimes instrumentally and sometimes in voice, as the sun came up over Fuji's ridge, like an incantation or a chant practically willing a new vision of collectivity into being:

> O sun, rise on the peak of Japan, rise where the flag was born
> We've been born at the peak of hallowed Fuji's nation
> O sun, rise on the peak of Japan, rise where the flags now wave
> We've been born at the peak of hallowed Fuji's nation [...]

The Fuji Nation seems to have emerged in the very moment of the dawn at Fumotoppara, as the relentless telling of different Japanese stories built into a fleeting new collectivity that was fused in the literal breaking of a new day. The Fuji Nation and "Japan," that is, are not quite the same thing—or if they are, they were so for only the briefest, most transient of moments. The impermanence implied here seemed to me to be both important and intentional: the story of the "Fuji Nation" could never simply become a new stasis replacing the old one. Its association with the vanishing moment of the sunrise and the unresolved chord progression that drives the song's chorus suggested that the story must continually be retold; becoming, not Being (Deleuze and Guattari 1998), put on endless repeat. In a weighty moment toward the end of the song, after the sun had fully risen, Nagabuchi silenced his band and spoke, uncharacteristically quietly, to his audience from the stage: "The wind is blowing; the flags are fluttering. If we work hard, if we put our hearts and all of our energies together, then we might just be able to make a decent country for our kids." Then, in a way that seemed to confirm the sense that the Fuji Nation had "been born" just moments earlier and was in fact comprised of those in attendance at Fumotoppara, he called out, ecstatically: "The sun has risen on the Fuji Nation!"

Some months later, I had the opportunity to converse with Junko (a pseudonym), a nurse from Kagoshima and at that time a member of the Ougoukai, an "unofficial" Nagabuchi Tsuyoshi fan organization that I consider in greater detail on track 5 of this book. Hoping to learn what her participation in the event meant to her, what it afforded her own life after the fact (DeNora 2003, 49), I asked Junko to reflect on her experiences at Fumotoppara. She said, in part: "At first, I didn't quite know how to take it. But the activism that the artists showed at Fuji—the antinuclear commentary, the alarm over Abe Shinzō and the security treaty—became an important trigger for me to think more carefully about decision-making at the national level. We can't just leave these things to the politicians—Japan's people [kokumin] have to grapple with these issues too, and Nagabuchi's performance on that stage provided an important impetus for that. His spending so much time making his case [are dake no jikan wo kakete uttaeru] on the stage makes me want to be more involved in politics, too, and make sure that I get to elections and so on. Young people often feel like their voice wouldn't count [muda] in elections—but Nagabuchi's political commentary made me rethink that."

There are many threads linking Nagabuchi and Junko here—their shared status as "Japanese" individuals in a moment of political anxiety in that country; their eagerness to see change; their shared presence on that field in the shadow of Mount Fuji, for that matter. But I want to focus on one particular thread running beneath all this, one that links Nagabuchi's performance at the foot of Mount Fuji and Junko's engagement with it. That thread is *storytelling*. Nagabuchi mounted his all-night concert at Fumotoppara with the intent of telling critical, destabilizing stories about "Japan" from its very conceptual center, unsettling dominant narratives—Japan's security relationship with the United States and drift toward the relegitimization of armed combat, the ongoing privileging of nuclear power, the authority and desirability of capitalism itself, among others—and telling new ones, reimagining the possibilities of collectivity. Junko, for her part, took Nagabuchi's musical storytelling and spliced it into the stories that she told herself about herself as a Japanese person, in ways that were politically productive, even if they didn't translate into the street-level "protests" that are often associated with critical political engagement. To be sure, some on that field were clearly invested in using the music and the contexts of its performance to reinforce more troubling, exclusionary stories of what "Japan," to them, is all about. A group of inebriated, middle-aged male concertgoers next to me, for instance, spent the aforementioned performance of "*Kazoku*" badgering the Okinawan and Zainichi Korean performers sharing the stage with Nagabuchi, hollering at them to "go home [*kaere*]"; although this can be a standard mode of heckling, particularly at "folk" concerts (I consider folk on tracks 2 and 3), such an interpretation didn't meld well with either the rock ambiance or the tone of the agitators, suggesting something more troubling. But for the most part, the event at Fumotoppara involved telling reflective, reimaginative stories about "Japan," something that presented exciting, if ambiguous, potentials. This sort of storytelling isn't an abstract exercise: as Junko's reflections showed, it can present real implications for the unfolding of everyday life itself. Junko, in fact, had an almost algebraic formula for how the storytelling emanating from Fumotoppara could unfold and reverberate. "This music causes people to *think*," Junko insisted to me in 2015. "It ripples out. First from the stage, then to the hundred thousand in attendance, and then to the people that they are connected to. You start with yourself, and then reach out to connect with your family, and then the circles expand out until they reach all of Japan." And although Nagabuchi, like others in this book, tends to distance himself from "politics," at least in the ways the term is usually understood, this is probably precisely the sort of formula that the artist had in mind when he put the event in motion in the first place—he'd likely be pleased to know that (his) storytelling matters.

Musical Storytelling as Method

At its most basic, the driving contention of this book echoes the conviction that propelled Nagabuchi Tsuyoshi's performance at Fumotoppara and underpinned Junko's reaction to it: *storytelling matters.* For the social actors I engage herein, storytelling matters because it affords a way to navigate, sing/speak back to, and sometimes redirect normative stories of social, (geo)political, economic, and artistic life in modern Japan. For me, storytelling matters because it provides a pathway into considering and revealing ongoing world-producing potentials in modern musical practice, including political potentials of the sort that are often assumed to have peaked in the so-called protest-folk boom of Japan's late 1960s and early 1970s and vanished shortly thereafter (I'll have more to say about this on tracks 2 and 3). Now, to argue that storytelling matters is in itself not a particularly original or provocative assertion; it echoes the insistences of cultural producers working in a variety of artistic mediums. Indian novelist Arundhati Roy (2003, 112), for instance, has famously argued that "[o]ur strategy should not only be to confront empire, but to lay siege to it … [w]ith our art, our music, our literature … and our ability to tell our own stories." In Japan, writer and activist Ishimure Michiko has placed storytelling at the genesis of different possibilities for living in the world (Allen 2013), while filmmaker and animator Miyazaki Hayao has insisted that "stories have an important role to play in the formation of human beings" (Mes 2002). Storytelling, in short, isn't "just" about fiction or film or entertainment. It's not merely *descriptive,* that is, but *generative:* a world-producing practice that propels history itself, and one deeply enmeshed in social and political life. Scholars have demonstrated this in a range of ways. Literature scholars Louise Young (1998), Faye Kleeman (2003), and Michele Mason and Helen Lee (2012), for instance, have shown how storytelling became a practice that helped generate and maintain the Japanese Empire (1868–1945). The practice of History itself, according to Cumings (2020, 122), can be understood as a mode of storytelling. Scholar of soft power Joseph Nye (2009, 162–163), meanwhile, has asserted that "success [in the geopolitical arena] is the result not merely of whose army wins, but *also of whose story wins*" (emphasis mine). The examples are numerous, putting *Homesick Blues* in well-established, accomplished company. In remixing storytelling with musical practice, I hope to contribute to the discussion by sketching out the contours of a useful framework for considering some of the practices of musical engagement in modern Japan, and their provocative, ambiguous potentials—by showing one more way that storytelling matters.

On the tracks that follow, I explore how social actors—artists like Nagabuchi, listeners/fans like Junko, others—use music to conjure and relay stories of everyday life in modern Japan and to navigate and intervene in questions of what it means to live in Japan, to "be Japanese" (or not). Although I'm of course interested in the musical stories themselves and offer detailed explorations of several of those stories herein, I'm more interested—as Eagleton (2008) is with literature—in *what people do with those stories,* how and why they're told in their lived historical contexts, what the telling of them reveals about social, economic, political, and cultural life in modern Japan, and what they help afford in disparate contexts. This is a form of musicking—that is, doing things with music (Small 1998)—that I call "musical storytelling" herein. For me, this is a broad term covering a range of practices. Sometimes, "musical storytelling" means storytelling engaged in by professional artists—Nagabuchi, for example—who use their own music in ways intended to infect the world with difference, via recording or in performance. At other times, it may be engaged in by amateurs, listeners, and fans, who find in music the lexicon to conceive of, articulate, and intervene in the realities of their own everyday lives. And sometimes, musical storytelling means the appeal to and depiction of music and its performing bodies by powerful third parties, who use these portrayals as means to other, sometimes disciplinary, ends. All these forms of musical storytelling are audible in these pages—sometimes simultaneously. Broadly, though, when I say "musical storytelling," I mean the use of or reference to music (including the portrayal of musical performance and performing bodies) by social actors—artists, fans and listeners, industry stakeholders, others—in conjuring and/or generating stories about oneself and/or others and the world, and the telling of those stories to oneself or others in ways often intended to intervene in the terms and conditions of everyday life: life under (geo)political modernity, life under capitalism. Musical storytelling sometimes *reinforces* those terms but more often (and more enticingly) *rearranges* them—scrambling them, to anticipate terminology that will appear frequently hereafter—and affords the telling of creative, critical, different stories about the world.

Musical storytelling never occurs in a vacuum—it's a process that is always embedded in and informed by the world. In a sort of feedback loop (Novak 2013), storytelling always promises/threatens to flow back into that world, disturbing, recalibrating, sometimes reinforcing its epistemological structure. This implies socially and politically generative potentials to storytelling that are, by now, well established. Culture itself, according to Geertz (1973, 448), boils down to nothing more (or less) than the stories we tell ourselves about ourselves; at the end of the day, "the truth about stories is that that's all we are" (King 2003). Michael Jackson (2013), following Hannah Arendt, finds in storytelling the means of "creating a viable social world," while Francesca Polletta (2006, 12) is even more precise: "In telling the story of our becoming, as an individual, a nation, a people," she argues, "we define who we are. Narratives may be employed strategically to strengthen a collective identity, but they also may precede and make possible the development of a coherent community or collective actor." And despite maintaining a markedly more cautious stance toward its potentials, Sujatha Fernandes (2017, 4) nonetheless urges the "[reclamation] of storytelling as a craft that … seeks to transform rather than reproduce global hierarchies and structures of power[.]" Storytelling, in short, constitutes one key process by which social life and the world itself can be generated, even as the nature of that storytelling is informed and channeled by the experience of living in the world.

To insist that storytelling matters, however, is not to ascribe to it a somehow universally emancipatory essence. Storytelling is *ambiguous*—it's contingent and contested, pursued by a range of social actors with a range of interests and desires, and is certainly no "magical elixir" leading ineluctably to "resistance" and revolution (Fernandes 2017, 3). As Fernandes has pointed out, storytelling under neoliberalism has served as a vehicle for reproducing economic and political hierarchies at the expense of different ways of conceiving of the world, as the "messy and inchoate experiences of everyday life are marshaled into compact and portable narratives that can be deployed … toward instrumental ends" (2017, 13). Polletta, meanwhile, has argued that while storytelling is an important resource in social and political movements, it also carries *risks*, arising from the limited story lines and structures made available to modern storytellers and the prevailing ways that storytelling is understood in the first place: "Popular beliefs about storytelling—about how authoritative it is, when it is appropriate, and how it is properly responded to—may curb the impact of otherwise compelling stories" (2006, 4). And sometimes, storytelling is quite plainly wielded as a blunt instrument for molding and maintaining specific geo-political and economic structures of power (I open the book with an exploration of just such a case, in fact). To explore storytelling, in sum, is often to confront what I call *storytelling regimes*—dominant, normatizing modes of storytelling that, even when not necessarily explicitly deployed to bolster received forms of power, still constitute "[s]pecifically institutional conventions of narration [that] operate alongside cultural conventions of emplotment to limit the kinds of stories that ha[ve] clout" (2006, 16). While it's clearly no preordained path-way to liberation, though, the caution urged by scholars like Fernandes and Polletta, along with the power of storytelling regimes themselves, actually helps elucidate storytelling's real-world stakes and implications. Storytelling matters, in other words, because it presents the possibility not merely of describing or narrating worlds, but of *producing* them—for better or for worse, and in a range of different ways.

Framing this book in terms of musical storytelling implies an intersection, a commonality between two practices—storytelling on the one hand, and musicking on the other. For me, this commonality is revealed in world-producing processes of *doing*. Scholars of storytelling maintain that "people do things with stories. They entertain and persuade, build social bonds and break them, make sense of their worlds, and, in the process, create those worlds" (Polletta 2006, 14). What is important is not so much "the story itself" as a purported reflection of an allegedly stable reality, but rather how the act of conjuring and telling that story intervenes in those contexts, and the "creat[ion of] worlds" that this affords, even when creating worlds simply means generating conditions within which previously authoritative sense-making terms and conditions of everyday life no longer make much sense. Scholars of musical practice and its stakes make similar assertions. It is a key tenet of ethnomusicology, for instance, that people "do things" with music (Small 1998; DeNora 2000; DeNora 2003; Jackson 2012; Wade 2014). Just as scholars of storytelling urge us to move beyond the story as a self-enclosed semiotic entity and consider the significance and stakes of conjuring and telling those stories in lived situations and con-texts, so, too, do ethnomusicologists insist that semiotic and textual analysis alone is not sufficient to grasp the range of meanings, significances, and poten-tial impacts that music may have. To do this productively, it's necessary to move beyond considerations of text and structure (as important as these also are) and explore the ways that music is actually put to use by social actors. Taken as one resource that is made use of in everyday life, music, like storytelling, can be appealed to in ways that afford extra-musical world making by orienting minds and bodies in the world: "Music can, in other words, be invoked as an ally for a variety of world-making activities; it is a workspace for semiotic activity, a resource for doing, being, and naming the aspects of social reality, including the realities of subjectivity and the self" (DeNora 2003, 39–40). What is key here is the "specific act of engagement with music [...] whether being made/ heard live or on record or imagined" (DeNora 2003, 49)—the doing with music, music's use in everyday contexts. As DeNora makes clear in her explication of the "music event," this engagement is a *process,* one that occurs across specific moments and contexts against the backdrop of preexisting conditions. What is of particular significance is the *outcome* of this process—what, if anything, engagement with the music in the contexts within which that engagement unfolded served to afford. And as is the case with storytelling, one of the things that engagement with music may help to afford is the production of social, cul-tural, and political life itself.

If we accept the premise that engagement with music affords the production of extra-musical worlds, then remixing musicking with storytelling can be helpful in clarifying one process by which this occurs—a process that may even be augmented by virtue of remixing one world-producing practice with another. Music, put simply, can be put to use in different ways by different actors in telling world-producing stories—a process that can generate outcomes worthy of our attention, "contribut[ing] to changing felt potentials for what the world can be" (Stirr 2017, 240). In a way that resonates with the "music event," musical storytelling unfolds in specific situations and against specific contexts and backdrops. It's informed by those contexts at the same time as it ultimately flows back into them, in ways that may afford specific outcomes. We might recall here how Nagabuchi Tsuyoshi used his own music to spin up critical sto-ries of everyday life in modern Japan at the foot of Mount Fuji in 2015, going so far as to practically incant a new collectivity into being at the event's climax—and how this went on to inform Junko's stance on the world. But one does not have to be a rock star, or a folk singer, or an *enka* crooner for this sort of musick-ing to be significant. Wade (2009) insists that we expand the category of "musi-cian" to include anyone who uses music, making it meaningful in the contexts of their own lives—and while I don't go quite that far in this book, I do put "musical storytelling" in the hands of a range of subjects and social actors, not just practicing, professional artists. These actors include folk singers and their crews, karaoke enthusiasts and industry stakeholders, rock stars and fans, reluctant idols and journalists, and even the U.S. military itself. To the extent that each of these actors uses music in "world-producing" ways, they are musi-cal storytellers par excellence. The most creatively critical among them—those who use musical storytelling to conjure and relay destabilizing or reimaginitive stories of everyday "Japanese" life—are those I understand as the singers of the Homesick Blues.

Singing the Homesick Blues

Like Nagabuchi Tsuyoshi and Junko, many of the singers of the Homesick Blues introduced in these pages engage closely with the idea of "Japan," in a range of different ways. In several cases, "Japan" is a locus of desire, what they're "homesick" for in the first place—even though they may never have left. But in this book, the idea of "homesickness" is deceptively tricky. As was the case at Fumotoppara (for the most part, anyway), singing the Homesick Blues does not mean indulging in restorative nostalgia (Boym 2001, 41–48) for a reified national Thing (Žižek and Herscher 1997, 64), resurrecting or returning to a past, pure, and usually imaginary "home" that has purportedly been lost—far from it. What the singers of the Homesick Blues are "homesick" for is what, in their eyes, "Japan" *can be,* not what it may have been in the past. Like Svetlana Boym's modern nostalgics, many of these individuals are "homesick" and sick of home, all at once—an ambiguous and potentially alarming state of affairs, to be sure. But just as storytelling is not necessarily emancipatory, being both "homesick" and sick of home does not necessarily need to be reactionary, either. Indeed, the tension that attends this duality—being homesick and sick of home; being dissatisfied with where one is at and striving to find something better—allows musical storytelling about "Japan" and everyday life there to unfold in reflective, often provocative ways. It's not *returning* to anything; rather, it's seeking out that which may not yet exist, even as it may go by the same name.

Again, what I'm describing here is tricky, even seemingly contradictory. How can musical storytellers like Nagabuchi, for example, persist in such a dogged adherence to notions of "Japan," yet simultaneously want to tell its stories so differently? Scholarly insight into storytelling is again helpful here. Jackson argues that storytelling is a key means by which we make sense of the world we inhabit. This sense making comes from "sharing our experiences with others in a form that they can relate or respond to, thereby reaffirming and consolidating our sense of belonging to a family, a circle of friends, a community or even a nation"—sharing stories of what it means to live in Japan, to "be Japanese," with others whose lives may be organized around the same narrative terms, and affirming "Japanese" collectivity in the process (Jackson 2013, 16–17). At the same time, however, "we also tell stories as a way of *transforming* our sense of who we are, recovering a sense of ourselves as actors and agents in the face of experiences that make us feel insignificant, unrecognized, or powerless"

(Jackson 2013, 17). What may seem here to be self-contradictory possibilities intertwine in this book in complex ways. As social actors who are always already embedded in a social ordering that, for better or for worse, orbits around the concept of "Japan"—"Japan is all [we] know," insists one of the Nagabuchi fans I'll introduce on track 5—the singers of the Homesick Blues are always engaged in a push and pull with the disparate material, geopolitical, historical realities of an everyday Japanese existence. "Japan," that is, is a key mechanism by which these social actors make sense of the world. But this can in no way be reduced to a simplistic dichotomy of submersion in and acquiescence to the national Thing on the one hand, or oppositional protest—actually an internal negation, as I'll explain in the next section—on the other. Rather, the singers of the Homesick Blues tend to reappropriate and scramble some of the conceptual terms by which everyday Japanese life is organized and narrated, telling the story of "Japan" very differently. Massey makes the crucial point that "there's the need to face up to—rather than simply deny—people's need for attachment of some sort, whether through place or anything else. ... The question is how to hold on to that notion of geographical difference, of uniqueness, even of rootedness if people want that, without it being reactionary" (1994, 151–152). Attending to musical storytelling—thinking about how different social actors sing the Homesick Blues—provides insight into considering how those actors themselves navigate this tricky ground, without necessarily becoming trapped by the rise of populism and the allure of the alt-right. Now, as I pointed out earlier, it's important not to idealize storytelling—its ambiguities derive from the desires of the everyday social actors who engage in it, and those desires can involve the freezing of the terms and conditions of social life according to nationalized or racialized terms, out of a desire to carve out a sense of stability and order amid turbulent conditions of everyday life under capitalist modernity. But as Jackson makes clear, storytelling can also simultaneously serve to *break down* order and set the stage for conceiving of collectivity anew. This is a sort of storytelling that "provides an opportunity for people to engage in a revision of the membership of their associations of life, affording an opening for the reconstruction of their identity" (Jackson 2013, 26).

The contingent, the contextual, and the situational are again important here—as is the playful. Jackson (2013, 14) urges a pivoting away from the *episteme*—reflections of knowledge, systems of understanding, the "story" as it stands alone—and toward the *techne,* the making and the doing that is context dependent and reminiscent of what de Certeau (1984, xx) calls "tactics." Exploring the stakes of storytelling as techne means attending to how and why stories are told in the contexts of social, political, economic, geopolitical, and material life—and for this reason, the book spends a great deal of time in ethnographic analysis, considering the storytelling tactics and strategies deployed by different actors in specific situations. Although buttressed by relevant scholarship throughout, the book's ultimate aim is to render the singers of the Homesick Blues philosophers in their own right, "explor[ing], on a case-by-case basis, what consequences follow from any behavior, and what effects our actions have upon our lives and the lives of others" (Jackson 2013, 21). And as I'll show on the tracks of this book, following these social actors across different situations as they make music meaningful in the contexts of their own lives (DeNora 2003, 39–40) and exploring "their strategies—intellectual and practical, magical and imaginative, affective and objective—for making their lives viable and fulfilling" (Jackson 2013, 21–22) can reveal a great deal about how they understand and deploy notions of politics, protest, and even "Japan" itself. "Japan" doesn't necessarily feature prominently or explicitly in all the instances of musical storytelling that I explore in these pages—but where it does, it's important to approach it on the storyteller's terms. To the extent that the "nation" is an imagined community (Anderson 1983), it can be imagined by philosophers of the everyday in contested, conflicting, contingent, and eminently *playful* ways. Musical storytelling is one of the processes by which this generative "imagining" occurs.

Storytelling as Politics, Politics as Storytelling

Insomuch as it helps to orient minds and bodies in the world, intervening in or reinforcing the normative terms by which the world is ordered and arranged, musical storytelling—like any production of knowledge—is a fundamentally *political* practice. Garon (1998, 117–118), citing Baker, argues that "'politics' [can be defined] in a relatively broad sense to include any action, formal or informal, taken to affect the course of behavior of government or the community," and as I'll show in different ways on the tracks that follow, the (re-)orienting of bodies and minds—one's own, others'—in ways that can impact their positioning and intentionality within the sense-making structures of social, cultural, political, and economic life is precisely what's at stake in musical storytelling. In that sense, this is a book about politics—but not about politics as we might imagine it. It's about the ways that social actors—fans, artists, others—tell stories about themselves (and others) to themselves (and others) in contexts of *everydayness,* understood here as the varied experiences of day-to-day life under conditions of capitalist modernity (Harootunian 2000a) and how that storytelling involves the conjuring and articulation of specific visions for living in the world. While the actors in this book do not necessarily understand themselves as "political" in terms of marches, placards, and slogans—indeed, at least one artist explicitly rejects this vision of politics in order to rescue what he sees as the political potentialities of his art—they are political nonetheless in that they are busily rearranging, and in some cases outright scrambling, the ways in which stories of everyday life in modern and contemporary Japan are conjured, told, and navigated. Attending to the Homesick Blues, that is, affords opportunities to reconsider some of the ways in which we've come to think about protest and politics in modern Japan to be sure, but—I hope—elsewhere as well.

The generally accepted story of critical political engagement in Japan has "protest" fading out in the early 1970s, after more than a decade of vociferous and often confrontational street-level dissent involving a wide spectrum of voices, from students to farmers to singer-songwriters. These turbulent years, of course, have their own history. In the aftermath of the Pacific War, and particularly after the Reverse Course (so named for the ways that initially progressive Occupation policies were reversed in the interest of fostering a conservative, pro-U.S. nation-state amid the perceived threat of communism in the late 1940s), Japan's story was recalibrated—by both Japanese stakeholders and American ones—to establish Japan as an ally and "friend" of the United States and a junior partner in a developmental global order. At the same time, Japanese history was itself subject to a rewiring, as Imperial links to Asia were erased and a new, closed-circuited story began to be told, one that established Japan as always already capitalist with "cultural" specificities and joined at the hip—wedded, sometimes literally, as I'll discuss on track 1—to the United States, simply marching toward the moment at which its own preordained economic "modernization" would be fulfilled. All this involved a limiting of possible story lines, a circumscription pursued, in part, in an attempt to seal Japan off and insulate it from the sort of radical rewriting whose potential alarmed U.S. and Japanese power brokers alike (Matsuda 2007, 54). This postwar reordering of a new Cold War world involved explicit and ongoing Japanese support of American geopolitical and economic prerogatives, the establishment and maintenance of U.S. military installations on Japanese soil, and perceived impingements on Japanese sovereignty. Combined with a rapid, disorienting swing toward urbanization and consumerism, all this bred anxiety, unease, and counterclaims on what "Japan" was or should be. The resulting tension erupted into widespread oppositional protest in Japan in the 1950s and 1960s, with the massive anti-AMPO (U.S.-Japan Security Treaty) uprisings of 1960 and the student movements of around 1968 constituting particularly visible manifestations thereof (Kapur 2018). Put simply, Japan's story wasn't yet understood as settled in the late 1950s and 1960s; this was a moment when claims to different prerogatives and priorities still played out in the streets and on university campuses around the country. When we think of critical political practice in modern Japan, these are often the moments that come to mind and that are celebrated—but that, in hindsight, are also mourned, as moments at which change was almost at hand but was allowed to slip away.

This sort of noisy, street-level political engagement did in fact recede in the early to mid-1970s. Numerous political and geopolitical phenomena, both domestic and regional/global, help account for this. The AMPO treaty, which had been a lightning rod for vigorous nationwide protest in 1960, renewed automatically and without debate in 1970; critical agitation against it never really dropped into gear the way it had a decade earlier. U.S.-occupied Okinawa reverted to Japanese political control in 1972, removing a hot-button issue that had often helped galvanize protest, while U.S. combat operations in Vietnam began to wind down around the same time. The student movement—already bogged down in what Oguma (2015) calls an "incomprehensible morass" of self-negation (*jiko hitei*) and the abstract rejection of "Japanese" subjectivity—lost most of its remaining public support after the 1972 Asama-Sansō incident, the violent siege of a mountain lodge in Nagano Prefecture that followed a deadly factional purge by young United Red Army members; both events involved loss of life, inviting perceptions of student action (and "protest" in general) as radicalized and violent. The state, meanwhile, worked to defuse critical energies by intervening in issues that had been important to protesters—pollution, for example—promising to resolve them through its own intercession and legislation.

Occurring in tandem with these more straightforwardly "political" developments, though—and particularly important for my discussion in this book—was the purported settling of the terms and conditions of everyday life in Japan that also occurred around 1970. In his seminal essay, H. D. Harootunian describes how "America's Japan"—meant to describe a Japan firmly embedded in a U.S.-led story of liberal rehabilitation, modernization, and capitalist development in earlier postwar moments—became "Japan's Japan" around 1970, once it became clear that "the goals of [postwar] modernization had been reached, income-doubling secured, and high economic growth realized" (Harootunian 1993, 215), and many Japanese individuals came to believe that they had entered the middle class (Nagahara 2017, 5). Japan's story, under this formulation, finally did become a closed and circular one—a storytelling regime par excellence—as cultural endowment was yoked into service to explain the fulfillment of Japanese capitalism, which in turn was cited as the predestined endpoint of Japanese "culture," and so on. In these general contexts, storytelling of the sort that could challenge the terms and conditions of everyday Japanese life was understood, with one or two notable exceptions, to have sputtered and stalled (Harootunian 2006, 116–119). For political scientists like Chiavacci and Obinger, the mid-1970s marked the start of a long dry spell, a multidecade moment of "invisibility" (2018, 1) in critical political engagement that would only really come to an end with the crises of March 11, 2011 (3.11), and the antinuclear (later anti-state and anti-rearmament) protests that reemerged in its wake (Manabe 2015).

But if critical political engagement after 1970 or so became largely "invisible," it certainly wasn't rendered inaudible. Far from forcing the story to an end, the purported fulfillment of capitalism and calcification of "Japan's Japan" around this moment and beyond actually became key factors sparking ongoing critical engagements with the terms and conditions of everyday Japanese life. The forms this engagement took, though, didn't always fit well into narratives that define protest and critique according to largely oppositional terms. The Homesick Blues, in other words, aren't exactly "protest songs." Rather than explicitly *opposing* Japanese social and political phenomena, the figures I consider herein often worked to force open the very "Japanese" stories that now seemed settled and beyond reproach, undermining their sense-making mechanisms, *scrambling* them—Nagabuchi's project at Fumotoppara, for instance. This doesn't render these voices apolitical—it just makes them political differently. Instead of outright opposition, critical musical storytelling for these figures means intervening in the various terms and conditions of everyday life, hijacking and redirecting the narrative in provocative, reimaginative ways. By considering such musical storytelling across a historical arc that includes but also transcends the celebrated moment of the late sixties and early seventies, and lingering in the very desert of "invisibility" in which critical political engagement was understood mostly to have fallen silent, my hope is that this book helps complicate how we, too, think about politics and "protest," about musicking and storytelling, and about cultural production and its possibilities in Japan writ large, especially after 1970 or so.

"Oppositional" politics and "protest" as they're commonly understood present a rather peculiar problem: in order for "oppositional protest" to be legible, it must simultaneously posit an entity that it can reject and whose authority is acknowledged and affirmed in the process of its negation (there is something here of Derrida's [1976] well-known critique of binary oppositions). This is what I, following Ivy and Žižek, call the "internal negation" (Ivy 2009, x) herein— what appears to be countercultural is not always the radical, reimaginative solution that it may seem to be, instead constituting the flip side of a coin that paradoxically helps cement the legitimacy of its target/object. Put more clearly in the terms of this book, it can be difficult for oppositional politics to tell new stories—such politics rely on existing stories to make sense, lending them a certain credence in the process. None of this is to dismiss or deny the legitimacy of oppositional protest—far from it. But it is to encourage a critical assessment of some of the ways in which it works and to insist that there are other modes of critical political engagement deserving of our attention. Storytelling—musical storytelling, in this book—offers a sort of third way beyond the linked binaries of protest and counterprotest, negation and affirmation. It affords a scrambling, not negating, of the stories that have been told about social, economic, and political life and the telling of new ones, often from the very seat of their purported (symbolic—like Mount Fuji—or literal) authority.

Musical storytelling isn't merely a precursor to politics (Polletta 2006, 6–7): it *is* politics. Indeed, it's a key contention of *Homesick Blues* that the now commonsensical assertion that critical political engagement in Japan withered and died around 1970, only to magically reemerge in the wake of the triple crises of 3.11, can be challenged by attending to some of the disparate praxes of musical storytelling that occurred across these moments—provided we can follow the figures engaged by this book and think about things like "politics" and "protest" in less formulaic, more expansive ways. That said, though, none of the musical storytellers whose voices I amplify herein necessarily have formulaic political ends in mind—pathways to revolution. What they do offer is a challenge to normative modes of storytelling, variously conceived—the powerful promise that stories can still be told differently, despite the purported settling of everyday life and the attendant demise of critical engagement in Japan after 1970 or so. The social actors I introduce in this book have valuable things to teach us—as storytellers ourselves, as scholars of Japan and East Asia, as researchers committed to the study of music, literature, and more—about political praxis, "protest," Japanese cultural production, and foregrounding the realities of everyday life in challenging stories of political and economic existence that seem to brook no claims of difference, only (internal) negation. These lessons are by no means applicable to Japan alone, as if that place were somehow removed, cut off from the flows of global history that inform everyday life practically everywhere. My hope is that readers of this book will find themselves inspired, to be sure, but also *rattled* by these voices—that we'll be willing to learn from them, to bring their insights "home" (Harootunian 2000a, 28) in ways that might trouble us, and spur us to think about how their tactics and philosophies might be redeployed in the contexts of our own modern everyday lives. Put slightly differently, and with apologies to Clifford Geertz, I hope that these voices will leak into and undermine some of the normative stories that we tell ourselves about ourselves, and about the world, that they will challenge our own assumptions concerning the nature of politics, protest, nations and nationalisms, and so on. I hope that readers will come away from this book better informed about Japanese popular music, even entertained—that they'll be inspired to seek these voices out, online or elsewhere, and hear them for themselves. But I also hope that they'll walk away inspired to think more expansively about musicking and storytelling, about different modes of politics and "protest," about how critical intervention in and the recalibration of everyday life become possible through musical storytelling—its perils and its promises.

Before you drop the needle on the record, dear reader, a caveat. All the musical storytellers I introduce in these pages are human beings and flawed individuals, in disparate and unique ways (aren't we all?). If I laud these figures and their work in these pages, I do so because I want to celebrate their contributions to musical storytelling and encourage a charitable (but still critical and thorough) assessment of those contributions, not because I consider them perfect or worthy of emplacement on a pedestal. My own position is tricky, too—as I amplify the voices that I've chosen to highlight in this book, positioning them as deserving of sustained critical and scholarly attention, I become a storyteller myself, relaying the interventions of others in ways that are constrained by considerations of length and theme, by my shortcomings as a researcher, perhaps even by my own unintentional biases. The intermeshing of the story and the storytellers—particularly when intermediated by yet another voice (my own)—is always messy and always imperfect; it's constantly open to critique and reimagination, to second-guessing and alternative interpretation. I hope, though, that I can beg the reader's patience and indulgence, that she'll forgive me for zeroing in on a limited selection of stories and limited aspects of these storytellers' lives and critiques at the expense of others. The only excuse I can offer is that the choices I make herein are all made in the interest of bringing these disparate voices to light in a monograph that doesn't spiral into unwieldy, unreadable length. A full-length monograph could probably be written about each of the figures I introduce herein; until that is done, though, the incomplete, even lopsided symphony that I compose in these pages will have to suffice.

Track List

Each track of *Homesick Blues* considers a different social actor or actors and explores the sorts of musical storytelling each pursues in different lived social, political, historical, and economic contexts. Taken together, I hope these voices gel into a sort of *concept album*—this is why I've chosen to call the components of the book tracks, not chapters. The book takes individual social actors as its main focus but does not limit itself to such figures—indeed, I open the book by considering the "storytelling" pursued by an exceptionally powerful institution and then gradually expand my focus as I incorporate the voices of individual musicians, industry insiders and stakeholders, amateur practitioners, and fans and listeners. On track 1, I consider a key geopolitical relationship that informs and underpins—in different ways—much of the musical storytelling that *Homesick Blues* goes on to explore: the U.S.-Japan security alliance. Rewinding to the end of the Occupation (1945–1952), I explore how music was appealed to by the U.S. military and its journalistic organs in telling stories of U.S.-Japan "friendship." Specifically, I show how the American military publication *Stars and Stripes* told stories of jazz singers like Peggy Hayama and Eri Chiemi in the 1950s in ways that could "teach" serviceman readers to conceive of the Japanese as friends and allies (especially in the context of the Cold War), and of themselves as "teachers," and go on to demonstrate how music was used strategically by U.S. forces in Japan to defuse critique and crisis later in the postwar period, particularly in the aftermath of the horrific rape of a twelve-year-old schoolgirl on Okinawa in 1995. I fade out by introducing "girls rock" royalty Princess Princess, showing how the band flipped the script on the normative story of U.S.-Japan "friendship" via a provocative performance that was held on the grounds of an American military installation in Yokohama in 1988.

On track 2, I take up the work of "protest folk" icon Takada Wataru (1949–2005) and consider how he developed a praxis of musical storytelling that interrogated everyday life—what the artist himself called "everydayness" (*nichijō*)—rather than relying on the oppositional critiques that tended to define his moment. I open the track by visiting an awkward conversation between Takada and well-known, critically minded journalist Chikushi Tetsuya (1935–2008) that took place in 2004 and propose teasing a more nuanced understanding of Takada's own critical project out of the dissonance that marred their encounter. Offering close readings of the artist's 1969 release of "*Akirame-bushi* [The Give-Up Ditty]" and his 1971 album *Goaisatsu* [Greetings], this track remixes Takada's voice with philosophical insights from Tosaka Jun, analyses of the LP record as medium, literary theory, and more as it reveals how Takada worked to establish new modes of critical storytelling that could not be reduced to what he calls "wishy-washy" forms of protest.

Track 3 explores the work of influential singer-songwriter (and Takada protégé) Kagawa Ryō (1947–2016). Kagawa is today remembered as a central figure in the late 1960s–early 1970s Kansai Folk movement, but he'd claim throughout his career to detest "folk," despite being indelibly associated with it. Relying on close readings of Kagawa's lyrical work and my own interactions and interviews with the artist shortly before his death in 2017, this track unpacks this apparent paradox, showing how Kagawa's musical storytelling retained its relevancy beyond the purported demise of "political" folk in the mid-1970s by reaching beyond explicitly oppositional politics and imagining something else, which the artist called "Japan's one more time." This involved, in part, a creative undoing of some of the terms and conditions by which Japan as nation-state was made to make sense in the first place—including, notably, gendered imaginings of authentic "Japanese" being, which the artist scrambles in his signature 1971 hit "*Kyōkun I* [Lesson I]." On this track I also begin to transition away from an exclusive focus on established bands and individual artists (as well as powerful bodies like the U.S. military), as I start to incorporate the voices of crews, colleagues, and other Kagawa Ryō insiders.

On track 4, I take up *enka,* a subset of modern Japanese popular music that is often ascribed the status of constituting the musical "heart and soul" of Japan. Continuing my pivot toward considerations of the uses of music and musical storytelling among everyday social actors, I travel to a major *enka* karaoke competition in Tokyo and to a local branch of a national *enka* appreciation society in 2010 to think about the ways that different people—individual karaoke contest entrants, judges and industry stakeholders, amateur aficionados enmeshed in precarious conditions of everyday life—make use of the music in telling their own stories and navigating the world. I show how *enka* and its uses, and the "Japan" that the music cites, are unstable and fundamentally contested and argue that "Japan" in *enka* (to the extent that it plays any role at all) can only be revealed a posteriori, through a consideration of the different desires that practitioners invest in the music in the contexts of their own everyday lives.

And finally, on track 5, I come full circle to return to the work of rock superstar Nagabuchi Tsuyoshi, with whom I opened these liner notes. Nagabuchi debuted in 1978 as a "folk"-inspired singer-songwriter, but his work quickly took on a much harder edge. From around the end of the 1980s—generally regarded as Nagabuchi's artistic heyday, and, not coincidentally, the apical moment of Japan's white-hot bubble economy—Nagabuchi embarked on vigorous interrogations of value, the nature of "Japan," and the nature and possibilities of collectivity itself. Relying on textual analysis, event participation and observation, and fieldwork in the artist's hometown of Kagoshima, I explore how Nagabuchi navigates thorny questions of locality and nationality as he both critiques "Japan" and invests it with new possibilities. As I prepare to close the track and the book, I shift the focus away from Nagabuchi himself and toward a select group of the artist's fans, with whom I spent considerable time starting in 2014. In this closing section, I consider some of the meanings these individuals take from the artist's work, and how the music becomes an important resource for them to understand, navigate, and tell critical stories of the terms and conditions of their own everyday lives.

There's one more "track" to attend to before I can move on from these introductory notes—the one from which I've appropriated the title of the book itself. "Homesick Blues" comes not from Dylan's "Subterranean Homesick Blues" but from a 1976 song by the aforementioned Kagawa Ryō. I've tapped Kagawa's "Homesick Blues" for my title in part simply to pay homage to a friend whom I was extraordinarily privileged to get to know in the final years of his life, before leukemia silenced his creative voice prematurely. But the song is also helpful in beginning to conceive conceptually and theoretically of some of the work that

I want to do in this book. It tells the story of a series of confrontations between Kagawa and random individuals over a long, nightmarish day in Tokyo. The song opens on a packed train, where the artist is accosted by a middle-aged man who grabs Kagawa by his long hair and accuses him of being a "spy" profiting from "illegal strikes." Kagawa jumps off at the next stop and takes shelter in a station bathroom, where he crosses paths with a drunk who declares him an "outsider" (*yosomono*) who is disrespectful of "democracy." Out on the street, he's stopped by a patriotic cop ("Sing *Kimigayo* [the national anthem]!" the cop barks), and then by a salesman with "a beard like Castro" who wants to teach him about Marx and Lenin, but who insists that happiness comes from encountering "Mister Donuts and McDonald's." The song clocks in at a whopping seven minutes and thirty-six seconds in length and is comprised of dueling musical styles: Kagawa sings of his own attempts to navigate the city in a subdued walking-blues style, which is repeatedly derailed by a loud, aggressive shuffle whenever he finds himself accosted. Everywhere Kagawa turns there's a new confrontation waiting, another story eager to swallow him up and define him according to terms that are somehow both unfamiliar and structural components of a broader story of everyday "Japanese" life in 1976. Bewildered and "homesick," he flees from each encounter and is finally found hiding and weeping in an alleyway by a "great rock singer," who promises to save him, but "first of all, you've got to decide if you're on the Left or the Right." Kagawa is skeptical of the rocker too—"Is all that Americanization really good for your body?"—and runs away again, eventually ending up back at the train station where it all started. It seems that he'll forever be hemmed in by closed-circuited storytelling, condemned to ricochet between established possibilities that are both "home" and very much not.

In the song's final moments, though, Kagawa's storytelling takes a twist. Back at the station and desperate to escape, he hears the stationmaster call out the names of possible destinations down different lines—"Kōenji, Kichijōji." "Must be temples or something," Kagawa mutters, referencing the -*ji* suffixes in these nouns. But of course, these are stations around Tokyo, dots along possible lines of flight that are playfully misrecognized as the song's walking blues fade out without establishing where Kagawa will go from here, or where "home" is in the first place. There's something important, I think, in Kagawa's tactical misrecognition of possible destinations, a suggestion that the Homesick Blues can be remedied not by going back, but by (mis)using some of the structures available (rail lines and station names in this case; recall here what Nagabuchi did with questions of "Japan" and the rising sun at Fumotoppara) to intervene in the sense-making stories of everyday life and imagine them differently, producing new worlds of possibility. The question of where Kagawa ultimately goes is never answered—it's left open. But perhaps that's precisely the point. This open-ended reimagining is a tactic deployed by many of the musical storytellers I introduce in this book—even as others, occasionally, use their own storytelling to discipline those very possibilities and keep them on more conventional frequencies. In all instances, though—critical and disciplinary—musical storytelling is deployed to world-producing ends. For better or for worse, that's what it means to sing the Homesick Blues.

"Friendship Through Music"

MUSICAL STORYTELLING AND
THE U.S.-JAPAN ALLIANCE

In 2021, as my writing of this book was getting underway in earnest, former U.S. deputy assistant secretary of defense for East Asia (2019–2021) Heino Klinck sat down with the American think tank National Bureau of Asian Research to share his thoughts on U.S.-Japan "friendship." Specifically, Klinck was reflecting on the U.S. response to the Great East Japan Earthquake of March 11, 2011, and its aftermath—a tragedy now generally referred to as 3.11— and the resonances of that response in geopolitical policy a decade later. This response, dubbed Operation Tomodachi, or Operation Friend, involved the deployment of a dizzying array of American military hardware—ships and helicopters, C-130 heavy transport aircraft and salvage units—and more than twenty-four thousand service personnel to northeastern Japan, where these assets took part in a wide-ranging rescue and recovery mission in the wake of the disaster. It was a mission that resulted in its own share of tragedy among those who took part: hundreds of sailors from the USS *Ronald Reagan,* for example, sued the Tokyo Electric Power Company in 2012 and 2017, alleging physical injury and even death resulting from their exposure to fallout from the Fukushima Dai'ichi Nuclear Power Station, placing them in a haunting sort of camaraderie with those they were there to assist (the lawsuits were subsequently thrown out). But for the most part, Operation Tomodachi is remembered by the U.S. military as a public relations success story, one afforded by the opportunity to engage in frontline humanitarian work—a visible, audible, and tangible manifestation of a binational "friendship" that had been asserted by the United States for more than seventy years and that has constituted an important touchstone of U.S. geopolitical policy since shortly after the end of the Pacific War.

In his recorded comments, Klinck insisted that

> Operation Tomodachi in particular demonstrated to Japan, and most importantly to the Japanese people, that you are an *ally.* [...] At the end of

the day, the United States martialed its forces in Japan to help the Japanese in every conceivable way. ... It was a visible symbol of our commitment to serving Japan and its people, and I think it helped a lot. Because frankly, more often than not, the only time you ever read anything about the U.S. military presence in Japan, it's usually something bad. [...] This massive operation demonstrated to the Japanese people the value of the alliance with the United States, at home. (National Bureau of Asian Research 2021)

Klinck began by talking about an American "commitment to serving the Japanese people" but quickly pivoted to what was really at stake in the operation: bolstering American geopolitical priorities. Indeed, Operation Tomodachi itself, despite its flowery moniker, was a sort of American soft-power offensive (Nye 2004), helping to quiet (for a time) critical Japanese mutterings over the actions and attitudes of U.S. forces in Japan and Okinawa, as well as popular criticism of the Japanese state's own ongoing economically and geopolitically motivated eagerness to continue hosting those forces (McCormack and Norimatsu 2012, 189–204). It was a performative reassertion of a closed-ended story that had been told and retold, in different ways, since shortly after the end of the Pacific War—a story of "friendship," alliance, and common interest; a geopolitical and strategic story masquerading as culture and sentiment. As the Cold War got underway, it was a story told with the broader aim of tucking Japan firmly under America's wing, underwriting ongoing geopolitical "cooperation" between the two countries with tales of common destiny and ensuring that Japan remained the last bastion against communism in East Asia. This is a geopolitical arrangement that has remained vital since the alleged end of the Cold War as well; to this day, Japan remains a key site for the projection of U.S. regional and global power, and as McCormack and Norimatsu (2012) and Dower (2017) point out, Japan is increasingly being looked to as executor of U.S.-led geopolitical and security priorities in Asia. Indeed, the 2015 "reinterpretation" of Japan's constitution that sought to authorize a more forward-facing military stance under the conceptual umbrella of "collective self-defense"— coming to the aid of an ally (read: the United States) under attack—was itself an example of how political prerogatives can often be underwritten by schmaltzy stories of "friendship"; unease over this shift in security stance became an important context for Nagabuchi Tsuyoshi's all-night concert at the foot of Mount Fuji in August of that year (see "Liner Notes"). To speak of the discourse of "friendship" between the United States and Japan in the postwar period, in short, is to discuss an inter-statial (Inoue 2017) geopolitical and economic strategy—one that unfolds and is buttressed not only in the halls of state power, to be sure, but at the level of everyday life and cultural production as well.

In his earnest exaltations of Japanese allyship, in other words, Klinck was simultaneously referencing, buttressing, and contributing to a storytelling regime that has helped further American geopolitical and economic interests (and Japanese ones, to be sure, though I'm mostly interested in the U.S. forces in Japan [USFJ] as the key actors here) in the Pacific and beyond since shortly after the end of the war. As I'll show on this track, this is a regime that has been facilitated in part through what this book calls musical storytelling. On this opening track, then, I want to explore how social actors—most significantly the U.S. military itself and its representatives—appealed to music and its performing bodies as they worked to compose a new world order in the aftermath of the Pacific War, using it to craft and articulate stories of U.S.-Japan "friendship" that could bolster geopolitical (and economic) prerogatives over a span of more than seventy years. Doing so will assist me in establishing the importance of musical storytelling as a theoretical and methodological framework, both as a "curated," normatizing strategy (such as that pursued by USFJ and its affiliated organizations) and as a tactic that "seeks to transform rather than reproduce global hierarchies and structures of power" (Fernandes 2017, 4). But just as importantly, this early attention to musical storytelling and the U.S.-Japan alliance will allow me to reveal and establish a geopolitical bass line whose overtones are audible—sometimes faintly, sometimes resonantly—in a great deal of the musical storytelling that I go on to explore in this book.

To conceive productively of this musical storytelling, I first explore early postwar reportage appearing in the *Pacific Stars and Stripes* (hereinafter the *Stripes*), a key journalistic arm of the U.S. military in Asia and the Pacific and particularly Japan. In doing so, I reveal how music and musical performances were cited as sort of benchmarks in the recasting and renarrating of Japanese bodies—frequently women's bodies—as *allies,* as more "like us," even as the distance between Japanese others and American selves required to justify and sustain (neocolonial) leadership of the latter over the former was strategically maintained. This was storytelling directed mainly at U.S. service personnel in Japan and the Pacific—in other words, those charged with enacting American geopolitical prerogatives on the ground. After 1962 or so, music went on to be cited more broadly and explicitly by USFJ in telling stories of U.S.-Japan "friendship," as "friendship through music" became a way of "softening" the ongoing American military presence in Japan, mitigating critique of its bases in particular and papering over protest with musical performance. This was largely about winning the hearts and minds of the Japanese people themselves. Despite the powerful institutions working to facilitate it, though, this storytelling regime was never immune to critique. At the end of the track, I pivot to show how eighties "girls rock" pioneers Princess Princess challenged this narrative not so much by *negating* it as by positioning their own critical, performing bodies within it and telling a much different story of U.S.-Japan "friendship" from within the grounds of an American military installation in Yokohama in 1988.

Princess Princess's intervention into this powerful storytelling regime—their scrambling of it from within the literal confines of its own authority—will help me set the stage for thinking productively about other modes and moments of musical storytelling that follow on subsequent tracks. The story of musical storytelling and the U.S.-Japan alliance, though, is one that spans decades—and to begin telling it, I have to hit pause on Heino Klinck's recorded 2021 exaltations of U.S.-Japan "friendship" and rewind all the way back to the U.S. Occupation of Japan (1945–1952).

Reading the *Stars and Stripes:* Musical Storytelling in the Occupation and Its Aftermath

The musical storytelling that I explore here finds its roots in the midst of the Occupation, as the relationship between the United States and Japan was being recalibrated from one of rabid hostility to one of strategic "friendship," and U.S. servicemen were being encouraged to conceive of Japanese bodies (and themselves) in new terms. Reframing the erstwhile enemy as "friend" was, in part, simply a necessary condition for the implementation of the Occupation in general, especially when the Japanese had been so ruthlessly dehumanized to prosecute an utterly merciless war (Dower 1986). But starting around 1947, in the context of emerging Cold War anxieties and especially with news of completed Communist revolution in China and the Soviet Union's successful weaponization of the atom in 1949, the story shifted in important ways. The so-called Reverse Course saw progressive reforms—America's "great experiment" in the democratization of Japan, its reconstitution according to ideals that America itself was never able to achieve—rolled back in the interest of promoting a strong, conservative Japanese state that would support U.S. geopolitical and security prerogatives, and the discourse of "friendship" took on new overtones. Now being "friends" with Japan meant establishing an ironclad alliance against communism (and in the service of capitalism) in East Asia. But while the establishment of this alliance certainly entailed geopolitical and diplomatic maneuvering, it also had to be engineered one fleshly body at a time. This engineering took place, in part, in the realm of culture and cultural production.

As Matsuda (2007) has argued, positing culture as a geopolitical and ideological front line in the Occupation and Cold War helped open important avenues for transforming the Japanese enemy into an ally, and Americans into teachers/leaders of a "free world" largely modeled on American values and norms. Indeed, during the Occupation "the American government in Washington and the Supreme Commander for the Allied Powers in Tokyo attached special importance to [its] cultural dimension in order to achieve the twin objectives of democratizing Japan and *turning it into a nation friendly towards the United States*" (Matsuda 2007, 19; emphasis mine). Even prior to the conclusion of a formal peace with Japan, the State Department assembled the Dulles Peace Mission—featuring Truman's special representative John Foster Dulles and business tycoon John Rockefeller—and dispatched it to Tokyo in January 1951 for the purposes of cultivating and strengthening "long-term cultural relations" between Japan and the United States; in other words, to develop "friendship" of a kind that would serve U.S. geopolitical interests (Matsuda 2007, 96). But while diplomatic interventions were of course important, this overarching geopolitical strategy—and its attention to "culture"—unfurled in more "popular," everyday venues as well, including the *Stripes,* the key storytelling medium that I want to explore in this section. The version of musical storytelling appearing in this publication helped to facilitate U.S. geopolitical prerogatives in this moment, providing a template by which U.S. service personnel in Japan (and others) could modify their conceptions of the erstwhile Japanese enemy through its portrayals of music and its performing bodies, and telling stories of a sexualized ally who was sensuous, desirable, like "us"—yet never quite equal, and always in need of "American" mentorship and tutelage. As I'll show in the pages that follow, this was storytelling that starred two women, Japanese singing sensations Eri Chiemi and Peggy Hayama, whose performances and very bodies were tapped to frame unfurling stories of U.S.-Japan "friendship," in very different ways.

The *Stars and Stripes* was first published in 1861, as a one-page paper, by Union soldiers during the American Civil War. It saw just four printings before being discontinued but was briefly revived in February 1918, in the context of the Great War. It was resurrected again during the Second World War, appearing first in the European theater in 1942, and later in the Pacific in 1945. It is this latter incarnation of the publication—*Pacific Stars and Stripes*—that I consider herein. Being a military newspaper, the *Stripes* writ large is of course deeply embroiled in American geopolitical prerogatives. The U.S. General Accounting Office clarified the paper's mission in 1986—it includes "bring[ing] DOD personnel ... news [that] makes possible the continued intelligent exercise of the responsibilities of citizenship [and] helps their morale and readiness by dispelling rumor and keeping them in touch with aspects of life in the United States while they live in unfamiliar surroundings," and, more centrally to my interests here, "provid[ing] applicable U.S. government, DOD, command, and *local news and information, which improves individual capability for mission accomplishment and brings a sense of joint mission purpose to ... personnel operating together to carry out the U.S. defense mission overseas*" (U.S. General Accounting Office 1986, 11; emphasis mine). As Elmore has pointed out, despite its avowed adherence to American First Amendment free speech ideals (U.S. General Accounting

Office 1986, 2–3), military intervention and editorial heavy-handedness have frequently characterized operations at the paper's Pacific edition, sometimes spilling into outright conflict between military leadership and civilian staff (Elmore 2010, 308–309). In other words, rather than constituting unfettered reporting or journalism per se, *Stripes* reportage in particular can be understood as oriented toward a deliberate furthering of U.S. geopolitical goals and security objectives (Elmore 2011). But it is precisely this heavy-handedness—reflecting a desire on the part of the military to lend the *Stripes* a sort of pedagogical function that could help bolster among readers "individual capability for mission accomplishment"—that makes it a useful storytelling medium to explore herein.

In this section, I pay particular attention to a regular entertainment column that appeared in the Pacific edition of the *Stripes* in the 1950s and 1960s called "On the Town." "On the Town" was conceived in January 1953 "to keep the servicemen and women informed about what was happening in the Japanese world of entertainment." The column declared itself to have "delved deep into Japanese show business and found it to be a refreshingly youthful thing, reminiscent of our own show world a few years back" (November 30, 1954)—a showbiz manifestation of the modernization theory perspective that would characterize U.S.-Japan relations across the same moment. The column's author and entertainment editor for the *Stripes*, St. Louis–born Al Ricketts, enlisted in the army in 1952 and drifted to the paper more or less by accident, initially as a movie reviewer. His column grew into a popular source of military-authorized information on the entertainment world in Japan and the Pacific and remained so until 1968, when Ricketts left the *Stripes* to join the *Honolulu Star-Bulletin* as a columnist (he died in Honolulu the following year at the age of just forty). Although aware of "restrictions" that were placed on him at "what is essentially a serviceman's newspaper" (*Time* 1961), Ricketts was an enthusiastic supporter of U.S. geopolitical prerogatives and seemed to relish his role within a journalistic and publicity organ that was oriented toward facilitating them. He evidently had little patience for musical expression critical of the American military: folk singers, Ricketts said, "should entertain and not crusade"; he even walked out of Joan Baez's Tokyo press conference when she called the Vietnam War "unpopular." Now, Ricketts's crankiness was a matter of some renown (*Time* 1961), and he subjected all sorts of cultural figures to critical attack, from Elvis to Judy Garland (January 10, 1969)—Joan Baez, that is, was far from his only target. The political priorities revealed in his dismissal of Baez are important, though, and we need to understand his writing on the Japanese singers that I take up herein in light of them.

Scholarship on Occupation and post-Occupation music in Japan has often starred singer Misora Hibari (1937–1989), and for good reason. Emerging in the immediate postwar period as a "jazz" and boogie-woogie singer in the style of Kasagi Shizuko (1914–1985), Misora was a vocalist of astonishing talent and skill who went on to be remembered as the most "Japanese" of singers of the postwar era. She enjoys a persistent pride of place in Japan's musical imaginary even now, decades after her death (Bourdaghs 2012, 49–84). But while Misora received some attention in the *Stripes,* she was never central to the musical storytelling that writers like Ricketts pursued—it was two other "jazz" singers, contemporaries of Misora's, who seem to have captured the American imagination, particularly in the immediate post-Occupation moment (1952 or so) and beyond. These singers were Eri Chiemi (1937–1982) and Peggy Hayama (1933–2017). Both Eri and Hayama were understood as "jazz" singers and narrated/appraised as such in the *Stripes,* but they performed a diverse range of genres, from country to pop, that were held together under this term. "Jazz" in this moment, that is, wasn't necessarily just jazz; the term encompassed a range of popular musical styles understood as American/Western in origin (Bourdaghs 2012, 15)—indeed, it was this "American" derivation of the music that tended to be important in *Stripes* discussions of these women and their performances. In what follows, I'll briefly consider the careers of Eri and Hayama and explore how they—specifically, their fleshly, singing, performing bodies—were positioned and portrayed by the *Stripes* in facilitating and narrating stories of the U.S.-Japan relationship through the early years of the Cold War and in encouraging those charged with carrying out American strategic prerogatives on the ground—American servicemen—to see Japanese bodies (and themselves) in terms amenable to its pursuit. What was at stake here was encouraging American service personnel and others to see the Japanese as "friends" and allies, and themselves as proper leaders/teachers of the "free world." It was this sort of musical storytelling that characterized Ricketts's column (along with other writing) in the *Stripes,* as Eri and Hayama became unwitting stars on an unfurling soundtrack propelling American stories of a new world order.

Eri Chiemi

Eri Chiemi was born Kubo Chiemi in what is now Taitō-ku, on the downtown side of Tokyo, in 1937. Her parents had deep musical roots—her father had been a musician and instrumental accompanist, playing piano and shamisen for *rakugo* (comedic storytelling) entertainer Yanagiya Mikimatsu (1901–1968). Her mother, meanwhile, was an actress and singer affiliated with the Yoshimoto Kōgyō entertainment conglomerate. By the end of the 1940s, though, Eri's father was unemployed and her mother was sick, prompting Eri to pursue her own showbiz career as a means of supporting her family. It was a good move:

Eri proved a sensation. Her career would see multiple hit records, dozens of film appearances (nine by 1955 alone), countless television appearances including a feature on Art Linkletter's *House Party* when the program visited Japan in 1954, a marriage to movie star Takakura Ken at age twenty-one (which prompted her brief retirement from show business in 1958; she returned only a few months later—hers was the bigger name at the time anyway), and an indelible association with the fictional character Sazae-san, whom she portrayed in the 1956 feature film of the same name and its nine sequels. She was also one of the well-known San'nin Musume (Three Young Maidens) trio of women entertainers, along with Misora Hibari and Yukimura Izumi. Although her career was wide-ranging, it was as a singer that Eri Chiemi would be most celebrated and most fondly remembered—and she got her start performing for U.S. military personnel during the Occupation and its aftermath.

In the spring of 1951, at the age of just fourteen, Eri approached one of the Japanese agencies specializing in dispatching entertainers to Occupation venues, looking for singing work. Her audition was so impressive that she was sent to an American camp the very next day. She sang the *tairiku merodī* (continental melody) hit "*Shina no Yoru* [China Nights]," a ballad originally performed by Watanabe Hamako and reprised in the homonymous 1940 film by Ri Kōran (by then newly reborn as American darling Shirley Yamaguchi), to great acclaim from the assembled GIs, who were left clamoring for more. As yet lacking much of a repertoire, Eri reportedly complied by singing "*Shina no Yoru*" again (*Sunday Mainichi,* April 25, 1954). As early as 1952, she was tapped to take part in the Occupation-backed All-Star Celebrity Show, hosted at the Ernie Pyle Theater, a Tokyo performance venue that was built in 1934 as the Tokyo Takarazuka Theater but requisitioned by U.S.-led General Headquarters (GHQ) in 1945 for the purposes of entertaining Occupation personnel. This show promised to "bring together the greatest number of Japanese and American service talent ever assembled on the stage of the Ernie Pyle" (*Stripes,* June 18, 1952) and constituted an early performative manifestation of the pivot toward collaboration, camaraderie, and friendship in the cultural world that would underwrite Cold War geopolitical prerogative in the political one. It was an auspicious beginning, and Eri became a hit on the base club circuit and beyond almost instantly, playing venues in Tokyo and in more distant places like Nagoya and Sendai. Eri Chiemi, in short, seemed to be everywhere in American-occupied Japan.

Eri's career as a professional singer, though, really took off when she recorded a cover of the 1948 country number "Tennessee Waltz," by Redd Stewart (1923–2003) and Pee Wee King (1914–2000), in 1952. According to legend, Eri was given a vinyl copy of the song—likely Patti Page's 1950 version—by a soldier at one of her performances. Enamored with it, Eri convinced King Records to let her record the song in November 1951 and released it as her debut single in January. Eri's cover—with its mix of Japanese- and English-language lyrics—proved a hit in Occupation-era Japan: the record went on to sell four hundred thousand copies, a sales record for King and a remarkable feat in a country where, according to the *Stripes*' enthusiastic assessment, "if a singer can sell 30,000 records … she is considered a ranking star" (January 30, 1955). By 1953, she was being introduced in the *Stripes* as "the Patti Page of Japan" (May 18, 1953)—a consequential characterization that I'll return to later on this track. She remained a regular at the Ernie Pyle—which continued to stage performances for U.S. personnel beyond the formal end of the Occupation in 1952—through at least 1954, and American informational organs continued to present her to listeners and readers enthusiastically: she was interviewed on FEN in February 1956, for instance—"[b]ouncy Japanese songbird Eri Chiemi pa[id] a visit to Far East Network's Iwakuni station and talk[ed] hit records" (February 16, 1956)—and was declared "Japan's Jazz Queen" by Ricketts in the *Stripes* in 1958. She was a "friend" to the Americans, an apt pupil, an erstwhile unknowable enemy now spliced into U.S. "culture" via the jazz she sang at officers' clubs and on bases. She was a musical darling of the U.S. military in Japan and a veritable regular in the pages of the *Stripes:* her name appears in the publication no less than 211 times between 1952 and 1983. But while Eri's prominence in this publication—and that of Peggy Hayama, whom I'll introduce momentarily—may have been triggered by their publicness as popular singers, in this historical moment it was thoroughly underwritten by their gendering *as women* (no male performers, for example, received anywhere near the degree of coverage that Eri, Hayama, and a few others did in this moment).

Scholars and artists alike have shown how the new inter-statial relationship between the United States and Japan that was built in the aftermath of the Pacific War was highly gendered, with America positioned in a dominant, "masculine" role and Japan placed in a submissive, "feminine" one (Igarashi 2000; Bourdaghs 2012; Hoaglund 2010). This played out in troubling ways during the Occupation and beyond, as Japanese women were positioned as fleshly incarnations of a sensuous, exotic "friend" in Asia, an available figure to be molded, enjoyed, played with, and in whom American benevolence and greatness could be reflected. Indeed, as Shibusawa (2006) points out, Japanese women in the Occupation and its aftermath were positioned as key facilitators of the newly emergent U.S.-Japan "friendship": encounters with women, narrating/telling stories about them in specific ways—as desirable, submissive, respectful, eager to learn—helped Americans to "transform … hostility into feelings of obligation and mercy toward Japan after a terrible war [and] begin to see a recently vilified enemy as a valued ally" (Shibusawa 2006, 51). The usefulness of these women in the conjuring and relaying of pedagogical stories of U.S.-Japan "friendship" and American leadership, that is, relied on their ability to be perceived as not only nonthreatening but also objectified and possessable, simultaneously familiar and exotic, thoroughly *doll-like* figures (Shibusawa 2006, 30; the figure of the "doll" is important here, and will continue to appear periodically throughout this track) who could be positioned for the pleasure and enjoyment of mostly male American personnel.

Sometimes, this positioning involved a relatively straightforward objectification and sexualization—a rendering of women like Eri and Hayama as *desirable* for the *Stripes'* serviceman readership. In September 1954, for example, "On the Town" introduced seasonal musical revues being mounted at Tokyo's Kokusai and Nichigeki Theaters—the latter featuring performances by Eri and Hayama—urging "[a]nyone who has never seen a Kokusai production … [to] make it a point to do so. Any lack of polish is usually overshadowed by the lavish settings and *takusan* girl-*sans* [many girls] scampering across the stage in every direction" (September 24, 1954). In December of the same year, the column promoted a musical ice revue titled White Christmas that "feature[d], besides *takusan* [many] girls on shiny blades, singer Peggy Hayama and others." Some months later, discussing Eri Chiemi's hugely successful two-night 1956 concert run at the Shochiku Theater in Fukuoka, Ricketts lingered over how the audience's "eyes bulged as much as the theater walls at Chiemi's tight-fitting Chinese red evening gown which practically defied description. A bolero flare at the bottom closed in tight at the knees and tapered upward to what might be called a 'low-cut strapless' at the shoulders" (January 29, 1956). In their vaguely belittling and objectifying terminology—conjuring a gaggle of young, bubbly "Oriental" women presented for consumption at the leisure of the audience, inviting a voyeuristic gaze upon the fleshly incarnation of pure sex onstage— these articles helped encourage a view of these performers (and, by extension, Japanese women more generally) as exotic, sensuous figures, to whom good-natured American paternal patience likely needed to be extended as well.

But often, the narrative positioning of Japanese (women's) bodies in a U.S.-led postwar order, and the reconstitution of those bodies as "friends" and the establishment of Americans as shepherds thereof, involved more than objectification and sexualization. Women like Eri and Hayama were also positioned by storytellers in varying degrees of proximity to an "American" ideal that was part of the "culture" that would save the free world. But as mentioned earlier, the discourse of "friendship" never involved the complete collapsing of distance between the Japanese and the Americans. In the U.S. gaze, conceiving of the Japanese as "friends" in this moment seems to have required both recognition of Japanese desire for assimilation to an "American" ideal and an intentional *distancing,* strategically keeping some Japanese at arm's length. This helped maintain a degree of difference and distinction between American selves and Japanese others that was useful in the continued justifying of U.S. leadership and authority in Japan—and this is where Eri and Hayama, who occupy oppos-ing (but complementary) points in this formula, begin to diverge. Eri was the successful assimilator, the unrivaled musical darling of U.S. forces in Japan. Her celebration in the pages of the *Stripes* seems to have been tightly bound not only to her desirability but also to her ability to successfully embody/perform (one version of) an American "us" as well—and this, in turn, was an embodi-ment that intersected with several thorny, interconnecting issues, including language, the voice, and especially race.

With the onset of the Cold War, and in light of Soviet criticism, the United States could no longer sustain—at least outwardly—the overtly racist vision of global politics that had marked its prewar (and wartime) perceptions of the world (Koshiro 1994, 322). *Stripes'* storytelling about Eri and Hayama, however, helps demonstrate that the centering of notions of race remained persistent in the 1950s, if, perhaps, more subtly so. As I pointed out earlier, the *Stripes* made a point of introducing Eri as "the Patti Page of Japan" as early as 1953. Now, Eri had had great success with her 1952 recording of "Tennessee Waltz," a song also recorded by Page, and in any event it's not uncommon (if also not helpful) for Euro-American discourse to describe artists from Japan and elsewhere accord-ing to their perceived "local" counterpart—this is something that persists even today. Given scholarly insights from Koshiro (1994), Dower (1986), and others on the persistence of racism and notions of white supremacy during the Occu-pation and its aftermath, however, it seems prudent not to dismiss Eri's forced transmutation into a (white) American performer out of hand. Transforming her into Patti Page in 1953 was a rhetorical move that could help reduce the racialized distance that had been established between Japanese bodies and "American" ones for the purpose of prosecuting a brutal, dehumanizing war. Ironically, though, overcoming the racist hatred that threatened to impede Japan's positioning as ally and last bastion against communism in East Asia apparently entailed not the actual *overcoming* of that racism but rather its reca-libration in a way that allowed/encouraged, in this storytelling, (some) Japanese to become "just like (white) us." This un-othering was deployed to narrate other Japanese singers in this moment as well, notably Kasagi Shizuko, who was "known [to the *Stripes*] as the Japanese Betty Hutton," another white performer (June 14, 1954)—and although the transformation could never *really* be com-plete (Eri's body, and Kasagi's, would of course always reveal their racialized "Japaneseness"; as I'll explain later on this track, this almost-but-not-quite incompleteness is precisely the point), what seems particularly significant here is that this conceptual re-racialization takes *white* women's bodies as its model.

Vocal expression—specifically, the articulation of English-language lyrics—was a key factor in this narrative transmutation of Eri Chiemi's Japanese body into an "American" one. In March 1954—relatively early in her career—Al

Ricketts in "On the Town" declared Eri to be a "standout," not primarily for her musicianship or her vocal ability, but because "[h]er [lyrical] diction is good" (March 2, 1954). Although she was occasionally admonished for perceived shortcomings in this regard—"[o]n that up-tempo stuff, Chiemi tends to swallow some of the words … and fluff a bit on her English," Ricketts chided in 1957, "but mostly she sounds great. There's *nothing wrong with her that can't be remedied*" (September 22, 1957; emphasis mine)—it seems that her (perceived) linguistic and expressive proximity to the Americans was a key factor keeping her in the latter's favor and in the *Stripes*' limelight. In fact, when she died in 1982, Eri Chiemi was remembered in a full-page obituary in the paper (which, incidentally, characterized her as a "Japanese Fanny Brice," yet another white performer) for her masterful ability to reproduce English-language lyrics, and was compared favorably to other Japanese singers of her moment who were seen by the Americans as insufficient, inauthentic "parrots"—merely imitators of a "real" American musical culture, not the real thing:

> When she started in the [Occupation] clubs, Chiemi had a precociously seasoned voice—although, when she first stepped onto a stage or bandstand in an organdy dress, a lot of customers groaned. Was this another one of the *no-talent parrots who sang English lyrics as if they were Sanskrit?*
> Then they watched and listened. (March 11, 1982; emphasis mine)

The musical authenticity lauded by Eri's eulogizers is entangled in language—but at the same time it *transcends* language, reaching something even more fundamental, more transmutative. This has to do, I think, with her perceived ability to traverse the racialized distance ascribed to her (and her contemporaries) by the very American commentators who lauded her performances, who celebrated her ability to reduce the distance between her own Japanese body and the purported American "real," a distance that could never be overcome by other Japanese singers dismissed as "no-talent parrots." The *Stripes* eulogizers' celebration of Eri's ability to rise above the status of "parrot" seems to have required what Lisa Barg (2000, 152), writing of Black voices and Virgil Thomson's American opera *Four Saints in Three Acts,* calls "the presumption of a white [American] vocal norm" (here again, Eri Chiemi as Patti Page, Eri Chiemi as Fanny Brice)—and Eri's perceived ability to embody that norm. For Eri, who was after all the occupant of a body racialized as "Japanese," this demanded a reconfiguration of the singer's body itself—at least at the conceptual level.

Murphy (2022) has argued that vocal expression was an important conduit affording radically recalibrated notions of bodily subjectivity in Imperial Japan, as singers like Kawabata Fumiko were able (or compelled) to occupy what Connor calls a "vocalic body," a process understood as the "projection of new ways of having or being a body, formed … out of the autonomous operations of the voice" (Connor 2000, 35–36). Eri's celebrated expressive authenticity at once afforded and was afforded by her occupation of an "American" (read, "white") "vocalic body" capable of authentic enunciation—a body that, in its genesis, seemed to provide the condition for her other, fleshly, racialized Japanese body to be shed and disavowed. If this new, somehow authentic "Americanness" is a "grain [that] is [her] body in [her] voice as it sings … [her] limb as it performs," the very materiality of her body as it speaks its (new) "mother tongue" (Barthes 1978, 182), that is, then this suggests a transmutation that has ripped Eri Chiemi out of her Japanese-speaking self, as it were, regenerating her very body as one that is sufficiently proximate (*only* proximate) to "us" to render her a valued incarnation of U.S.-Japan "friendship." But here it gets tricky. The process is never complete: when American listeners hear her and praise her diction, they are in fact hearing *two bodies*. Eri's nearness to a "white [read, "American"] vocal norm," that is, can be celebrated only if her "Japaneseness" is not allowed to fade away entirely, if it lingers as a reminder of the distance she has been able to overcome in the first place. As a result, we are confronted with a disorienting double-engendering of Eri Chiemi's vocalic body—a "Japanese" one, formed of her inclusion within a racialized musical community of "no-talent parrots who sang English lyrics as if they were Sanskrit," and an "American" one, formed out of authentic enunciation and/as proximity to a "white vocal norm" and her *escape* from that community. Each body needs the other in order to make sense, and Eri finds herself simultaneously disembodied and doubly embodied, somewhere in between. From the perspective of American musical storytellers in the *Stripes*, however, the point remains that this dis/re-embodiment begets a nearness to an American "us" via the generation of a "vocalic body" and its proximity to "white vocal norm[s]," and it is this nearness—even as (or precisely because) her Japanese body continues to lurk in the background—that renders her an ideal fleshly incarnation of U.S.-Japan "friendship."

Finally, and most abstractly, *Stripes* writers cited the question of *feeling* in positing Eri as an exemplary singer of American music and "friend" of the United States. In her performances, *Stripes* writers heard what they understood as their own musical "culture" echoing back to them, in a closed-ended sort of geopolitical call-and-response—and presented this echo to their serviceman readers. In 1954, for example, when the monthly Japanese music magazine *Swing Journal* crowned the then seventeen-year-old Eri top female vocalist in Japan, Ricketts declared that "[m]any of those in the business attribute the bouncy brunette's skyrocketing popularity to her Stateside trip last March" (March 10, 1954), while in 1955 her musicianship and performativity were described as "exceptionally good, showing the impact of her recent visit stateside [and] enough to send Doubting Thomas Americans away with a new outlook on Japanese entertainers" (August 25, 1955). Although she also sang Japanese numbers on the camp and club circuits—including Kasagi Shizuko's "Tokyo Boogie-Woogie" and Takamine Hideko's *Ginza Kankan Musume* [The Ginza Can-Can Girl]," by jazz composer Hattori Ryōichi—these were understood as "American" in style and feel: GIs reportedly loved the songs, with their swing beats and blues idioms, even singing along (Hayama and Shiozawa 2014, 159). As a result, the fact that the songs were Japanese in compositional origin didn't undermine the assertion that the absorption of "American" musical idioms—"feel"—was the key condition affording Eri's popularity and skill (the erasure of Blackness in this appropriation/"Americanization" of jazz and blues and assertion of "feeling" is an important issue that I must attend to on another occasion). But as I also suggested earlier, rather than "turning her American" outright (were this to happen, there would be no basis for inter-statial "friendship" between different—and unequal—actors in the first place), what seems to be at play here is a certain displacement of Eri's otherness and the opening of a transparent channel of perceived knowing, on the basis of shared "American" musicality and according to "American" standards. Precisely because racialized distance could never be collapsed completely (Koshiro 1994, 321–324), this displacement of the otherness of the other (Sakai 1992), of "the Japanese," rested at the core of much U.S. policy vis-à-vis Japan through the immediate postwar period and into the Cold War, as Japan was transformed from a vicious, utterly unknowable enemy into what it had purportedly always been since the beginning of time—an American protégé working its own way along a modernization arc toward the end of history (Fukuyama 1992), a few steps behind to be sure, but always fundamentally "America's Japan," at least until those normative expectations supposedly became thoroughly internalized around 1970 and America's Japan became "Japan's Japan" (Harootunian 1993). I'll have more to say about this on the next track.

In these ways, then, Eri Chiemi became a musical medium in and through whom stories of U.S.-Japan "friendship" and American leadership that would underpin geopolitical prerogatives during the Cold War and beyond could be articulated, justified, and made to make sense. Music provided a conduit by which Eri could be conceived of as almost like "us" (but not quite), an apt pupil of the United States and its music who had successfully reoriented herself toward America at the level of the body itself. In point of fact, this reorientation was often compulsory and even implicitly violent, the result of a strategic storytelling that demanded Japanese bodies (and especially Japanese women's bodies) be reconstituted in specific ways. But it was understood in military publications like the *Stripes* as a welcome effect of American influence and benevolence. At the hands of Al Ricketts and others, Eri became a sort of pinup girl for the American readership of the *Stripes*, a *doll*, an idealized, fleshly representation of a rehabilitated (or at least rehabilitating) Japan who eagerly subjected herself to what Shibusawa has called "liberal paternalism" and the tangible incarnation of a story that "journalists and others fell back on … to explain to the American public [and service personnel] SCAP's [Supreme Commander for the Allied Powers; the core of Occupation authority in Japan] policy to reintegrate Japan into a U.S.-led liberal capitalist order" (Shibusawa 2006, 25).

The *Stripes* continued to follow Eri Chiemi eagerly until the mid-1960s, in a way that probably sustained—reflexively—her ongoing musical involvement with the American military apparatus in Japan more broadly. She continued to be hailed by Al Ricketts as "Japan's jazz queen" (August 13, 1958) and as "Japan's top jazz singer" (August 2, 1962)—that is, as the star pupil and replicator of what was understood to be "American" musical culture (Atkins 2001, 171–174). Later, as the American military and U.S. geopolitical priorities were coming under intensifying criticism in the mid-1950s and 1960s, and even more so with the onset of the Vietnam War, USFJ and writers at the *Stripes* turned to Eri as the embodiment of an ideal moment when American "leadership" was uncontested, as the poster child of an idealized, and rapidly decaying, mode of global geopolitical organization that featured a malleable, submissive, eager-to-learn Japan as an America-in-training and the last bulwark against communism in East Asia. In 1963, for example, not long after the anti-AMPO upheavals of 1960, the Meiji Club held what it called an Old-Timers Night, featuring Eri and others in a salute to what it called "the grand and glorious 'Golden Era' in Japan, circa 1945–1955," an event that the paper claimed "should bring tears to the eyes" of the old-timers (January 17, 1963). Following her death in 1982, her *Stripes* eulogizers wailed that "Chiemi Eri belonged to us"—a revealing articulation of the ways in which the U.S. military appropriated women's bodies in the postwar period, molding them into conduits for U.S.-Japan "friendship" by recasting them as fleshly incarnations of a (re-)feminized Japan that was once again sensuous, submissive, and eager to learn. And in 1983, Eri appeared—posthumously—in the pages of the *Stripes* one final time, in a mournful article grieving what its author (not Ricketts) perceived as the decline of Iwakuni—once a bustling hub of military activity, and where Eri herself was interviewed for FEN in 1956—as an American base town:

> Where is the harmony and thunderburst of that song, and the deafening drift of rock 'n' roll? Roger Miller was once King of This Road. It was a Hard Day's Night for the Beatles and a Japanese pop singer, Chiemi Eri, charmed Americans with her chirrupy voice. And there was always Duane Eddy and Marty Robbins and …
>
> Is there nothing now, not even a faint echo of Elvis, no remote cry or loud shaft of light from the past? (January 28, 1983)

Framing this nostalgia sonically and musically is an intriguing move, and one that serves to reveal just how central musical storytelling was to the fostering and maintenance of a world order that placed the United States and its military at its center and that relied on the conjuring and ongoing telling of stories of "friendship" between the United States and Japan. This geopolitical vision, at least into the 1960s, saw America as a paternalistic teacher and was sustained by presenting the Japanese as desirable "friends" and eager pupils. But as I've already suggested, while the pupil should certainly be apt, she can never fully attain the level of expertise of the teacher—otherwise, how can the story of the teacher's supremacy be justified and maintained? In the next section, I'll focus on Eri Chiemi's contemporary and musical colleague Peggy Hayama and show how her portrayal in the *Stripes* as perpetually almost-but-not-quite "American" helped sustain the distance required for the maintenance of a sense of U.S. leadership and superiority, which in turn helped reconstitute the Japanese not as enemy but as potential friends and allies in need of benevolent guidance.

Peggy Hayama

Peggy Hayama was born Kotakari Shigeko on December 9, 1933, in the Ichigaya section of Tokyo, and was not yet twelve years old when the Pacific War ended. Her family was in Hiroshima in 1945, but at her father's insistence Shigeko had evacuated to the Fukushima countryside as the war was nearing its conclusion, thus narrowly escaping the atomic bombing of the city. After the end of the war, Shigeko and her family returned to Tokyo; her father, quickly surmising that English-language abilities would be an important resource in postwar Japan, had his daughter tune in regularly to the *Kamu Kamu Eigo* [Come Come English] program hosted by Hirakawa Tadaichi on NHK Radio from February 1946 to February 1951. Shigeko's radio time, however, was not spent solely in study—in due course, she encountered WVTR (Armed Forces Radio) and began listening to its jazz broadcasts. For the young Kotakari, this encounter with "American" music would prove both formative and liberating— the music that she initially encountered on WVTR, she recalled, afforded her the possibility of orienting her own body *differently,* around pleasure and dance and away from wartime *kokutai* (national body) ideology of collective struggle, suffering, and sacrifice (Hayama and Shiozawa 2014, 156). But she would soon find herself entangled in a different sort of geopolitical snare, as American forces tapped her as another fleshly conduit for strategic storytelling about the nature and terms of U.S.-Japan "friendship."

Kotakari's professional name—Peggy Hayama—came about entirely by accident and was itself the result of interactions with an American soldier.

A friend of Hayama's from a relatively wealthy family owned a phone that—being linked into a common exchange—would frequently receive "wrong number" calls. One day, a call came in from an American soldier, with whom Hayama's friend—a student of English, like Hayama and many during the Occupation—had a brief conversation. Having secured the soldier's name and barracks telephone number, the girls would subsequently call him occasionally to practice speaking English. One day, the girls asked the soldier to give them "American names." In Hayama's recollection, "[h]e gave us each names, on the basis of the feeling of our voices ... 'How about my voice?' I asked him, and he said, 'Your voice seems ... definitely like a Peggy.'" Hayama never met the soldier—but the name stuck (Kadota 2017, 224–227).

It was through the intervention of that same friend that Hayama began to sing professionally. The friend's elder brother led a Hawaiian music band and had secured a part-time gig over the summer of 1950 playing for GIs—but was short a vocalist (Kadota 2017, 228). The brother tapped Hayama for the role, and the rest is history. Although she started on the bases, she didn't stay there: "jazz" was booming in popularity in Japan at the time (Kadota 2017, 232), and Hayama played gigs at other venues around Tokyo as well. Upon graduating from high school, she joined tenor sax player Watanabe Hiroshi's band Stardusters, becoming their third lead vocalist (immediately following Nancy Umeki, who would go on to have a successful career as a singer in the United States), and started combo work with pianist Akimitsu Yoshitaka, who'd go on to play for Peggy for six decades (Hayama and Shiozawa 2014, 159; Kadota 2017, 232). In 1952 she recorded "Domino," a song made popular in the United States in 1951 by Tony Martin and Bing Crosby, as her professional debut, and she'd hold a prominent place in the Japanese musical imagination until her death in 2017, albeit mostly as a singer of Japanese pop and *enka,* not jazz. The breadth and depth of her career, however, were more or less ignored in the pages of the *Stripes* in favor of a tight focus on her engagements with the U.S. military and its representatives—and, more specifically, on her ability (or lack thereof) to embody idealized imaginings of "American" musical culture and expression. Like Eri Chiemi, Peggy Hayama would go on to be featured frequently in the pages of the *Stripes,* where she became a medium for American musical storytelling that sought to teach servicemen (and other readers) about their new Japanese "friends"—but also about the burden of their own leadership and superiority in a bifurcated Cold War world.

Peggy Hayama first appears in the *Stripes* on May 8, 1952, just after the formal end of the Occupation, in the context of an announcement for a "battle of the bands" event slated to be held at the aforementioned Ernie Pyle Theater. This event fronted American acts, drawn from within service ranks—but featured Peggy Hayama (then eighteen years old), who had already "proved a sensation" at earlier Occupation-backed events, as a "guest star." The following year she'd go on to give performances backed by the 293rd Army Band (which also facilitated the event at the Ernie Pyle) and sing at a special dinner at the Washington Heights officers' club celebrating the 151st anniversary of the founding of the West Point military academy on March 16. She was a regular at the Ernie Pyle through 1954 and played Camp Drew (in Gunma Prefecture) in 1956 alongside drummer George Kawaguchi and the Big Four (February 25, 1956). In 1957 and 1958, Yokosuka's Club Alliance—"billed as the largest enlisted men's club in the world" (December 4, 1957)—put together jazz extravaganzas that headlined Hayama (as well as Eri Chiemi). And in 1958, Hayama—alongside none other than Al Ricketts—was even featured on a Far East Network radio comedy program titled *The Feeneys USAF*. In the episode in question, American Bert Feeney—the central character—boasts to anyone who will listen that he's good friends with all the Japanese superstars in Tokyo. When the NCO Wives' Club in Tachikawa (site of a major airbase; I'll visit Tachikawa again momentarily) wants to invite Peggy Hayama to play at a charity bazaar they're hosting, they turn to Bert for help. Bert, of course, doesn't actually know any superstars, so he appeals to Al Ricketts, who saves the day by lining Hayama up for the event—with the Yokosuka Navy Band backing her. At the end of the episode, Bert Feeney, Peggy Hayama, and Al Ricketts even sing a song together (November 15, 1958).

In this way, Peggy Hayama enjoyed a prominent place both in base-centered musical culture in the 1950s and early 1960s and in the pages of the *Stripes* (her name appears in the paper no less than 345 times, mostly before 1965). Like Eri Chiemi, she was rendered a *doll* at the hands of the *Stripes* and USFJ, a sensuous, sexualized plaything representing a feminized "Japan" that was no longer a threat but a potential ally, one eager to be of service to the United States. One of Hayama's earliest appearances in the newspaper, for instance, came in the context of the publication's "Guide to Tokyo Night Life." The guide explained that at the field-grade officer's club in the Dai-Iti Hotel, "there's a voice that makes love to you, and Peggy's got more than a … lovely voice, she's cute and beautiful which is quite a trick for a little girl." A photo of American officers dancing to a Hayama performance was captioned: "What's the fun of being a colonel if you can't take time out to listen to something as lovely as Peggy?" (August 25, 1952). The fact that the objects of this sort of storytelling were Japanese women helped new (heterosexual, patriarchal) stories about Japanese bodies to be told, rendering them desirable, attainable, and possessable, and far from the threat that Japanese male fighting bodies had been during the war. This also afforded an erotic fantasy of intimacy on the part of serviceman readers, one that carried geopolitical implications as well. Strategic storytelling about these women, that is, invited the American (and mostly male) readers of the *Stripes* to conceive of Japan as a close, feminized ally in a gendered bina- tional relationship in the context of the burgeoning Cold War. To that extent, Hayama was as celebrated in the pages of the *Stripes* as Eri Chiemi was.

But although they were both presented as "friends" of the United States— or, more precisely, useful exemplars of the new, desirable Japanese ally, reha- bilitated through an American intervention that sought endlessly to rescue them from the "aberration" (Harootunian 2019, 336) of Japanese militarism and fascism and draw them closer to a liberal, democratic "us"—the treatment afforded Eri and Hayama at the hands of Al Ricketts and the *Stripes* diverged in important ways as well. Like Eri, Peggy Hayama was broadly considered one of the "jazz" greats in 1950s and 1960s Japan—she was even one of the dignitaries on hand to greet Benny Goodman when he arrived at Haneda Airport for his tour of Japan in December 1956. But even as she periodically received rave reviews for individual performances, the persistent story line of "On the Town" seemed to be that she was somehow never quite good enough, never quite as adjacent to the American "real" as Eri Chiemi was. In January 1958, for example, *Metronome* magazine—a prominent but now defunct American music maga- zine that focused on jazz—ran an article on jazz in Japan that singled out Hayama and Eri (as well as fellow San'nin Musume Yukimura Izumi) as exem- plary Japanese jazz singers. Al Ricketts, cranky at the best of times, hit the roof. "The article is not factual and in the best interests of Japanese jazz, we'd like to clear up a few points," he wrote. "Peggy Hayama tries, but isn't a jazz singer ... Chiemi Eri [is] the only female vocalist with true jazz potential. She has *the feel- ing for jazz that no other Japanese singer can match* [emphasis mine]. [...] [I]f Peggy Hayama's recording of 'Itte Shimau Onna' is 'the grooviest vinyl treat on the record shelves in Japan,' then all is lost. But really lost" (February 19, 1958). Now, it's worth pointing out that Ricketts had earlier declared Japanese "jazz," which in his mind had peaked at the apex of the Occupation in 1952, to be generally in decline as of 1956. "Jazz," he wrote, "which hit its peak and had to come down sometime, has come down with a resounding thud; Japan has reached a saturation point and its musicians are now standing still" (June 5, 1956). But his eagerness to anchor the insufficiency of Japanese jazz squarely in the body of Peggy Hayama is nonetheless remarkable, and revealing.

Whereas Eri Chiemi was largely celebrated as a star student of the United States and its musical culture, even to the degree that her otherness was dis- avowed in the interests of conjuring a Japanese version of "us," Hayama could never quite seem to catch up. But the (perceived) distance that persisted between Hayama and American musical/cultural ideals was itself an important mecha- nism for telling and sustaining stories of U.S. leadership and benevolent tutelage—so much so that, despite Eri Chiemi's apparent status as the superior act (in the *Stripes*' eyes, at least), it was Hayama who appeared in the paper more frequently. At times, she seemed to be referenced simply to remind readers of the distance from "American" norms/ideals that Eri had successfully overcome. In 1955, for example, another *Stripes* column titled "*Ongaku* [Music]" discussed then twenty-one-year-old Hayama's planned tour of the United States, which, after some delay, eventually got underway in March 1955. Private First Class Robert Sweeney, author of that column, described Peggy as a "second or third rated canary in the land of sake and soba." According to Sweeney, "[h]er one big attribute, her gimmick, is *the fact she's Japanese*—so she'll play it smart, and play it Eastern from the start. […] As a kid in kimono Peggy ought to cause quite a stir in Lindy's" (January 16, 1955; emphasis mine). Whereas the "Japaneseness" of Eri Chiemi's body was *de*-emphasized, that is, in the interests of generating a sense of nearness to a (white) American "us," Peggy Hayama's body—draped as it is in what Sweeney earlier in the column called "Oriental garb"—is *re*-emphasized as Japanese, and her performance is framed in those terms. She can thus only ever be a "second or third rated canary in the land of sake and soba"; any attention she garners on tour in the United States will be due to her "Japaneseness," not to any musical prowess. In his consideration of sixties rockabilly star Sakamoto Kyū, Bourdaghs reminds us that (musical) borders are not easily crossed, and that the success of figures like Sakamoto relied on his ability to project an imagined "Japan" to an American audience through largely shared musical forms (Bourdaghs 2012, 85–112). Although she never enjoyed the success abroad that Sakamoto did, something similar attended Sweeney's discussion of Peggy Hayama's impending tour of the United States in 1955. And yet, Eri Chiemi's positioning in the (erotic) U.S.-Japan geopolitical fantasy seems to rely precisely on her ability to transcend borders, broadly conceived; to be drawn close into an "American" musico-cultural embrace. Where Eri is permitted to cross borders, that is, Hayama was often left on the far side of them, in ways that remind one of their very existence and the ways in which they're patrolled. What this speaks to, perhaps, are two sides of a geopolitical coin: to make Eri Chiemi's border crossing (and de-emphasized racial otherness) meaningful in discourses of U.S.-Japan "friendship," the existence and persistence of those borders (and the distance they imply) must be periodically highlighted—and that task, it seems, fell to the perennially not-quite-enough Peggy Hayama.

This can be further clarified by considering the very questions of vocalization and language that attended Eri Chiemi's aforementioned crowning as "Japan's jazz queen." In my discussion of Eri, I explained how her ability to embody an "American jazz" grain endeared her to service personnel, and specifically to commentators at the *Stripes,* who rebroadcast this embodiment through their writing and celebrated her "feel" for the music, situating her as (almost) one of "us." Her embodiment of the music—that is, her emplacement within a "vocalic body" formed around the enunciation of "white vocal norm[s]"—allowed *Stripes* writers to conceive of Eri as transcending the (imagined) gaps between authentic and inauthentic musical expression, putting her in a different league from those groan-inducing "no-talent parrots who sang English lyrics as if they were Sanskrit," and affording her portrayal as a musical figure who had traversed what had seemed just a few years earlier to be irreconcilable distance between the United States and Japan. Peggy Hayama, on the other hand, seems to have been made to embody the very distance that U.S.-Japan "friendship" in this moment demanded be transcended—a pedagogical role no less essential, but one that required her story to be told rather differently. Commenting on a musical revue held at the Kokusai Theater in Asakusa in March 1956, and that featured performances by Hayama, Ricketts chastised her in precisely the terms that Eri Chiemi had been praised. "Also in the show," he wrote, "[is] Peggy Hayama, who sings 'come arong and risten to the rurrabye of Broadway.' She knows better" (March 4, 1956). The following year, this general line of attack made an appearance once again, this time in the context of a review of a jazz performance by Hayama at the Shinjuku Koma Theater. "Peggy Hayama, a good-looking gal with a lot of talent, could be so much better than she is," Ricketts declared. "Peg gets so wrapped up in stalking around the stage that her 'rs and ls' come out all wrong. She knows better" (June 27, 1957). The portrayal is petty and belittling and makes use of racialized stereotypes deployed to ridicule and dehumanize the Japanese enemy during the Pacific War. (And we might return briefly here to Barg [2000, 151], who reminds us of the insidious and racist belief that "[B]lack faces rendered [B]lack voices incapable of producing the correct (read white) enunciation to sing opera"; the "white vocal norm," in this way, is about vocality itself, but it is also very much about language and its enunciations.) In this way, although she didn't face condemnation as an irredeemable "parrot," Peggy Hayama's distance from authentic musical expression and the American "us" as revealed in the "white vocal norm" remained considerable.

All this, though, leads me to a related point. Even more consequential than Ricketts's lingering on Hayama's articulation of *r*'s and *l*'s here, I think, is the other repeated phrase: "*She knows better.*" This phrase speaks volumes about how the Americans saw themselves in this moment in Japan, and about the roles ascribed to musical figures like Eri Chiemi and Peggy Hayama in conjuring notions of U.S.-Japan "friendship," under benevolent American tutelage in the Cold War. The Americans tended to fancy themselves as paternal *teachers* (Shibusawa 2006, 25), guiding an erstwhile enemy toward "freedom" and "democracy" (the latter in particular tended to be associated with "whiteness" in this moment [Koshiro 1994, 321]). Now, to Shibusawa, the paternalism apparent in the U.S.-Japan relationship over these moments was a liberal paternalism, not a colonial one: "Different from colonial paternalism, this liberal paternalism tried to foster quicker growth and development from a 'backward' state toward a democratic political economy" (Shibusawa 2006, 19). That said, though, Peggy Hayama's incorporation into *Stripes'* strategic narratives in this moment does open pathways to understanding American curated storytelling as a (neo)colonial exercise, aimed in part at reassuring those charged with executing American economic and geopolitical prerogatives of its fundamental superiority and its nature as a centripetal focal point to which Japan (and the "free world") was to draw near for the prosecution of the Cold War. This is particularly clear in Ricketts's lingering on Hayama's articulation of *r*'s and *l*'s, and the question of language—what this lingering helps to produce and narrate is a linguistic (and racial) hierarchy, common in colonial contexts (Migge and Léglise 2007, 1; Naregal 1999, 3446). What Hayama's lagging place in this hierarchy seems to reveal is *the distance itself*: the justification, that is, for Americans to continue their pedagogical (Shibusawa 2006, 17) mission in Japan (the inverse echo of this, of course, is Eri Chiemi's embodiment of the possibility of the fulfillment of the American "teacher's" task). American storytellers—such as those at the *Stripes*—needed Japanese women like Peggy Hayama who could be cast as struggling but not irredeemable pupils, worthy beneficiaries of American benevolence and friendship who "kn[ew] better" even as the distance between them would never be completely closed. In order to validate the U.S. pedagogical mission, these "dolls" needed to constantly struggle to catch up, to leave the space necessary for American paternalism, guidance, and indeed supremacy/ superiority to continue to make sense in the first place. Women like Hayama (and Eri Chiemi), that is, needed to be close—but not *too* close. The musical storytelling that unfurled in *Stripes* served in part to position these women at differing degrees of proximity to a white, American, and democratic ideal, narrating a play-by-play of their relative success—articulated musically—in becoming "just like (white) us," even as they'd always remain Japanese (Koshiro 1994, 321–323). This helped make Japan's "subjugation appear as natural as a geisha's subservience to a male client, while picturing Japan as a child emphasized its potential to 'grow up' into a democracy" (Shibusawa 2006, 5)—that is, into a true "friend."

For all of her disciplining at the hands of Al Ricketts and the *Stars and Stripes,* Peggy Hayama was apparently still useful and was still posited as a "friend" of the United States—particularly later in her career, as the storytelling emphasis on the part of the U.S. military shifted away from pedagogical paternalism and the training of service personnel to see the Japanese as desirable "friends" (and themselves as "teachers") and toward something more closely resembling inter-statial "friendship." Although she had mostly faded from its pages by 1964 or so, Hayama made one last appearance in the *Stripes* in

1971—at the height of the Vietnam War, and, more pertinently, near the apex of the harsh criticism of American military policy that attended it. "Peggy Hayama crossed her shapely legs in the Spanish room of her $200,000 home located in an exclusive section of Tokyo's Shibuya district … ," it opened, "smiling as she credited 'G.I. Joe' with making her famous and independent." After a whirlwind tour through Hayama's career and some of her accomplishments—punctuated by pictures of the singer positioned alongside American musical figures: Hayama with Pearl Bailey, Hayama with Johnnie Ray, Hayama with Connie Stevens—the feature-length story concluded: "It may be 'Knock America Week' every week for some but Peggy's not buying it. For Peggy Hayama, G.I. Joe's kind generosity overrides his faults, and she knows him well. In response to his warm applause through the years, she sings him a vote of confidence with every note ringing true" (June 27, 1971).

Peggy's own ascribed "faults," by 1971, had been largely cut from the narrative in the interests of telling a straightforward story of embodied inter-statial "friendship"—one that orbited around musical camaraderie and around a Japanese artist's gratitude to the kind, benevolent Americans who made her what she was. Particularly in the context of the Vietnam War, it's a story that displaces criticism of the American war in Southeast Asia and Japanese support thereof, and replaces it with a story of U.S.-Japan allyship, told via appeal to music and performing bodies. In the next section, I'll continue to explore this evolving musical storytelling by focusing on what U.S. military organs would eventually term "Friendship Through Music"—a strategic articulation of U.S.-Japan commonality and common destiny that has served to deflect critique from the U.S. military presence in Japan (particularly its network of bases), especially in moments of crisis, by providing different templates by which the orientation of American and Japanese bodies can be understood.

Friendship Through Music and Its Discontents

There are probably several intersecting reasons behind the gradual disappearance of Eri Chiemi and Peggy Hayama from the pages of the *Stars and Stripes* in the mid-1960s. Musical tastes were changing and evolving, as "jazz" (even as a catchall for "American" popular music in the early postwar moment) was fragmenting into mambo, rockabilly, rock, folk, and more and contending with these for listenership. Hayama was moving in different musical directions, having recorded "*Nangoku Tosa wo Ato ni Shite* [Leaving Behind Tosa, That Southern Land]" in 1959—a decidedly *enka*-sounding song with roots on the front lines of Japan's war in China, where it was sung by troops hailing from the Kōchi area (Tosa)—and bolstering her "Japanese" musical presence around it.

(Prime Minister Ikeda Hayato, apparently, was a fan; Al Ricketts reported on December 16, 1961, that he'd performed an impromptu duet of the work with Hayama at a private gathering the night before.) Eri Chiemi, meanwhile, had stopped performing altogether by 1968, due to polyps on her vocal cords. In the background, Japanese jazz—actual jazz, to the extent that it was also part of Eri's and Hayama's repertoires—was moving out from beneath the American umbrella and beginning to stand on its own (Atkins 2001, 255), making it less appropriate, perhaps, as a yardstick for measuring Japanese performative and musical (that is, cultural) proximity to an embodied American ideal (an undertone, perhaps, to Al Ricketts's grumpy declaration that Japanese jazz hit its peak in 1952 but was in serious decline by 1956).

But there were historical changes afoot, too. By the late 1950s and early 1960s, Japan's new positionality as "ally" had, in American minds, likely become much more commonsensical than it was in the immediate aftermath of the Pacific War, rendering servicemen less in need of guidance in conceiving of Japanese bodies in ways that aligned with their state's geopolitical prerogatives. At the same time, the U.S. military was increasingly susceptible to critique, both within Japan and beyond it, due to a range of issues including Cold War American imperialism, nuclear testing, and especially the presence of American military installations on Japanese soil, widely seen as an infringement on Japanese sovereignty (Kapur 2018, 12–13). This shift in the political winds intensified as the 1950s wore on, but it was underway even before the end of the Occupation. Kapur points out that the first large-scale, organized Japanese protest targeting a U.S. military installation took place at Uchinada, Ishikawa Prefecture, from late 1952 into 1953 (Kapur 2018, 14), but anti-American civil unrest—involving thousands—was actually occurring in different spots around Japan and alarming U.S. officials earlier than this. In February 1952, for example, a flurry of anxious, confidential dispatches were transmitted from Tokyo to the Foreign Office in Washington describing "Anti-Colonial Day" rallies that had been held on February 21 "in 26 places in Japan, involving about 6,000 protestors in all, and [that] led to a number of clashes with police." The confidential telegram continued: "In Nagoya on 20th February [1952] a rally of a definite anti-American kind was held in which participants, mostly students, carried posters saying 'Get Out Yankees,' 'Drive out U.S. soldiers who prostitute our sisters,' 'No Security Forces,' etc. Participants in all these rallies appear to have included, as well as members of the Communist party, students, trade unionists, and others who oppose the security pact and rearmament" (U.S. Foreign Office, Tokyo 1952).

These events were alarming enough that they were included in a U.S. government Daily Intelligence Briefing, marked "secret," on February 27, 1952: "Although 1952 marked the third anniversary of 'anticolonialization day' in Japan," it read, "this was the first time that the demonstrations were so widespread, and pointedly anti-American" (Office of the Director of National Intelligence 1952). This demanded attention—and quickly.

The U.S. response to burgeoning anti-American critique in Japan in the fifties, sixties, and beyond was multifaceted, but one of its key prongs involved an ongoing strategic centering of culture (Matsuda 2007, 55). Here, I want to explore one specific aspect of that: the strategic appeal to music to tell and reaffirm stories of U.S.-Japan "friendship." At around the time that Eri and Hayama were fading from the pages of the *Stripes*, a perceptible shift arose in the way music was being used by U.S. forces in Japan. Rather than "helping" service personnel tasked with enacting geopolitical relationships in the Pacific to see Japanese bodies as familiar (but not quite "us"), as sensuous allies and earnest pupils of the United States, the emphasis seems to have shifted toward winning the hearts and minds of Japanese people themselves. As DeNora (2003, 57) and Wade (2009, 20–22) point out, music can be used to help orient bodies and minds in the world in specific ways. In its strategic deployment on the front lines of a cultural offensive aimed at counteracting intensifying critiques of the U.S. presence, prerogatives, and actions in Japan in the 1950s and beyond, it's apparent that music was often used quite explicitly to position fleshly bodies in relationships of collaboration and camaraderie with American strategic interests and pivot them away from (potential) protest. Of course, music can never be reduced to a simple tool of social or political control; any meaning or affordances it may have are dependent upon the contexts that those engaging with the music find themselves in, their desires and perceptions of the world, and so on (DeNora 2000, 2003). The simple fact that U.S. forces may have *wanted* to use music in certain ways, that is, presents no guarantee that those objectives would be achieved—indeed, as I bring this track to a close I'll discuss how other actors can gum up the works by hijacking and redirecting the very musical storytelling that they were tapped to facilitate. But by the very same token, the strategic desires of musical storytellers can't be dismissed out of hand, either. For the time being, I continue to focus on USFJ as the key storyteller in question. To the extent that music can be put to use as a powerful facilitator of togetherness (Cavicchi 1998, 158–183; DeNora 2000, 123; Fox 2004, 21–24), it was ideally suited to helping further American geopolitical imperatives centered on U.S.-Japan "friendship" in this moment and beyond.

Cyclical Crisis and the Strategic Appeal to Music

By the time the Anti-Colonial Day protests were becoming a matter of serious concern in 1952, American officials in Japan were already trying to counteract and defuse what they saw as alarming political tendencies among Japanese social actors by appealing to discourses of U.S.-Japan "friendship." Although the ferociousness of the 1952 protests may have caught them off guard, Anti-Colonial Day itself did not come as a surprise to American authorities in Japan—as the briefing cited earlier makes clear, it had already been held twice, in 1950 and 1951. As tensions simmered ahead of the protests in early February, U.S. Army colonel and assistant secretary of state for Far Eastern affairs (and, later, president of the Rockefeller Foundation and secretary of state under the Kennedy and Johnson administrations) Dean Rusk made the following comments, worth quoting at length, at a luncheon meeting of the America/Japan Society held in Tokyo:

> Our two Governments have decided that it would serve the cause of peace and our mutual security if, "as a provisional arrangement" for the defense of Japan, American armed forces remain for a time in Japan after the effective date of the Treaty of Peace. [...] I have no doubt that each of us shall do everything possible to reduce or remove irritations and obstacles standing in the way of complete and cordial cooperation in this field. [...]
>
> If I may quote from the opening remarks made by the distinguished representative of Japan, "Friendly association among peace-loving nations is predicated upon the existence of friendly relations between individual nations. Friendship arising out of mutual respect, mutual trust, and mutual understanding must be the keynote of our associating with each other, and it is on the bedrock of such friendship that the Security Treaty between your country and mine must rest in order to serve its wider international purpose. I am sure that we are all in full concurrence that our common task here is to work out arrangements which will best serve the purpose of promoting effective cooperation between our two countries." (General Headquarters Far East Command, Public Information Office 1952)

In these remarks, made in the lead-up to the April 1952 enactment of the Treaty of San Francisco and the U.S.-Japan Security Treaty, we can already see American (and Japanese) power brokers appealing to "friendship" as a means of underwriting geopolitical prerogative and diverting impediments thereto—"irritations"—by framing the ongoing U.S. military presence in Japan, and Japanese state support for it, as a natural outcropping of "mutual respect, mutual trust, and mutual understanding." This semantic maneuvering by Rusk reveals American unease at the cracks already appearing in the wall buttressing Reverse Course U.S. geopolitical policy that centered on maintaining Japan as the last bastion against communism in East Asia—and a desire to patch those cracks up before they became irreparable.

Rusk's unease, of course, would be justified and exacerbated just a few weeks later, when the third Anti-Colonial Day exploded into protests across the country. This sort of street-level criticism against the new regional/global order that he elucidated—and sought to anchor in lofty notions of "friendship"—would continue to intensify over the course of the 1950s. It would hit its first boiling point (many more would come) with the so-called Sunagawa Struggle of 1955–1957, which began as a localized protest by farmers against the appropriation of their land for the purposes of extending runways at the nearby Tachikawa Air Base but soon "became a nationwide media spectacle ... [that] expanded rhetorically to encompass larger goals of upholding Japan's pacifist constitution and opposing American imperialism" (Kapur 2018, 15). In tandem with other "incidents" of this moment (Kapur 2018, 16–17), the late 1950s saw a developing crisis in U.S.-Japan relations that threatened to derail American geopolitical prerogatives in East Asia. A way had to be found to redirect the narrative. One way the U.S. military responded to this crisis was to double down on the sorts of performative articulations of "friendship" that Rusk had already tried out on his closed-door luncheon audience. In a way that set the stage for a strategy that the Americans would pursue for years to come, music came to be deployed more and more frequently, in a range of ways, as an important linchpin in this effort.

In 1959, for example—two years after the Sunagawa Struggle, which had been centered on the Tachikawa Air Base—Tachikawa Base Command mounted a Cherry Blossom Festival, which welcomed more than two thousand visitors and featured "a spring fashion parade by 10 of Japan's top models and entertainment by Peggy Hayama. ... More than 2000 [people] watched the 1½ hour show given at 3PM and 7PM in the Festival Building [on base]" (April 22, 1959). Although military installations in Japan had welcomed visitors from surrounding communities since as early as 1950, when inaugural Armed Forces Day celebrations were held at bases around the country, these tended to foreground American military hardware, procedures, power, and presence—in other words, precisely that which was falling under intensifying public critique in this moment (Camp Tokyo in 1954, for instance, hosted one such celebration under the rather domineering moniker Power for Peace). The Tachikawa event saw a localized shift away from a *military* focus and toward the *cultural* in localized articulations of "friendship" between the United States and Japan—again, with women's fleshly and performing bodies taking center stage—and a particular foregrounding of music in that effort. The Tachikawa Cherry Blossom Festival, that is, constituted an important first step in the pivot toward telling stories of what USFJ would go on to call Friendship Through Music—a pivot that was launched with Peggy Hayama as one of the key musical figures of the Occupation and its aftermath but that would go on to incorporate a much wider range of musical actors, both American and Japanese.

Friendship Through Music as American geopolitical strategy seems to have first been clearly articulated in September 1962. The timing is important. As the 1950s drew to a close, protests continued to intensify against the U.S.-Japan security arrangement and Japanese measures put in place to shield it from critique—organized action against then prime minister Kishi Nobusuke's Police Duties Bill in 1958, for example, which sought to "enhance the government's ability to obstruct and disrupt left-wing protest movements," bled into the very anti-AMPO upheavals they were meant to prevent. The anti-AMPO protests of 1959 and 1960 brought millions of bodies into the street, heightening American worries that bases in Japan "could rapidly be rendered unuseable by popular resistance" (Kapur 2018, 17–19). The U.S. military presence on Okinawa and its still-occupied status made it an important conceptual center for these upheavals, and in a way that echoed Tachikawa's response to the Sunagawa Struggle, American forces on Okinawa launched a small cultural counteroffensive in their aftermath. This again involved inviting Japanese musical figures to perform in a U.S. military context—but this time in a collaborative performance with American military musicians. On September 16, 1962, the 558th Air Force Band from Kadena Air Force Base performed with the Naha Philharmonic Chorus for "a special program on AFRTS-TV [Armed Forces Radio and Television Services] … designed to promote Ryukyuan-American *friendship through music*" (September 15, 1962; emphasis mine). This performance, which featured a mixture of American and Japanese tunes, was intended as a televised broadcast, not as a live event, but even at the time it was mounted "[t]he two musical groups [were] also planning concerts for Ryukyuan audiences in the near future." In 1962, then, in the aftermath of AMPO, music was being used in Okinawa in a very specific way—as a means of portraying camaraderie and rewriting the story of American-Okinawan relations as one of "friendship" and collaboration rather than domination and dependence. This rewriting involved the strategic presentation of scenes of American and Okinawan bodies making music *together,* as opposed to confronting each other, whether literally or figuratively.

More generalized cultural initiatives with a focus on (binational) "togetherness" began popping up around this moment on other U.S. military installations in Japan as well. In 1960, for example, Camp Zama, in Kanagawa Prefecture, hosted a *bon-odori*—a community dance held in memory of the dead, a common occurrence each August across Japan—as an on-base "open house" event. Coming in the immediate aftermath of the June 1960 AMPO uprisings, this event was intended to "celebrate the 100th anniversary of the United States-Japan treaty of amity and commerce" and featured "700 members of Zama women's clubs [performing] Japanese dances in competition for prizes donated by the USARJ [U.S. Army Japan] Special Services and Civil Affairs Offices" and the "USARJ band [playing] Japanese music for the Japanese and American spectators during the intermission and before the show" (August 16, 1960). The same year, the naval base at Yokosuka held an open house for the Japanese community, featuring "[a] parade, music, and a football game" (October 31, 1960). Later, in 1988, Misawa Air Base in Aomori Prefecture launched its "America Day," framed as a way to introduce "American culture" to the local community; later iterations of this event involved occasion for "cultural exchange" with the surrounding communities as well, allowing "people [to] ask questions and see our commonalities and unique differences" (April 3, 1988). In these ways, the cultural dimensions of the efforts to establish and sustain U.S.-Japan "friendship" that got underway as early as the Occupation continued well beyond it, with the key difference being that rather than high-level state strategy and diplomacy, they tended to play out locally, on bases and within impacted communities. The intent was to modify how Japanese people conceived of the interactions between American and Japanese bodies (political and fleshly ones) at the level of everyday life, often—though not always—through the mediation of music and musical storytelling. And like a sort of cyclical feedback loop, these efforts tended to expand and intensify in response to what the Americans perceived as geopolitical crisis.

Friendship Through Music as a specific strategic initiative—one that was first instigated in the aftermath of the various AMPO-related struggles of around 1960—would come roaring back in the mid- to late 1990s and remains an important cornerstone of the U.S. cultural offensive in Japan through the present day. In 1996, musical arms of the American and Japanese militaries—the III Marine Expeditionary Force Band and the 15th Brigade Band of the Japan Ground Self Defense Forces, respectively—reprised the collaborative musicking of 1962 in a joint concert held (once again) on Okinawa. By 1997, this event had been officially named the Friendship Through Music concert; it was held that year in the auditorium of Kubasaki High School (a U.S. Department of Defense school for the dependents of service personnel), located on Camp Foster in Okinawa City. The concert was a two-hour affair, free and open to the public, and featured "Broadway show tunes, popular Japanese and American selections and patriotic music" (September 17, 1997). Pointedly, the evening was capped by a collaborative performance of "The Stars and Stripes Forever." In a parallel development that same year, USFJ in collaboration with Japanese state officials instigated what the forces called "Yūkō Day"—"friendship day," actually a monthlong series of events, imagined as a means of "build[ing] friendships and boost[ing] the image of American forces in Japan" (June 26, 1998)—and rolled the Friendship Through Music concert into it. This move clarified the aim of what now became an annual music event: to promote a sense of U.S.-Japan "friendship" and mitigate critique of the American presence and priorities by showcasing American and Japanese bodies engaged in a collaborative display of musicking. The link connecting music, "friendship," and geopolitics was thus cemented and elucidated in a whole new way, providing a script for telling stories of the alliance between the United States and Japan.

There's a historical reason why all this maneuvering occurred around 1997. If Tachikawa's Cherry Blossom Festival and the first made-for-TV installment of what would eventually become the Friendship Through Music concert series in 1962 can be understood as responses to moments of perceived crisis in the U.S.-Japan relationship, the 1997 establishment of Yūkō Day and the resurrection of Friendship Through Music as geopolitical strategy can as well. The crisis portending these latter developments was triggered by a particularly horrifying event: the abduction and gang rape of a twelve-year-old Okinawan schoolgirl in the town of Kin, home to Camp Hansen, by two U.S. Marines and a sailor in September 1995. The sheer viciousness of this crime—kidnapping and tying the arms and legs of a young child, raping her repeatedly on a dark, rocky beach not far from the American base, leaving her there for dead after carefully disposing of her bloodied underthings—is almost unthinkable in its brutality. But as Angst (2003) has discussed, the facticity of the child's rape—its sheer violence at the level of an individual, fleshly body; the trauma of the victim and the culpability of her attackers—has tended to be muted in favor of amplifying much more generalized discussions of its geopolitical consequences and ramifications. Put differently, the child's body—and the violence visited upon it—was repurposed to different ends, as actors in the United States, Japan, and Okinawa scrambled to tap and redirect the story line, each for different purposes (Angst 2003, 141–143). State actors in the United States and Japan, for their part, saw the rape as a "political bombshell" (Kawato 2015, 76) that presented a broader existential threat against the maintenance of the AMPO alliance itself—a threat that was revealed in the extensiveness and ferocity of the protests to the U.S. military presence on Okinawa that erupted after the fact. The rape, that is, while ultimately and most importantly an act of unspeakable violence against the body of a young girl, also rocked the body politic, relighting the fuse on explosive Okinawan (and Japanese) discontent over the American presence and the U.S.-Japan security alliance itself and sending tens of thousands into the streets in protest in October (Angst 2003, 138). This was a serious crisis. To deflect some of the seething criticism of the American presence on Okinawa and in Japan, and to shield the alliance from potential collapse, different stories about how American and Okinawan (as well as Japanese) bodies intervolved had to be told.

Convinced that they needed to do "something big" (Kawato 2015, 76) in the aftermath of the rape, American and Japanese officials established the Special Action Committee on Okinawa (SACO) in November 1995, a body whose stated purpose was to "reduce the burden on the people of Okinawa and thereby strengthen the Japan-U.S. alliance" (Ministry of Foreign Affairs of Japan 1996). In the end, SACO's main tangible accomplishment was to reach an agreement to close and return the site of the contentious Marine Corps Air Station Futenma, in Ginowan City, although its relocation to Henoko Bay (an ecologically sensitive site in the north of Okinawa) constitutes more of a shuffling of pieces on a geopolitical chessboard than any meaningful reduction of the burden on Okinawa. As Kawato points out, however, the establishment of SACO was also a *performative* act, intended to "capture the attention of Okinawa and the rest of Japan, and show they were doing something about the base problems" (Kawato 2015, 77). A key facet of this performativity involved the reassertion of U.S.-Japan "friendship" as the foundational condition for decidedly unfriendly strategic and military maneuvering: that is, the "enhance[ment of] mutual understanding between US forces and local Japanese communities" (Ministry of Foreign Affairs of Japan 1996). Yūkō Day was a direct "outgrowth" of the committee's final report and recommendations, issued in December 1996. "Officials from the U.S. and Japanese government," the *Stripes* reported on June 26, 1998, "felt annual *yuko* [*sic*], or friendship, observances would build closer ties between civilian and military communities." Musical storytelling, particularly the visible/audible foregrounding of American and Japanese bodies engaged in collaborative musicking in continuing events like the Friendship Through Music concerts, became a crucial mechanism through which that "friendship"—*yūkō*—could be demonstrated and performed.

Although Okinawa would remain the key site for the annual Friendship Through Music event, the emphasis on music as a means of conjuring and sustaining stories of U.S.-Japan "friendship" soon manifested at other sites around Japan as well. In 1998, U.S. officials opened Yūkō Park, or Friendship Park, a combined outdoor concert venue—the Sakura Shell—and playground erected on an erstwhile soccer field near Yokota Air Base, just to the west of Tokyo. "Kids can come back here and play on the super playground while the adults can seriously watch and listen to the music," the second lieutenant in charge of project development told the *Stripes* on the occasion of the park's opening. The dedication event was engineered as a celebration of "[f]riendship between GIs and their Japanese neighbors at Yokota Air Base" (May 26, 1998) and featured four hours of music, including a concert by the Air Force Band of the Pacific (Asia), performances by Japanese musicians, musical tributes to Glenn Miller (here again, the specter of a "grand and glorious 'Golden Era'"), and even songs from American actor and marine veteran Wilford Brimley (1934–2020), who emceed it. Sakura Shell remains active as a base-affiliated concert venue, and in fact hosted the awkwardly named Tomodachi-stock (clearly a play on Woodstock) in April 2011, held as a disaster relief fundraiser in the aftermath of 3.11. But the Friendship Through Music concerts seem to have remained the cornerstone of this particular facet of the American cultural offensive in Japan. In a rather on-the-nose article published in 2019, for example, the Defense Visual Information Distribution Service—which connects global media outlets with U.S. military operations and prerogatives worldwide—told an extended story of the literal, actual marriage between a (male) sergeant euphonium player in the III Marine Expeditionary Force Band and a (female) Japan Ground Self-Defense Force French horn player in the 15th Brigade Band, the participating ensembles in the Friendship Through Music concert series. This article, which celebrates fleshly American and Japanese bodies literally intertwined in music and marriage and/as the U.S.-Japan security alliance (and obscures the violent rape of an Okinawan schoolgirl with images of consensual sexual entanglement), removes any lingering uncertainty over the nature and rationale of the geopolitical framing and use of music as a means of conjuring and telling stories of U.S.-Japan "friendship." "The combined band concerts are to strengthen the Japan-U.S. relationship and express the friendship that the countries have today through music," it explained. "Music binds those with different backgrounds and cultures, and those who speak different languages. Music can act as a universal tool which creates friendships and new alliances" (Defense Visual Information Distribution Service 2019). The collaborative concert series continues on Okinawa as of this writing and is featured regularly and prominently in military publications (see, for example, Defense Visual Information Distribution Service 2023).

Musical storytelling, then, has been a key strategy underpinning the fostering and maintenance of the U.S.-Japan security alliance over a period of several decades. It's followed a gradual crescendo as it was deployed as one means of counteracting recurring crises and their broader geopolitical and strategic ramifications across the historical moments discussed herein. Placing a spotlight on American and Japanese military bodies that engage in collaborative musicking and that sometimes literally embody the postwar U.S.-Japan "love story" as fleshly performing bodies intertwined in marriage; transforming military installations into concert venues where Japanese and American bodies can sway in unison, taking pleasure from music and displacing potential protest with that pleasure; building base-adjacent sites such as Yūkō Park that are specifically designed to facilitate community gatherings and military-civilian "friendship" through music—all this affords occasion for bodies to move in different ways, away from the streets and the sorts of clenched-fist performances of protest that began alarming American authorities as early as 1952 and toward collaboration, common enjoyment, "friendship." In the wake of the rape of the schoolgirl in Kin in 1995, this strategy became a means of distracting from the horrific violence visited upon an Okinawan schoolgirl's body and establishing different modes of storytelling according to which American, Japanese, and Okinawan bodies could be situated (actually or imaginatively) *differently.* None of this is to say, of course, that the performative centering of *yūkō* or the annual Friendship Through Music events cause everyday social actors, especially those on Okinawa, to simply forget, and abandon their critical impulses to musical enjoyment. But in the imagination of policy makers, this at least seems to promise to buy a little space and shift the narrative that alarmed Klinck in 2021—"more often than not, the only time you ever read anything about the U.S. military presence in Japan, it's usually something bad"—in a direction that is more amenable to the maintenance of the U.S.-Japan security alliance and to American geopolitical prerogatives more broadly. As was the case with the depiction and narrative positioning of singers like Eri Chiemi and Peggy Hayama, this musical storytelling has tended to be deliberate and strategic, with an eye to conjuring and sustaining worlds amenable to American (and Japanese, to be sure) geopolitical and economic interests over the longer term. But USFJ has also made more ad hoc, spur-of-the-moment use of music when such opportunities presented themselves. On what remains of this track, I'll explore one such occasion—but as I'll show, contested claims on the nature of U.S.-Japan "friendship" on the part of its key performers meant that this event likely didn't go quite as its USFJ hosts had anticipated.

Dolls in Action: Princess Princess Flips the Script

In 1988, a new rock band was garnering a great deal of attention in Japan. Known popularly as Puri-Puri, or P2—variations on the group's actual name, Princess Princess—the five-member "girls rock" band actually got its start in 1983, when the young women who would comprise it (Konno Tomoko [b. 1965], keyboards; Tomita Kyoko [b. 1965], drums; Watanabe Atsuko [b. 1964], bass; Nakayama Kanako [b. 1964], guitar; and Okui Kaori [b. 1967], lead vocals) responded to and ultimately passed an audition process held by TDK Records, which was looking to put together a rock-infused "idol" unit. Initially named Akasaka Komachi by TDK and promoted as a "quintessential contemporary high school girl–style band," the group—as a commercial creation engineered to both splice into and stimulate sexualized fantasies of "intimacy," marketing tactics common in idol manufacturing and promotion (Galbraith 2018)—was subjected to a familiar eroticization. Dressed scantily in the rather bizarre music video for their first single, a chirpy synth-pop number called *"Hōkago Jugyō* [After-School Lessons]," the women were presented with cardboard cutouts of vinyl records placed over their breasts and a stern male principal working futilely to keep them in line, and pictured cavorting in swimsuits in idol magazine articles that emphasized their physical (breast, hip, waist) measurements far more prominently than any discussion of their music. In a way reminiscent of

Eri Chiemi and Peggy Hayama, that is, these women were initially "sold" to their (mostly male) consuming public as *dolls*—sensuous, possessable representations of Japanese girl/womanhood upon which desire could be projected and through whom erotic fantasies could be told (Nagaike 2012). Though the geopolitical and historical underpinnings differed, the ways that Akasaka Komachi seemed shoehorned, through their packaging and engineered presence, into confirming certain heterosexual, patriarchal conceptions of the (Japanese) world in the 1980s shared much with the more overtly political storytelling pursued through reference to the fleshly presence and performativity of early postwar figures like Eri and Hayama. And like Eri and Hayama, these women would later find their careers intersecting with the musical storytelling pursued by U.S. forces in Japan.

Around the middle of the 1980s, though, Akasaka Komachi were busy pushing back at the stories that were being told about and through them by TDK and maneuvering toward being able to tell musical stories of their own. Unlike many contemporary idols—for whom musical skill is an afterthought, if it's valued at all (Stevens 2008, 50)—the young women who would go on to comprise Princess Princess were all talented, accomplished musicians (Okui Kaori, who fronted the group, recalls getting her start playing keyboards with bands in high school [Okui 1998, 23]). Being marketed as "dolls" was proving tedious and frustrating. Before long, the women began covering songs by Roy Orbison and the Rolling Stones at events they were dispatched to and made it known that they were interested in writing and playing their own music as a rock unit, not embodying others' fantasies as idols. The audaciousness of this led to the women bouncing among talent management firms for a time, but in late 1986 they finally settled at Shinkō Music Entertainment and met Massachusetts-born Michael Kawai, who would oversee the band's rebirth out of CBS Records as Princess Princess and produce much of their material. "The first thing that I did when I was put in charge of Princess Princess was to ask the group's members, who had originally been marketed along 'idol' lines, what their thoughts on music were," Kawai recalled years later in a 2012 interview with Hiroshima FM. "And I learned that they wanted to be a rock band, to write and sing their own songs. [...] I thought that Puri-Puri should aim to become a 'girls rock' band with listeners across the spectrum [as opposed to the goth-styled ZELDA and the Japanese metal band SHOW-YA, both popular at the time], so we got to work writing songs that we hoped would bring people out to live performances" (Hiroshima FM 2012).

The strategy was successful. The band-centered, wall-of-sound style (as much a musical hallmark of the eighties in Japan as it was elsewhere in the world) that Princess Princess presented proved popular, and the group earned a following playing live houses and small venues in Japan starting in 1987, moving to progressively larger houses and bigger crowds as they toured. In February 1988 the band released its fourth single—"19 GROWING UP"—which, with its power chords, heavy synthesizer, driving percussion and bass line, and Okui's soaring vocals, cinched their popularity. Their third album—*HERE WE ARE,* an LP featuring energetic pop-rock tracks that was clearly composed with live performances in mind—peaked at number eight on the Oricon sales charts in February 1988, and tickets for their April performance at Tokyo's Shibuya Kōkaidō (a prominent, medium-sized live music venue in the capital that, like the much larger Nippon Budōkan, which I'll visit on track 5, bestows a status of having "made it" in Japan's popular music world when one plays there) sold out in just two hours. In late 1988 and early 1989, Princess Princess would release the power ballad "M" and the upbeat crowd-pleaser "Diamonds," both of which helped cement the band in Japanese popular memory as one of the greatest musical acts of the 1980s and 1990s—and indeed, in 1990 they would go on to play the Budōkan, making history as the first all-women's unit to do so. By later in 1989, their albums were hitting the top spot in the Oricon charts and staying there: five consecutive LP releases between November 1989 and January 1993 hit number one, with the first of these—*LOVERS*—achieving million-seller status. But in mid-1988, Princess Princess were still on tour paying their dues. Eventually, they'd collide with USFJ in Yokohama on August 31, with an event that the band titled Panic Tour Summer '88 Seaside Concert at North Pier: Dear My Best Friend.

In 1988, as Princess Princess's star was on the rise, the city of Yokohama was preparing to celebrate the one hundredth anniversary of the formal establishment of its municipal government. As part of these celebrations, Kanagawa-ku—the city's central district—was marking sixty years since its own (1927) incorporation as a city "ward." Kanagawa's history, however, predated its absorption into Yokohama in important ways. Geographically oriented along Tokyo Bay, a stone's throw from Edo (later Tokyo), Kanagawa-ku was where the Tokugawa shogunate and Townsend Harris, representing the United States, concluded the Treaty of Amity and Commerce between the United States and the Empire of Japan in 1858; it was also designated one of the "open ports" under this treaty. Concluded at cannon-point and designed mostly to facilitate American economic interests in the Pacific, the unequal Treaty of Amity and Commerce also granted extraterritoriality to non-Japanese persons in Japan, thereby shielding Americans from the oversight of local laws. In this way, it foreshadowed the infringements on Japanese sovereignty that attended Japan's experiences hosting U.S. forces after 1945 under the U.S.-Japan Security Treaty (and that, indeed, made prosecuting the servicemen who gang-raped the schoolgirl on Okinawa such a complicated issue [Kawato 2015, 68–71]). Kanagawa-ku, in short, was a key site through which much modern Japanese history and geopolitics flowed—particularly that concerning relations with the United States—and this history was celebrated in 1988 with a series of events titled Kanagawa: A Festival of History and of the Future '88. Perhaps fittingly, the celebrations circled back to intersect with the ongoing American presence in Yokohama—and this intersection was facilitated through *music*. On April 26, city officials announced that a Seaside Concert would be held on August 31 as the crowning event of the festival (*Yomiuri shinbun* 1988a, 22). What made the announcement and the event itself noteworthy was the fact that it was to be held at North Dock—at the time an active U.S. military installation, home to the U.S. Army's 836th Transportation Battalion.

Originally named Mizuho Wharf by the Empire of Japan, North Dock is a shipping and port facility built on reclaimed land not far from Yokohama Station and across the water from the city's distinctive Minato Mirai oceanfront development project. Construction began on the facility in 1925, but it wasn't completed until twenty years later; immediately after the war in 1945, the occupiers appropriated the pier complex and turned it into a marine transport hub. The idea to mount the Seaside Concert at North Dock came from within a Yokohama municipal events planning committee, whose staffers framed the event as an opportunity for fostering "U.S.-Japan friendship." Now, the planners didn't really expect that the proposal to hold a concert at North Dock would be approved by USFJ (*Yomiuri shinbun* 1988a, 22). This was, after all, an active U.S. military installation, a place normally off-limits to everyday Japanese civilians (at least for most of the year). Much to their astonishment, however, the American authorities responded enthusiastically—even eagerly—when the committee sought permission for the concert from the Camp Zama headquarters of USARJ (U.S. Army Japan). Initially, the planners had proposed a modest, fifteen-hundred-person-capacity event, to be held on a small corner of North Dock. USARJ, however, urged them to go bigger. Already in April 1988, army authorities were suggesting that planners work toward a three-thousand- to five-thousand-person event. In the end, somewhere between eight thousand and ten thousand people made their way to North Dock via special shuttle bus for the concert; the army even provided AV hookups and offered up its own personnel to staff food and drink stands, "enveloping the venue in a sort of 'American feeling'" (*Kanagawa shinbunsha* 1990, 170–171; *Yomiuri shinbun* 1988b, 14). The Seaside Concert featured performances by both amateur and professional Japanese and American bands, lasted for three hours, and was, according to Kanagawa Ward's subsequent report on the event, epoch making: "We are told," the report read, "that a concert held by Japanese artists for a Japanese audience within the grounds of a U.S. military installation is an unprecedented event" (*Kanagawa shinbunsha* 1990, 171). The Japanese artists tapped to headline this "unprecedented event" were none other than emergent supergroup Princess Princess.

Although scholars have pointed to the (ultimately canceled) 1992 concert by rock unit the Alfee at Naval Air Facility Astugi as the first performance by a Japanese popular music group to be arranged on an active American military installation in Japan (Stevens 1999, 58–59), in fact it was Princess Princess who accomplished this feat with their 1988 show at North Dock. This show has something of a legendary status among the band's fans. The women played a high-energy eighteen-song (including encore) set, featuring crowd-pleasing pop-rock numbers like "*Sekai de Ichiban Atsui Natsu* [The Hottest Summer in the World]," which remains their signature hit even today, the irreverent "GO AWAY BOY" ("I'll take your bullshit pickup line and give it right back to you, tied up in a silk ribbon," the lyrics sweetly snarl), and the early rock hit "19 GROWING UP." Sadly, a full recording of the show doesn't exist (or, at least, isn't publicly available), but the limited visual records that do show a confident quintet of women, fully in command of their art and of their audience, fronted by Okui Kaori and Nakayama Kanako, who strut up and down the massive outdoor stage with the sea breeze blowing through their equally massive eighties hair against the Yokohama skyline. It was, by all accounts, a great success. But to get at some of the contested musical storytelling that was at play in this unusual event, we have to look a little closer.

The city planners charged with putting the Seaside Concert in motion may have been surprised by USARJ's receptiveness to the event—indeed, their outright eagerness to host it—but by this point in my discussion, I hope that readers of *Homesick Blues* are not. Despite being an "extremely rare case" of an event that was facilitated within a U.S. military installation by "everyday citizens [*ippan shimin*]" (*Yomiuri shinbun* 1988a, 22), the way that the concert fit into a longer story of American uses of music in promoting camaraderie and collaboration between Japanese social actors and USFJ should by now feel familiar. The event, bringing together base stakeholders and the local Japanese community (particularly its youth) in a highly visible event headlined by one of that moment's hottest musical acts, presented a golden opportunity to literally stage performative notions of U.S.-Japan togetherness, friendship, and what Dean Rusk decades earlier had called "complete and cordial cooperation." It transfigured agents of state-sponsored violence into music promoters and North Dock into a concert venue, in ways that could help deflect protest and shield the U.S. military presence writ large from critique. Small wonder, then, that USARJ should have all but coproduced the event. As Japanese media coverage from the morning after demonstrates, they made the right bet. In an article titled "Rock Instead of Tomahawks?! 8,000 People Get the Fever," the Yokohama *Yomiuri* reported that "[i]n a way that struck a sharp contrast to the naval base at Yokosuka, where organized demonstrations against the deployment of two Aegis [Arleigh Burke–class] destroyers could be seen on the same day, North Dock saw young people swept up feverishly in the intense rhythms of rock." The Seaside Concert, it seems, afforded the reorientation of Japanese bodies in a city (one of many) still under partial occupation by U.S. forces, displacing the potential for protest and replacing it with pleasure. The very authorized, planned presence of these bodies on North Dock, their envelopment in what the *Yomiuri* called an "American feeling" (*Yomiuri shinbun* 1988b, 14) as they "r[o]de the rhythm with abandon in a wide-open space" (*Kanagawa shinbunsha* 1990, 171), seemed to help *reconstitute* them, transmutating them from potential critics of American and Japanese geopolitical prerogatives into fleshly incarnations of and conduits for the very "friendship" that those prerogatives relied upon.

But nothing in music and its uses is ever quite so simple. The story that USARJ wanted to tell through this event is straightforward enough, but at North Dock critique wasn't simply an outside element that could somehow be neutralized at the gate as the amps were cranked up and bodies began dancing "with abandon": it came from within the enclosures of the event itself. Princess Princess were not yet publicly revealed as headliners when the Seaside Concert was announced on April 26, but by June the band had begun discussing the upcoming show on televised music programs. During one such appearance on *All-Night Fuji*, a late-night program on the Fuji TV network, lead vocalist Okui Kaori said:

> This summer, on August 31st, the last day of our tour, Princess Princess will be holding a concert at a place called North Pier [another name for North Dock], an American military base. This is a place that Japanese people can't get into normally; it totally feels like an America within Japan … once you go over the bridge, and through the gate, there's all this—like, barbed wire? It's a really, um, lovely place. Seriously, even if not for a Princess Princess concert, it's really a place worth going to, and just looking around, so please, this August 31st, come onto an American military base and raise the roof [*matsuri sawagi*] with Princess Princess! (*All-Night Fuji* 1988)

In these pre-concert comments, Princess Princess already seems to be inviting critical reflection on the existence of U.S. military bases in Japan and the nature of that existence—they're "lovely place[s]" strewn with barbed wire, exclusion zones that "Japanese people can't get into normally," not really Japan at all but "an America within Japan"—and urging listeners to think about how these places might be "occupied" differently by exuberant Japanese bodies engaged in musicking on their own terms.

During the concert itself Princess Princess kicked this up a notch. The tenth song of the set was a medium-tempo, piano-centered ballad called "SHE" (the title is in English), with words by Nakayama Kanako and music by Konno Tomoko. It's a mournful reflection on a friend—"Dear my best friend," the song addresses her in English; recall here the band's own title for the event, as opposed to the official one—who has become utterly unrecognizable after falling in love with an American serviceman on a U.S. forces base in Japan. The friend is whisked away to the United States, is married to the soldier, and enters into a world that fundamentally *changes* her (again, the specter of marriage and/as geopolitics). The song takes the form of a sort of recollection, spurred by the arrival of an airmail letter from the erstwhile friend, and is carried along on a simple, sad piano melody. The lyrics read, in part:

> It changed every single thing about you
> That base camp, on Saturdays
> You changed your uniform
> Got all prettied up [*o-share wo shite*], put in your earrings
> And the two of you hurried off [...]

> Watching you and him
> Laughing at incomprehensible jokes [*shiranai jōku*]
> You go, in beyond the barbed wire, while I
> I'm just, I'm just left standing here [...]

> Dear my best friend
> I push your happy-looking snapshot away
> Dear my best friend
> Please, be well, beneath unknown skies.

The choice to perform this particular song at this particular show was an intriguing—and loaded—one. DeNora's conceptualization of the "music event" (DeNora 2003, 35–58)—an analytical framework that informs much of the thinking that I do in this book—can help us think productively about this choice and about the stakes of performing "SHE" at North Dock. Deploying the "event" as analytical framework demands that we pivot away from discussions of what music purportedly "does," means, or reflects, and toward considerations of *what people do with music*—including fans and listeners, of course, but artists themselves, too. This "doing," or use, takes place in specific situations of many types—from individuated listening to literal "events" like the Seaside Concert. The preexisting contexts within which the music is deployed, the moment of musical engagement itself, its resonances after the fact—all are crucial to specifying any "meaning" or significance that engagement with the music might produce. And here, always, resides the potential for one mode of storytelling to interfere with—even derail—another. The city of Yokohama and USARJ positioned Princess Princess as part of a plan to retell a specific story—that of U.S.-Japan "friendship." But the band seemed to hijack those plans, using their own music in ways that the planners likely didn't expect and generating a nuanced critique by embedding "SHE" into a preexisting social and geopolitical context informed by a decades-long maintenance of U.S. military installations on Japanese soil. Indeed, "SHE" only really made sense within that context, and its significance was turboboosted by the fact that the band chose to deploy the song in a performance on an active military installation. The band's own musical storytelling, articulated in "SHE" and performed within the purview of precisely the sort of militarized apparatus that was the main beneficiary of curated stories of U.S.-Japan "friendship" in the first place, seemed to subtly complicate the strategic desires held by USFJ in authorizing their concert there. What the event, and the performance of this song in particular, may have afforded attendees after the fact is an important question— but one that's hard to answer some thirty-five years after the show. At the very least, though, even in the absence of event-specific fieldwork, we can appeal to history, geopolitics, Okui's own pre-event commentary, and so on to show how Princess Princess used their own performance of "SHE" at North Dock to make USFJ's stories of "friendship" make just a little less sense. The band's musical storytelling, in short, generated the potential for envisioning or producing a new world, by chipping away at and destabilizing the old one.

Princess Princess refused to accept the stories that their first label, TDK, told about and through them. They rejected those stories and wrote new ones of their own. I can't help but think that there's something similar underpinning "SHE," and the band's show at North Dock in particular. Although tapped to headline an event that was unmistakably intended to continue a long, varied history of strategically framing and performing U.S.-Japan "friendship" though music, the band took those worn-out stories of "friendship" and *scrambled* them. Like Eri Chiemi and Peggy Hayama, the five women comprising Princess Princess had been expected to become fleshly conduits for U.S.-Japan "friendship"; dolls, after a fashion. If questions of inter-statial "friendship" between the United States and Japan are regularly displaced—in different ways—onto women's fleshly bodies for the purposes of sustaining and pursuing geopolitical prerogatives, then Princess Princess displaced them yet again, routing the story through the body of an actual friend (the song, reportedly, is based in actual experience) that they then tell/sing using their own, showing how U.S.-Japan "friendship" can derail *actual* friendship, warping (Japanese) lives and bodies—"it changed every single thing about you"—and rendering them unrecognizable. This provocative take on "friendship" gummed up the mechanisms of officially sanctioned storytelling *from within its very stronghold,* helping expose it to critical reexamination. Their critique was subtle and complex, anticipating and resonating in important ways with the creative, reimaginative—as opposed to outright "oppositional"—musical storytelling pursued by other artists and social actors I'll visit in this book. At North Dock, that is, Princess Princess revealed themselves as singers of the Homesick Blues in their own right, imploring listeners to come, to see, to think, to conceive critically of this "America within Japan," and by extension of "Japan" itself. And like others whom I'll engage on the tracks that follow, Princess Princess managed to develop this thoughtful critique not by negating from without but by rewriting the story from within.

Reprise

In the spring of 2011, as the American military was assembling thousands of tons of military hardware and tens of thousands of bodies for deployment to the Tōhoku coast, Princess Princess were developing other plans. Although they'd broken up in 1996, the women put the band back together in 2012, playing stadium venues in a fundraising tour meant to support post-3.11 recovery. It was a massive success. The monies raised by Princess Princess and their fans—more than five hundred million yen—went to several different organizations in Iwate, Miyagi, and Fukushima Prefectures, the regions hardest hit by 3.11. Large sums went to training programs for nurses, for example, and thirty million yen went to Tōhoku Fukushi University in Sendai. The biggest portion of the money, however—some three hundred million yen—went to building Sendai PIT (standing for Power Into Tōhoku), a live-music venue that opened on the former site of the largest post-disaster emergency housing complex in Sendai. "We've been a group that does music, so we'd always wanted these funds that we were able to collect through playing music to go to a project that has something to do with music," said lead vocalist Kishitani (formerly Okui) Kaori when the group's funding of the project was announced on August 27, 2015. "If lots of folks gather here from outside the region, it'll connect to the revitalization of Tōhoku." Sendai mayor Okuyama Emiko was enthusiastic: "The venue can ... be a place where new power and new potentials are cultivated," she said (*Sports Nippon,* August 28, 2015). Sendai PIT eventually opened on March 11, 2016—five years to the day from 3.11—and featured, of course, an inaugural performance from its benefactors, although the women insisted that despite appearances, this performance didn't constitute another comeback. Their career as a unit, Kishitani said, had come to an end with Princess Princess's appearance on NHK's *Kōhaku Uta Gassen* [Red and White Song Competition] on New Year's Eve 2012, sixteen months or so after Heino Klinck's flotilla had wrapped up its own work and sailed on from the coast of Japan.

I opened this track by considering Operation Tomodachi, one moment in a very long story of U.S.-Japan "friendship" whose promulgators have regularly made extensive and strategic use of music. I end with a group of women who used their own music to intervene in this storytelling regime, scramble its story lines, tell them differently. In a way, these threads intertwine in northeastern Japan—but their resonances are very different. When America's military hardware showed up off the coast of Tōhoku to begin its humanitarian mission in March 2011, it was there to reassert a closed-ended story, one that had already been conjured and told many times over. Princess Princess, on the other hand, established a local performance site "where new power and new potentials [could be] cultivated," where musical storytelling could be started anew, its possible affordances open-ended, not closed. To be sure, the band is not in any sort of direct conflict with the United States or its aims here—but their post-3.11 work did help to reveal and clarify a different sort of vision for musical storytelling and its potentials than that which had been pursued as (geo)political strategy by America since the Occupation, and that finds one logical endpoint in Operation Tomodachi. And it was, in the end, Princess Princess's own version of musical storytelling that afforded the band's challenge to curated American visions of U.S.-Japan "friendship" at North Dock in the first place.

If we un-pause the tape on Heino Klinck's 2021 comments about U.S.-Japan "friendship" and let it play again, then, we should now find our listening marred by an uncomfortable—or revolutionary—dissonance, an undertone that introduces a disharmony into a storytelling regime that has calcified into a sort of "common sense" over a period of nearly eighty years. The story of U.S.-Japan "friendship" has been told and retold, and as I showed earlier, musical storytelling has constituted an important means through which it's been made to unfurl, its forms and specificities shifting and morphing according to historical moment and geopolitical context. But the hegemonic limit of this storytelling was reached—the script flipped—when Princess Princess dared to rewrite the story from within the very structures they were tapped to sustain, via musical storytelling of their own. This is what accounts for the unsettling dissonance and is surely what Fernandes has in mind when she insists on the "reclaim[ing] of storytelling as a craft that … seeks to transform rather than reproduce global hierarchies and structures of power" (2017, 4). This isn't "protest," per se—rather, it's a negation of the negation (Bourdaghs 2012) that protest requires, an insistence on scrambling the sense-making mechanisms of received storytelling regimes, and a stance that demands we conceive of "politics" differently in order to imagine everyday life anew. As I'll show on the tracks that follow—starting with late "folk" sensation Takada Wataru, who insisted on prioritizing interrogations of what he called "the everyday" over formulaic notions of "protest"—this is precisely what characterizes the singers of the Homesick Blues, each in disparate, sometimes surprising ways.

Takada Wataru, Kansai Folk, and the Tactical Conjuring of the Everyday

A FOLK singer and a journalist walk into a bar.

It's early summer 2004, and a characteristically warm day in the Kichijōji neighborhood of Tokyo. The folk singer (Takada Wataru [1949–2005], generally regarded as a founding figure of the Kansai Folk movement of the late 1960s and early 1970s) and the journalist (Chikushi Tetsuya [1935–2008], generally regarded as one of Japan's greatest critically oriented investigative newsmen) make their way to a quiet corner table upstairs at the Iseya Sō-Honten, an unassuming and inexpensive yakitori joint and watering hole just down the street from Kichijōji Station. The window is open; a breeze floats in. The sun is still high in the sky, but Takada wastes no time getting the party started. He orders oolong tea and a glass of *shōchū* spirits on the rocks from a waiter who clearly doesn't need him to spell out the order—Takada's face is a familiar one here. "I've been coming to this place for thirty-five years," he boasts to Chikushi as they make their way in from the street. "Nearly every day." Comfortably settled now, they begin a conversation that will go on to be featured on the July 3 episode of Tokyo Broadcasting System (TBS)'s *NEWS23*, a nightly news broadcast anchored by Chikushi until 2007 (Takada 2004).

The conversation deepens and the glasses empty (and are refilled), and the folk singer and the journalist talk of many things. They chat about Takada's daily routines and his penchant for getting into the *shōchū* in the early afternoon if he's got nothing else going on. Takada shares his love of people watching, particularly the retirees and pensioners making their way around Kichijōji in the middle of the day (this attention to the mundanities of everyday life is central to Takada's critique and is an issue that I will visit in some detail later). They discuss a brand-new documentary by director Tanada Yuki, titled *Takadawataruteki* [Takada Wataru Style] (2004), which explores Takada's life and career and of which Takada himself heartily approves. Several cups of *shōchū* in and thoroughly inebriated by this point, Takada jovially turns to the camera and, peering into its lens, offers its operator something to eat (the operator, of course, refuses). And finally, evidently deeming Takada sufficiently warmed up, Chikushi drops the question that he really wants to ask. "Takada-san, they're fighting a war over in Iraq right now. That old song of yours—'*Jieitai ni Hairō* [Let's Join the SDF].' Folks are out there singing it. I hear that you're not happy about that."

Freeze the frame. Well-known to scholars and fans of modern Japanese music alike, Takada's "*Jieitai ni Hairō*" (written in 1968, released in 1969) is a bouncy, upbeat, and bitingly satirical work that presents itself as a call to "join, join, join" the Self-Defense Forces, or the SDF—Japan's de facto military. Textually comprised of lyrics by Takada placed atop the melody to Pete Seeger and Malvina Reynolds's 1962 work "Andorra"—which sings of the small, independent European territory of the same name, where "[t]hey spent four dollars and ninety cents/on armaments and their defense … [a]nd if anyone comes with a war budget/they throw the rascals out"—Takada's work invites listeners to "[c]ome on over to the SDF any old time … your body itself is capital … With some help from our American buddies, [l]et's go get those nasty Soviets and Chinese." The whole thing, of course, is done entirely tongue in cheek. Given Japan's Imperial/militarist misadventures in the late nineteenth and early twentieth centuries, public perception of the SDF during the Cold War tended to be characterized by mistrust, particularly in the context of 1960 revisions to the Treaty of Mutual Cooperation and Security between the United States and Japan (better known as the AMPO treaty), which saw Japan entangled ever more extensively with U.S. geopolitical prerogatives and colored by fears of remilitarization (Satō 2012; Midford 2011). And yet, the SDF was growing precipitously in the late 1960s, often relying on relative rural (and sometimes urban) impoverishment and the disavowed unevenness of so-called high-speed economic growth as it maneuvered to expand its ranks (Sasaki 2015, 33; Satō 2012) and offer a place of refuge for "[a]ll of the tough guys, the men among men [who could] join up with the SDF and scatter like the petals of a flower." Within a decade or so the SDF—established, ironically perhaps, with the encouragement of the United States, which was eager to see its new "friend" and ally (see track 1) rearmed in the geopolitical and security contexts of the Reverse Course and the Cold War (French 2014, 87)—had swelled from the relatively small National Police Reserve (1950) and National Safety Force (1952), with 75,000 and 110,000 troops, respectively, to a force of around 250,000, roughly its size today.

All this added up to danger for Takada. It was less than twenty-five years from the end of Japan's disastrous war, and Japan was tethered to the United States through Cold War security arrangements as yet more Asian blood was being spilled in Indochina (Japan's de facto logistical support for the Korean

War the previous decade had already generated critical reflection on the part of many Japanese; see Havens 1987 and Lichten 2012 for more on the intersections between race, war, and geopolitics in these moments). Takada was compelled to respond—but his move wasn't to compose the sort of oppositional "protest song" that was becoming fashionable by 1968 (I discuss this trend in more detail on track 3). Rather, in "*Jieitai ni Hairō*," Takada Wataru spun up critical musical storytelling that shunned straightforward denunciations of the SDF and centered some of the terms and conditions of everyday life in this moment instead, highlighting how the "story" of the SDF was told within them—a move that was particularly significant given the aforementioned sticky ways in which the SDF and its rapid growth were entangled with everyday life and with survival itself, at least for some. These conditions included the geopolitical and security contexts of the song's moment, to be sure, but also the viscerality of capitalist modernity ("your body itself is capital"), its materiality and mundanities, untimeliness, unevenness, and upheavals (Harootunian 2000a, 54), all of which were also factors establishing the circuitry within which the SDF was embedded in 1968 and that enabled its growth. As I'll show on this track, this sort of tactical (de Certeau 1984, xx) foregrounding of the everyday would go on to both characterize Takada's musical storytelling and make him something of an outlier in his own historical moment and artistic tradition. Despite being remembered as a late sixties cultural icon and "protest singer," that is, Takada tended to defy the sixties-style oppositional politics that trended toward the negation of a vague "established system" (Oguma 2015), and that itself constituted a storytelling regime of sorts. This defiance, however, opened up the possibility of a different sort of politics that demanded a grounding engagement with the materialities of the here and now. I'll have much more to say about this in the pages that follow.

Takada's tongue-in-cheek representation of the SDF in 1968 was so insightful and observant—so effective at appropriating and redeploying the stories that the SDF told itself about itself—that it was, bewilderingly, initially taken as supportive of the SDF. In fact, urban legend has it that the song was so warmly received by representatives of Japan's Ministry of Defense after it was featured on a June 1968 episode of the TBS television program *Madame Bola's News* that Takada was approached by a member of the agency for permission to use it in a recruiting campaign (Mitsui 2013)—a request that was, probably on more careful reflection, subsequently withdrawn. But today, "*Jieitai ni Hairō*" is universally understood by scholars and commentators as a "protest song." In a sense, of course, it is. Tōru Mitsui goes so far as to declare that "[o]f all the anti-war songs that were written in 1968, [this one] became the most popular" (Mitsui 2013, 89). But as we rejoin the conversation between the journalist and the folk singer and unfreeze the frame, we learn that Takada Wataru was less than impressed with its deployment by Japanese anti-war activists as a "protest song" in the context of the Iraq War—also known as the second Gulf War—in 2004. The context—the specifics of everyday life—had changed.

Back, then, to summer 2004. Stung by harsh criticism from the United States that the country had shirked its "international responsibilities" (themselves a product of the purported end of the Cold War and its concomitant bipolar ordering of the world) by committing monies but no manpower to the first Gulf War (1990–1991), Japan under the leadership of then prime minister Koizumi Jun'ichirō was eager to commit personnel to the second one, at least to the extent that an acrobatic interpretation of the AMPO Treaty would allow. Japan thus conjured and deployed the Japanese Iraq Reconstruction Group, a largely humanitarian endeavor that seemed to be designed more with soft power than with military power in mind. Many Japanese individuals, however, were alarmed by the first forward deployment of Japanese personnel to a combat zone outside of United Nations auspices since the end of the Pacific War, and tapped "*Jieitai ni Hairō*" as a means of articulating their anxieties and angst. But the only real bridge here connecting the song to the circumstances of its composition is the specter of militarism itself—not the context, not the everyday, which in 2004 was informed by a post–Cold War multipolar ordering of the world, the rise of neoliberalism, and so on. Responding to Chikushi's query, Takada explained, "When I first wrote this, I took everything that they [the SDF, the state] were saying at the time and threw it back at them, right? Thinking that that sort of thing can't be allowed to stand. They're saying that [protest is] fashionable right now, that's why they're singing the song today. But it's wrong. They've got the guts of it [*naiyō*] wrong." What irritated Takada, it seems, was the attempt to use "*Jieitai*" as a sort of transhistorical wrench that could be deployed to critique a militarism that is understood to be transcendent and unmoored from the material realities of everyday life, and part of a vague "established system" that is, paradoxically, reinforced in the very effort to negate it.

Takada continued. "What I try to attend to is the surroundings that we're part of. … Being in those surroundings, the act of singing them—that's what it really means to critique war. Just raising your fist and yelling 'no war!'—that's wishy-washy; it's not enough. Singing the everyday—portraying the everyday [in song], interrogating it, and asking, okay, exactly what is this thing called 'the everyday'? That's what's needed." As he spoke, the folk singer leaned intently over the table, his eyes and voice betraying a desperate desire for the journalist to understand his stance. The awkward silences in the exchange, however, seem to indicate that Chikushi did not, or at least that he struggled to. Though just one moment in a longer conversation, the palpable disconnect between Takada and Chikushi here spoke volumes and seemed to point to a gap between received assumptions of what protest and critique "should be," on the one hand, and the critical praxes of (some) artists and social actors, on the other. It also suggests a different stance on politics itself—a divergent assessment of "what's needed" and how to get there. In this exchange, in short, Takada Wataru was laying out an ethics of musical storytelling that requires a little unpacking.

Despite his criticism of the "fashionable" deployment of "*Jieitai*" in 2004, I don't want to suggest that Takada is somehow ascribing a frozen sort of authenticity to protest, or even to this song itself, that is somehow only viable in 1968. As I'll show on this track, Takada himself appropriated voices from the past in order to articulate critiques in vastly different moments, and at any rate, he is well accustomed to one of the central conundrums of songwriting: "[J]ust like shit and piss," he said in the interview, "once [music's] out in the world there's not a goddamned thing you can do about it." Rather, Takada Wataru—like other voices in this book—invites a careful engagement with the stories that songwriters (and others) tell, and a consideration of how this might inform how we think about critical musical storytelling, or "politics" itself. Takada's musical poesis tells stories of politics and protest and of living in the world that do not mesh well with dominant understandings of the nature of oppositional "protest" and of how it should work, especially in music, and particularly in Japan's critical folk music of the late sixties and early seventies. The silent yet palpable dissonance that marred the discussion between the journalist and the folk singer at its most crucial moment, that is, marked a gap between the ways that Chikushi understood protest, folk, and perhaps even Takada Wataru himself, and the ways that Takada understood the same. As I'll discuss later, critical, often anti-war "folk" in Japan finds itself entangled in a very powerful storytelling regime of its own, one that is both understood as emanating from (some of) the music and, reflexively, ensnares it. Authoritative in both popular and scholarly discourse, this regime understands "folk" largely as oppositional "protest songs," often ones that negate war or what Oguma Eiji has already called, earlier, the "established system." But for Takada, "*Jieitai ni Hairō*" isn't an "anti-war" or "protest" song at all—it's a song about everyday life. And yet, in being a song about everyday life, it is also, necessarily, an anti-war song, a protest song—a song about politics thought differently.

On this track, then, I take this productive communicative misfire between two of modern Japan's most respected political and cultural commentators as a stepping-off point to unpacking the mechanisms of Takada Wataru's musical storytelling. Specifically, I aim to theorize the space of dissonance that opened up between the folk singer and the journalist when they sat down in that smoky Tokyo watering hole, and tease out of it an understanding of Takada's tactical centering of everydayness not merely as a pathway to critical politics but *as critical politics itself,* in a way that I hope will allow Takada to be heard on his own terms. Takada's moment of around 1970 was marked by powerful, contested claims to the authority to tell the story of what it meant to "be Japanese." These emanated from the state and from capital, to be sure, but also from cultural producers like Takada and others, who aimed to disrupt the congealing developmental narratives—themselves storytelling regimes—that were on the verge of being naturalized as Culture by centering (increasingly disavowed) stories of everyday life, a "transgressive" musical storytelling practice that could help to "redefine people's interests and identities in ways that create entirely new lines of contention" (Polletta 2006, 16). In what follows, I'll show this transgressive storytelling at work by considering how Takada Wataru used his recording of "*Akirame-bushi* [The Give-Up Ditty]" (1969) to upset the received narrative of capitalist History by disturbing the flow of teleological, developmental time. I'll go on to discuss how he worked to reset the parameters of critical political engagement by presenting a riotously polyvocal foregrounding of the everyday via his 1971 LP *Goaisatsu* [Greetings]. Takada's aim is not to *overcome* the everyday, but rather to center it as a means of thinking critically about phenomena such as war and their enabling conditions. What I hope to demonstrate is a (re)imaginative, exuberant, toxic, critical conjuring of different histories, one in which the medium—in the case of the *Goaisatsu* LP—is as important as the message.

Birth of a Genre: Takada Wataru and the Rise of Kansai Folk

Along with rock, the electric guitar (*ereki*) boom, Beatles-inspired "group sounds," Japanese pop (*kayōkyoku*), and the newly emergent *enka* (see track 4), U.S.-inspired folk music—which became known as *fooku,* but which I'll continue to refer to as "folk" in the interests of simplicity and consistency—was one of the musical forms that became a soundtrack of sorts for Japan's 1960s and early 1970s. Much like *enka,* and to a lesser extent rock, it became a key musical arena wherein practitioners worked through questions of what it meant to live in Japan, to "be Japanese." Although it would find its heyday around 1970, folk really began to take root in Japan beginning earlier in the sixties, as recordings of U.S. artists like Dylan, Baez, the Kingston Trio, and Pete Seeger found favor with students on university campuses. This was the so-called college folk boom—students with guitars would get together with friends and play copies of mostly U.S. folk standards. Although this form's popularity inspired a few commercial successes (Mike Maki's [b. 1944] "*Bara ga Saita* [The Rose Blossomed]," released in 1966; the 1968 Folk Crusaders single "*Kanashikute Yarikirenai* [I'm So Sad I Can't Go On]"; among others), it was not noted for any of the organic, critical commentary that folk later would be. By the end of the decade, however, more explicitly critical "protest folk" was being composed by songwriters in and around the Kyoto and Osaka region. This was so-called Kansai Folk, and it tapped into both the conditions of everyday life in late sixties Japan and the global spirit of revolt that was so palpable around 1970, spooling out critiques of entrenched political power, the war in Vietnam, and the consequences and contradictions of high-speed economic growth and urbanization that many Japanese individuals, especially students, were experiencing. This was the newly emergent musical form within which Takada would find his own voice after a childhood of poverty, sadness, and struggle, earning fame as one of its most influential, exemplary figures even as he simultaneously helped build it from the ground up.

Takada Wataru was born the son of a poet and former Communist Party member in Gifu Prefecture on New Year's Day 1949, the youngest of four children (Fujimoto et al. 2007). Losing his mother to illness at an early age, the young Takada moved to Tokyo with his father, who worked as a day laborer to support his children. At the age of sixteen, Takada encountered the music of the American folk music revival of the mid-1960s and came to be particularly influenced by Pete Seeger (1919–2014), who played his first shows in Japan in 1963 and heralded the Japanese "folk boom" that was to come. He was so enamored with Seeger, in fact, that Takada—who was by now learning the ukulele and the guitar—enlisted the help of his junior high school English teacher to compose and send the artist a letter in June 1966, wherein he appealed to Seeger for his guidance in writing lyrics and songs. Some two months later, a response arrived from Seeger himself. In it, the artist encouraged the now seventeen-year-old Takada to hone his songwriting skills by studying Seeger's scores and lyric writing via Sing Out! magazine and other publications, and to develop strong musical sensibilities of the sort that would keep audiences coming back to hear him. But one line in Seeger's letter stands out as particularly influential in Takada Wataru's development as an artist and a musical storyteller. "[Y]ou can learn more from your own neighbors and friends," Seeger wrote, than Takada could ever learn from him (Satō 2019). That Takada should have received this advice from Seeger seems, in hindsight, rather ironic, given that it appears to have been a key factor steering him away from Seeger's commitment to established, international leftist solidarity movements and toward the more complex political stance that Takada would go on to develop in his own musical storytelling. I'll describe that stance below.

In any event, Takada was encouraged and invigorated by this encounter with his musical hero, and he continued in his songwriting with renewed determination. Evidently more interested in lyrics/stories than in music—or, put differently, seeing the latter mainly as a vehicle for the former—Takada wrote prose and poetry furiously and for a time dreamed of becoming a man of letters. But in early 1967, tragedy struck his family yet again. Takada's father, Yutaka, his body worn down by years of hard physical labor as a *nikoyon* (a slang term deriving from the approved wages for day laborers in Tokyo in 1949—240 yen: two hundred-yen bills, *ni-ko,* and four ten-yen ones, *yon*), died on January 5. The young Takada, still a minor, was compelled to start working at a printing press to make ends meet and found shelter with his brother for a time. Eventually, he moved to rural Saga Prefecture in Kyushu to stay with an aunt there, helping out in the family's pharmacy during the day and attending night school in the evenings. He kept up with both his writing and his music, though, apparently under the watchful eye of Pete Seeger himself, who looked down from a poster that Takada had hung on his wall. Aware of her nephew's dream of becoming a storyteller and of the implausibility of fulfilling that dream in rural Saga, Takada's aunt urged him to return to Tokyo. Takada did so, and clearly articulated his dreams (which focused more on the literary than on the musical in that moment, though as Takada himself helps us see there's not necessarily a great deal of difference between them) in a diary entry from August 1967:

> This is the dream that I have today. First, I'll graduate from high school, and see if I can enter the Literature Department of a university somewhere. Then *I want to write the story of the paths that our family has lived,* and be able to release that as a book. I don't want to become salaryman-ized, like my brother.
>
> I want to spread my wings. I want to do more of what I want to do than my father was able to, to spread my wings and live an unexpected life. [...] I want to live a more human, more free, poorer (I mean this in monetary terms as well), richer (in spiritual terms) life. Large and wide, to live as a flowing river. (Satō 2019; Takada and Takada 2015)

Spurred by Seeger's exhortations to hear the voices of his own neighbors and friends and filled with the desire to "write the story of the paths that our family has lived," Takada wrote voraciously as a night school student at Ichigaya Commercial High School upon his return to Tokyo (Satō 2019) and was eventually presented with the opportunity to perform some of his lyrics for a small audience there (Fujimoto et al. 2007, 21). Word of the unique song he played—"*Jieitai ni Hairō*"—began to spread, and his reputation as a songwriter began to grow. In August 1968 Takada headed to Kyoto with fellow folk musicians Endō Kenji (1947–2017), who would eventually earn acclaim for his melancholy number "Curry Rice," and Minami Masato (b. 1944) to take part in the Third Kansai Folk Camp, organized by Christian pastor Murata Taku. He brought the house down with "*Jieitai ni Hairō*" and was invited to join the Takaishi

Jimusho music production office, which was preparing to launch URC, the Underground Record Club, a subscription service that would transform music distribution in Japan by delivering records directly into the hands of club members. Takada thus became one of the label's first featured artists; indeed, the first LP distributed by URC was a compilation of recordings by Takada and his contemporaries, folk group Itsutsu no Akai Fūsen (the Five Red Balloons), and included "*Akirame-bushi* [The Give-Up Ditty]," which I'll consider later. In this way, Takada was borne along on the contingencies of his own life to become both heir to and architect of Kansai Folk, and one of its most recognizable names, releasing thirteen original albums and an autobiographical book over a thirty-six-year career, in addition to being made the subject of the aforementioned documentary film in 2004. Although Takada's main medium would not—despite his dream in 1967—be the book, his storytelling impulse is clear: throughout his career, Takada Wataru would tell precisely the stories of crisis and possibility—the stories of everyday life—that his family lived, that Pete Seeger urged him to turn his ear to, and that, as I'll argue later, challenge normative, ideological narratives of developmental History, storytelling regimes that Endo has called "nothing but capitalism itself" (Endo 2012, 1032).

I linger on the particularities of Takada's life to stress the fact that his formative years were wholly enmeshed in the contingencies and contradictions of contemporary capitalism. His experiences narrate a story far removed from that of high-speed economic growth and emergent universal Japanese middle-classism, the story of the purported fulfillment of capitalism itself that would gain traction around 1970. The contingencies of Takada's own everyday life, in other words, challenge dominant, developmental imaginings of History and insist upon telling a different history altogether—the histor(icit)y of the everyday. This is what Takada, in his inebriated afternoon chat with Chikushi Tetsuya, called *nichijō*—"the everyday"—and it's what he insisted on centering in his musical storytelling. This is where the complexities of Takada Wataru's critical praxis begin to reveal themselves. Like other singers of the Homesick Blues that I consider in this book, what Takada Wataru presents in his musical storytelling is not an internal negation of taken-for-granted structures of power, but rather the negation of that negation, a critical reimagining of the terms and conditions of everyday life itself. This is achieved through challenging dominant stories by remixing them with, or simply telling, different ones. As I'll show presently, Takada Wataru had little regard for the developmental economic narratives that tended to dominate his moment around 1970, narratives that muddled everydayness in favor of foregrounding a linear, closed-ended History whose terms and conditions were already defined in antiquity and whose outcome—the fulfillment of capitalism—was already determined. The musical storytelling pursued by Takada centered the very experiential,

Figure 2.1 Takada Wataru backstage at the Haruichiban music festival in Osaka, 1975. Photo by Itokawa Yōji.

visceral, material, mundane, and bluntly *present* everydayness that History disavowed, a tactic that promised, through a forthright grappling with its terms, the possibility of conceiving of history—and living in the world—differently.

"*Akirame-bushi* [The Give-Up Ditty]" and the Undoing of History

Takada Wataru picked up his guitar in the midst of a debate that was already raging in Japan's music world—the so-called rock in Japanese debate. For some time, musicians and critics had been grappling with the question of whether the Japanese language was an acceptable medium for rock and roll, with the general consensus that it was not. Some bands, notably the four-man unit Happy End, resisted this consensus and earned renown for performing and recording rock in the Japanese language (Bourdaghs 2012, 159–194). But Happy End was an important presence not only in Japanese rock, but in Japan's developing folk world as well. The band would back Takada Wataru on the recording of his 1971 album *Goaisatsu*, discussed in the next section, and Takada's protégé Kagawa Ryō on his own 1971 LP *Kyōkun* [Lessons] (I consider Kagawa and *Kyōkun* on track 3). Equally important to the musical overlap between these figures in this moment, however, is the overlap in philosophies of *language*. The development of what would come to be known as Kansai Folk—much of it under the influence of Takada—owes a great deal to the determination to tell original musical stories of/to "Japan" in Japanese that was shared by Happy End and others in the rock world. This also helped distance Kansai Folk from the straightforward translations of American folk standards that tended to mark the college scene in Tokyo and elsewhere and that were—by virtue of being translations—unavoidably removed from everyday Japanese life. Now, scholars have asserted that much critical folk in Japan was informed by a desire for "indigenous ... authenticity," in a moment in which sovereignty itself seemed to be under threat (Bourdaghs 2012, 161). Takada Wataru also insisted on telling his stories in Japanese, and to a certain extent, this desire for authenticity can be detected in that insistence. But like Happy End, Takada had little interest in resurrecting a transcendent authenticity based on an idea of an established *Volk* that could oppose the ills of modern society—in other words, simply negating the existing frameworks of "Japan" itself. Rather, just as the use of the Japanese language decentered the apparent unilingual authority of rock, Takada's musical storytelling—and the best of that which came after him— sought to scramble the so-called authentic altogether and imagine it anew. Indeed, even where translations did play a role in Kansai Folk and in Takada's work specifically (something that did occur, as I'll discuss later), this tended to involve the creative repurposing of literature and poetry, for example, as opposed to translated appeals to the authority of American folk masters. Just as rock in Japanese disrupted linguistic hegemony and expanded the authority to tell stories in that genre, that is, centering the Japanese language in ways that were not reducible to citations of a translated American "authentic" helped Takada and other architects of Kansai Folk develop a critical musical storytelling of "our own" and become singers of the Homesick Blues.

Perhaps ironically, Takada Wataru's determination to tell musical stories of Japan in Japanese owes a great deal to his interactions with his American hero, folk icon Pete Seeger. In his autobiographical *Bourbon Street Blues*, Takada recalls that "[h]e taught me ... that it won't do to simply sing foreign songs just as they are. I have to sing my own songs, songs as manifestations of the Japanese language [*Nihongo to shite no uta*], and that's what I'm experimenting with right now" (Takada 2008).

As I pointed out earlier, Takada had earlier aspirations of becoming a different sort of storyteller, of telling the stories of his own everyday through the medium of the book. A series of contingent encounters pulled him off that course and toward a more focused and ultimately permanent engagement with songwriting and musical storytelling. But as was the case with Happy End and Japanese rock, the storytelling that Takada wanted to pursue—with its emphasis on the everyday experiences of Japanese individuals ("learn … from your own neighbors and friends," Seeger urged) and recourse to the Japanese language, as opposed to the translations of American standards that characterized "college folk"—was *new*: there was no ready-made score or template to refer to. So, he turned to voices of the past for help. In late 1966, one of Takada's own teachers, music critic and folk afficionado Mihashi Kazuo, counseled the eighteen-year-old Wataru to appeal to the critical musical storytellers of the Meiji (1868–1912) and Taishō (1912–1926) periods for inspiration—a suggestion that Takada took seriously (Fujimoto et al. 2007, 92). Just two days after his conversation with Mihashi, Takada would write "A Declaration of a Folk Singer Singing *Enka* Over Traditional North American Melodies" and in 1968 would perform and record "*Akirame-bushi* [The Give-Up Ditty]," a work by turn-of-the-century poet and musician Soeda Azembō (1872–1944).

Soeda Azembō spent his early years as a day laborer in the work camps that marked Japan's capitalist transformation (Soeda 2009), emerging as a cultural figure in the late 1880s and initially gaining renown as a poet and wandering minstrel (*enkashi*). *Enkashi* were figures who might be understood as very early singer-songwriters, of sorts—as I'll discuss later, they had key roles to play in the enunciation of critique at this time. Though he was long dead by the time of its emergence, Soeda and his compositions would go on to have an important second life in the musical storytelling unleashed by Takada Wataru and others nearly a century later. But although this second life seems to intersect with the summoning of an authentic indigenous precedent for folk that scholars have identified in this moment (Bourdaghs 2012, 161; Dorsey 2013, 99), Takada's citation of Soeda in "*Akirame-bushi*" is not about the (re)animation of the vanishing authentic at all. Rather, it's about tapping voices of the past to unleash a jarring sort of *untimeliness* that would play a significant role in the temporal aspects of the critique conjured in his artistry. For Takada Wataru, in other words, past masters like Soeda Azembō aren't oracles, pointing toward vestiges of lost authenticity as monuments to be recouped from an idealized yesteryear. Rather, Soeda's voice is deployed in a tactical scrambling and questioning of History and "progress," as a malleable terrorizer of the now.

As I discuss on track 4, *enka* today are a subset of modern Japanese popular music that tends to be viewed as a bastion of conservatism and as "the heart/ soul of Japan" (Yano 2002, 4). At around the turn of the twentieth century, however, *enka* packed an explicitly critical punch. Growing out of the Freedom and People's Rights Movement of the 1880s, early *enka* were "protest songs," after a fashion—and it's this music that Soeda Azembō would take up as a composer and lyricist. Performed on the streets, *enka* provided a means by which those who "were not allowed to speak their opinions … [could] sing them" (Wilson 1993, 287), and although these *enka* predated the possibility of mass distribution via modern recording technologies, advances in print technology and modernizing transportation networks saw leaflets of the *enkashi* performers' lyrics—whose sale provided an income to the performers—reach far beyond the street corners. Some works of this period, such as the "*Dainamaito-bushi* [Dynamite Ditty]" of 1885, advocated outright violence as a means to wrest political rights and freedoms from the state (Malm 1986, 188; Treat 1996, 112), and it was in the shadow of and in response to such critical musical storytelling that political parties were founded and a National Diet formed in 1890. These appeasements, however, actually helped nudge political *enka* into a gradual decline after 1890, a decline that was hastened by evolving political and economic circumstances. Students in the cities singing different sorts of *enka* that spoke of urban loneliness and longing for the countryside, the importation of Western musical forms and advances in recording technologies that helped to spur a greater interest in the music than its message, and (much more ominously) the High Treason Incident of 1910, which saw anarchist writer Kōtoku Shūsui hanged, all helped chip away at *enka* as medium for critical musical storytelling. Soeda Azembō, however, would continue composing and performing critical *enka* throughout this period. Among his compositions was "*Akirame-bushi* [The Give-Up Ditty]," which Soeda recalled in his memoirs (2009, 119) having composed in 1906.

Scholars tend to emphasize the 1920s as a defining moment of Japan's modernizing upheavals (Silverberg 2006; Harootunian 2000b). Soeda himself, after fading from the *enka* scene as the genre continued to decline and reinvent itself, reemerged in this moment as an ethnographer and analyst of modernizing Asakusa, in Tokyo, providing inspiration and data for Kawabata Yasunari in the writing of his *Scarlet Gang of Asakusa* (Silverberg 2006, 184). But as important as the 1920s are, this is not the moment of "*Akirame-bushi*," and it's important to consider what was happening in Japan at the work's much earlier juncture around 1906.

Capitalist economic development in Japan did not occur at a uniform pace in the decades leading to the 1920s—it was erratic and relatively slow, moving in fits and starts in accordance with geopolitical contingencies such as the first

Sino-Japanese War of 1894–1895, and the Russo-Japanese War of 1904–1905. Until the outbreak of World War I—which "removed most of Japan's advanced, industrial competitors from both domestic and world markets," particularly in heavy industry, and resulted in "an unprecedented stimulus in all sectors of the economy"—the traditional sector remained predominant in Japan (Harootunian 2000b, 3). This does not mean, however, that significant changes were not underway, many of them viscerally experienced by Soeda himself, who, as I mentioned, emerged from labor camps in this period. In the three decades between 1883 and 1913, for example, Japan's workforce grew from twenty-two million persons to twenty-six million. While the bulk of this increase remained in the traditional sector, the burgeoning modern sector also quadrupled during this relatively short period of time. Meanwhile, landowners were consolidating their economic and political grip on the land: consolidated farmland was increasingly leased to tenants, which led to an "accelerated tenancy increas[ing] to about 45% of the farming population by the time of World War I. By 1900 landowners were collecting rents equivalent to almost a quarter of Japan's rice crop," allowing for the investment of capital in local enterprise and the maneuvering of wealth into political power (Harootunian 2000b, 5). Expanding tenancy and the commodification of labor power—among other material conditions— became key factors informing the visceral experience of everyday life in modernizing Japan, and it was frustration over the conditions of Japan's capitalist transformation writ large that Soeda put to music in his "*Akirame-bushi*."

"*Akirame-bushi*" as musical storytelling eviscerates the political-economic conditions of the song's moment—the everyday implications of an emergent capitalist modernity. It speaks to the very frustrations felt by Soeda and others amid a capitalist modernization in which determinations of conditions of life and terms of survival felt increasingly removed from the hands of social actors themselves. But the song also articulates what at first glance seems a certain resignation and deference to the new order. The lyrics read, in part:

> Landlords, the rich—they're all selfish people
> And officials, they're there to put on airs
> Such is this floating world that I was born into
> So I give up, and chalk it up to my own bad luck. [...]
>
> The sweat is wrung out of me, and all my livelihood drained
> Every drop of blood sucked out, and then, on top of that,
> They toss me to the curb, and step on me
> So I give up, chalking that up to my own bad luck, too. [...]
>
> No use meddling with our betters;
> No one can win against a crying kid or a capitalist.

Poverty is just bad luck, and illness a sad burden
And I give up on worrying about them, knowing it can't be helped.

Soeda here invokes precisely the increased tenancy, burgeoning power of the landlord class, expanding wage labor, and commodification of labor power that I noted earlier in my brief historical overview of the period. Until its very end, the work appears more a lament than a critique, a way to give voice to conditions of life under a congealing capitalist regime that are described elsewhere in the lyrics as "suffocating." But in its very last moments, Soeda takes the work's repetitive refrain of "giv[ing] up" and deploys it to turn the tables:

Give up, now; go on and just give up
It'll be better in the long run if you just give up
But I'm an animal that was born free, so
I give up on the idea of giving up [*akirame kirenu to akirameru*].

By suggesting "giv[ing] up on the idea of giving up," Soeda here wrests open a portal for a tactical critique of the apparently already hegemonic terms of life for many in Japan in 1906—and he does so by wryly deploying the very resignation required for its continuous reproduction. The idea of "giving up" feeds back onto itself, becoming a double negative that threatens to eat away at the very normalization of capitalism and "progress" that gave rise to it. Later in life, Soeda apparently succumbed to the lure of survival secured in the bosom of the state, as evidenced in his highly overblown poetic salute to Kishi Nobusuke's 1940 New Order, titled "Advance, New Order, Advance!" (Soeda 2009)—a composition that seemed to celebrate the emergence of fascism itself. In "*Akirame-bushi*," though, we have Soeda at his critical best. It was this Soeda who would be channeled by Takada Wataru in the latter's own critical musical storytelling, as Kansai Folk began to emerge in the late sixties.

Takada recorded Soeda's "*Akirame-bushi*" in 1968, including it on the aforementioned inaugural album from URC that was released the following year. The work is presented in live-recording format, from a performance that, as Takada's framing comments reveal, occurred somewhere around October 1968. "There are only around two months left in the year Meiji 100," the artist deadpans in the recording before launching into the work, "so I'm going to sing through this one carefully [*jikkuri utawasete itadakimasu*]." He goes on to apparently lambaste his compatriots' willingness, at least in his view, to "just give up": "This song is the best one that there is for expressing the disposition of the Japanese people [*Nihonjin no seishitsu*]." Importantly, though, we might also understand Takada here as articulating the very highest of hopes in the collective critical capacity of those compatriots, given the work's concluding twist, whose impact is evident in the chuckling gasps of understanding caught by the recording at its very end.

In a move that seems intended to forefront the lyrical content of the work over the musical, Takada delivers Soeda's poetry over the repetitive, chorusless melody line of the "Black Mountain Rag," an American traditional tune with roots in the Ozark Mountains. Takada's choice of an American tune as the melodic basis for this most "Japanese" (in his view) of works is itself significant. On the one hand, this choice seems to reference the omnipresence of America, a specter haunting the everyday crises that frame Takada's musical storytelling in this moment (the growth of the SDF, the consequences of the Cold War in Asia, the effects of capitalism and high-speed economic growth). On the other, it introduces a sort of conceptual dissonance that is itself destabilizing and reimaginative, anticipating a tactic that I'll revisit in my discussion of the 1971 LP *Goaisatsu,* in the next section. But what is perhaps more important than *what* is being sung about here is *when* it is being sung. I've already noted that Takada, in his redeployment of "*Akirame-bushi,*" pointedly claimed that the year of his performance was Meiji 100—in other words, the one hundredth year of the Meiji era, which commenced in 1868, enveloped the capitalist upheavals detailed earlier and Soeda's 1906 response thereto, and in fact ended in 1912 with the death of the Meiji emperor and the ascendance of the Taishō regent, for whom the ensuing era was named. This claim, of course, is entirely false. The Taishō (1912–1926) and Shōwa (1926–1989) eras, each associated in its own way with "progress," are erased from the historical annals here, and the suggestion seems to be that no real departure was managed from the turbulence and crises of Japan's early forays into capitalism. (Notably, though, this trick also serves to eradicate fascism, the Pacific War, and Soeda's apparent collusion therewith, a potentially more troubling omission that I acknowledge but must leave to the side for now.) And indeed, the very fact that this temporal critique is being mounted in the late 1960s—in the very midst of Japan's period of high-speed economic growth, which lasted from 1955 to 1973— makes it a powerful challenge, along with other highly critical works like Oka-bayashi Nobuyasu's 1969 "*San'ya Burūsu* [San'ya Blues]," to the normative terms of Takada's historical present, with its emphasis on income doubling, emergent universal middle-classism, and the purported overcoming of the contradictions and consequences of capitalism in the achievement of a "miraculous" economic regime whose particulars were somehow hardwired into Japanese DNA. And unlike the New Left critics of this moment, who took "the ravages of the growth-oriented state" (Dower 1993, 22) for granted as precondition to mounting an oppositional critique thereof, Takada's temporal critique resets History in order to scramble the idea of "progress" in the first place.

Takada Wataru's redeployment of "*Akirame-bushi,*" taken intertextually with the artist's own framing commentary, seems to tell a story that draws temporal links between Soeda Azembō's 1906 and Takada's own 1968. It's a story that denies the developmental, teleological narrative that was being strategically deployed to define History in this moment, as contingency and unevenness (that is, everydayness) were on the verge of being made to vanish into claims of capitalism as Culture. This vanishing marked the coagulation of a storytelling regime that Harootunian (1993) has called "Japan's Japan," which in turn marked the moment around 1970 when the stories of capitalist development that had largely been told by America about Japan earlier in the postwar era—"America's Japan"—finally became the stories that Japan told itself about itself. But despite—or, probably better, precisely because of—the much-touted high-speed economic growth of this moment and the purported fulfillment of capitalism and emergence of a universally middle-class Japanese society, unevenness persisted in ways that troubled ideological claims to even development everywhere. High-speed economic growth itself relied upon the maintenance of unevenness between urban centers and rural locales, as evidenced by the notorious *shūshoku ressha*—"employment trains"—that hauled young members of the industrial reserve army out of peripheral prefectures (including Saga, where Takada had spent time in his youth) and into the metropole between 1954 and 1975 to feed economic growth with inexpensive labor power, largely funneled into industry. There was, in short, more than a passing resemblance between everyday life (for some) in the late 1960s and the sorts of everydayness articulated and eviscerated by Soeda in his moment of writing in 1906. Others sensed it, too: writer and lyricist Itsuki Hiroyuki, for example, found in the reimagined, reemergent *enka* of the late 1960s traces of "the sound of groaning coming from someone who is being oppressed, discriminated, and trampled on; someone who is suffering under that weight and yet is attempting to resist it with their whole body" (Nagahara 2017, 202). But for his part, claiming 1968 as "Meiji 100" allowed Takada to disturb the ideological trajectory of modernization theory that held such sway in this moment and that fed notions of an emergent universal middle-classism. It allowed him to propose a different sort of history—not a teleological, national History built on the ideological promise of even development everywhere, but an everyday history founded in the consistent, repetitive violence of capitalism. "Progress," in this history, is revealed to be a lie.

Like Happy End and others, Takada Wataru found himself navigating thorny questions of "authenticity" that animated Japan's popular music scene around 1970. He insisted on telling stories of Japan in Japanese and seemed to turn to the prestige of voices of the past—like Soeda Azembō's—to do so authoritatively. But this wasn't the appeal to transcendent, native authority that it might seem, nor did it amount to reprising a score that had but to be rescued from the muck of modernity in order to be played "better." Rather, in an appeal to untimeliness made all the more powerful for the moment in which it unfurled, Takada turned to Soeda to accentuate the unevenness of his own here and now and highlight some of the contingencies and material realities that persisted in his moment despite intensifying claims of the fulfillment of a universal middle-classness that was purportedly in sight on the horizon. To the extent that Takada sought an "authenticity," it was an authenticity of everyday life that challenged and destabilized teleological narratives of History in favor of emphasizing the untimeliness and unevenness of the present and illuminating the avenues for critical engagement that this opened up. This was a project that Takada would continue to pursue—albeit in different ways—on his 1971 LP *Goaisatsu* [Greetings].

A Politics of Form: *Goaisatsu* [Greetings] (1971) and the Potentials of the LP

After the releases of Takada Wataru's debut single—"*Jieitai ni Hairō*"—and his first URC LP (which featured "*Akirame-bushi*"), the popularity of Kansai Folk continued to surge. The Nakatsugawa Folk Jamboree—also called the All-Japan Folk Jamboree—evolved out of the more modest Kyoto Folk Camp that had helped to launch Takada's career; it was held each year between 1969 and 1971, drawing thousands to an outdoor concert site in rural Gifu Prefecture (Takada himself played all three installments). In 1971, the Haruichiban springtime concert series kicked off in Osaka under the guidance of music producer Fukuoka Fūta. Haruichiban would become an annual event through 1979 and reemerge in the wake of the Hanshin-Awaji (Kobe) Earthquake of 1995, bringing critical musical expression in the form of folk, rock, and other forms to new and old audiences alike. Ironically, folk's own exploding popularity helped to bring about its relative decline after 1972 or so, as countercultural purists found themselves unwilling or unable to reconcile "folk" expression and commercial success. But for a moment, folk (and especially Kansai Folk) was the soundtrack for "protest" in Japan around 1970, as artists wrote and sang songs opposing the Vietnam War, the emperor system, the exploitative nature of capitalism, and more.

Beyond music, as well, these were years in which maneuvering to lay claim to the authority to tell stories of what it meant to "be Japanese" continued unabated. The state, for example, worked to solidify stories of universal Japanese middle-classism by pursuing former prime minister Ikeda Hayato's (1960–1964) so-called income-doubling plan, a strategy instigated in the wake of the upheavals of 1960 in an attempt to deflate some of the material motivation for protest ahead of the next AMPO Treaty renewal in 1970. It was largely successful. U.S. president Nixon got into the game as well, narrating the Japanese in economic terms as "courteous yet ungrateful rivals, a frugal, calculating, hard-working, and superbly regimented people" (Frankel 1971). Many individual social actors remained profoundly, and often violently, dissatisfied with such normatizing modes of "Japanese" storytelling and moved in different ways to counter them. In January 1971, for example, a young salesman from Yokohama burned down the emperor's villa at Hayama. That same year, protestors bombed the home of the head of the Police Affairs Division and set off an explosive device that had been attached to a Christmas tree in Shinjuku. Throughout 1971 a coalition of farmers, leftists, students, and local Chiba Prefecture residents stood against the state and its attempts to appropriate farmland for the construction of New Tokyo (Narita) International Airport, itself a Cold War project whose ends were understood to lay ultimately in the service of capitalism (the airport eventually opened in 1977). And a year earlier, in 1970, famed writer Mishima Yukio (1925–1970) committed ritual suicide at SDF headquarters in Tokyo, having failed to convince the troops to rise up and join him in reclaiming their essential "Japaneseness." The question of what it meant to "be Japanese" around 1970, that is, was far from settled.

But amid it all, Takada Wataru seems to have paid little regard to formulaic notions of counterculture or established modes of protest, preferring instead to keep on telling everyday stories of "Japan" to itself. Like his protégé Kagawa Ryō, whom I'll discuss on the next track, Takada maintained a skepticism toward 1968-style "protest," preferring instead to keep the focus on questions of everyday life and the possibilities of its recalibration through musical storytelling. Unsurprisingly, he responded acerbically and sharply to those who wanted to reduce critique to performative calls to overcome the sort of vaguely defined "established system" mentioned earlier. By 1969, for example, Takada was already expressing impatience with the sorts of formulaic, oppositional actions organized by many self-described "folk" aficionados. In a way that would foreshadow his disdain for the deployment of "Jieitai ni Hairō" in 2004, Takada took aim that year at the so-called Tokyo Folk Guerrilla, a group that had made a name for itself occupying the underground passage leading to the West Exit of Shinjuku Station in Tokyo and filling it with amateur song. The B side of the single release of "Jieitai ni Hairō" featured an acidic ditty titled "Tōkyō Fooku Gerira no Shokun-tachi wo Kataru [Speaking of the Young Men of the Tokyo Folk Guerrilla]," which featured uncharacteristically harsh, tightly wound guitar work and vocals and seemed to encourage a critical appraisal of the membership of that movement.

> ... I'm sure that you know all about them
> those guys from the West Exit of Shinjuku Station
> Called the Folk Guerrilla

Those cool, good-looking elites
Those cool, good-looking heroes
One of them let slip the other day …
"There's a warrant out for my arrest, you know.
Kansai Folk—it's just a fad. It's pretty much reached its limits.
Songs by Takaishi [Toimoya] and Okabayashi [Nobuyasu], just artifacts from a
past age."
And saying this, they started to sing—
Ancient songs from the Kansai Folk repertoire.
A TV news crew was there, filming it …
"Mass media go home!" they said,
Posing for the camera.

What is apparent here is a critique of a certain emphasis on form over content, on a perceived valorization of oppositional politics as fashion. What is lost in this sort of performativity, it seems, is a thorough grappling with the terms and conditions of everyday life, the sort of stance exemplified (in Takada's eyes) by artists like Okabayashi Nobuyasu (b. 1946), who eviscerated the social relations of capitalism in the aforementioned "*San'ya Burūsu*" and who was singled out for a backhanded sort of praise by Takada in "*Tōkyō Fooku Gerira*." In 2004, this critique would translate into what Takada would call the "wishy-washy"— "[j]ust raising your fist and yelling 'no war.'" Already in 1969, in other words, the twenty-year-old Takada was searching for a way to do critical politics *differently*. One of the places that he found it was in the tactical deployment of the long-playing record (LP) and in the remixing of music and his first love: literature.

Takada's appeal to Soeda Azembō for "*Akirame-bushi*" in 1968 anticipated a general tendency in folk in Japan and around the world—the interplay between music and poetry/literature. It's well-known, for example, that Pete Seeger's 1963 recording of "Guantanamera" is based on a turn-of-the-century poem by Cuban revolutionary philosopher and author José Martí. The lyrics to the Byrds' Vietnam-era (1965) "Turn! Turn! Turn!," meanwhile, are taken from the Old Testament, and specifically the book of Ecclesiastes. In Japan, poets were participants in the early "folk camps" that helped launch Takada's career. And as I pointed out earlier, it's been suggested that the appeal to past poetic masters like Soeda Azembō constituted an attempt to "resuscitate" (Mitsui 2013, 91–92) authoritative voices of the past who could help authorize critical praxis in the here and now. But although Takada would turn repeatedly to Soeda as he continued to develop as an artist, this sort of appeal to the stasis of a transhistorical critical authenticity (Eckert 2003) doesn't seem to speak well to the nature of Takada's project. As I showed earlier, Takada both objected to citations of ahistorical authority (his own, in the case of "*Jieitai ni Hairō*") in critical musical storytelling and, simultaneously, appealed to the voices and contexts of past masters like Soeda Azembō to skewer the stories of capitalist fulfillment that were circulating around 1970. But this is not the contradiction that it may seem. Takada's appeal to Soeda in "*Akirame-bushi*" was rooted in a different kind of storytelling—it amounted to a *remix,* an appeal to voices of the past that helps scramble the developmental narrative of the present by centering the everyday, not transcending it in a narrative of indigenous authenticity that is itself similarly ahistorical.

These approaches to musical storytelling—resuscitation on the one hand and the remix on the other—are vastly different, and they imply very different relationships between "literature" and "music." The resuscitative appeal to transhistorical authenticity implies a *buttressing* of the borders between them. Critical authority—what other scholars cited herein call "indigenous precedent" (Dorsey 2013, 99)—is always already contained within the confines of literature in this formulation; music is simply a means of accessing it. At the very moment that literature is tapped for its authority, the gap between literature and music becomes unbridgeable, the site of the distance that gives literature its perceived authority as a source of indigenous precedent in the first place. Music can merely cite and repeat this "precedent" in a claim to critical authority that's never really its own at all, but always the purview of literature. It's a closed-ended formula, one that tends to face toward the past, or worse, face outside of history altogether in its rote recitation of lessons handed down by past masters. Takada Wataru appealed to literature and music to tell everyday stories in a different way, one that involves *breaking down* the boundaries between these forms in order to generate something else entirely. This is exemplified in Takada's 1971 LP *Goaisatsu* [Greetings], which I take up in the next section as a textual (and temporal) site at which vastly different poetic voices can be remixed in a way that both centers everydayness in the now (as was the case with "*Akirame-bushi*") and reveals what wartime philosopher Tosaka Jun (1900–1945), writing in a much earlier moment, would call the *there*-ness, the *da-charakter* of the political—as opposed to its transcendence in a vague "established system"—by embedding it within that very everyday. As I'll discuss in more detail later, Tosaka—in developing a theoretical intervention that he referred to as *yuibutsuron,* or materialism—insisted upon conceiving of the political as situated firmly within everyday life, a move that renders it malleable by forcing its descent from stratospheric conceptual realms of transcendence and emplacing it within its own material contexts. The relentless literary and lyrical citations of material, mundane everyday life that animate *Goaisatsu*—eating ice cream, riding a bike, getting coffee—allow Takada to make precisely this sort of move, as he assembles the stories that comprise his album into a broader political intervention that is made possible precisely because of the nature of the intertextual assemblage at play. Polletta has argued that "[s]tories are bracketed in a flow of discourse; they call the listener's attention to what they reveal" (Polletta 2006, 9). As I'll show later, the LP becomes the very site at which this "flow" is given form, as Takada's stories of the everyday call attention to the malleable politics of the now. This is what amounts to remixing literature into a concept album.

Remix: The Riotous Polyvocality of *Goaisatsu*'s Grooves

Takada Wataru's third LP—*Goaisatsu* [Greetings]—was released in 1971. By this time, Takada had left URC and was signed to King Records, which would soon beget Bellwood Records, a relatively short-lived (1971–1978) label that hosted many of the folk and post-folk voices of the 1970s, including Komuro Hitoshi (b. 1943), Iwai Hiroshi (1944–2000), the group Hachimitsu Pie, Happy End, and Kagawa Ryō. The album is vintage Takada. Backed by instrumentals from Happy End and supported by guest vocals from artists like Kagawa Ryō, folk singer Nakagawa Gorō (b. 1949), and others, it features Takada's exquisitely laid-back, nasal tenor meandering through sixteen tracks—forty-two minutes—of some riotously diverse lyrical material, singing lazily atop talking-blues lines and different variations on twelve-bar blues structures for the most part—although different musical forms (including a French chanson) creep in from time to time.

The album, in short, is a study in polyvocality—especially in terms of lyrical authorship. The opening cut, for example, is a short talking-blues number consisting of poetry from Tanikawa Shuntarō (b. 1931), one of Japan's most widely published poets and translators, who has won acclaim for his plain-spoken, straightforward, yet highly sophisticated writing. Although he wrote the lyrics to one of the most recognizable works of Japan's "protest folk" era—"*Shinda Otoko ga Nokoshita Mono Ha* [What the Dead Man Left Behind]," recorded by folk pioneer Takaishi Tomoya (b. 1941) and others—and has been a strident voice in the post-Fukushima push to abolish nuclear power in Japan (*New York Times*, December 11, 2020), Tanikawa understands himself as having tacked a different course from the dominant oppositional politics of these moments, preferring instead to grapple with questions of lived experience (Poetry Foundation, n.d.). Track 3, "*Nenrei / Haguruma* [Age / Gears]," features Takada's signature acoustic fingerpicking and is built around poetry by Arima Takashi (b. 1931), a Kyoto native and renowned modernist poet who himself became involved in the Kansai Folk movement and contributed lyrics to singers including Iwai Hiroshi (1944–2000) and Nakagawa Gorō (Hikihara and Kuzell 1993, 149). For track 8, "*Burūsu* [The Blues]," Takada turns to a Nakajima Tamotsu translation of the American poet Emily Dickinson (1830–1886), putting her short poem "Life's Trades" ("It's such a little thing to weep / So short a thing to sigh / And yet by trades the size of these / We men and women die!" [Todd 1896, 20]) to a tune that again features Takada's fingerpicking and that's just a minute or so in length. Analysts of Dickinson's work note the ways in which her writing explores the intricacies and trivialities of everyday life (Ackmann 2020), making Takada's choice to include her voice in this album a revealing one. Soeda Azembō makes an appearance on the LP as well—he wrote track 15, "*Shirami no Tabi* [The Louse's Journey]," which Takada transforms into a driving rock song (complete with electric guitar, bass, and drums) sung from the perspective of a louse as he navigates and tries to survive the filthy, precarious conditions of his own existence. And Yoshino Hiroshi's (1926–2014) "*Yūyake* [The Sunset]," with its delightfully attentive and somehow forlorn snapshot of an evening streetcar ride and the depiction of a young woman's struggle between her sense of duty and her sense of comfort robbing her of the chance to take in the beautiful sunset just beyond the window, becomes track 12. In sum, Takada makes broad appeal to poetic commentators on and philosophers of everyday life, in a way that stitches together a diverse and detailed portrait of different moments of immediacy and lived experience. And importantly, in many instances, these musical storytellers speak of nothing but the simple, the visceral, the mundane.

Takada's own lyrical contributions follow a similar sort of tack. In "*Kōhī Burūsu* [The Coffee Blues]," he sings of heading to Inoda Coffee at Sanjō-Sakaimachi in Kyoto to enjoy a cup of joe and see a "cute girl"—likely a waitress—that he was infatuated with (Takada in fact spent a great deal of time both at Inoda Coffee and at the Rokuyōsha, an underground café a bit east of Inoda along Sanjō Street, when he was living in Kyoto). In "*Jitensha ni Notte* [Riding a Bike]," he sings about "riding a bike, ringing the bell, over to that open field to continue our game of baseball; then I'll wash my feet in the river on the way back, riding a bike all the way home." And in fan favorite "*Aisu Kurīmu* [Ice Cream]," Takada delivers a sparse dozen words or so—describing, from a feminized standpoint, how both ice cream and lovers can go bad if left out for too long—over a three-finger picking melody reminiscent of the guitar work of Mississippi John Hurt (1893–1966). There is some confusion over the authorship of the lyrics of "*Aisu Kurīmu*," which are in fact credited to a Kinumaki Shōji, who doesn't seem to exist—fan conjecture suggests that this might in fact be novelist Kinumaki Seizō (1900–1978), but it also may be a white rabbit left in the album by Takada. In any event, none of these tracks explicitly suggests a topical, oppositional stance on anything; rather, they tend to highlight and make present the mundanities of everyday life, which, with the possible geographical restrictions imposed by the specificities of the café in "*Kōhī Burūsu*," are arguably accessible to all. But as I'll suggest later, this apparent apoliticality begins to look rather different when we stand back and consider the album as a cohesive whole.

Goaisatsu taps Takada's well-established concern with political-economic questions as well. Intentionally placed sardonic songs needle the costs of the growth of Japan's consumer economy around 1970. In *"Neage* [Price Increases]"—track 11 of the album, with lyrics by the aforementioned Arima Takashi—Takada adopts the voice of a capitalist who can't keep his story straight. Explaining pricing policy for a commodity that is unspecified in the poem/song, the voice literally changes its tune with every line, moving from "We aren't thinking of price increases at all" to "We don't plan on adopting price increases right away" to "Some are saying that price increases are unavoidable" through "Price increases are unavoidable / We're moving ahead with price increases." Though nowhere near the alarming, double-digit spikes that would arrive by the middle of the decade, inflation in Japan in 1971 was already greater than 6 percent, and we can note here a familiar citation by Takada of the challenges of everyday life under capitalism. And as an ironic sort of indication of both the longevity of Takada Wataru's work in modern Japan and the persistent growth of the costs of capitalism, it's worth pointing out that in 2016, the Akagi Nyūgyō Company used *"Neage"* to announce and "apologize" for raising the price on its GariGari-Kun, a massively popular and inexpensive iced treat found in convenience stores around the country, from sixty to seventy yen—the first "price increase" on the product in twenty-five years, and one that came in the context of different sorts of everyday challenges, amid growing socioeconomic unevenness in Japan.

But there are more explicitly political cuts on the record as well—or, put differently, cuts that might be more readily associated with dominant understandings of the "political." Tracks 2, *"Shitsugyō Teate* [Unemployment Benefits]," and 9, *"Onajimi no Mijikai Tegami* [That Familiar Short Letter]," are adapted from works by Black American jazz poet and social activist Langston Hughes (1902–1967), which in turn were translated into Japanese by Kyoto-based poet and lyricist Kijima Hajime (1928–2004). At first glance, Hughes seems a commonsensical choice for inclusion on an album that ultimately aims to mount a critical intervention into questions of politics, history, and the nature of "Japan" itself—it's well-known, for instance, that Hughes was detained by the Tokyo Metropolitan Police during a visit to Japan in 1933; he was suspected both of being a Communist spy and of collaborating with other leftist figures in the country. Hughes made no bones about how he saw Japan in this moment: "Japan [is] a Fascist country," he'd declare in an interview on his return to the United States (Huh 2017, 204–206). At the same time, though, the two Hughes works selected for inclusion on the *Goaisatsu* LP also reveal a subtler political intervention at play on the part of Takada—one whose effect is to draw attention to the mundanities and materialities of everyday life. Track 2, adapted from Hughes's 1942 poem "Fired," seems to extend the attention paid by Takada to the commodification of labor power (such as with Soeda's "*Akirame-bushi*") and the existential challenges of capitalism (such as with Arima's "*Neage*"), but in a different, delightfully unconcerned sort of way. Hughes's original—translated nearly verbatim by Kijima—reads:

> Awake all night with loving
> The bright day caught me
> Unawares—asleep.
>
> "Late to work again,"
> The boss man said
> "You're fired!"
>
> So I went back to bed—
> And dreamed the sweetest dreams
> With Caledonia's arm
> Beneath my head. (Hughes et al. 1994, 260)

Like Soeda, Hughes—and Takada via Hughes and Kijima—cites the allegedly unavoidable imperative of selling labor power to survive, arguably the corner-stone of capitalist modernity. Soeda, as I've discussed, offers "giv[ing] up on the idea of giving up" on critiquing its purported authority as a method for challenging this norm. In a similar sort of move, Hughes offers a decidedly bright and unconcerned vision of the consequences of turning one's back on capitalism's dominant exchange (Karatani 2014). What is apparent here is a recalibration of value; as I've argued elsewhere in an examination of a different narrative mode (Aalgaard 2019), rejecting the authority of this exchange as the mechanism through which value is defined and turning to find it elsewhere is itself a form of storytelling that disturbs the terms and conditions of capitalist modernity. Unemployment, in this recalibrated value matrix, presents benefits of its own.

"*Onajimi no Mijikai Tegami* [That Familiar Short Letter]" presents an even more complex critique, through an intertextual remixing of verse by Langston Hughes and music by French musician and writer Boris Vian (1920–1959). Hughes's poem "Little Old Letter," originally published in 1943, tells a chilling story of receiving devastating written correspondence in the mail. The precise nature and content of this correspondence is not revealed, but it is so harsh as to be murderous: "Just a pencil and paper," Hughes writes; "don't need no gun nor knife— / A little old letter / Can take a person's life" (Hughes et al. 1994, 271). Since his receipt of the letter is associated with the fact that "I was born black[,]" it is not difficult to conceive here of the dehumanizing, incapacitating physical and psychological trauma associated with institutionalized racisms targeting the Black community in 1940s New York. And since the short communiqué is written in pencil, it is not difficult to imagine a scrawled letter stuffed into a mailbox announcing a racially motivated intent to harm, or kill.

Takada's move here is to deliver Kijima's translation of Hughes's verse atop music written by Boris Vian for his "*Le Déserteur*." Written in 1954—at the tail end of the first Indochina War between French colonialists and the Viet Minh— "*Le Déserteur*" is a contemplative ballad with occasional hints of French chanson, with lyrics constituting a letter rejecting military service that is sung to the French president: "I am not on this earth to kill wretched people … my decision is made, I'm going to desert. […] Refuse to obey / refuse to do it / don't go to war / refuse to go." The impetus for this defiant declaration lies in Vian / the narrator having "just received / my call up papers / to leave for the front[,]" a different sort of "little old letter" that similarly carries the threat of ending the recipient's life. Versions of "*Le Déserteur*" were subsequently recorded by American folk acts including Peter, Paul and Mary (1964) and Joan Baez (1980), with the effect of articulating a straightforward, pacifist, anti-militarist critique in the context of intensifying conflict in Southeast Asia in the 1960s. But there is more to Takada's project than a straightforward oppositional critique of conscription in the moment of the Vietnam War. First, as he did with "*Akirame-bushi*," Takada taps allegedly overcome histories to reveal their persistence in his own everyday. The life-ending letter here carries echoes of the *akagami* (red letter) draft notices that reached many millions of young Japanese men during the Pacific War, in a way that intersects with Japanese critiques of the SDF in this moment of alarm over aggressive recruitment and the specter of revived militarism (placing it squarely in the orbit of "*Jieitai ni Hairō*"). Second, Takada's remix of Hughes and Vian also helps him to articulate the interrelations among capitalist modernity, racism, and the militarized state. This certainly resonates with the alarm being sounded by some Japanese over the racial dimensions of the U.S.-led Vietnam War in 1971 (Roberson 2011, 593–620) and the tendency for Japan's own Imperial history to be both forgotten and repeated under the racializing auspices of the American military umbrella during the Cold War (Lichten 2012, 1–24). But it digs around at something more fundamental as well. Although Takada's lyrics do not include Langston Hughes's important citation of Blackness, by assigning Hughes's verse to Vian's music, "*Tegami*" becomes a critique of the ways in which militarism is enabled by modes of discrimination—in Japan's case in this moment, class and regional discrimination, as the SDF in this period became a shelter for the industrial reserve army and those mired in poverty in the midst of so-called high-speed economic growth, particularly in rural sites like Kyushu. In short, close attention to this two-minute track reveals critical musical storytelling that is both domestic and global in scope and that points beyond calls for pacifism toward an engagement with the conditions of everyday life that feed militarism in the first place.

But by far the most prevalent poetic voice on *Goaisatsu* belongs to Ryūkyūan (Okinawan) poet and author Yamanokuchi Baku (1903–1963), a figure probably best-known for his 1938 novella *Mr. Saitō of Heaven Building*. A frequent and vociferous critic of geopolitics in the 1960s—particularly pertaining to Okinawa's positionality in the U.S.-Japan Security Treaty—Yamanokuchi wrote "Unsinkable Aircraft Carrier Okinawa" in 1964, a poem that satirizes former prime minister Nakasone Yashuhiro's valorization of the "heroic" role assigned to Okinawa in the context of the Cold War, where it was (and continues to be) situated at the front lines of American security interests in the Pacific and beyond, and indeed of the U.S.-Japan alliance itself (see track 1). For Yamanokuchi, the reality of this alliance in Okinawa is that "800,000 wretched lives / have been driven into a corner of the deck / with no way to grow rice / on the steel and concrete" (Rabson 1998, 221–222). Although Yamanokuchi penned several of the lyrics that became *Goaisatsu* tracks—including the bouncy, Carter Family–esque *"Seikatsu no Gara* [The Essence of Everyday Life]," a frequently performed and rerecorded Takada Wataru staple that sings of a narrator who "grew tired of walking / and hunkering down in the space between / the earth and the night sky / fell asleep amidst the grasses"—his most pointedly critical contribution to the LP is probably *"Maguro ni Iwashi* [Sardines for Tuna]," which grapples with the *Lucky Dragon No. 5* incident of 1954. (Yamanokuchi's original poem, repurposed verbatim by Takada for the *Goaisatsu* LP, appears in Yamanokuchi 1964.)

The *Lucky Dragon No. 5* incident is well-known. On March 1, a tuna trawler—the *Lucky Dragon No. 5,* or *Daigo Fukuryū Maru*—out of the port of Yaizu in Shizuoka Prefecture, with twenty-three souls aboard, was fishing around the Marshall Islands in the South Pacific. Not far away, at Bikini Atoll, the U.S. military was preparing to conduct the Castle Bravo atmospheric thermonuclear weapons test, which would be remembered as the largest nuclear weapons test to date. Despite being outside the published danger zone designated by U.S. military authorities, the *Lucky Dragon No. 5* and its crew encountered the fallout from the Castle Bravo test—falling in the form of ash—and although the vessel quickly exited the area, all twenty-three crew members would be stricken with acute radiation poisoning. One, radio operator Kuboyama Aikichi, ultimately succumbed to its effects in September of that year. In addition to inspiring one of the most venerable monster-movie franchises of all time—Honda Ishirō's film *Gojira* [Godzilla] would be released by Toho Studios in late 1954—this tragedy rocked a Japanese public that was increasingly wary of its positionality in the Cold War global order, and of its purported protection under the American nuclear umbrella a scant nine years after the atomic destruction of Hiroshima and Nagasaki.

"*Maguro ni Iwashi*" is a complex, multilayered poem, which Takada sets to music atop an unhurried three-quarter-time waltz rhythm, with appeal to acoustic guitar and accordion. It tells the story of a wife—and, eventually, her husband—who want to draw a line of demarcation between the human world and the natural one and lay claim to an essential, top-of-the-food-chain sort of humanity by consuming tuna *sashimi*. The work begins:

> I feel like eating
> Tuna sashimi
> Said my wife,
> Sounding like a human
> And having been told thus, I too
> Put on human airs
> And began dreaming
> Of tuna sashimi, but
> Got annoyed, and said
> If you don't mind dying,
> Then go ahead and have some
> My wife pouted,
> And turned away, but
> Husband and wife are both
> Tuna, after all.

The poem here clearly references the tuna trawler and its irradiated catch, with a warning about the consumption of contaminated seafood. But there's a hint of a sort of self-destruction here, as well, of death arriving not only in radioactive toxicity, but also on a misrecognition of humanity as somehow fundamentally separate and removed from the natural order despite its embeddedness therein (Latour 1993) and the attendant, lurking threat that the consumption of the other is always actually the consumption of the self. The poem continues in a similar vein:

> Everyone walking this earth, we're all tuna
> Tuna despise nuclear bombs
> And are threatened by hydrogen bombs
> We live this modern world
> Full of anger, full of anger, full of anger.

The rhetoric of harnessing the atom—of the military deployment of nuclear weaponry and the "peaceful" use of nuclear power—has long been wrapped up in the "modern" drive to subjugate nature and harness it for human uses, and the struggle articulated in "*Maguro ni Iwashi*" might be understood as the struggle between the desire to sustain that claim and the recognition of the deadliness inherent in the impossible attempt to do so. And although there's a fleeting recognition at this midpoint in the poem of the interconnectivity of the human world and the nonhuman and the ramifications that the harnessing of nuclear power have for all, it doesn't last.

> One day I peered down at my plate,
> And said to my wife
> "Ash from Bikini is all over this."
> My wife flipped her chopsticks around
> And took it back to the kitchen,
> And poking at the head of the burned sardine, muttered
> "It's just the ash from the grill."

> I feel like eating
> Tuna sashimi
> The husband started in as well,
> Sounding like a human.

The flickering recognition of the commonality of the human and the nonhuman, and of the fallacy of exerting a terrifying utility over a purportedly external natural world, fades in this disheartening conclusion. Sardines are, of course, food both for humans and for tuna, and in disavowing the toxicity of the Bikini ash that sickened the crew of the *Lucky Dragon No. 5* and poisoned its catch—"It's just ash from the grill"—the human impulse here disavows its own susceptibility to the toxicity of the very tools used in the domination of the natural order and reignites a promise of self-destruction. Despite "[s]ounding like a human," the "husband and the wife are both tuna, after all," and the poisoning of the tuna is the poisoning of themselves. In the very attempt to separate the human world from the natural in order to facilitate its domination and lay claim to "humanity," that is, humanity devours itself. The quest to dominate and extract surplus value from the natural world has been one of the driving forces of capitalist modernity, and from the methylmercury poisoning of the sea at Minamata in the 1950s to the irradiation of the land at Fukushima in 2011 and beyond, history has demonstrated its dangerous fallacy (Walker 2010). In "*Maguro ni Iwashi*," this key transaction of modernity is foregrounded (along with the shadows of geopolitics and the militarist state), centered in a way that can help facilitate a critique thereof, and of the everyday life that both envelops and is defined by them. This making present of the mundanities, terms, and conditions of everyday life—a consistent thread connecting all the tracks of *Goaisatsu*—is central to Takada's critique, something I'll explore in more detail later. Here, let me stress simply that "*Maguro ni Iwashi*" establishes Yamanokuchi Baku as an incisive philosopher of the everyday—of Takada's *nichijō*—making him very much at home on *Goaisatsu*. Takada would remain a great fan, producing an album later in his career (1999) that was comprised entirely of Yamanokuchi lyrics (called, simply, *Baku*). The combined literary and musical efforts of Yamanokuchi and Takada led critics to appraise *Baku*'s tracks as *yunta,* or Okinawan labor songs (Takada 2015)—an unsurprising assessment given Takada's unrelenting interrogation of the material terms and conditions of the everyday.

Synthesis: Situating *Goaisatsu*'s Cuts as Components of an LP

I am left, then, to think about how we might synthesize *Goaisatsu*'s tracks and think productively about the LP's intertextuality and polyvocality, and how doing so might help to clarify Takada Wataru's ethics of musical storytelling. Given Takada's reputation as a founding figure of Kansai-based "protest folk," the cuts on *Goaisatsu* that grapple explicitly with structural, historical, and political-economic questions (like "*Maguro ni Iwashi*") seem more or less at home on the album. The more intriguing question concerns the ways in which these interrogations of militarism and marginality, the terms and conditions of the capitalist everyday, and of nuclear power—and, by extension, of the geo-politics of the Cold War and the U.S.-Japan security alliance—are made to sit alongside mundane musical stories of riding a bike, getting coffee, and enjoying an ice cream. There seems to be, in short, an odd copresence of the political and the apolitical on this album. At first glance, this can seem a (partial) sidestep-ping of the political (Bourdaghs 2012, 161–162), a betrayal of the critical prom-ises of the musical tradition that Takada himself helped to establish. But I want to suggest that there's something more complex going on here. The dizzying topical, chronological, and geopolitical heterogeneity narrated by these tracks—poems, in many cases—is sutured together by Takada in a way that in fact both articulates the presentness, the *there*-ness, of everyday life, and, in a temporal unfurling potentiated by the long-playing (LP) record, presents a messy, chaotic challenge to the orderly, teleological narrative of everyday life that was circulating around 1970. On *Goaisatsu,* diverse literary interventions from different moments, locales, languages, and traditions are rendered musi-cal and compiled into an LP—a *concept album*—in a way that both reveals and invites a confrontation with the terms and conditions of everyday life, and "grounds" politics in the process.

Takada's son, Ren—himself a singer-songwriter—explained this approach in an interview in 2015. "My father debuted with '*Jieitai ni Hairō*,' but from the time he moved over to Bellwood Records and released *Goaisatsu,* he made a point of *packaging the political differently,* shifting his gaze to everyday life, to what regular people are seeing, hearing, how they're living" (Takada 2015). As I'll explain momentarily by pivoting back to wartime philosopher Tosaka Jun, what may appear to be a sidestepping of politics in an embrace of the abstract and the rejection of the directly topical is in fact better understood as a tactic aimed at rendering the political *present, there*—and thus malleable. By 1971, this was a tactic that was growing in importance as the historical moment continued to change. Lacking the key anchor points of (for example) the AMPO revisions and already devolving into an anti-modernist, existential sort of angst, critical politics in this moment was becoming unmoored from material specificities and was drifting toward the negation of a vague "established system" that had to be overcome, even as that system was part and parcel of the negating Japanese self and its embeddedness in History. As Oguma Eiji (2015) has pointed out, this circular self-negation became a key factor fueling the collapse of organized, street-level protest in the early 1970s as many Japanese lost patience with what was seen as an "incomprehensible morass of childish rebelliousness," performative and unmoored from the material realities of life—indeed, echoes of Takada's critique of the Shinjuku Folk Guerrilla can be detected here. Takada's critical musical storytelling seems to have sought to resolve this rendering abstract of the political by literally remixing politics and the mundane—by centering the everyday and rendering politics a material, accessible, malleable part of day-to-day life. This centering of the everyday both challenged the claims of a transcendent, conceptual History and—via its embedding in the mundanities of everyday life—rendered politics specific, near, and subject to critical examination.

This remixing as it's manifested on *Goaisatsu* relies on the structure of the recording itself. As scholars have repeatedly pointed out, the medium matters. David Novak, for example, has shown how the creation and sharing of mixtapes became part of the circuits of exchange between listeners and artists that both removed production authority from the hands of record companies—leading to what he calls a "democratization" (Novak 2013, 203)—and helped to define the contours of a scene called Noise. The material, low-fidelity *sound* of cassettes as well—with their repeated over-recording and attendant hissing and popping—helped to establish its aesthetics. Exploring an earlier moment, Kerim Yasar argues that recorded sound became a key modality by which Japan itself was imagined, in both its presences and its absences—on the one hand, the partnership between radio programming and recorded music in the processes of nation making in early modern Japan helped to create a "shared culture … that shaped the sensibilities of entire generations" (Yasar 2018, 24), while the conspicuous *absence* of recordings of the emperor's voice during the Pacific War helped to generate an aura that was shattered when his recorded voice was broadcast to announce the war's end. And in a different geopolitical context, Michael Schmidt—taking up the LP rerelease of works by American jazz great Louis Armstrong—demonstrates the ways in which the LP both produces and is ascribed a significance that is more than the sum of its grooves (Schmidt 2018, 304–331). In order to conceive productively of Takada Wataru's critique, it's important to consider the specific natures and uses of the LP as a storytelling medium, and I'll linger with Schmidt for a moment to do so.

The 33⅓-rpm long-playing (LP) record was developed by Columbia Records in 1948. Initially, the LP was used mainly as a repackaging mechanism for the 78 rpm singles that had been the norm in recorded music to that point—it was a new technology deployed mainly as a means of (re-)selling musical commodities in the context of a postwar economic slump (such as, according to Schmidt, with the early Frank Sinatra LPs). But as time went on, different uses of the LP would open up different ways for the medium to carry and ascribe meaning and significance, depending on the ways in which it became embedded in the world. When Louis Armstrong's hot-jazz 78 singles from the 1920s and early 1930s were repackaged in LP format in 1951, for example, the sonic frequencies of the tracks remained the same, but they were nonetheless *transformed* into objects ascribed a new sort of value and collectability on the basis of their commodification by those authorized with the capital (economic and otherwise) to declare such distinctiveness. The ways in which the tracks fed back into shifting historic, economic, and racialized moments begat different articulations of worlds of significance. Cover art, liner notes, everything became part of the process that made the LP something greater than the sum of its parts: "Albums needed to be created in a way that made sense within the terms set out by jazz criticism and history. The organization of the tracks, the categories used, and the type of information given all had to speak to the specific categories and knowledge of jazz listeners" (Schmidt 2018, 317). As a cohesive whole, LPs "defined their own individual sounds while simultaneously linking those recordings to a larger set of recordings, ideas, material, practices and institutions [and] whatever else in the customer's experience can be related to the album at hand" (Schmidt 2018, 322). A "music event" of sorts in its own right (DeNora 2003), the LP thus became a medium that could both afford the imagining of worlds and take its own enduring significance from the contexts that it is spliced into. The LP as a wholistic entity, in other words, could be tapped to tell a historically and contextually specific story, and one that could be quite distinct from that suggested by its individual parts, in ways that the 78, with its limitations of space, simply could not. And importantly, this was a story that *unfolded in time,* as track ordering and so on invited an appreciation (in the case of Schmidt's example) for Louis Armstrong's development as an artist, and so on.

The LP format arrived in Japan in March 1951, initially as media that could afford longer, uninterrupted listenings of recorded classical music. But the format ended up being widely utilized in other genres as well, including folk. When the Underground Record Club (URC) was established in 1969, subscribers would receive two singles and a full LP at each semimonthly distribution, for a subscription fee of two thousand yen (as I've noted, the first LP distributed by URC was in fact a compilation by Takada Wataru and folk group Itsutsu no Akai Fūsen and featured Takada's live recording of Soeda's "*Akirame-bushi*"). Takada himself seems to have preferred the LP format—over a thirty-six-year career, he released just nine singles, compared to thirteen full-length LPs (six more compilation LPs would be released after his death). *Goaisatsu* itself would generate just one single in 1971, when "*Jitensha ni Notte*" was released in EP format, coupled with "*Kōhī Burūsu*" on the flip side. *Goaisatsu,* that is, was meant to be listened to as an LP, not as a series of stand-alone singles.

There's a reason for this. As I discussed earlier in the context of the rerelease of Louis Armstrong's singles—and as is evidenced by the eagerness with which the LP was taken up as a medium for classical music to deliver on the desire for an uninterrupted, unfolding listening experience—the LP format lends itself more productively to musical storytelling. Takada Wataru was certainly not alone in using the medium of the LP in this way. At around the time of his debut in 1969, the *concept album*—which aims to present and articulate a cohesive whole and conjure a narrative that unfolds in time (Stimeling 2011, 399–404)—was gaining credence as expressive form in the rock world, and artists in other genres were experimenting with it as well. The same year that *Goaisatsu* was released in Japan, for example, American singer-songwriter Willie Nelson released the concept album *Yesterday's Wine,* which explored the idea that, in Nelson's terms, "life on earth is a quest for returning to God" (Stimeling 2011, 394). Despite the album's being more or less doomed to commercial failure, RCA (Nelson's label at the time) extended its support to Nelson for the project because it was seen as tapping a desire among the "emerging countercultural country audience" for a more cerebral narrative reflection on the nature of life and the metaphysical—that is, a desire for more in-depth stories. Nelson himself, meanwhile, "insist[ed] that *Yesterday's Wine* be approached as a complete and unified musical and narrative expression"—in short, as musical storytelling (Stimeling 2011, 397).

Meanwhile, closer to home for Takada, Happy End released the LP *Kazemachi Roman* [Romance in the City of Wind] in 1971. *Kazemachi,* broadly considered to be a standard-bearer for concept albums within Japan and beyond, tells an expansive story of Tokyo prior to the transformations visited upon it with the Olympics of 1964: "With the Tokyo Olympics in 1964, the house that I'd been living in to that point became a road," recalls Matsumoto Takashi, lyricist for Happy End, discussing the album in a 2019 interview. "As a student, I'd figured that it's more important to nurture [*taisetsu ni shinaito*] the city that exists in my memory than the one that's actually there in the world" (Matsumoto 2019). Concept albums of the sort that were circulating around 1970, in short, foregrounded a consciously narratory approach; deploying this form presented an explicit challenge to the econocentric logic of three-minute singles that could meld well with the complementary structures of radio airplay and sales, but also allowed for a story to be built. While neither the elder nor the younger Takada, to the best of my knowledge, has explicitly characterized *Goaisatsu* as a concept album, I want to suggest that we can best understand it, and best conceive of Takada Wataru's critique, by conceiving of it in those terms.

If Willie Nelson's *Yesterday's Wine* consists of a "complete and unified musical and narrative expression," *Goaisatsu*'s unity is in its disunity. As I outlined earlier, the album starts with a greeting—*goaisatsu* in Japanese, the album title itself—and then immediately begins unfurling a series of tracks that are dizzying in their disparity. These tracks address matters as politicized as the Cold War and nuclear power, at one end of the spectrum, and as mundane as eating ice cream or riding a bike, on the other. The verses come from everywhere—disparate authors, disparate times, disparate histories, disparate linguistic and geopolitical contexts—and are sutured together in a Japanese narrative articulated by the gentle voice of Takada Wataru, which unfolds over a span of forty-two minutes or so (plus the time required to flip the LP). Working back from Takada's desperate 2004 attempt to have Chikushi Tetsuya understand his critique not as negation or opposition but as a confrontation with the terms and conditions of everyday life, we can begin to think about how the album—and the specificities of the LP as medium—potentiates this confrontation. Each of the lyrical contributions of the album, in all their temporal and geographical diversity, is repackaged by Takada within a slice of aural time to both present an audible vision of the everyday and intervene in "hegemonically ordered everyday life" (Marotti 2013, 99) by positing a self-enclosed temporality of the type that could only ever be afforded by the LP, one that is simultaneously distinct from and embedded in the world. This is a temporality that's almost irredeemably messy and untimely rather than linear and teleological—here again are echoes of the tactics deployed in "*Akirame-bushi*"—but that also insists upon the materiality, the *there*-ness, of the everyday for its embeddedness within it. In other words, *Goaisatsu* presents itself as a story that both challenges the authority of History and imagines history differently, one that unfurls in defined time as it marks the contours of material, everyday space.

I can better demonstrate the common concept at work here, I think, by appealing to philosophical insights on the nature of the everyday, and its critical potentialities. Though their moments and modes of engagement are radically different, I want to suggest that we can get a better grasp of Takada's ethics by returning to philosopher and intellectual Tosaka Jun and exploring his insights on *everyday space*. Tosaka was born in 1900 and graduated from the Department of Philosophy at Kyoto University, having studied under the guidance of (and gone on to critique) Nishida Kitarō, a key figure in the Kyoto School of philosophy. Tosaka's work was driven by rigorous critiques of political economy and everyday life, and his engagement with the question of space was informed by a "historical materialism centered on the concept of the everyday ... [and an] insistence that practice needs to be centered in the here and now." Importantly, this materialism rejects both notions of space-time parallelism and notions of an uninterrupted, detached sort of stream-of-consciousness temporal flow (Bergson's [2011] *durée*), insisting instead that "time [be brought] into the realm of 'thereness' and practical activity" (Kawashima et al. 2014, 132). Time, motion, and matter find a dialectical unity in Tosaka's conceptualization of materialism—*yuibutsuron*—meaning both that time unfolds in tandem with material practice and, depending upon the nature of this unfolding, that the present moment of practice is always potentially "available as a moment of intervention *within* history" and the (contingent) totality of historical time (Kawashima et al. 2013, 126). This contingent site of materiality, practice, and unfolding temporality—the space of everydayness—becomes "the space where history is made" (Kawashima et al. 2013, 136). And as I suggest later, this assertion of practice and/as historical intervention in the face of the purported authority of the transcendent and conceptual, and in resistance to the claims of an already completed History (Kawashima et al. 2013, 138), helps to unlock the politicality of the *Goaisatsu* LP around 1970.

History is important in understanding Tosaka's interventions. Writing in a moment marked by the ascendance of fascism in Japan, Tosaka's project was, in part, to undo the authority of a spatial means of conceiving of the world that was oriented toward the transcendent and the conceptual, and conducive to what he would elsewhere call "Japanism" (Kawashima et al. 2013, 59–69). Refusing to defer to the authority of transcendent space as the vessel determining and defining human existence—Martin Heidegger's *Dasein,* an anchoring and ultimately ahistorical Being-in-the-world that left traces in modernity and that could be tracked in order to pursue and access an authentic self—Tosaka insisted upon revealing the *da-charakter,* the *there*-ness, of living in the world. This is the methodology that he called *yuibutsuron*—materialism—that revealed everyday space, which was, for Tosaka, "none other than the field of practice" (Kawashima et al. 2013, 133). The actual structure of everyday space could be articulated in what Tosaka called *extension,* which is, in turn, comprised of dimension, continuity, and length. These take shape as materiality and practice unfold within time: everyday space, that is, takes shape as social actors interact with and reproduce the mundane, material conditions of their own lives. "[P]ractical human action," for Tosaka, "must be grounded in the specific social, cultural, and political mediations produced by the forces and relations of production" (Kawashima et al. 2013, 142). The various exchanges required for the maintenance and growth of capitalism and the time it took to perform them, to put it crassly, were also what gave form to everyday space and what underpinned the mundane, visceral experientialities of everyday life. We might think about the generation of extension as roughly equivalent to blowing up a balloon—if the balloon is the material conditions (space itself) in which our everyday lives are founded, the breath or air going into that balloon interacts with the material conditions that both constrain and give form to its existence, gradually expanding it, both spatially and temporally (since the balloon gradually takes shape throughout the process of blowing into it). What we are left with is a tangible, material delineation of extension as everyday space, as history (not History) itself.

Though admittedly oversimplified, this analogy allows us to conceive of the *materiality* of a phenomenon whose understanding is too often (in Tosaka's assessment) abandoned to the realm of the mysterious or the metaphysical. But it also allows us to see something else, something that is of vital importance both to Tosaka and to Takada Wataru: *the balloon can be popped.* Having been given accessible, malleable, material form, everyday space is now open to constructive (or even destructive) intervention—it is no longer an all-encompassing phenomenon that affords only the possibilities of acquiescence or protest (what I've already called internal negation). For Tosaka in 1931, this material rendering of the spatial—and the deauthorization of the omnipresent, all-capturing conceptual "Japanism," which could be and indeed was deployed as a transcendent, unapproachable truth that demanded sacrifice in the interrelated names of capital and empire—was a matter of life and death. Indeed, the philosopher would pay for his critical insights with his life when he died in police custody in 1945, just days from the end of the Pacific War. But for Takada, too, this recalibration of history became a crucial methodology for wrestling claims on the nature of everyday life away from teleological, modernization-theory narratives of what Japan was all about around 1970 and the moment of "Japan's Japan." In *Goiasatsu,* Takada insists on revealing the materiality of everyday life by emphasizing its sheer mundaneness and practical visceralities (riding a bike, getting iced cream), but also by intersplicing that mundaneness with political-economic reality and with what we'd more readily recognize as "political" questions. In so doing he knocks those questions down to size, embedding the political in the realm of the mundane with a thud and rendering it accessible, malleable, subject to critical intervention. This is made possible precisely by remixing it with the mundane in the context of the sort of unfolding temporal narrative (also, as we've seen, crucial to Tosaka's vision of everyday space) that the LP as medium affords. Critique for Takada Wataru does not come from *opposing* an already authorized, all-encompassing conceptual politicality (in other words, the "established system") or its manifestations (the SDF, for instance), in the form of an internal negation that may paradoxically reinforce that authority by virtue of acknowledging and opposing/negating it. Rather, critique for Takada Wataru means working to reconceive of the political as part of, and intertwined with the practices of, everyday life. It means defining the political by the mundane, reworking it as a component materiality of a balloon that can be popped.

To be clear, I am not asserting here that Takada Wataru was a student of Tosaka Jun's critical philosophy, or that he explicitly sought to model his own interventions around the latter's insights. Rather, I want to show how attending to Tosaka's work helps us to conceive of the critical potentials of Takada's insistence on confronting and centering the everyday, and to make sense of Takada's tactic of defining the political by the mundane. Scholars of social movements have revealed important points of intersection between the mundane and the political. Fernandez, Marti, and Farchi, for example, writing of Cooperativa La Juanita in Buenos Aires, describe a social movement that grew out of visceral experiences of precarity in Brazil—unemployment, the inability to pay utility bills (Fernandez et al. 2017, 201–223). The Cooperativa temporarily ballooned to link into a broader national movement but then shrank back down to the neighborhood level, where it became characterized by an ongoing engagement with the material terms and conditions of everyday life (the Cooperativa generated local economies that challenged ongoing Histories of development and the commodification of labor power—textile workshops, a bakery, a neighborhood school). Neither organized politics nor infrapolitics—the politics of the weak— the Cooperativa exemplified mundane, everyday life *as* politics. Though Takada's project and the Cooperativa clearly differ in scope and in aim, each shares a rootedness in Tosaka's everyday space, and the ever-present potential for its materialities to generate feedback loops that splice into and generate political engagement. For Takada, it seems, this generation is precisely the point—it's an important move in shifting politics from the trap of the internal negation of the vague "established system" whose critique animated the student movement in 1968 (a critique that was misdirected toward the transcendent and conceptual even as it was, ironically, informed by the viscerality of everyday life), and opens the door to a radical reimagining of "what it really means to critique war" is all about.

As I pointed out earlier, Takada Wataru's original ambition was to become a writer, a storyteller according to a different mode. Given the makeup of *Goaisatsu,* and given Takada's original literary ambitions, we are left to consider, I think, whether this LP constitutes a musical endeavor—or a literary one. The answer, I think, is simultaneously neither and both. On *Goaisatsu,*

Takada appeals to a riotous polyphony of different (mostly literary) voices to sketch out an audible vision of everyday life, one whose radical geographic, linguistic, and historical heterogeneities reject any effort to draw a teleological narrative of an already completed History. The choices he makes, the voices he taps, help articulate—each in different ways—embedded, experiential, and material practices of everyday life that both foreground the mundane and bring Politics (as transcendent, as encompassing, indeed as a mode of Culture) "down from its metaphysical heights to its moment of production in the space of everydayness [… and] subject it to the historical, material, and political character of its own period, a period with a specific relationship to the whole of historical time" (Kawashima et al. 2013, 138). It is precisely *Goaisatsu*'s cacophony of heterogeneous voices that is required to do this effectively. Poetry alone is already perfectly capable of facilitating a political engagement with the world. The form and practice of poetry themselves are political—there is no simple distinction to be made between history and the words on the page; indeed, "[f]orm is not a distraction from history but a mode of access to it" (Eagleton 2007, 8). But the musical articulation of these literary voices adds an important dimension. In part, broadened potentials for significance and meaning are simply an outcome of the dialectical mixing of originary textual sources belonging to different modes. As Takada Ren would point out decades after its release, for example, in discussing the aforementioned "*Onajimi no Mijikai Tegami* [That Familiar Short Letter]," "there's no way to discern the contents of that letter just by reading the lyrics of the song. It's once they're placed atop the melody [to Boris Vian's "*Le Déserteur*"] that my father's message comes through." But unpacking *Goaisatsu* is not just a matter of attending to its intertextuality. I have argued elsewhere that making the printed word itself *sonorous*—imbuing it with sound—helps to center it in the experience of readers, rendering its critique present in a way that can interfere with or short-circuit other ways of conceiving of the world (Aalgaard 2019). Transposed into music itself, and placed on an LP, this effect is expanded and amplified. Disparate literary interventions such as those comprising *Goaisatsu* are afforded a unity and a temporality that is particular to music and specifically to the LP, revealing an unfurling moment of everyday space that is both informed by and, it seems, engineered to inform the world of which it is a part. These voices unfurl in a definable moment that can challenge the ideological claims of History precisely because they steal its form, becoming an unwinding temporal narrative of its own—and it is music in general, and the LP in particular, that affords this potential (DeNora 2000, 66–68). Takada's appeal to the mundane is thus not a disavowal of politics at all—rather, it is politics done differently, an appeal to the *there*-ness of politics in everyday life that renders both material, not conceptual, and thus malleable and susceptible to rearrangement and redefinition. What makes *Goaisatsu* work is the productive breakdown of the barriers between literature and music, and their remixing into something new, a mode of storytelling that cites both literature and music in a way that aims to tell—and potentiate—different histories.

There is a certain ambiguity to the everyday and the mundane, and it is certainly not my intent to essentialize or romanticize praxis itself as a portal to necessarily utopian possibility. As Marotti, Harootunian, and others have shown, everyday life can become the site where capitalist accumulation is obscured and normalized in the repetitive daily practices of modernity, in the ever-new in the ever-same. The mundanity of money and its exchanges, for example, is precisely what avante garde artists like Akasegawa Genpei sought to disrupt, thereby revealing and challenging the modes of "domination" that lay behind them (Marotti 2013). In the 1930s, thinkers like Yanagita Kunio sought to locate precisely the transcendental life of the (Japanese) folk whose narrative authority Tosaka sought to disavow by tapping "the everyday life and practices of peasants" and "authoriz[ing] the performance of folk rhetoric in the construction of a new communal order" (Harootunian 2000b, 298). But on the other hand, and by the very same token, the mundane can point to the experiential visceralities of everyday life that both exceed and trouble the Nation's claim on the authority to narrate it, articulating the radically embedded outlines of life that cannot be subordinated to ideological narratives of (national) History. Revealing the mundane *there*-ness of everyday life, that is, can present a serious challenge to taken-for-granted structures of power (of which money, for example, is a part) by moving perspective from History to history, from ideology to materiality. And when politics are spliced into this material everyday—the move that Takada Wataru accomplishes in *Goaisatsu*—then politics are *demystified,* dislodged from a transcendent sort of position that only allows for acquiescence or internal negation (potentially the same thing) and rendered an accessible, *there* part of experiential life that is susceptible to reconfiguration and reimagination. This, it seems, is what the folk singer meant when he told the journalist in summer 2004 that "[s]inging the everyday—portraying the everyday [in song], interrogating it, and asking, okay, exactly what is this thing called 'the everyday'? [is] what's needed."

Afterlives

Takada Wataru collapsed after a concert in the town of Shiranuka, not far from Kushiro in eastern Hokkaido, on April 3, 2005. He was baptized as a Catholic the following day, and passed away on April 16, less than a year after holding court with Chikushi Tetusya over *shōchū* and chicken skewers at the Iseya Sō-Honten in Kichijōji. I had the incredibly good fortune to see Takada play the

Fukushima Prefectural Culture Center, front-row center, in August 2003, when he performed at a special event alongside folk superstars Iruka, Komuro Hitoshi, and Minami Kōsetsu. Even then, he was unsteady on his feet, leaning on handlers for support as he made his way to his foldable chair and boom microphone stand for a fifteen-minute set, which he navigated with frequent recourse to a tall glass of water that was most likely not water at all. And yet, he held everyone—audience and fellow musicians alike—in thrall with his dry, acerbic wit, his unassuming manner, and his musical conjuring of the everyday. Takada's quiet musical presence was towering in life, and it remains so in death, as young acts like neo-folk duo Humbert Humbert bring his masterpieces of the mundane like "*Seikatsu no Gara*" to new audiences.

For the most part, Takada Wataru's critical legacy is taken to be "*Jieitai ni Hairō*." This is true both within Japan and beyond it—as I discussed at the opening of this track, this was the work that Chikushi Tetsuya evoked in his (ultimately shaky) attempt to understand Takada's critical stance, and the song tends to be celebrated in non-Japanese scholarship as an exemplary "protest song" of Japan's 1960s as well. In a sense, of course, that's exactly what it is. But the song's treatment as an exemplar of oppositional politics tends to obscure the actual politics of Takada's songwriting and storytelling practice. Takada himself left the song on the sidelines for most of his career; it was only very rarely that it would have any presence at all in his live performances. By shifting his perspective to the everyday, Takada was able to unmoor his art from the moment of around 1970 and develop what I'd like to call, in closing, a *trans-sixties critique*—critical attention to the everyday, that is, allowed Takada to grapple with this often romanticized, dehistoricized moment as a plot along a longer arc of historical materiality, one that began (in his work) as early as 1906, traversed 1968 and 1971, and continued to have resonance well into the new millennium, when works like "*Akirame-bushi*" continued to be carried forward by Takada's student and protégé Kagawa Ryō, whom I'll consider on the next track. What looks here like a contradiction in light of Takada's criticism of the appropriation and deployment of "*Jieitai ni Hairō*" by activists in 2004 actually reveals the truth of his engagement with the everyday—it is precisely the unchanging violence of capitalism, despite claims to its overcoming in universal middle-classism and even development everywhere, that validates the trans-historical deployment of "*Akirame-bushi*" and the remixing of everyday philosophers in *Goaisatsu* as an unflinching critique of the terms and conditions of everyday life. As the younger Takada pointed out in 2015, this is by no means an abdication of the political. It's simply politics done differently.

Reflecting on his father's legacy, Takada Ren (2015) concluded that "[r]eading my father's diary, it's clear that he had a clear vision—at seventeen—of what 'folk singer Takada Wataru' must be. As a Japanese person, to press forward using the expressions of the Japanese language." For Takada Wataru, singing the Homesick Blues meant telling the stories of everyday life in Japan to his compatriots, in Japanese, in ways that ascribe a *there*-ness to the material minutiae of everyday life, digging around at their roots and exposing them to critical consideration and reimagination. This focus on the material conditions of everyday life, for Takada, was what held the key to exposing and critiquing the terms and conditions of the social—and this, in turn, was prerequisite to a useful critique of war, and avoiding its reduction to an internal negation of power. Though separated by moment and by context, this is where the philosophies of Takada Wataru and Tosaka Jun intersect. On the next track, I'll add one more voice to the mix—that of Takada's student and protégé Kagawa Ryō—and consider the ways in which he built from Takada's critical, destabilizing storytelling in order to begin retelling stories of Japan itself.

TRACK THREE

A Most Unusual "Lesson"

KAGAWA RYŌ, ANTI-FOLK, AND "JAPAN'S ONE MORE TIME"

I**N** the summer of 2015, Japan was in an uproar. Earlier in the year, Abe Shinzō (1954–2022)—prime minister at the time, as well as prominent member of the far-right historical-revisionist political and cultural "think tank" Nippon Kaigi (the "Japan Conference"; see Mizohata 2016), grandson to former Liberal Democratic Party (LDP) hawk and prime minister Kishi Nobusuke (1896–1967), and grandnephew to former LDP prime minister Satō Eisaku (1901–1975)—had submitted legislative bills to the Diet, aimed at reconfiguring Japan's regional security posture. Widely known as the *sensō hōan*—the war bills—this proposed legislation sought to "reinterpret" Article 9 of Japan's postwar constitution (the so-called anti-war clause, which forbids Japan from maintaining or deploying externally oriented military forces, formally limiting the Self-Defense Forces to a defensive stance) and authorize action overseas in the event of an attack on an ally: so-called collective self-defense, largely to the benefit of the Americans. This "reinterpretation" served multiple functions and fit into multiple histories, at once. On the one hand, it marked a continuation of the drift toward rearmament that had been underway (largely at the behest, or at least with the blessing, of the United States) since the establishment of the National Police Reserve (1950) and National Safety Force (1952)—antecedents of the Self-Defense Forces whose ballooning presence and contexts would be so sharply critiqued by Takada Wataru in his "*Jieitai ni Hairō* [Let's Join the SDF]" in 1969 (see track 2). On the other, though not a broad renunciation of Article 9 itself, the move would allow Abe and his allies to reanimate Abe's grandfather's dream of a remilitarized state and reverse Japan's perceived castration at the hands of what many hawks understood to be a foreign-imposed, pacifist constitution. Much of the Japanese populace, however, was having none of it. Bodies filled the streets across the country and occupied space in front of the Diet buildings in some of the largest and most raucous street-level protests to occur in decades. The stage was set for a summer of clashes and tension, with Abe relentlessly insisting on the need for an updated security posture in a new, post–Cold War world, and many individual Japanese rejecting this vision and the renewed militarism it portended, calling on Abe to quit—or even to die (Shibuichi 2017, 148).

By summer's end, the tension was reaching a fever pitch. Rocker Nagabuchi Tsuyoshi—who would hold a massive concert at the foot of Mount Fuji in mid-August, as anxieties over state action soared (see "Liner Notes")—warned of "feel[ing] that war's on the horizon" (*Sankei Sports,* July 19, 2015). Newly emergent student groups like SEALDs (Students Emergency Action for Liberal Democracy) were active in both street-level protests and campus teach-ins at places like Kyoto University, which had in fact already been the site of scuffles between students and state agents in recent months: in November 2014, for example, a plainclothes public security officer (*kōan,* often regarded as the descendants of Imperial Japan's dreaded thought police) infiltrated the Yoshida campus, leading to a multihour standoff with police when students exposed his identity (*Sankei West,* November 8, 2014). In cities and towns across the country, groups large and small marched through city centers and up and down major thoroughfares, waving the *"Abe yamero* [Resign, Abe!]" cards that had become ubiquitous fixtures at the protests by that point. Public broadcaster NHK broadcast the Diet deliberation proceedings live each day; these were dissected by the evening news shows each night. Throughout, public opinion remained solidly against the proposed legislation—an Asahi Newspaper poll in mid-September, for example, put public support for Abe's bills at just 29 percent (*Japan Times,* September 19, 2015). In a way reminiscent of the AMPO upheavals of 1960, state prerogatives and public sentiment surrounding national security and the U.S.-Japan security relationship were sharply, vociferously at odds.

But as was the case in 1960, the state would ultimately have its way. The LDP, enjoying a commanding majority in both governing houses, rammed the legislation through the Diet on September 19, effectively declaring an end to seven decades of (reluctant) pacifism as state policy (Yoshida and Aoki 2015) and clearing the path for broad Japanese engagement in the Asia-Pacific arena on behalf of U.S. interests, heralding a new phase of U.S.-Japan "friendship" (see track 1). In fact, Abe had boasted on a state visit to Washington, DC, in 2013—long before the bills actually passed—that "Japan is back": boosted defense expenditures and constitutional reinterpretations in Japan, that is, would both support American defense postures in the Pacific (Singh 2015, 51) and enhance Japan's security profile, allowing Japan to (re-)establish itself as what Abe and other state leaders loudly, but shortsightedly (Dower 2017), called a "normal country." The upheavals of 2015, in short, represented a significant plot development in the ongoing and contested jostling for the authority to tell stories of what it means to live in Japan, to "be Japanese." The state, clearly no more beholden to the voices of organized protest in 2015 than it had been in 1960 (White 2016), had won another round.

Amid the disappointment and despair that followed, however, a concert clip appeared on a usually quiet social media page belonging to a prominent singer-songwriter named Kagawa Ryō, who is generally associated with the critical Kansai Folk music boom that I discussed on track 2. It was a moment of (virtual) musical storytelling that seemed to capture and channel the frustration and fear of that early autumn day perfectly.

> We have one life; we live but once
> So don't go and toss your life away
> When we panic, it's so easy to stumble
> When they tell us that "it's for the sake of the Nation."
> Turn pale, take cover;
> Run away and hide.

The song featured in the clip was Kagawa's 1971 hit "*Kyōkun I* [Lesson I]," a work that would have been instantly recognizable to many. Featuring a gentle, repetitive melody well suited to the folkish guitar-and-voice compositional format of its moment, along with puzzling, rather jarring lyrics that I'll have much more to say about later, "*Kyōkun I*" is one of the best-known and most resilient songs of Japan's folk boom. It's been adapted and rerecorded by artists working in a diverse array of musical milieu, from "traditional" *enka* artists like Hatakeyama Midori (b. 1939) to neo-folk pop stars like Humbert Humbert to groups like Japanese rock unit Gopchang-Jeongol, a "cover band" fronted by Korea-based guitarist and musician Satō Yukie (b. 1963) that mostly performs Korean-language rock tunes (Satō 2013). The version that appeared online in the wake of the passage of the *senso̅ hōan,* though, was an acoustic performance by Kagawa himself, backed by Sugino Nobu on steel guitar, from a large outdoor concert in Nagoya in September 2004. Were it another artist with another song from folk's heyday that interjected into the 2015 post-*hōan* malaise, the story might simply end here, with a shrugged acknowledgment of a nostalgic turning away from a bruising political moment and a yearning for a moment when "politics" in Japan were somehow different, more receptive to public outcry (they never were, of course, at least not in any meaningful way). But "*Kyōkun I*" could as easily have been written as a direct response to Abe's antics in 2015 as it was a commentary on the terms and conditions of everyday life in 1971. The question, then, is how and why this voice of the past—reluctant heir to critical folk, a musical tradition thought long dead (save, for example, occasional nostalgic rereleases and commemorative projects)—was able to tell a musical story that resonated as strongly in the aftermath of the passage of the *senso̅ hōan* as it did in 1971, to say nothing of historical points in between.

As I also discussed on track 2, there tend to be fairly explicit correlations drawn between "folk" music in the 1960s and early 1970s, on the one hand, and oppositional protest—especially anti-war protest—on the other. Put even more bluntly, "folk" is often taken as the musical manifestation of oppositional protest itself (Mitsui 2013, 82). This is understandable, especially in a Japanese context. Although the English-language term "folk" covers a range of musical practices, "folk" in Japanese tends to be associated quite closely with protest music and what is called *hansen fooku*—anti-war folk. Indeed, when I discuss "folk" (and later "anti-folk") in these pages—and the ways that artists like Kagawa Ryō conceived of it—that's the sort of resonance that I'm tapping. *"Kyōkun I"* tends to be remembered as a *hansen fooku* anthem, and in a way, of course, it is—that's what lent the work such poignant meaning on September 19 in the first place. And yet, it's much more than the straightforwardly "anti-war" anthem of folk's heyday that it's often asserted to be. To be sure, Kagawa Ryō shares with Takada Wataru a reputation for being one of the central figures of the critical Kansai Folk boom of around 1970. But this characterization never sat well with the artist himself, at least in terms of the ways in which folk's critical project tended to be understood. Kagawa Ryō, like Takada before him, viewed "oppositional politics" and "protest" with a good deal of skepticism ("I never did like those raise-your-fist-and-yell things," he said in a *Chūnichi* newspaper interview in 2007). Careful attention to *"Kyōkun I"*—which I'll explore in detail on this track—helps to reveal a great deal of complexity in Kagawa's musical storytelling, a complexity that cannot be reduced to labels like "anti-war" or "protest singer" (characterizations that both Kagawa and his family—following his untimely death from leukemia in 2017—strenuously resisted). Understanding this complexity and the tactical choices Kagawa made in his songwriting can help us both conceive of the tenacious resonance of Kagawa Ryō's musical storytelling in modern and contemporary Japan and reassess the dimensions of a musical form that is often evaluated according to its contributions to "oppositional politics."

On track 2, I showed how folk icon Takada Wataru tapped poetic storytelling traditions from different moments and contexts to develop a critique that privileged *everydayness* over oppositional protest and de-emphasized the internal negation of what I, following Oguma, called a vague "established system" (Oguma 2015). This was a tactic that appealed, in part, to the technology of the LP record to render politics present, there (*da*), and susceptible to critique by remixing politics with the mundane realities of everyday life. By insisting on the inextricable entanglement of politics and the everyday, Takada's critique pushed "folk" beyond topical, oppositional "protest" to pry open the possibility of what I called a "trans-sixties critique." Here, I take up the artistry of Kagawa Ryō, who was Takada Wataru's most adept pupil and protégé, and who built on the work that his teacher began. Like Takada, Kagawa sought to scramble the sense-making mechanisms of everyday life and encourage a rethinking of what it meant to live in the world. But in ways that exceeded Takada's mild impatience for the "wishy-washy"-ness of oppositional politics, Kagawa's interventions relied upon an explicit disdain for "folk" itself, which, although clearly not literal, I still insist on taking seriously in order to understand his critique.

In what follows, I attend closely to Kagawa's development as an artist and to his signature "*Kyōkun I*" to reveal a critical stance that I term "anti-folk"—a playful, yet deadly serious, destabilization both of the terms and conditions of everyday life and of the authority of "folk" to negate them (what I call "anti-folk" is unrelated to the "alternative folk" coming out of New York in the 1980s and 1990s that has sometimes gone by the same name). I'll argue that Kagawa explicitly and tactically rejected the oppositional ethos of folk, even as he embraced its critical and political potentialities—and that this had wide-reaching implications, including for the music's longevity and resonance beyond its brief heyday of around 1970. Negating folk's own negations of some of the dominant phenomena of around 1970—the newly fortified nation-state; war; "the existing social, political, and cultural framework of Japan" itself (Bourdaghs 2012, 161)— allowed Kagawa to spin off into provocative new directions, developing critiques that could be reimaginative, strange, even shocking. At the same time, spinning up critiques that did not need to affix themselves to historically contingent phenomena to be legible also meant that Kagawa was able to survive the historical shifts that robbed many folk acts of their relevance, ensuring that his work continued to resonate in, for instance, the aftermath of the passage of Abe's war-bills legislation in 2015. By building on the "trans-sixties critique" developed by Takada Wataru in ways that tactically rejected the historical entrapments and oppositional ethos of folk, in other words, Kagawa Ryō was able to expand folk's possibilities and transcend what he seems to have understood as its limitations. This had everything to do with scrambling dominant stories of everyday Japanese life, as the artist worked toward a vision of what he'd articulate later in his career as "Japan's one more time."

The Summer (and Winter) of '69: The Making of an (Anti-)Folk Legend

Kagawa Ryō was born Kosai Yoshihiro (he would not become "Kagawa Ryō" until 1970) in Hikone City, Shiga Prefecture, on November 21, 1947. His first dabbling in music came as a student at Kyoto Sangyō University, where Kosai was active in amateur popular music circles, performing as a vocalist in so-called copy bands covering English-language rock tunes by the Rolling Stones, the Beatles, the Animals, and the Kinks (Nagira 1999). He recalls being sidetracked into a more structured musical world entirely by chance. In the summer of 1969, as a senior in college, Kosai was working part-time at a masonry at Imabari, on the western shore of Shikoku. On his way to the ferry port at Nankō, in Osaka, to catch the boat to work, Kosai found himself with some time to kill and stopped in at a "live house" in Umeda that was featuring daily performances of the then ubiquitous folk music. Takaishi Tomoya (b. 1941), remembered today as one of the earliest figures to emerge onto what would become the Kansai Folk scene, was playing. Kosai listened more or less disinterestedly—"so this is what's popular these days," he recalls thinking to himself (Muramoto 2003, 10–18). But on his way out, looking for something to read on the ferry, he bought a copy of *Folk Report*, a seasonal publication featuring folk-related news and articles that was put out by the loose federation of music industry companies that included the Underground Record Club (URC) and, later, Ongakusha. The group was presided over by Hata Masa'aki (1930–2003), an event production and promotion entrepreneur who had established his own company, called Art Promotion, in the mid-sixties and taken up the management of Takaishi, farming him out to events hosted by Rō'on (the National Workers Music Association) and labor union gatherings and later becoming a key figure fostering and facilitating many of the events, artists, and frameworks of Japan's folk movement. Toward the back of the magazine was a job advertisement for Art Music Publishing, another arm of Hata's music-industry endeavors, and it caught Kosai's eye: "Won't you come and work with us?"

The ad stuck with Kosai. Nearing the end of the summer and facing the need to commence the formal job hunting—*shūshoku katsudō*—that is part and parcel of the end of the college experience in Japan, he decided to send in a résumé at around the end of August. Kosai was offered a job at a subsequent in-person interview with Hata; he took it, he says, because the company seemed "out of the ordinary." He was originally charged with crafting "spots" for new releases: he'd listen to the music and identify the thirty seconds that best encapsulated the song (Kagawa, personal communication, 2015), write up a snappy intro for it, and run the results over to the studios of Radio Osaka, where a DJ would record the spot for release on the airwaves. He was also put in charge of editing the very *Folk Report* that had led him to the job in the first place (Nagira 1999, 117) and was involved in some aspects of album production as well—he recalls running recordings by ferry to Kyushu for mixing because the Osaka offices lacked the requisite equipment. But Kosai's most consequential encounters in his new work would undoubtedly be with Kyoto-based folk artist and banjo player Iwai Hiroshi, and, via Iwai, with Takada Wataru.

Iwai Hiroshi (1944–2000), like Kosai, started out as an employee with Art Music Publishing. But in addition to being an office employee, he was also an accomplished banjo picker. Iwai backed the recordings of some key folk figures around 1970, including Okabayashi Nobuyasu, the aforementioned Takaishi Tomoya, and Takada Wataru (Iwai in fact plays banjo on the recording of Takada's "*Jieitai ni Hairō*"). He played all three installments of the Nakatsugawa Folk Jamboree and eventually put out an LP of his own through URC in 1970 called *Boku no Shirushi: Warabeuta* [A Sign of My Existence: Nursery Rhymes]. Kosai was tasked with promoting this album, taking copies round to radio stations and so on. He recalls growing particularly close to Iwai during the winter of 1969. Iwai taught him to play the guitar, for example, and the pair would hang out with other URC figures—including Takada Wataru, who also enters the frame at this point—in a tatami flop room at the Osaka offices of Art Music Publishing (Muramoto 2003, 13). Since Takada was a URC artist, Kosai was tasked with developing spots for his recordings as well; Kosai's relationship with Takada, both professionally and personally, gradually grew and would prove crucial in the development of his own songwriting and emergence as an artist. Now good friends, the three men—Iwai, Kosai, and Takada—regularly spent time at Takada's boardinghouse at Yamashina, which would become a crucial node in the development of Kansai Folk in its own right for the interactions, conversations, and discoveries that occurred there. (Later, as an established artist in 1972, Kagawa Ryō sang of the boardinghouse in his celebrated "*Geshukuya* [The Boardinghouse]," a song characterized by a conversational storytelling—as opposed to singing—of all lyrical content except the chorus.) Later, they'd even perform together as the so-called San-Baka Torio, or "Three Stooges." In any event, the winter of 1969 saw a strong bond develop among these three men, who found themselves enmeshed, in different ways, in the business of musical storytelling. They'd continue to influence and inform one another's musical praxes for decades to come.

But in early 1970, there was not yet an artist named Kagawa Ryō—there was only Kosai Yoshihiro, who was slowly awakening to new modes of musical expression in a moment animated by an emergent critical folk, under the influence and tutelage of two of its most prominent figures. The contingencies of Kosai's employment with Art Music Publishing and his closeness to Iwai and Takada, however, were propelling Kosai toward a debut of his own. In the spring of 1970, the trio would bring their guitars to Okazaki Park in Kyoto, jamming together and rehearsing for Takada and Iwai's appearance at the second Nakatsugawa Folk Jamboree in August. During these sessions, the more experienced musicians began promising—threatening—to bring Kosai onstage at Nakatsugawa. In the end, it was a threat that Takada and Iwai made good on (with the approval of Hata), pulling Kosai onstage and backing him with mandolin and banjo, respectively. He sang a three-song set—"*Sono Asa* [That Morning]," based on the Carter Family's 1964 recording of "Will the Circle Be Unbroken"; "*Akai Tsuchi no Shita De* [Under the Red Earth]"; and "*Kyōkun I.*" With that performance, Kosai Yoshihiro became Kagawa Ryō, making his official debut to vociferous acclaim from audience and artists alike (fellow Nakatsugawa performer and folk artist Nagira Ken'ichi, for example, would later recall how Kagawa "mesmerized the crowd" with his unique vocals and delivery, leaving no doubt among those in attendance that a new star had been born [Nagira 1999, 118]). I'll have much more to say about "*Kyōkun I*" later.

Kagawa's success at Nakatsugawa in August 1970 did not immediately release him, however, from the music-business machinery whose contingencies had propelled him onto that stage in the first place. He had more dues to pay before being allowed to stand on his own two feet as a professional recording artist. In the wake of Nakatsugawa, Hata sent Kagawa on nationwide tours with Takada and Iwai (the Three Stooges trio mentioned earlier), sometimes with Okabayashi Nobuyasu, others with folk supergroup Itsutsu no Akai Fūsen (the Five Red Balloons), for whom Kosai had been a gofer and baggage boy just one year previously. He was farmed out as "celebrity host" of the MBS late-night radio program *ChaCha Young,* which aired from 1:30 a.m. to 5:00 a.m. from 1970 to 1973, and recalls being told that this work fell within the defined duties of his employment at Art Music Publishing—he received no additional remuneration, or even transportation costs for these gigs ("You're a fucking company employee!" Hata barked when Kagawa asked whether transportation, at least, might be covered). Eventually, at Hata's prodding, the recording of Kagawa's debut album, *Kyōkun* [Lessons], got underway in Tokyo in March 1971. Kagawa recalls sleeping on Hayakawa Yoshio's (of psychedelic folk-rock band the Jacks) floor during recording; the label declined to spend any money on a hotel room for him. Though the point is ancillary, it's worth stating that Kagawa's recollections paint a rather different picture of URC than that which is often presented in scholarship and generally rosy commentary on the label—while URC certainly pioneered novel distribution practices in its subscription format and direct sales agreements with dozens of record stores across Japan, helping it to sidestep the constraints of (self-)censorship, it was clearly not quite the revolutionary facilitator of countercommercial musical creativity that it's often made out to be in popular discourse, at times sounding more like a precursor to the "idol" factories that would emerge in the mid-1970s than an economically disinterested bastion for the defense and preservation of musical "authenticity." (Indeed, it was at least partly the contradiction that URC embodied that led to the collapse of "folk" from the inside out in the early to mid-1970s, as evidenced in what would become the rather riotous proceedings of the 1971 Nakatsugawa Folk Jamboree.) In any event, however, Kagawa Ryō continued paying his dues until late 1971, when he finally stopped having to go to the office, thus recognizing himself for the first time as a professional singer-songwriter and performer in his own right.

Over the ensuring four and a half decades, Kagawa would release sixteen solo and collaborative studio and live recording albums, which incorporate a remarkable diversity of musical styles ranging from folk to country to rock. He'd collaborate with the late playwright Higashi Yutaka (1945–2000) in theater troupe Tokyo Kid Brothers' 1975 production of *The October Country* (Kagawa contributed music and lyrics to the production), make occasional television appearances, and move beyond Japan to play concerts in China and, much later, North America. Though he's never been a million-selling artist (a status that he was largely uninterested in anyway), Kagawa has been an inspirational figure and teacher in his own right to some of the biggest-selling figures of Japan's New Music / singer-songwriter era, including Nagabuchi Tsuyoshi, fellow Nakatsugawa alumnus Yoshida Takurō, and Hokkaido folk rocker Matsuyama Chiharu. His importance to "folk," and to modern and contemporary Japanese popular music writ large, simply cannot be overstated.

And yet, at the very same time that he found a career as a "folk singer," he explicitly and vociferously rejected "folk"—or, perhaps more precisely, the compartmentalization and characterizations that "folk" implies. In 1973, for instance, he released a live recording of a work dryly titled "*Fooku Shingaa* [Folk Singer]," in which the narrator (Kagawa himself) vows to travel the length and breadth of Japan to track down and kill a man who'd had the gall to call him a "folk singer." As the chuckling that's audible throughout the live recording of "*Fooku Shingaa*" helps establish, Kagawa's murderous rage is of course in jest—but at the same time, it's not. There's something there, something that I want to take quite seriously. He sought to distance himself from folk in the ways that he told the stories of his own musical engagement as well: "All music for me is 'rock,'" Kagawa told me in conversation in Tokyo in June 2016. "It doesn't matter if it's *enka,* or jazz, or nursery rhymes [*dōyō*]—if the music hits my heart, like a drum, then it's rock." He went on to denigrate the periodic revivifications of aging folk icons in televised programming like public broadcaster NHK's *Za Fooku Songu: Seishun no Uta* [Folk Songs: The Music of Our Youth], and his distaste for what he called *dōsōkai*—class reunions. "Those things are boring," Kagawa complained. "They make me want to change the channel. Why would I participate in something that makes me want to change the channel? … It's the new generation's turn now." Kagawa's disdain for "folk," in short, was real—but like so many aspects of his musical storytelling, this also isn't quite what it seems.

In one sense, Kagawa Ryō's (self-imposed) positionality in a liminal cultural space that was somehow both within the purview of "folk" and beyond it helped ensure his success as a URC artist in a crowded and shifting musical landscape. This liminality, in the recollection of former Art Music Publishing manager Muramoto Takeshi, helped shield Kagawa from the upheavals and controversies surrounding folk's "authenticity" that played out in 1970 and 1971 and that reached a sort of climax at the third Nakatsugawa Folk Jamboree, positioning Kagawa for ongoing success in a moment when folk was already starting to implode. But there's more to it than this. "I was a person who originally didn't even know the term 'folk songs,' and my departure point was a completely different one from the folk movement," Kagawa recalled in 2003. "If I'd been enthralled with [Itsutsu no Akai] Fūsen or with Okabayashi [Nobuyasu], I wouldn't be here today. There's a strength to not knowing [folk]. Hata [Masa'aki] knew that I wasn't the sort to sing as part of a 'movement'" (Muramoto 2003, 17). By "movement," Kagawa is referring here to the topical oppositions and overt "protest" stance—that is, the musical negations of a vague "established system," a storytelling regime in its own right—that characterized much of Japan's critical folk music of the late 1960s and early 1970s, a mode of curated storytelling (Fernandes 2017) that Takada Wataru critiqued and recalibrated in his own way and that Kagawa dedicated much of his own energy to scrambling and reconfiguring. Art Music Publishing "was an odd place, and the employees were all eccentric. It was a place where people were free to do what they wanted," Muramoto (2003, 18) says. "But even within that context, Kagawa Ryō stood out as a person who found his own way, and pursued it." Kagawa's ethics of "anti-folk"— his "own way"—carried political implications of its own, as he worked to undermine both the terms and conditions of everyday life and folk's negations thereof in pursuit of what he would later in his career call "Japan's one more time" (*Nihon no mou ichido*). This required dismantling the predictability of folk and adopting the strange, the surprising, and the new, telling different stories not only of "Japan," but of what it meant to be a "folk singer" in the first place. In so doing, he worked to tell stories that weren't about the oppositional "protest" of his moment at all—but were critically and politically potent nonetheless. As heir apparent to folk, it seems, Kagawa Ryō spent his career determined to save the music by pushing it beyond its limitations and presenting something else in its stead. This is the musical ethics that I call "anti-folk." It's not a mere *negation* of folk but, rather, a negation of the negations (Bourdaghs 2012, 159–194) that folk tends to enunciate, and the articulation in their place of something quite different. Nowhere is this adventurous, irreverent musical storytelling more apparent than on Kagawa's 1971 debut LP, *Kyōkun* [Lessons].

The *Kyōkun* LP

Kagawa Ryō's debut LP is "legendary" (Nagira 1999, 120) among music aficionados and artists alike. The record foregrounds Kagawa's sometimes laid-back, sometimes forceful and tightly wound high-tenor vocal delivery, along with his already accomplished acoustic guitar fingerpicking techniques. But the album was also supported by a veritable who's who of the music world in Japan around 1970; indeed, although it's primarily a showcase for Kagawa and his work, the LP can be understood as exemplifying the contingent encounters that culminated in Kagawa Ryō's emergence as an artist in the first place. In addition to Takada Wataru and the rock band Happy End (who provide the bulk of the album's instrumentation), *Kyōkun* is backed by singer-songwriter and music producer Suzuki Kei'ichi (b. 1951), who also founded the rock band Moonriders; folk-rocker (and later actor) Agata Morio (b. 1948) of Hachimitsu Pie; Murakami Ritsu, who would go on to back rocker Nagabuchi Tsuyoshi on albums and in performance; and more. These figures helped Kagawa tell a wide range of intriguing musical stories, via appeal to a wide range of instrumentation and sound. Indeed, even considered solely in terms of sound and musicality, the *Kyōkun* LP confounds attempts to pin it down as a "folk" record—with its disorienting appeals to rock, accordions, and even a revamping of Takada's "*Akirame-bushi* [The Give-Up Ditty]" that sounds suspiciously like a French chanson, *Kyōkun* doesn't sound much like a "folk" album at all, at least as "folk" was being imagined around 1970.

But lyrical expression is what truly lies at the heart of Kagawa's tactics of "anti-folk." Playful, provocative poesis animates nearly all the cuts on the *Kyōkun* LP—and this expressivity can be traced back to a fascination on Kagawa's part with the Japanese language itself, which in turn led to his diving into songwriting in the first place. I must digress here to consider the artist's awakening to what he came to see as the "deep" possibilities for being "playful" with the Japanese language (Sakamoto 2007), because this philosophy of language ties directly to his philosophy of music, and specifically to the playful, provocative critiques that he spools up on the LP, particularly in the title track, which I'll examine in some detail later.

As discussed on track 2, numerous artists around 1970 were exploring the potentials of pursuing musical expression via the medium of the Japanese language, including Takada Wataru. Under the influence of Takada—who was committed to telling musical stories of everyday life in Japanese and who was in fact working on a book of poetry of his own in this moment (Muramoto 2003, 12–13)—Kagawa Ryō (then still Kosai Yoshihiro) was developing an interest in telling strange, provocative stories through music with appeal to the Japanese language. Indeed, the artist told me in conversation in 2015 that his experience crafting a spot for Takada's bouncy, fingerstyle interpretation of the Animals' 1964 recording of "House of the Rising Sun," "*Asahirō*," from the latter's 1969 solo album *Kisha ga Inaka wo Tōru Sono Toki* [At That Moment When the Train Passes through the Countryside], was particularly significant: "I was amazed that someone could do that with the Japanese language. It moved me, made me cry [*naketekuru*]." The common resource of the Japanese language opened, for Kagawa, avenues for musical participation and creativity that had long seemed foreclosed: "[A]nybody could make songs, anybody could become a singer." In an earlier interview, Kagawa elaborated on the importance of the discoveries that this former ventriloquist of Anglo-American rock songs was making in terms of the possibilities of the Japanese language, in the context of his collaborations with Takada and Iwai, to his own burgeoning songwriting: "This person who knew nothing but English-language songs, I started thinking that wow, Japanese is really something. I started buying up the mimeographed poetry and lyrics collections that people were selling in the underground passageways [in Osaka]. Iwai-san helped me think about how I might put that sort of poetry to music … encouraging me to develop melodies, even just by humming out ideas. [...] The fact that I became interested in the possibilities of the Japanese language was really important in my case" (Muramoto 2003, 13).

It was, in short, a fascination with (Japanese) language and its expressive possibilities that drew Kagawa Ryō to songwriting in the first place. But as was the case with Takada Wataru, this had nothing to do with reanimating the linguistic authenticities of past masters. Rather, it seems to be the surprising and the destabilizing (the "wow") that grabbed Kagawa's attention and that he sought to reproduce in his own music.

Now, just what it was that Kagawa Ryō found so amazing about Japanese is hard to quantify. It's clear that he had great respect for Takada and for the originality of the Japanese lyric writing that he was engaged in, itself happening in the same moment that the rock-in-Japanese debate was being propelled in new directions by pioneers like Happy End (see track 2). Kagawa was very heavily influenced by Takada and assisted him in his lyrical work. But while Takada's obsession involved spotlighting and centering everyday Japanese life via both his own lyricism and an appeal to a pantheon of poetic maestros, for Kagawa Ryō the emphasis was more on what he saw as the *playful possibilities* of Japanese, and on making the language do strange, unexpected things. This philosophy melds nicely with his philosophy of music itself. In discussion with me in June 2016, asked to share what "music" is to him, Kagawa pressed back against the idea that he even "does music" at all, preferring to describe himself as engaged in something called *ongaku-teki na mono,* or "something akin to music." Pressed to describe his ideal sort of music, he immediately described a sonic experience that is capable of presenting the surprising, the unexpected. "Music is something that drifts to me out of a crowd, out of an open window on a street, overcoming all of the background noise out there," he said, waving his hand in a gesture that encompassed the busy open café that we were seated in as well as the busy Shinagawa Station concourse below us. "It might be a song that reaches out and grabs me, coming out of a *pachinko* parlor or something. Or it might be in the sounds of voices, or the sounds of the streets. If it excites me, if it makes me stop and say 'what the hell is that [*nan nano, kore*]?,' then it's music." It seems that what Kagawa sought in music was something puzzling and unpredictable, unusual and strange, something that requires active engagement—and both music and words, it seems, offer this promise. As the artist himself explained to me through a clearly intentional allusion to joking and to play, when the punch line is already apparent with the opening notes, then "song," at least as understood by Kagawa Ryō, lacks value. Language and/as lyrical expression is an important part of this overall framework.

The tracks on *Kyōkun* provide important insights into Kagawa's musical and linguistic philosophies, and how he saw startling, provocative deployments of language potentiating startling, provocative critiques. This is particularly true of the title track, "*Kyōkun I.*" Although this song is indelibly associated with Kagawa Ryō—and vice versa—its lyrics are in fact adapted from a 1967 book by poet and children's author Ueno Ryō (1928–2002), titled *Chotto Kawatta Jinseiron* [A Slightly Odd Philosophy of Life], and specifically from a brief chapter therein titled "*Kyōkun Sono Ichi* [The First Lesson]." It's the first of three "lessons" included in the book, all of which deal with questions of patriotism, nationalism, and war; the text was quoted in a pamphlet Kagawa purchased from activists in the passageways beneath Osaka's Umeda Station, and he was drawn to it immediately, thinking that "this could be a song" (Ueno 1985, 92–111). "*Kyōkun Sono Ichi*" is composed in a decidedly jarring fashion, making extensive use of the katakana orthography—a Japanese phonetic "alphabet" reserved mostly for foreign loanwords and in which extended prose would not normally be written—and turning the linguistic rules of Japanese inside out, presenting loanwords that katakana is usually tasked with depicting (the English-derived "spare," for instance; see the lyrics, following) as hiragana, the phonetic orthography for scripting so-called native Japanese words. The specific effect of this, in part, is to generate a total reversal, a photographic negative; it's a textual tactic that also helps anticipate Kagawa's broader critique (I'll return to this later). Overall, the text is staccato, stuttering, and altogether *defamiliarizing*: the orthographic form of Ueno's chapter alone, in other words, was enough to capture the attention of an artist committed to engaging with the puzzling and the strange. Indeed, it appears that Kagawa fixated on the work largely because of the strangeness of its structure and composition, in addition to the provocativeness of its subject matter; it was, to Kagawa, "cool" (*share*), something that he became intent on rendering musically. It reads, in part:

教訓その一　命ハ一ツ. 人生ハ一回. ダカラ, セメテ, ダマシタリ, ダマサレ タリシテ, コノ命, ステナイヨウニシヨウ. アワテルト, ツイ, フラフラトシテ,

オ国ノタメ——— ナドトイワレルト, ポント, ソノ一ツキリノイノチヲ, ソマ
ツニ投ゲダスヤツモデテクルガ, 考エテモミタマエ. オ国ハ, オレタチガ死
ンデモ, ノコリマス. 少ナクトモ, ズットアトマデ, ノコリマス. 「アッ, マチガ
ッテマシタ. シツレイ」ト, イッテクレルカモシレナイガ, イノチノすぺあーハ
アリマセンヨ. [...] 死ンデモ, 神様ダーーーートイワレルヨリ, 生キテ, バカ
ダーーーートイワレルヨウニ, ツネニ心ガケルベキデス. [...] モシ, キミノ
ソバデ, 美クシイコトバデ, 「イノチヲステテ男ニナレ」ナドトイウ人ニ出会ッ
タトキハ, ブルブルトフルエマショウ. [...] イイエ, アタシャ女デケッコウ. 女
ノクサッタノデ, カマイマセン」ト, 青クナッテ, シリゴミスルコト. [...]

Lesson number one. We only have one life. We live once. So, at the very
least, let's do our best not to throw this life away in deceiving others, or
being deceived ourselves. When we panic it's so easy to stumble, when
they tell us that it's for the sake of the Nation—just like that, poof, some
will frivolously toss this once-around life away, but think about it for a
minute. Though we might die, the Nation will remain. It will remain at
the very least for a very long time. "Oops, made a mistake. Sorry," they
might say, but life doesn't come with a spare. [...] We should always commit ourselves to living and being called stupid, rather than dying and
being called gods. [...] If you encounter someone who appears beside you
and calls upon you, using beautiful words, to "offer up your life and be a
man," that's the time when you should start trembling. [...] "No, I'm perfectly happy as a woman; being a rotten woman suits me just fine," you
shall say, and turn pale and run away. [...] (Ueno 1967, 229)

In Kagawa Ryō's hands, Ueno's chapter became "*Kyōkun I* [Lesson I]." It
begins:

命はひとつ　人生は1回	We have one life; we live but once
だから　命を　すてないようにネ	So don't go and toss your life away
あわてると　つい　フラフラと	When we panic, it's so easy to stumble
御国のためなのと　言われるとネ	When they tell us that "it's for the sake of the Nation." [...]
青くなって　しりごみなさい	Turn pale, take cover;
にげなさい　かくれなさい	Run away and hide.
御国は俺達　死んだとて	After we're dead, the Nation will be just fine
ずっと後まで　残りますヨネ	It'll last on and on—and on.
失礼しましたで　終るだけ	"Sorry 'bout that," they'll say, and that'll be the end of it
命の　スペアは　ありませんヨ [...]	Life doesn't come with a spare. [...]

In composing this work, Kagawa was appealing to an already well-established folk practice of adapting literary works in song—a tactic extensively pursued by Takada Wataru, under whose tutelage Kagawa was exploring songwriting. The chapter's second life as a song, however, came as news to its original author, Ueno Ryō. In later writing, Ueno recalled that Kagawa and Iwai Hiroshi came to visit him in December 1972 to apologize for appropriating his work for the "*Kyōkun I*" lyrics—a visit made more pressing by the recent RCA release of *enka* artist Hatakeyama Midori's recording of the song, with lyrics credited to Kagawa Ryō (the Hatakeyama version was titled "*Kyōkun*," or "Lessons," but the lyrics remained the same). The pair were apparently profusely remorseful, but Ueno did not really know why, or how to respond. In Ueno's thinking, Kagawa had *amplified* the work, modifying it in ways that allowed it to overcome its own limitations as written text. Responding to the contrite songwriters, Ueno insisted that "even if it was the case [that you appropriated my work], it's you who attached music to it, right [*kyoku wo tsuketa no ha anata desho*]? The written word is different from song, you know. Regardless of how many good words I might be able to write out, they just become type and reach a limited subset of readers. Song is a different sort of culture altogether [*ishitsu no bunka*]" (Ueno 1985, 92–111).

What Ueno is pointing to here is the way Kagawa Ryō's composition simultaneously cites and *transcends* the materiality of printed text—and its limitations—in ways that both enhance it and force it to do something different. In other words, Kagawa becomes a sort of node in an expressive network: affected by a textual encounter, he takes the text and amplifies it beyond the confines of the page, giving it a sort of musical life and resonance beyond itself and generating an intertextual entity that is simultaneously new and an expanded and enhanced modification on the original (Dell and Kynes 2014). Now, as I've already suggested, it's likely that Kagawa—in his attraction to the strange, the surprising, the provocative—was drawn mainly to the *orthographic/textual* oddities of "*Kyōkun Sono Ichi*," finding in them the destabilizing sorts of possibilities that Deleuze and Guattari find in so-called minor language, a transgressive use of the "language of masters," a hatred for it, a recalibration of language from a signifier of power to the signified itself, capturing the reader within a self-enclosed grappling with language that demands a confrontation with language as *system,* and its relation to the system outside of it (Deleuze and Guattari 1986, 16–27). In Ueno's chapter, textual language and orthography become both signifier and signified: the jarring, destabilizing text calls attention both to itself and to the storytelling regime that it's embedded within. In this regime, authorized uses of national language—Deleuze and Guattari's "language of masters"—are linked to authentic expression of a national self (Lee 2009; Gottlieb 2005, 39–54); in scrambling the former, Ueno's text helps challenge the sense-making authority of the latter (I'll have more to say about the disciplinary connotations of "national language" on track 4). The tactical, even subversive playfulness of the text helps both frame and augment the meaning of Ueno's "lesson," with the effect that commonsensical notions of national belonging, nationalism, and patriotism are challenged on two fronts— the semantic and the systemic—and sacrifice in the service of the nation-state is deglorified. This, broadly, is the work that Kagawa Ryō's adaptation of Ueno's "lesson" in "*Kyōkun I*" sets out to do as well.

In a way, though, Kagawa is limited here by his own voice. He cannot reproduce the orthographic particularities of the text in his singing, for example, and even the liner notes for the *Kyōkun* LP render his lyrical adaptions in a more "standard" Japanese. Precisely because he could not reproduce the "strangeness" of Ueno's orthography in voice, a change in tactics was called for—sense making had to be scrambled in other ways. This involved an appeal to the very fleshly body that allowed Kagawa to emit a voice in the first place, and, more specifically, to its orientation within the discourses of Nation that Ueno's chapter also sought to challenge. Kagawa Ryō's playful appropriation and amplification of Ueno's strange text, that is, generated a wide-reaching, enduring challenge to the terms and conditions of everyday life under the modern nation-state precisely because it was delivered vocally, via his own body. Part of this involved giving voice to scrambled notions of gender.

"*Kyōkun I*" and the Tactical Scrambling of Gender

Ueno Ryō's "*Kyōkun Sono Ichi*" was never intended to be a folk song—but it became one in the hands of Kagawa Ryō. As a folk song, however, "*Kyōkun I*" went directly against the grain of the storytelling regime that folk had established for itself by 1971, a regime built around notions of "protest" and struggle. This is probably most apparent when "*Kyōkun I*" is placed alongside other representative songs of this moment. In October 1969, for example, Takaishi Tomoya released a Japanese translation of British artist Ewan MacColl's 1954 "The Ballad of Ho Chi Minh." Takaishi's rendition deploys a sparse, mournful guitar-and-banjo melody to tell a story of the Vietnamese revolutionary and his efforts to "forge and temper the army of the Indochinese people": "Every soldier is a farmer/Comes the evening he grabs his hoe/Comes the morning, he swings his rifle on his shoulder/That's the army of Uncle Ho." In April of that same year, Okabayashi Nobuyasu's lively, thoroughly irreverent "*Kusokurae-bushi* [The Eat Shit Ballad]" was finally released through the URC label, after being pulled from a planned release on Victor a year or so earlier in the wake of the Recording Industry Ethics Regulatory Commission's flagging it as a "popular song warranting caution." As Dorsey (2013) has discussed, the song was so pointed in its topical, oppositional critiques of authority that every verse promised to offend—and, potentially, to bring unwanted controversy to Victor. And at around the same time, Takaishi and Okabayashi were combining their efforts in recording the well-known folk anthem "*Tomo Yo* [O Friend]," a work that typified Japan's critical folk moment with its "Internationale"-style exhortations to "stoke the flames of battle/for the dawn is nigh/and on the other side of this darkness/a shimmering tomorrow awaits." All this musical storytelling was occurring amid mounting alarm over the escalating conflict in Southeast Asia, in the contexts of the ongoing student movement, and so on. The "protest"-oriented musical interventions mounted by Takaishi, Okabayashi, and others around this moment required the contingencies of history to be legible (this will become important momentarily)—and paradoxically, these contingencies were defined and clarified in part by the very musical articulations that denounced them.

Kagawa Ryō, though, pursued a different sort of path. As I discussed earlier, Kagawa remained insistent throughout his career that his musical storytelling remain distinguishable from what was called "folk" around 1970. "I don't want to be painted with the same brush as those guys [*issho ni saretakunai*]," the artist told me in conversation in Tokyo in 2015, referencing the key gatekeepers of Japan's "critical folk" tradition—such as Takaishi—without doing so by name. In our discussion, he lambasted very specific turns of phrase that are associated with folk's heyday and that often surface in "folk" anthems like "*Tomo Yo*" and "The Ballad of Ho Chi Minh": "*Te wo toriatte* [let us join hands]," "*yoake wa chikai* [the dawn is nigh]," "*sensō hantai* [no war]," and so on. In rejecting such turns of phrase, Kagawa was rejecting a specific vision of oppositional "protest" (centered on the New Left, for example, or the student movements) in Japan around 1970—and given the ways that this vision has been able to dominate discussions of what politics and critique in Japan and elsewhere have been all about, it's not surprising that the artist, with different visions thereof, felt the need to reject the label of "protest singer."

But as I've already pointed out, Kagawa's rejection of dominant notions of "protest" doesn't equate to apoliticality. Like his teacher Takada Wataru, Kagawa Ryō was political—he was just political *differently*. Part of this is likely historical. By the time of Kagawa's impromptu debut at Nakatsugawa in August 1970, for example, the ink was dry on the 1970 renewal of the AMPO Treaty—this event did not generate the 1960-style protests that had been hoped for, both revealing and reinforcing a gradual waning of organized, street-level action. Okinawa's status was another important factor. Although its actual handover would not occur until 1972, Okinawa's "reversion" to Japanese rule was agreed upon between U.S. and Japanese authorities in 1971, thus removing another hot-button protest issue from public discourse (although thousands of Chūkakuha [Japan Revolutionary Communist League, National Committee, Middle Core Faction] students still took to the streets of the Hibiya district of Tokyo and burned down the Matsumoto-rō restaurant in protest of the terms of the reversion). The student movement was waning as well, as was public patience for "radical" protest in the context of a perceived swing toward radicalism and violence on the part of protesters—this patience would collapse more or less entirely with the United Red Army factional purge in Gunma Prefecture and subsequent hostage crisis at the Asama-Sansō mountain lodge in Nagano in February 1972, which left a combined total of fourteen Red Army members, two police officers, and one bystander dead. Although none of this meant that critical engagements with questions of what it meant to live in Japan, to "be Japanese," were finished, and although critical politics was far from dead in 1971, it did mean that the specific modalities of grappling with those questions were changing, as insightful and imaginative critics like Takada Wataru were growing skeptical of "protest" and turning toward critical engagements with the everyday (see track 2). Although his specific tactics were not the same as Takada's, Kagawa Ryō's storytelling tactics and political stance should nonetheless be conceived of in this light.

Ueno Ryō's poem afforded Kagawa the chance to tell a musical story that worked against folk's dominant "protest" ethics and, at the same time, articulated a powerful critique of some of the terms and conditions of everyday life. This is probably rendered clearest in the repetitive refrain of "*Kyōkun I*": "Turn pale, take cover; [r]un away, and hide." The refrain articulates a general ethics of fleeing, including from the violence of war—but most specifically, it's urging flight from what Kagawa, via Ueno, calls "*o-kuni*," a term vaguely evocatory of "country" that, in this context, suggests a sarcastic deference to the national Thing (Žižek 1993, 201–202). I've translated "*o-kuni*" here as "the Nation," but it can be understood as standing in for the state as well. In this repeated exhortation to "[r]un away, and hide," the critical thrust of the work runs completely perpendicular to the songs by Takaishi and Okabayashi that I introduced earlier, which call—in different ways—for struggle and opposition. But this is no nihilistic giving up. Rather, what "*Kyōkun I*" seems to advocate for is a withdrawal from any engagement with the Nation at all, a refusal to enter into exchange with it (Karatani 2014)—even if that exchange is oppositional, hostile. Such a withdrawal also, by its very nature, refuses to lend the Nation any sort of legitimacy or authority; in so doing it opens new avenues for rethinking what it means to live in the world, and under what terms. This seems particularly important in a moment—1970–1971—when the state was fortifying its position in Japanese social life and, in effect, taking the place of the bodies that were steadily retreating from the streets and appropriating narratives of social and political change through passing pollution laws, arranging Okinawa's reversion to Japanese rule, and so on. But despite its expanding footprint, the Nation didn't quite win the day here—rather, its shifting positionality and ballooning claims to authority helped create the conditions for telling new, thoughtful stories that involved a distancing both from the state and from the validation thereof via its internal negation. "*Kyōkun I*" is one such story, par excellence.

To be sure, an ethics of "run[ing] away and hid[ing]" does suggest a critique that can be thought of as more explicitly and formulaically anti-war. This is what allowed the *Kyōkun* LP's U.S. distributor, for example, to proclaim the song a "life-affirming anti-war ballad" in its own advertisements for the album. Indeed, much of the work pivots on an exhortation to listeners to not "go and toss your life away," the implication being that one stands to lose that life in battle; it also insists that "[r]ather than dying and being called 'gods'" it is better to "live and be called stupid," a repudiation of wartime rhetoric centered on the positionality of Yasukuni Shrine as a final place of respite and glory for fallen soldiers. But it's crucial to bear in mind that the chief object of the work's critique is not war per se but rather what Kagawa calls "the Nation" as war's potentiating framework. The call, in other words, is not so much for a rejection of war, full stop, but rather for a reconsideration of the ways that modern life is ordered around the specter of the Nation, and the sacrifice and death that it demands, especially in war. It's not (only) war that needs to be rethought, that is, but the Nation itself—and given its ubiquity in modern life, "fleeing" the Nation and its sense-making mechanisms is something that can only be accomplished by scrambling the stories that it tells and undermining their authority.

"*Kyōkun I*," then, is productively thought of as a "lesson" that rejects the commonsensical mechanism of the Nation outright, rather than being drawn into a legitimizing relationship with it as its internal negation. But this scrambling of the Nation as a taken-for-granted anchor for modern life involves more than simply turning one's back on it: the very act of "run[ning] away, and hid[ing]" must be actualized by a body that is no longer suitable to the Nation's uses, and that can avoid being (re-)appropriated into it. For Kagawa, this next-level scrambling pivots around telling stories of *gender*. Although hints of gender-bending are sprinkled throughout the work (mostly linguistically, through a tactical deployment of what scholars have called "feminine Japanese speech"—I'll come back to this later), Kagawa's provocative appeal to gender is rendered most explicit in the third stanza:

"Offer up your life—be a man!" they say
And when they do, then it's really time to start trembling
That's right, I'm perfectly happy as woman—
Being a "rotten woman" suits me just fine!

Kagawa has occasionally faced vigorous criticism for some of the lyrical content of "*Kyōkun I*"—specifically, for his invocation of what the song, following Ueno's poem, calls the "rotten woman." The idiom in the original Japanese is one that is used to "link women with certain character faults" (Cherry 1987, 32), implying that a man who is *like* a rotten woman—*onna no kusatta yō na*—is inadequate or "unmanly." As Cherry points out, this "is an insult hurled at Japanese men by accusers of both sexes" (Cherry 1987, 32), but it relies upon misogynistic assumptions of the inferiority of women for its efficacy. Kagawa has been taken to task for repeating what is generally understood to be a slur against women and has been put on the defensive on multiple occasions: when he played the University of Chicago in October 2016, for instance, Kagawa changed this line at the very last moment—from "*onna no kusatta*" to "*otoko no kusatta*," or "rotten man"—likely out of fear of being misunderstood on the occasion of his first North American performance. Now, misogyny has been a serious problem in Japan throughout the years of Kagawa's career, and the blowback that he faces for his musical redeployment of Ueno's phrasing is understandable. But these criticisms, while undoubtedly well intended, fail to consider the actual utility of questions of gender in "*Kyōkun I*." What some view as a lyrical shortcoming, that is, actually holds an important key to unpacking the complexity of Kagawa's critique in the work and to the ongoing resonance of that critique across different historical moments. To make this argument persuasively, I need to digress for a moment and tell some of the (gendered) story of the Nation in modern Japan.

As scholars have shown in different ways, Japan as modern Nation—in its disparate incarnations, including Empire—has been deeply and indelibly gendered. Indeed, gendering is an important framework upon which different strategies for the Nation's maintenance and expansion are built and its story told, from gendered divisions of labor aimed at reproducing capitalism in times of "peace" to gendered exhortations of sacrifice in times of war. This has been true across an array of historical moments and has involved conjuring stories of both womanhood/femininity and manhood/masculinity. The Imperial Precepts to Soldiers and Sailors of 1882, for example, admonished military personnel not to "become effeminate and frivolous" lest they be subjected to scorn and "the contempt of the world." The "limbs" of the Imperial body (Ota 2008, 155), it seems, were to be precisely the "men among men" whom Takada Wataru would sardonically assure of a place in the Self-Defense Forces some eighty-seven years later. The Meiji Civil Code of 1896, meanwhile, explicitly sought to structure the families that would be the building blocks of the new, "modern" Imperial state around the authority and superiority of the husband: "Fundamentally, a wife is bound to serve her husband and to put the household affairs in order," the code instructed. "Therefore acts such as may injure the feelings of her husband, or important acts in respect to property, cannot be done by a wife at her option but must be done with the permission of her husband" (de Becker 1909, 17). Silverberg argues that this "ideal Meiji woman of the late 1800s had served as a 'repository of the past,' standing for tradition while men were encouraged to radically change their way of politics and culture" (Silverberg 2006, 70). In the 1920s, when women challenged these dictates as Taishō Democracy (and its attendant upheavals) swept through Japan, the media and anxious conservatives responded by conjuring the figure of the so-called Modern Girl—part fantasy, part fleshly contemporary woman—as an object of discipline, proclaiming her un-Japanese and demanding that she reassume her proper position within the family state. The Nation's social order could be steadied, the story went, if women could be put back in their place. In the postwar period, women's fleshly bodies have been made to stand in for the body politic itself, as concrete instances of sexual violence—such as the rape of the Okinawan schoolgirl that I discussed on track 1—were tapped and ultimately displaced by patriarchal narratives seeking to posit a generic female body to be equated with geopolitical soil to be guarded (Angst 2003). And in the contemporary, neoliberal moment, women are tasked with the impossibility of bolstering capital on two fronts—as provisors of inexpensive, precarious labor power in the marketplace and as reproducers of "Japan" (as labor power) at home. Indeed, women are regularly harangued by LDP politicians for neglecting their "Japanese" duty of reproducing the Nation through childbirth (Holloway 2010, 4). As King has pointed out, "gender, specifically femininity, is a discipline that produces bodies and identities and operates as an effective form of social control" (King 2004, 30).

This telling of gendered stories of "Japan" has played out in cultural production as well, across diverse moments and through a range of texts. As Japan expanded its colonial foothold in Asia, for instance, women sometimes found themselves working cooperatively within patriarchal Imperial power structures as a strategy to improve their own standing within the Empire. Kono points out that a Japanese woman seeking valuation as an active agent of empire building in the colonies understood that her own "recognition as national subject is contingent upon her successful performance of the officially-sanctioned role of motherhood" (Kono 2012, 234), hence self-congratulatory stories of literally raising subjects for the emperor such as those detailed in Koizumi Kikue's 1936 story "Manchu Girl." After the war, amid an influx of Occupation-era American culture and fleshly excess understood by some as posing a threat to the (masculine) body politic itself, filmmaker Kurosawa Akira made strategic appeal to diegetic classical music in films like *Drunken Angel* (1948) to lay out an audible vision for the overcoming of what was perceived as national castration and the recentering of rational, masculine subjectivity (Bourdaghs 2012, 24–29).

And in 1966, Mishima Yukio—a writer generally acknowledged to have been obsessed with questions of masculinity and its purported role in upholding Japanese "tradition"—released the film version of his 1961 novella *Yūkoku* [Patriotism]. *Yūkoku* is a story of idealized gendered performativity (both male and female) in the context of the attempted Shōwa Restoration coup of February 26, 1936, involving the literal embodiment of "masculine" discipline and sacrifice on the part of Lieutenant Takeyama Shinji of the Imperial Japanese Army, and unquestioning "feminine" obedience and determined, sacrificial loyalty (recall here the Meiji Civil Code) on the part of his wife, Reiko (indeed, the case might be made that it is Reiko who is the central character in the story, and not the lieutenant at all—that *Yūkoku* is a story of how to be a Japanese woman as much as how to be a Japanese man). Mishima, of course, would go on to stage this bodily discipline and reassert masculine "Japanese-ness" in the midst of the Cold War global order as he reenacted the conclusion to *Yūkoku* in gruesome fashion, in a bloody spectacle aimed at revealing and overcoming Japan's purported estrangement from its "tradition" (Sone 2010, 32) in his ritual suicide at SDF headquarters in November 1970, just three months after Kagawa's debut and shortly prior to the release of the *Kyōkun* LP.

Finally, to set the stage for Kagawa Ryō's storytelling in *"Kyōkun I,"* let me bring my focus in one step further and consider how this gendered storytelling of Japanese subjectivity played out in music. I can do so by attending to just one song—albeit a song with many lives. In 1937, King Records released a rousing, march-tempo *gunka* (songs exhorting war, the military, and sacrifice for the nation that were ubiquitous during Japan's Imperial period) titled *"Otoko Nara* [If You Are a Man]," with lyrics by Nishioka Suirō (1909–1955, the "poet laureate of Nagasaki," known mostly for his works about that city) and music by Kusabue Keizo (1901–1982, who is largely unknown beyond this single work). Although the work predates the desperate, self-destructive strategy deployed by the state near the end of the war, *"Otoko Nara"* is popularly known as the ballad of the *tokkōtai* (the "special attack forces," known in popular discourse as the *kamikaze*), and it predictably calls for men to find glory in smashing themselves to bits for the National cause:

> If you are a man, if you are a man
> No matter where you end up, or what you may roar
> Take the burning passion of your young blood
> And go—holding the Rising Sun close to your breast
> You're a man; go get it done
>
> If you are a man, if you are a man
> Leave no regrets behind, not for this floating world
> The petals are scattering now; men, call on your brass balls

If you toss your life away, there's nothing left to fear
You're a man; go get it done

Although it started as a *gunka*, "*Otoko Nara*" would go on to have multiple second lives after the end of the war—not as a militaristic call to arms, but as an exhortation for Japanese men to rescue a "Japan" that lost its way in the postwar period via an appeal to and practice of masculinity. Takakura Ken, for example—an actor and recording artist strongly associated with notions of stoic, "Japanese" manhood, and who, in case Japan needed a reminder of this, released a compilation LP in 1974 (also through King Records) titled *Otoko no Sekai* [The World of a Man]—rereleased "*Otoko Nara*" in 1966, strategically modifying lyrics here and there to dilute resonances with the *tokkōtai* but keeping the overall spirit of the work intact: "[T]here's no use in fearing the rain and the wind/cut through the waves of this floating world/with a man's determination as the vessel/if you are a man, give it a shot." In January 2011, "*Otoko Nara*" was resurrected yet again, this time as an *enka*-tinged post-bubble critique of a capitalist precarity that can somehow be overcome via a restoration of "Japanese" manhood. "Turn against the teachings of Fukuzawa Yukichi [a figure generally regarded as a facilitator of post-Tokugawa (1600–1868) "modernity" in Japan and who advocated a wholesale adoption of Western learning]," this newest version exhorted, "and smash this uneven society [*kakusa shakai*] to bits … reclaim your Yamato Spirit! If you are a man, give it a shot!" Of course, the revivification of "*Otoko Nara*" at the hands of Takakura and Nishikata tapped into questions of masculinity in ways that were different from the original song's summons to sacrifice in the service of the Imperial state. And yet, it still sought to tap an essential National Self that was still there and lying dormant in male (and sometimes female) Japanese bodies, but whose awareness and agency had been dulled by geopolitical and economic flows. Rehabilitating this authentic National Self and rescuing it from history was the point, and gender was appealed to as a key means of effecting this rehabilitation.

As I zoom back out, it becomes clear that this musical storytelling was itself part and parcel of a broader gendering of the Nation and National subjectivity that can be traced back to some of Japan's earliest modern moments. Gender, that is, is a key mechanism by which the story of the Nation has been told, musically and otherwise. Now, as I've already argued, Kagawa Ryō's critical project in "*Kyōkun I*" lay in troubling "the Nation" as the potentiating framework for war and in urging a critical reassessment of the ways that modern life is ordered around its purported authority. But this is deceptively tricky. Different modes of negation (including self-negation) pursued within the purview of the Nation as fundamentally unchallenged author of the terms and conditions of everyday life offered no solution: such tactics risked veering into an attempted romantic overcoming of modernity (Harootunian 2000b) and an assertion of "authentic" Japanese-ness that is itself narrated in gendered terms—as in Takakura's and Nishikata's revivification of "*Otoko Nara*," and especially in Mishima's *Yūkoku*—at best, and devolving into an "incomprehensible morass of childish rebelliousness" at worst (Oguma 2015). Either way, the authority of the Nation would be left largely intact, either through its modification or through an internal negation that in fact defined itself by the Nation's ubiquitous authority. Kagawa, it seems, saw just one viable path before him. To unsettle the authority of the Nation, he set out to scramble questions of *gender,* a key modality through which its stories have been told. To accomplish his critique, in other words, Kagawa had to disturb the (gendered) framework that has underwritten so many iterations of the Nation across Japan's modern moments (e.g., Tamanoi 1998), a framework that was yoked into the service of the Imperial state on the one hand, and appealed to as a means of negating the state-led postwar order and restoring an authentic, patriarchal "Japan" on the other. In short, he had to wipe the slate clean and start again—and tell different stories of what it meant to occupy a body in modern Japan.

Ueno's chapter provided Kagawa with the opportunity to tell such a story. Kagawa accomplished this through his musical rendering of Ueno's original text, to be sure, but also through his performing something of a productive impossibility in the process—embodying and voicing, as a "Japanese man," an outright rejection of what it has meant (according to some) to be a "Japanese man," and utilizing the very questions of gender that have been deployed to undergird and reinforce the Nation to blow the entire narrative to pieces. In a way that speaks to Kagawa's penchant for the strange and the provocative, "*Kyōkun I*" purposely unsettles the question of the gender of the narrating/singing voice. On the one hand, the "we" of the work—"[a]fter we're dead, the Nation will be just fine"—is articulated as *ore-tachi,* which is itself based in *ore,* generally understood as a "stereotypically masculine term" (Okamoto 2006, 321) for referring to the self. But at the same time, the only time that "I" (presumably a component of the "we") makes an appearance in the work, it is as *atashi*—a self-referential term that, as Itakura notes, is closely associated with so-called feminine Japanese speech (Itakura 2008, 468). Further, as Ohara, Saft, and Crookes and Okamoto point out, the sentence-final particle *ne* is also associated with feminized expression, potentially all the more so when combined with other particles like *yo,* and "the most prominent difference between masculine and feminine Japanese is that feminine Japanese is considered more polite" (Ohara et al. 2001, 107). This combination of sentence-final particle and "polite" speech points to an evocation of the feminine in the work's exhortations to "really start trembling" (*furuemashō yo ne*) and "[l]et us live and be called 'stupid'" (*iwaremashō yo ne*). Importantly, these linguistic combinations are *not* part of Ueno's original text—they're voiced by Kagawa for the first time in the recording of "*Kyōkun I*." In this way, Kagawa amplifies a gender "remix" that blends Ueno's original work and his own voice in a way that undermines the binary gendered structures that reinforce both the Nation (as in, say, Nishioka's 1937 *gunka*) and internal negations of versions thereof (as in the works by Mishima, Takakura, and Nishikata).

Now, I want to stress that I'm not suggesting a simple reversal—the internal negation, and thus, unintentionally, the validation—of the very binary (and sometimes clichéd) linguistic norms that themselves tend to reflect and reinforce gender inequality in Japan. Reducing language use to gendered caricature is a dangerous folly. It's important to point out—as other scholars have done—that the barriers between "masculine" and "feminine" Japanese are not as clear-cut in practice as they might seem: indeed, "[i]nstead of merely reducing language to a dichotomy of male and female speech, [recent empirical studies] have made the point that Japanese possess the ability to *use* language in innovative ways and create for themselves different and diverse gendered identities" (Ohara et al. 2001, 108). The key, that is, lies in how language is used in practice, rather than how it's characterized in the abstract. But this—the innovative use of language to effect political critique—is precisely the point. As far as I'm aware, and as essays written by the artist around this moment seem to attest (Kagawa 1972, 81–83), Kagawa Ryō did not identify as transgendered; the gendered performativity apparent in "*Kyōkun I*," that is, should not be taken as a literal rejection of his own masculinity. Rather, Kagawa's deployment of scrambled gendered language seems intended to confound the gendered performance of his own "Japanese" subjectivity, his slotting into the sorts of narratives of "masculinity" (or "femininity," for that matter) that are themselves such important components of National storytelling. (Butler [2004, 124], for instance, has explored how gender and heterosexuality become embroiled "in the building of a certain fantasy of state and nation.") Kagawa's performance of the productive impossibility through his manipulation of language, that is, seems to offer a line of flight around the gendered storytelling regime put to use both in conjuring the Nation and in naturalizing the sacrifices made in its name ("[y]ou're a man; go get it done"). It's a transgressive performance of gender that helps to reveal and clarify what Butler (1990, 141) calls "the performative possibilities for proliferating gender configurations outside [of] restricting frames of masculinist domination and compulsory heterosexuality"—and the structures of power and violence that they help to uphold.

If gender is "not expressive but performative [and] effectively constitute[s] the identity that [it is] said to express or reveal" (Butler 1990, 141), then Kagawa's interception and scrambling of the binary, heteronormative stories that have been deployed to bolster and sustain the Nation across the historical moments described earlier also allows him to conjure into being, to give voice to, possibilities for inhabiting a "Japanese" body *differently*. This is an ethos of "run[ning] away, and hid[ing]" from dominant (gendered) discourses of the Nation, to be sure, but it's not a negation per se—rather, it seems to me to be an exploration of different possibilities for living in Japan, for "being Japanese" (this will become all the more important later on this track, when I explore how Kagawa takes this song on the road in pursuit of what he called "Japan's one more time"). In his refusal to hew to the heteronormative stories of Nation-craft, Kagawa is able to start dodging the storytelling structures that seek both to constrain and to Nationalize the possibilities of his own fleshly existence. But there's more. Importantly, what's at stake in Kagawa's performance of the productive impossibility is not to simply flip the tables and embody the internal negation of the masculine—in a way, this was precisely the strategy pursued by hypermasculine sentimental nationalists like Mishima (Sakai 2006, 186) in their attempts to negate what they saw as a variously feminized, illegitimated postwar Japan (Igarashi 2021). Rather, Kagawa steps beyond the frame entirely in his musical storytelling—crucially, not (merely) declaring a positionality as "woman," but as "a *rotten* woman." The impossibility that Kagawa performs, in other words, is the impossibility of remaining a (Japanese) man while rejecting both Nation-sanctioned terms of masculinity *and* its internal negation in sanctioned "womanhood." This tactical distancing is what is achieved via his explicit citation and redeployment of the notion of the "rotten woman" and what places this purportedly problematic intervention at the very core of the song's critical project.

Now, as I pointed out earlier, Kagawa has faced criticism for his lyrical invocation of the "rotten woman [*kusatta onna*]," mostly due to the general intent of the idiom—to criticize men by equating them with a "rotten" (i.e., inferior) woman. But the "rotten woman" is not set here as a yardstick, insufficient in her own rights, against which to measure and declare the inadequacies of men. In this song, neither the singing/storytelling "I" (Kagawa, but not just Kagawa) nor any other man is *like* a rotten woman; rather, "I" proudly adopts the subjectivity of a so-called rotten woman, *becoming* one: "Being a rotten woman suits me just fine." At first glance, Kagawa's tactical grappling with gender in this song risks being derailed into a performance of "womanhood" as the internal negation of "manhood"; this is a trap that risks opening up an endless, closed-ended vacillation between the binary bookends of a broad gendered narrative that is of perfectly good use to the Nation and that ends up reinforcing it. As I discussed, "woman" is yoked to the service of the Nation in important ways as well, and appealing to gender to destabilize it is a tricky line to walk. Kagawa solves this conundrum by explicitly becoming a figure who is doubly outside the norms of the Nation: unmanly, "rotten," and entirely unuseful to it, confounding the expectations placed on his body as a fleshly component of the Nation entirely. In a way that echoes some of the textual strategies apparent in Ueno's original chapter (I think here specifically of the upending of the roles ascribed to katakana and hiragana, described briefly earlier), Kagawa's embodiment and vocalization of "*Kyōkun I*" help turn some of the gendered expectations for "being Japanese" inside out, like a photo negative. It's a masterful, critical performance that resonates strongly with what Butler (1990) has called, broadly, "gender trouble"—the intentional, performative confounding of dominant gender norms—and that seems rooted, to come full circle, in Kagawa's fascination with the possibilities of the Japanese language. And the effect of this playful destabilization, of refusing to engage the Nation's use of gender either through affirmation or through (internal) negation, is to urge a complete reimagining of what it means to live in the world, to "[r]un away, and hide" instead of "stok[ing] the flames of battle."

"Japan's One More Time" and Kagawa Ryō's Music Events

Kagawa Ryō remained closely engaged with history and the shifting terms and conditions of everyday life across the arc of his four and a half decades in music. Different works, different albums, demonstrate this in different ways. Kagawa's sardonic lampooning of patriotic fervor in the context of the Pacific War and sarcastic (or not) call for renewed "war" against the United States in the context of former prime minister Satō Eisaku's Cold War collaboration with the same in his somber, funereal-sounding "*Sensō Shimashō* [Let Us Go to War]" (1971) can be seen as anchoring one end of this historical arc; "*Shiawaseō na Hitotachi* [Happy-Looking People]," a pensive, somehow mournful song recorded by Kagawa as the last song on his final album, 2016's *Mirai* [The Future]—itself compiled against a backdrop of growing unease in the wake of 3.11, the "state secrets law" of 2013 (which criminalizes asking about state secrets, themselves more or less arbitrarily defined, regardless of whether or not one knew they were "secrets" in the first place [Manabe 2015, 5]), and Abe's "war bills" of 2015—sat at the other ("People need to open their eyes [*mikiwamenaakan*] … they don't have a clue about the dangers facing them," Kagawa told me in June 2016 as he reflected on these moments. "*Minna shiawaseō ya mon* [Everybody just looks so goddamned happy!]"). But the anchor of Kagawa's diverse musical storytelling would always be "*Kyōkun I.*" He rerecorded the song repeatedly throughout his career, modifying the musical framework in ways that could appeal to different audiences: it became a hard-rock tune in a 1996 collaboration with Te-Chili, for example, and it took on a different sound yet again in recorded sessions with steel guitarist Sugino Nobu in 2002 and 2007. But the lyrics never changed. It's hardly surprising that "*Kyōkun I*" has remained powerful, resonating across decades and in different historical and geopolitical contexts: as long as the Nation and its gendering framework remain key conditions of everyday life, the song will have a place. In an interview in 2007—when Abe Shinzō was prime minister, but years before the second Abe cabinet, when alarm over the prime minister's intentions truly began to spread, culminating in the uproar over the "war bills" and the tense summer of 2015—Kagawa explained what he saw as the contemporary relevance of "*Kyōkun I*" in these terms: "I'm a human being who doesn't know a goddamned thing about politics. I have no idea what they mean by 'Beautiful Country,' and I probably couldn't even spell the words 'Abe Shinzō's Cabinet' properly. But I do think that Japan has become quite the ballsy country over these past few years. Words like 'state policy' and 'patriotism'—words like that get thrown around these days as if they were nothing. Before we even knew what was happening. So it seems to me that singing an 'unpatriotic' song like ['*Kyōkun I*'] is important these days" (Sakamoto 2007).

The language is crass, likely intentionally so (recall the explicit appeal to "brass balls" articulated in Nishioka's original "*Otoko Nara*," cited earlier). A big part of what makes "*Kyōkun I*" "unpatriotic," of course, is its insistence on troubling the gendered narratives that the Nation relies upon for its very survival. This reliance upon notions of "masculinity" (and "femininity") was evidently as much a part of the makeup of the Nation in 2007—when Japan became, in Kagawa's assessment, "quite the ballsy country"—as it was in 1970. Interrupting these gendered mechanics of Nation making, as I described earlier, was precisely what made Kagawa's critical musical storytelling in "*Kyōkun I*" make sense—and what's kept it relevant.

Kagawa's tactic of intervening in the way that the Nation, as a key underwriter of the terms and conditions of everyday life, made sense in the first place, rather than merely opposing its actions or character—a musical stance that I've been calling "anti-folk"—was a novel one to take as a folk singer. Troubling folk's historically isolated claim to critical vocabulary and authority by speaking/singing in unauthorized terms—a sort of heresy—even earned Kagawa the ire of some of his artistic contemporaries, at least one of whom was reportedly exasperated enough to tell him, in his recollection, to "get with the program." But these transgressions against "folk's" storytelling regime have been precisely what allowed Kagawa's own musical storytelling to remain relevant when other "folk"—such as that dealing with the Vietnam War, for example—has struggled to do so, or has been relegated to the realm of nostalgia in what Kagawa himself called televised "reunions" of old folk hands. This heresy is at the core of "anti-folk" as Kagawa's critique—and it's a heresy that is exemplified in "*Kyōkun I.*" It is thus perhaps not surprising that Kagawa, in the 2007 interview cited earlier, vowed to "keep singing [the song] until I die." But despite the frequent rerecordings of "*Kyōkun I*," pursuing this critique was never something that could remain confined to an album's grooves or to liner notes. Singing "*Kyōkun I*" "until I die" meant singing it on the road.

Kagawa Ryō spent a great deal of his career on the road, following a practice of what he called *tabi*—"travels." Superstardom was well within Kagawa's reach in the early 1970s, when, as folk-rock star Matsuyama Chiharu recalled in a televised interview in 2000, the music world waited to see whether it would be Kagawa Ryō or his contemporary Yoshida Takurō who really "made it big" (Matsuyama 2000). But this was a contest that Kagawa largely forfeited (Yoshida, meanwhile, remains a superstar to this day). Rather than pursuing a career of stadium shows and commercial successes, Kagawa pursued his musical storytelling in small "live houses," playing for crowds of a few dozen to perhaps a few hundred (in 2015 he estimated that he was playing around one hundred shows per year). These cramped, smoky venues constituted a vital part of Kagawa's musical storytelling—they were where his strange, disruptive "anti-folk" ethics leapt out of the abstract and off the LP and spilled into performance spaces as part of a collaborative "world-producing" (Stone 1982) practice. In Kagawa's preferred venues, the distance between performer and audience member was reduced to practically nothing, generating a "closeness" that was of great importance to him. "These shows are not something that I create on my own, and just hand to people," Kagawa told me in 2016. "We make them together." The very physical attributes of his preferred performance places, in other words, helped facilitate what Kagawa called "liveness"—a sort of collaborative co-creativity pursued by social actors (both performer and attendee) embedded in the world (Condry 2006, 137) and that relies on challenging received stories of the world, and telling new ones.

"*Kyōkun I*" remained a staple of these shows throughout Kagawa's career. As far as I'm aware, every Kagawa concert—including the considerable number that I took part in—featured the song, usually near the end of the evening. For the most part he stuck with his lyrical claim to "rotten woman[hood]" in those performances, including as a "guest" performer at a 2015 performance by contemporary neo-folk/pop duo Humbert Humbert, where he emerged from backstage to take over vocals from female vocalist Sano Yūho for that line—and only that line. Sometimes, in ways clearly intended to enhance the "meaning" of the work intertextually, he'd place it alongside other key songs in the set list. At a performance that I attended in the spring of 2015, for example, Kagawa set up "*Kyōkun I*" by softly plucking out the mournful guitar notes that open "*Sensō Shimashō* [Let Us Go to War]," discussed briefly earlier. "Oops," he muttered. "Wrong song." But of course, the "mistake" was intentional. The entire episode lasted perhaps five or six seconds, but the aim was clear: to enhance the

Figure 3.1 Kagawa Ryō performs at a small "live house" in 2014. The artist recalled playing more than one hundred such shows per year at this point in his career. Photo by Yoshimura Teruyuki.

critical punch of "*Kyōkun I*" among a group of socially and historically embedded listeners at a particularly fraught political moment, when the Nation seemed on the verge of running amok. The audience knew and instantly recognized the work—the uneasy gasp/chuckle that rippled through the room was proof enough of this. Its referencing of war—the ultimate folly of the Nation—helped to amplify the critique of "*Kyōkun I*" in a moment marked by the imminent passage of the "war bills" and anxiety over the prospect of remilitarization (Muto 2016). The song, that is, among its community of listeners in 2015 made as much sense as (if not more than) it had in 1971. It's probably not surprising, then, that after the show a regular audience member expressed frustration to me with the general inclination to memorialize folk and contain it to a moment now past: "The time for listening to Kagawa Ryō's music," the audience member insisted, "is *now*."

At around this moment, Kagawa added another staple to his live performance set list—"*D no Tsuki* [Waxing Moon]," a contemplative, medium-tempo work recorded in simple triple time and the only Kagawa original to be included on his aforementioned final album, *Mirai* (the rest of the tracks are covers, songs that Kagawa deemed particularly important in this moment). "*D no Tsuki*" contains an important lyric, which—crucially—is not inscribed in the liner notes/lyrics card, but which the artist never failed to sing in performance: "[L]ook for me; for me, and for Japan's one more time." The move here seems to push beyond the destabilization of the Nation afforded by "*Kyōkun I*" and think about the *reassembly* of "Japan" according to different terms (Latour 2005)—a project that is simultaneously lyrical, performative, and even geographical, as I'll discuss later. By intentionally excluding the lyric from his own album's printed liner notes, Kagawa ensured that the call to "look ... for Japan's one more time" was legible only aurally and accentuated in performance, in the co-creative, collaborative music events through which artist and audience work to destabilize the terms and conditions of the Nation and imagine "Japan" anew. It's a playful storytelling tactic that harkens—albeit in a different way— to Kagawa's fascination with the possibilities of language and expression that drew him to Ueno Ryō's original "*Kyōkun Sono Ichi*" in the first place, and resonates with Ueno's enthusiastic assessment of his appropriation of the chapter and its redeployment as "*ishitsu no bunka*"—a "different sort of culture"—that could transcend the limitations of textuality and become amplified, expanded, "overheard" (Yano 2002, 7). It was a complex approach to critical musical storytelling that caught not only my attention but that of some of his most dedicated listeners as well.

Asked for their thoughts on this line and Kagawa's performative strategy— which sounds on the surface like the articulation of a nostalgic longing for a forgotten past—the insights of some of those in Kagawa's immediate orbit were enlightening. Kitagawa Yoshio, for example, Kagawa's Kansai-area "road manager" (a largely volunteer position; nobody, including Kagawa, was making much money with these gigs), suggested that "it *seems* nostalgic, but what did Ryō-san actually want to say? Where have we come from? Where are we going? What sort of 'future' [*mirai;* the name of the album] is waiting for us? That's what I take from it, anyway." Sakamoto Masayoshi, musician and frequent Kagawa collaborator, told me that "Ryō-san's been watching this country in real time since the sixties, walking through it. He's seen the times change before his very eyes; he's sung about it. This isn't about nostalgia; for me, it's about the possibility of having exciting *new* times." And for concert promoter Mikado Haruki, Kagawa's call for "Japan's one more time" was about a future-oriented recalibration of everyday Japanese life in the wake of the ongoing crises of March 11, 2011. In each case, the call to "look for ... Japan's one more time" seemed to become part of the ways that these social actors understood Kagawa's overall critical stance and their own potential role(s) within it—not in the singular, importantly, but in the plural (Kitagawa's "us," Sakamoto's "this country"). The call resonated as an invitation to find in the scrambled Nation of "*Kyōkun I*" the promise of a collective way forward, of different histories and possibilities for living in the world.

For all these figures, then, what may sound at first like a restorative call to the past was actually the opposite—the focus here, following Boym's more general insights on the ambiguities of nostalgia (2001, 49–50), "is not on recovery of what is perceived to be an absolute truth, but on the meditation on history and passage of time" in the interests of "open[ing] up a multitude of potentialities" and imagining "Japan" in new, productive ways. And "*Kyōkun I*," of course, as "un-patriotic" masterpiece and destabilizer of the Nation, helps generate the scrambling that renders this reimagining, or *reassembly*, possible in the first place. Kagawa, in short, seems to call here for a redemption of "Japan" that is not about restoration, but rather about reflection on the patina of time and the (L)essons of history; about what might be, not what was. And by ensuring that the call for "Japan's one more time" was only vocal, never textual, he ensured that it avoided the centripetal pull "to pin down the voice to the letter, to limit its disruptive force, to dissipate its inherent ambiguity" (Dolar 2006, 49), that it remained always open-ended, always pointed toward the future. As a tactically and singularly *sonic* resource, that is, the song—and this crucial line specifically— could circulate among the historically embedded bodies gathered in Kagawa's performance places (like Kitagawa, and Sakamoto, and Mikado), "help[ing] audiences imagine a community of ... listeners" (Novak 2013, 30) and be rendered susceptible to capture in the collective, not just the (reading) singular. This communal capturability seems particularly vital when considering Kagawa Ryō's live shows as *events*.

Kagawa's understanding of his own performances—"[w]e make them together"—resonates strongly with Jackson's conceptualization of "musical events, understood as dynamic and processual, [as] a space in which performers and other participants interact and negotiate their relationships with each other as well as with other events that have occurred in the past ... musical meaning is what emerges from the shared and variable understandings that participants bring to and create through participation in musical events" (Jackson 2012, 7–15). To keep on singing "*Kyōkun I*" "until I die," then, and to seek the possibility of "Japan's one more time" through the inmixing of "*D no Tsuki*," was to continue to tell musical stories that trouble the singular sense-making authority of the Nation across moments in which it remained a key element of everyday life, both for Kagawa and for everyone else in his performance spaces, and that generated "meaning" that was both critical and reimaginative. To be sure, this generation of "meaning" and shared critique takes place in defined places—for Kagawa, the smoky, intimate "live houses" that were his preferred venue. But music events can also feed back (Novak 2013) into the very lived historical and political circuity looping through and lending meaning to the collaborative musicking engaged in by artist and audience in the first place, spilling out into social life. That the critiques spun up in Kagawa's event spaces could be captured simultaneously by those populating them as sound, as *music,* is important, and points to the ways that music can help to establish and reveal the contours of "scenes that afford different kinds of agency, different sorts of pleasure and ways of being" (DeNora 2000, 123). It also begins to point the discussion back toward what Kagawa Ryō, on the surface, appears to reject: the collective potentialities of "folk."

McKay points out that collaborative events such as the ones I'm describing here help "create … a time and space of celebration, a site of *convergence* separate from everyday routines, experiences and meanings—ephemeral communities in place and time" (McKay 2015, 3). But to the extent that such events feed back into their own potentiating conditions—becoming "world producing"—the possibilities of the event can exceed its own physical confines and ephemerality and seep into everyday life itself. As the physical reactions to the music on the part of attendees help to show—the uneasy gasps and chuckles in response to "*Sensō Shimashō,*" for instance, or the anxious urging on the part of the listener I encountered earlier that Kagawa's music must be listened to *now*—participants in music events can be drawn into the "flows" of performances, and "[o]nce inside those flows, it becomes possible for them to see new ways of understanding, manipulating, and mastering the materials, situations, and constraints presented to them in performance and daily life" (Jackson 2012, 7). Deployed in specific performative settings, the music is appropriated by and pulled into the everyday lived realities of social actors already drawn to the critical musical storytelling that Kagawa engages in, accruing meaning among the co-constituents of an event in ways that can set the stage for a (re-)thinking of the terms and conditions of social life (I'll continue to discuss this on tracks 4 and 5). In this way, "it is perfectly reasonable to speak of music as material of social organization, because styles of movement, emotional and social roles come to be associated with it and may issue from it" (DeNora 2000, 121–125). This is not to say, of course, that music (Kagawa's or anyone else's) *causes* anything at all—it doesn't. But it is to point to the very real ways in which music, particularly among a community of listeners already deeply invested in a critical musical storyteller like Kagawa, can be drawn on as a resource for (re-) orienting thoughts and bodies among such historically embedded social actors. In these ways, Kagawa's performative practice and pursuit of "Japan's one more time" resonated with scholarly thinking on the music event. But the specificities of Kagawa's artistic and musical practice offer the opportunity to expand our thinking on the event as well. In Kagawa's case, it's informative to pay attention not only to the event as an enclosed space of interaction (Stone 1982), but to *where* and *how* those events unfurled as well. This has to do with Kagawa's own body and its movements on the road.

As I argued earlier, "*Kyōkun I*" isn't a "protest song" as such works are generally understood. Rather, it's a critical reflection on the implications of occupying a gendered Japanese body and on the possibilities of scrambling those norms to imagine "Japanese" life differently. The song works, in large part, precisely because it dares to undermine the gendered norms imposed on Japanese bodies by the Nation and to suggest that the body can be occupied in ways that are not susceptible to its reach. But this centering of the fleshly body intersects with Kagawa's critical practice in other ways, too. As I've already mentioned, Kagawa Ryō spent a great deal of time on the road, in a practice that he insisted on calling *tabi*. These *tabi* took him on lengthy, circular tours of the archipelago, as he traced overland routes—often with PA equipment and his signature electro-acoustic guitar slung into the trunk of a car—punctuated by stops at "live houses" along the way. I asked Kagawa's longtime partner Fujiko to reflect on Kagawa's insistence on staying on the road, on its implications. Her response was revealing.

> It's not so much that Kagawa loved the road, I think, as it was that he loved people. He had a lot of love for the people that he met in different places across Japan, and loved the places where they lived. [...] He actually took me and our son to many of those places, and introduced us to the folks who lived there. I remember him telling our son many years ago, "you know, your dad knows some folks who are incredibly rich, and others who can barely get by." He told me that he wanted to take our son to meet all sorts of people, that by doing so he'd learn that there are all sorts of ways of living in the world.
>
> Through his concerts he was able to go to all sorts of places, and get to know the incredible spots around Japan that the locals there would take him to. The more he toured, the more he came to love this country called "Japan."
>
> Live shows = *tabi*. *Tabi* = people.

For forty-six years, then, Kagawa's "live houses" became nodes in a network whose contours were traced in the process of the artist's own travels. *Tabi*, for Kagawa, seem to have involved tracing the outlines of a "Japan" rooted not in the normatizing dictates of the Nation, but rather in diverse locales and everyday lives, in the possibilities of living differently, and sometimes in living off the page entirely (Harootunian 2000a, 157). His tracing of a "different" Japan, that is, seems to have been geographical as well as lyrical. In conversation, Kagawa described intentionally selecting "off the path" sites for his events as opposed to, say, regular performances in places like Tokyo or Osaka (although these cities did appear in his performance schedules). The aim, for Kagawa, was to draw people out and have them populate—even if just for a night—places away from Japan's main centers: "[F]olks will come out [to see some of these places] if I'm playing in a town they think I'll never be back to again." The "Japan" that he found (even engineered) on the road, to put it simply, did not necessarily equate to the Nation that was the object of his critique. Rather, it seems likely that the "Japanese" possibilities that Kagawa discovered through *tabi*—through "making [musical events] together" with like-minded individuals—helped to generate the possibility of calling for "Japan's one more time" in the first place: "The more he toured, the more he came to love this country called 'Japan.'"

Kagawa's incessant traveling throughout Japan, that is, physically linked him to people in communities across the archipelago, literally connecting the dots of a "Japan" that was not always already there, but that was always in the process of being produced through his musical storytelling, broadly conceived. Returning relentlessly to his career-anchoring "*Kyōkun I,*" and later adding in "*D no Tsuki,*" Kagawa facilitated critical music events at these locations across the country, "mak[ing]them together" with those who came out to take part and performing "Japan" in ways that didn't so much *negate* it as spin up a critical rethinking of its terms and conditions. Kagawa's own declaration of the occupation of a "Japanese" body in a way that can upset the gendered rules of the Nation—Butler's "gender trouble"—is at the core of the critical practice articulated in "*Kyōkun I.*" But intentionally gathering bodies together in the radically intimate, off-the-path places preferred by Kagawa and spooling up critical music events—generating a "scene"—can move critique from the singular to the collective, generating the potentiating condition for "Japan's one more time." Scholars have shown how such events often have "the fundamental purpose of envisioning and crafting another, better world ... [Such an event] at its most utopian is a pragmatic and fantastic space in which to dream and to try another world into being" (McKay 2015, 3). For Kagawa, it seems, "Japan"—not the Nation—still carried the potential of being such "another world": this is probably close to what Kagawa had in mind when, reappropriating and repurposing Abe Shinzō's "beautiful country" rhetoric at the end of his 2007 interview, he said: "Accepting each other; loving each other. That might be the sort of thing that 'Beautiful Country' means to me." And with every stop along the *tabi* route—with every dot that was connected as bodies assembled in cramped bars and halls—Kagawa drew closer to sketching the contours of a critical collectivity that emerges from the shadows when the Nation is undermined and something else is summoned to take its place: a community of the "all sorts."

Following his concert at the University of Chicago in 2016, Kagawa Ryō sat for another feature-length interview—this time with the *Chicago Shinpō*, a Japanese-English bilingual newspaper serving Chicago and the Midwest region of the United States. The article resulting from the interview was titled "*Fooku Buumu Kara 40 Nen, Kagawa Ryō ha Ima mo Koko ni Iru* [Forty Years from the Folk Boom, Kagawa Ryō Is *Still Here*]" (emphasis mine) (Urayama 2016). By "folk boom," the article meant to reference the critical, "protest" folk of around 1970 that's most often associated with the term and that I've been referencing herein; its subtext, of course, was surprise at Kagawa's resilient presence on the music scene some four decades on from the purported end of critical folk in the mid-1970s. The assumption that critical folk faded away after this moment, as I described earlier, is commonplace and not particularly surprising. Music, after all, helps orient minds and bodies on the basis of the contexts within which it's referenced and used (DeNora 2003, 49–50), and as the songs became divorced from their own affording conditions (the Vietnam War, for example, to return to the example cited earlier), their critical punch and perceived relevance necessarily waned—it's for this reason that so much folk is relegated to the realm of the nostalgic in the contemporary moment, musical artifacts to be trotted out once in a while on NHK and wistfully sung along to as the "music of our youth." Kagawa, though, used music and language to tell a much different sort of critical story than that which was in vogue in his moment, and in so doing ensured that his critique would survive the shifting historical contexts of the mid-1970s and beyond. Kagawa Ryō was not alone in surviving the death of "folk"; other key figures continue to play as well, such as Okabayashi Nobuyasu, whose "*San'ya Burūsu* [San'ya Blues]" similarly articulates a political-economic critique that is not isolable to the contingencies of around 1970. But in his explicit, avowed disdain for "folk"—a disdain that we can now begin to understand as actually constituting a deep love—Kagawa was perhaps the most vociferous advocate for expanding folk's potentials, and not allowing it to fade with the turning of history's page. By zeroing in on the underlying, potentiating conditions of many of the contingent, topical critiques of around 1970 and de-emphasizing their symptomatic manifestations (the echoes of the work of Kagawa's friend and teacher Takada Wataru, discussed on track 2, are too clear here to miss), Kagawa in "*Kyōkun I*" exemplified an "anti-folk" stance that helped to save "folk," or at least the best of its critical impulses, from itself. The song remains an "un-patriotic" masterpiece that negates folk's negations while still upholding its promises, working instead to dig around at the roots of the terms and conditions of everyday life that make the Nation and its internal negation legible in the first place. And probably more than any other work, it helps explain why Kagawa Ryō—even in death—is "still here."

"Love Songs"

In his 2007 interview with the *Chūnichi shinbun,* Kagawa Ryō denied—as he often did—knowing anything about, or having any interest in, "politics." But this needs to be taken with a grain of salt. When Kagawa says "politics," he means the sort of street-based activism that defined much of his moment of around 1970, and that he worked against as a practitioner of what I've been calling "anti-folk." Kagawa remained keenly aware of the potential and necessity of challenging the stories that the Nation told itself about itself—and telling new ones in their stead. It's what kept him singing "*Kyōkun I*" quite literally until he died. But despite all the political potential that I've been ascribing to it in these pages, "*Kyōkun I*" wasn't a "protest song" at all. It was a love song. Or, perhaps more precisely, it was a love song that compels us to think about—and affords—"protest" in different ways.

One year after his death in April 2017, Kagawa's family organized a "tribute concert" in his memory, featuring Ariyama Junji (b. 1953, formerly of the aforementioned folk unit Itsutsu no Akai Fūsen, later Kagawa collaborator in Te-Chili), singer-songwriter Kanamori Kōsuke (b. 1951), rocker Kaneko Mari (b. 1954), the gnkosaiBAND (featuring Kagawa's son, Genki), and others. The event was titled Love Songs. This title came about in part as the result of Kagawa's partner Fujiko's own attempts to navigate and resolve the contradiction of a folk singer who was so avowedly "anti-folk." "Kagawa debuted with '*Kyōkun I*,' but he always hated being categorized as an anti-war folk singer [*hansen fooku*]," Fujiko wrote to me in autumn of 2020. "I'd always thought that the contents of his early stuff [like '*Kyōkun I*'] made it unavoidable that they'd be thought of as protest songs—but he'd always mutter 'no, that's not it. They don't get it.' It was the first year after he passed away that I realized that *every song he sang* was a love song. […] Kagawa wrote love songs, he sang love songs. Love songs directed at living itself, love songs for every life out there. I told Genki that I wanted to title the event 'Love Songs,' and he got it right away—'That's perfect!' he said. So, we gave the tribute event the title *Love Songs.*"

To love life is, in a way, to distrust—if not outright hate—the Nation. But this cannot be reduced to a negation of "Japan." Rather, it's to love the people and the places that comprise it, to sketch out different contours and visions for it, to stay hopeful for "Japan's one more time" that is never about making Japan great again, but rather about organizing future-oriented hopes for different possibilities that can still be gathered under its signposting. As I write this track in 2022, more than fifty years after the debut of "*Kyōkun I*," seven years since its tactical deployment in the wake of Abe's "war legislation" in 2015, and five years on from the death of Kagawa Ryō himself, the song is enjoying a resurgence of popularity in Japan. Actor, singer, and model (as well as daughter to well-known actor Ken Watanabe) Anne, for example, caused something of a stir in summer 2020 when she posted to social media video of herself singing "*Kyōkun I*," finding its call to "run away, and hide" as particularly meaningful in the context of the devastating global COVID-19 pandemic (Watanabe 2020). It's perhaps an odd reading, focused just on a line or two ("run away, and hide") rather than the broader content and contexts of the work. But none of that fazes Kagawa's partner. "Once a song has left the hand of its composer and goes out into the world, it starts walking on its own," Fujiko says, echoing Takada Wataru's rather more crass assessment from track 2. "The rest [meaning, significance] is up to the person who hears it." But particulars of interpretation and use aside, the song is, for Fujiko, a love song at its core. She continued: "As long as there are people out there who find in the music their own encouragement, their own solace, their own consolation, as long as there are people for whom the music provides a leg up and a gentle nudge from behind, well, then I guess I have to say that that's because somewhere in the music, deep down, there was love." Fujiko's assertion here carries resonances of the insights of music scholars who trace the ways that social actors can find strength, solace, and possibility in specific songs, depending on the lived contexts that those actors find themselves within. But awakening to possibility is *itself* a political act—one that relies on a realization that the story is not as finished as it may seem, that it can be told differently, that doing so can point toward a different Future (*Mirai*, Kagawa's aforementioned final album). The undiminishing resonance of "*Kyōkun I*"—of Kagawa Ryō himself—finds its source in the promise that things *can* be different, that we can do more than simply negate the already given terms and conditions of everyday life and simply rely on the tired stories that we already have, as oppositional as that reliance may be. It's the promise of "anti-folk," of a disdain for protest-oriented "folk" that was never really disdain at all—rather, it was a determination to see the promise of "critical folk" through and, by pivoting from "protest" to a love song, to save it from itself. And it's the promise of being able to tell the story of what it means to live in Japan, to "be Japanese," in new and open-ended ways.

Singing My Song

KARAOKE POLITICS ON THE EVE
OF JAPAN'S DARK SPRING

I walk the streets of the Shiba district of Tokyo in the early summer humidity of 2010, beneath a thick bank of cloud that threatens to obscure the top of nearby Tokyo Tower. I'm searching for Tokyo Shiba Melparque Hall, site of the twenty-sixth Japan Amateur Popular Song Festival (Nihon Amachua Kayōsai, hereafter the Kayōsai), an annual karaoke competition produced by the Nihon Amachua Kayō Renmei (Japan Amateur Popular Song Federation, hereafter NAK), a highly organized Japanese popular music "appreciation society." Established in 1982, NAK had roughly thirty thousand members in 2010; as of this writing, that number remains more or less the same. The Kayōsai is the organization's signature event, and I've been invited to attend this year as an observer by an NAK producer sympathetic to my desire to explore musical storytelling among karaoke enthusiasts. Unsure of what to expect but vaguely envisioning another incarnation of the small- to medium-scale amateur singing contests regularly held in villages, towns, and cities across Japan, I am stunned to turn a corner and find a massive banner displaying NAK's logo and the title of the event draped over the entrance to a towering concert hall. From the rather intimidating door managers inspecting entrants' tickets to the dozen or so "congratulatory" floral arrangements that have been sent to the venue by an array of record labels and professional recording artists, the pre-entrance ambience gives every indication that, while the performers in today's event may be amateur, its production is most certainly not.

Armed only with my e-mailed invitation from the producer, I'm briefly detained by the suspicious security detail at the main entrance before being rescued by my NAK contact and ushered inside. The grand scale of the Kayōsai is immediately apparent in the vibe that pulses through the venue—the lobby is a maelstrom of costume hawkers, CD and cassette vendors, production staff bustling about in industry-standard dark suits (complete with radio earpieces), and participants who have come to this corner of Tokyo from across Japan and as far away as Hawai'i and Brazil to take the stage and be heard. The Kayōsai, which is open to participation by all NAK members, is held annually in this large-scale concert hall in the heart of the metropolis. It's a massive, nine-hour marathon of music that features 150 contestant-performers who have cleared preliminary elimination rounds in their home regions (NAK has more than one hundred chapters across Japan and around the world) and reached the final showdown of the passionately dedicated and enormously talented. It's professionally produced and emceed and features guest performances by well-known recording artists. The atmosphere is somehow carnivalesque, reminiscent of a summer festival with its stalls and kiosks and booths, and is marked by a thrumming undercurrent of palpable excitement. And as the background music, the record vendors, and the clothing stalls—selling glittering evening gowns for women, tuxedos and garish "gangster suits" for the men, even a kimono or two—make clear, this is first and foremost a festival of *enka,* a modern popular music form that purports to tell the story of the "heart and soul of the Japanese" (Wilson 1993, 286). *Enka* and its practices—the way it gets wrapped up in musical storytelling—is the music(king) that I explore on this track.

To write of *enka* is to refer to vastly disparate modes of musical storytelling across Japan's modern moments. In the late nineteenth and early twentieth centuries, for instance, *enka* referred to a wandering minstrelsy of sorts; individual artists—*enka-shi*—would use their own music in often biting ways, articulating in song critiques of the state (for example) that they were not permitted to say (Wilson 1993, 287; Treat 1996, 112). Soeda Azembō belongs in this camp; I explore Soeda and his work on track 2 of this book. Later, in the 1960s, writer Itsuki Hiroyuki would celebrate what were often panned as the gloomy, sentimental characteristics of *ryūkōka*—"Japanese" popular song—and rename the music *enka* (Wajima 2014, 78). This was a countercultural (actually counter-countercultural) move, meant to challenge the "developmental," and implicitly "Americanizing," storytelling of the established Left (I'll return briefly to the question of "counterculture" later). But since the 1970s, *enka* has been ascribed the role of representing—in music and performance—notions of authentic, "traditional Japan" itself, and of constituting a key site at and through which the Nation is imagined, its story told. Musically, there is little about the genre that would suggest "tradition"—indeed, the claim is itself thoroughly modern, and part of an attempt to define "Japan's music" against the incursion of musics understood to be "foreign," such as rock and folk (Treat 1996, 111). Although *enka* works do tend to employ vibrato-laden, *nakibushi* (crying-style) vocals and a *yonanuki* pentatonic scale, both of which are ascribed the status of being sonic representations of what might be called rhetorical Japaneseness (Stevens 2008, 17–20), *enka* recordings themselves tend to be hyperproduced along familiar pop-musical lines and feature electric guitars, synthesizers, saxophones, drum machines, so-called Western musical idioms, and so on. Regardless, however, like country music, *enka* has become tightly bound to vague ideas of authenticity and the *Volk* and deeply implicated in telling stories of "Japan" as imagined national community.

In popular (and some scholarly) discourse, in other words, *enka* are saddled with a rather heavy ideological weight. Industry gatekeepers, media commentators, even some amateur practitioners and fans tend to describe the music as constituting nothing less than the musical manifestation of the "heart/soul of [the] Japanese" (Yano 2002, 7). As such, *enka* and its practices seem to constitute the very antithesis of the reimaginative, destabilizing, and political musical storytelling that I'm exploring in this book. But a consideration of *enka* and its practitioners is not as out of place among other singers of the Homesick Blues as it might appear to be. As I mentioned briefly earlier, scholar Wajima Yusuke has argued that *enka* at its birth around the late 1960s could be understood as a sort of *counterculture*. New Left activists (and others) appealed to the gloomy, sentimental strains of *enka*'s *ryūkōka* forebears precisely because they were met with disapproval by the established Left, who tended to find the music reactionary; early *enka* were the antithesis of the brighter, "cheerful and wholesome" (Wajima 2014, 74) sounds of "American" music that established progressives wanted to promote. Nagahara locates a similar sort of countercultural critique in forerunners to *enka* in the 1950s and 1960s, when the music's purported vulgarity was linked to an earthy, outlaw sense of "Japaneseness" that challenged the "political, economic, and cultural irresponsibility of the ruling class" in an era of "mass society" and alienation in the face of prevailing economic and geopolitical prerogatives (Nagahara 2017, 202–203). Now, for Wajima, the countercultural potentials of *enka* had largely faded by 1970 or so, as the music's "countercultural implication[s] seem to have given way to a naive inclination toward a nostalgic representation of the nation's past" (Wajima 2014, 81). The moment around 1970, in other words, marked a juncture at which the music was co-opted into a different sort of storytelling regime, one interested in closed-ended assertions of Japanese "authenticity." My aim on this track is not quite to negate this assessment and posit a post-1970 continuation of the "countercultural" possibilities that Wajima and Nagahara find in early incarnations of *enka*. I am, however, eager to delve deeper into the question that lies at the base of Wajima's insights on *enka* as counterculture in the first place—the question of how the music is *used* by specific social actors in specific contexts, at specific times. Attention to this question of use allows me to push beyond vacillating descriptions of *enka* as a medium through which closed-ended notions of the Nation are imagined and produced, on the one hand, or as enduring "counterculture," on the other (itself a bifurcated, codependent set of possibilities that relies on mutual negation to be legible), and think about some of the ambiguous ways that the music is deployed in everyday practice. And while not quite counter-cultural, this does point to a certain *tension,* as *enka* are yoked into service—by aficionados and amateur performers on the one hand, by the music's gatekeep-ers on the other—in ways that we might not expect, as a medium for telling (sometimes critical, sometimes disciplinary) musical stories of what it actually means to these actors to live in Japan, to "be Japanese."

On this track, I pivot away from a focus on powerful institutions (track 1) and individual artists and their critiques (tracks 2 and 3) to begin thinking about how everyday social actors—fans, amateurs, industry stakeholders—deploy music as part and parcel of their own musical storytelling practices (I'll continue in this vein on track 5). By spending some time with the membership of the Nihon Amateur Kayō Renmei—both within Melparque Hall and beyond it—I consider some of the ways that *enka* and the mode of musicking known as karaoke are used by different practitioners in telling stories of their lives. Let me finish my warm-up, though, by clarifying my own approach to the music of "Japan." Given the weighty baggage that has been ascribed to *enka* since the 1970s, it's not surprising that scholarly interrogation of the music has tended to take imaginings of "Japan" as both starting and ending points. "Japan," that is—in a way that reaffirms the stories that *enka* stakeholders tell themselves and others about the music—is taken as an a priori potentiating condition for the genre, one that is itself regenerated and reaffirmed by its practitioners in a way that sketches those practitioners within its already sealed discursive space. But although I will certainly reach "Japan" in the course of my discussion, to do so productively I cannot take it as my starting point, as the informing condition of a closed-circuited analysis, lest I simply end up right back where I started. Rather, I need to think about how we get there, when we get there, and why. Rather than centering "Japan" as an a priori condition of analysis, in other words, I want to emphasize different praxes of musical storytelling that make use of *enka* and see what this reveals about how "Japan" gets wrapped up in *enka* musicking after 1970 in the first place. This will, I hope, allow me to hear different stakeholders singing the Homesick Blues in ways that can be unpre-dictable, surprising, and maybe even open-ended. In order to begin telling this story, I have to rewind to the moment of modern *enka*'s emergence and con-sider the history of karaoke, which is, after all, what I've come to Melparque Hall to observe. It constitutes a medium for musical storytelling par excellence.

Prelude: Thinking about Karaoke

This book takes the moment of around 1970 as an important waypoint for con-sidering different modes of musical storytelling in modern Japan—and karaoke is certainly part of the history of this moment. Other scholarship has described the birth of karaoke in Japan—its emergence in a Kobe establishment called Crescent around 1970, its subsequent evolution from a (male-centered) part of Japanese nightlife into a pastime with much broader appeal, whose popularity would explode with the rise of private karaoke "boxes" in the 1990s and remain formidable into the present day—and has positioned the practice along a longer historical arc of "Japanese culture" and engagement with song. This is well-trod ground (Mitsui and Hosokawa 1998; Yano 1996, 1–17) and needs no repeating here. Instead, I'd like to consider karaoke in terms of some of the musical and political contexts of the moment of its emergence and think of it less as a musical rearticulation of patterned culture or identity and more as a medium for embodied, participatory musical storytelling.

In 2002, three very well-established "old hands" in the *enka* world—composer and one-time singer Tokuhisa Kōji (b. 1948), who wrote music for *enka* megastars like Ishikawa Sayuri and Misora Hibari; lyricist Mozu Shōhei (b. 1938), whose lyrics have been sung by household names including Itsuki Hiroshi and Yashiro Aki; and producer and former chief adjudicator for the Japan Record Awards (est. 1959) Konishi Ryōtarō (b. 1936)—sat down to reflect on karaoke, the conditions of its emergence, and the state of popular song in modern Japan more broadly (NAK 2002). In their assessment, karaoke's emergence constituted a game changer in the nature of musicking in modern Japan. While amateur singing associated with nightlife had existed in Japan prior to the rise of karaoke, it generally took the form of procuring the services of instrumental accompanists, usually acoustic guitar or accordion players—*nagashi*—who wandered the bar districts plying musical services to bar proprietors and patrons, providing a live soundtrack for aspiring vocalists. The pump was thus already primed when karaoke emerged later on—although ironically, karaoke would threaten the livelihood of these wandering *nagashi* forebears in that the less talented / more "amateur" the singer was, the more likely they were to seek out recorded karaoke soundtracks, rather than live instrumentals, as backing for their singing.

But the rise of karaoke was also fueled by ongoing changes to engagement with modern popular music writ large. During the roundtable, Mozu asserted that the practice of popular music among the "masses" (*taishū*) in Japan saw important developments beginning around the middle of the 1950s, in terms of both form and engagement. Now, musicking in Japan had already been undergoing significant change prior to this, especially around the end of the Pacific War and the start of the Occupation and the "liberation"—variously conceived—of individual bodies from *kokutai* (national body) ideology (Bourdaghs 2012, 11–48). But Mozu still makes the point that there were important shifts toward embodied participation and coproduction of music and musical events that were specific to the 1950s. The latter half of the decade, for example, saw the explosion of rockabilly. In February of 1958, the First Nichigeki Western Carnival was held, drawing thousands of fans to its weeklong run: attendees rushed the stage; young women clawed at emergent male stars; frantic motion and bodily engagement were everywhere (Bourdaghs 2012, 85–87). This wasn't merely a *reaction* to the music—it helped *create* the rockabilly atmosphere and the youth culture that solidified around it. In the mid-1960s, so-called group sounds—in the style of the Beatles, for example—would reign, then rock and folk, which involved their own modes of embodied participation and engagement among audiences and between audiences and artists. "With the explosion in popularity of the youth-centered rockabilly, rock, and folk-song scenes," Mozu explained, "people who had been on the 'listening side' of the equation suddenly found themselves singing and dancing along with the artists in the concert halls. The element of 'participation' came to be included in songs." This element of embodied participation would prove an important potentiating factor in the rise of karaoke as well.

The record companies' claim to creative and production authority was also being challenged around this moment—by folk (I explore folk in detail on tracks 2 and 3). During the roundtable, Konishi suggested that musical trailblazing by so-called labor youths (*rōdō shōnen;* his term) in the context of a charged political moment on the eve of the impending 1970 AMPO treaty renewal, combined with the accessibility of inexpensive acoustic guitars (compared with, say, the prohibitive equipment costs of the Ventures-inspired *ereki,* or electric guitar, boom of the same moment), allowed for folk to explode in the way that it did. It was the participatory, individuated, embodied nature of folk and its propensity to break the authority of records (Dorsey 2013) that helped it to redefine creative authority in Japan's music world around 1970, dislodging it from the grip of record companies and placing it in the hands of individual artists like Takada Wataru and Kagawa Ryō, smaller, subscription-based labels like URC, and amateurs like the Shinjuku Folk Guerrilla. The landscape of musical engagement for many in modern Japan, in other words, was changing and was allowing for musical storytelling by anyone with a guitar and a voice— a shift that would also pave the way for the rise of the singer-songwriters in the mid-1970s and onward, including Nagabuchi Tsuyoshi, whom I'll consider on track 5.

But these changes didn't encompass everyone. Whether one got carried along by them or left behind in their wake depended largely upon one's musical tastes, which were in turn often connected to generation. In Mozu's assessment, so-called adults—by which he means mostly middle-aged men who did not identify with youth music culture—tended to be left behind in these shifts toward participatory musical engagement. These "adults" found themselves feeling abandoned by the transformations in musicking in this moment, many with cash in their pockets (recall here that 1970 marked the endpoint of then prime minister Ikeda Hayato's largely successful income-doubling plan and an important moment in the growth of Japanese capitalism) and time on their hands. The emergence of karaoke in the early 1970s provided a solution, becoming a means to launch what Mozu called a "counterattack" (*gyakushū*) against a youth-centered, embodied, participatory music culture (Bourdaghs 2012, 87) that was leaving "adults" in the dust. Importantly, though, this "counterattack" was ultimately a *generative* one, affording "adults" the opportunity to claim a mode of embodied, participatory musical storytelling of their own, one that tended to be articulated through "Japanese" popular song—*kayōkyoku* (like *ryūkōka,* a broadly encompassing term for "Japanese" popular music; this is the *kayō* of Kayōsai) and, later, *enka.* Now, the notion of "embodiment" is important here and will remain so throughout this track. As danah boyd (2007, 128) and others have pointed out, the body is both a key means of participating in culture and an important storytelling resource: "In conveying who we are to other people, we use our bodies to project information about ourselves." But this is not as straightforward as it may seem. The actual experience of occupying and using a body is contextually specific, individuated, and potentially subject to the discipline of others, especially in a context like the Kayōsai. Indeed, embodiment—of the specificities of one's own life, of *enka* as musical form, of how these intersected and collided in performance—emerged as a key flashpoint among participants and stakeholders at the event. I'll describe this in more detail later. Broadly, though, it was precisely the sort of embodied musical storytelling described herein that animated the amateur performances at Melparque Hall, some forty years after karaoke's birth.

Of course, karaoke wouldn't maintain its generational and gendered exclusivity for long. In the nearly five decades since its appearance, karaoke has become an integral part of youth culture, providing inexpensive gathering and drinking spaces that have become ubiquitous across Japan. It is as enjoyed by women as it is by men—if not more so. But it continues to be defined by the participatory and performative (that is, embodied) aspects that Konishi, Mozu, and Takehisa described and that have drawn scholars' attention since the 1980s. This performativity, though, is usually understood as occurring within fairly narrow, prescribed limits. Existing scholarship on karaoke—and especially on karaoke that involves *enka*—tends to emphasize patterned reproductions of form, which take place (affirmatively or subversively) within the confines of discursive regimes of gender or identity or "culture." DeNora (2000, 119), for example, points to how karaoke performance can become a way of representing imagined ideals of gender. Brown (2015), meanwhile, has explored how karaoke can be an important medium that affords both the articulation and the subversion of "identity" among participants. And writing specifically of the case of

Japan, Yano (1996, 3) argues that "[k]araoke may be thought of as a technological reification of *kata*-driven expression, a kind of hardware of patterned form." Although individuated expressivity does exist, "the self-expression afforded through karaoke exists within preestablished *kata*. ... The degree of self-expression is limited to what is permissible within a set form which includes ornamentation, dynamics, and, for some, even bodily gestures" (Yano 1996, 9). This applies to the specific case of *enka* as well: "'Doing *enka*' becomes synonymous with embracing an organized, hierarchical arrangement of social roles [and] daily activities. ... A song extends into a way of life through which an *enka* fan can live the imaginary" (Yano 2002, 147). Each of these perspectives resonates, in a way, with storytelling—they allow us to conceive of the ways that stories of gender or patterned identity are re-presented in ways that may posit a self within their discursive confines, or, alternatively, negate them. But at the same time, these perspectives also suggest a sort of *stasis* that doesn't meld well with the embodied, participatory impulses that helped propel karaoke's emergence in the 1970s, or with how it was actually used by contestants at the Kayōsai.

As a mode of musical storytelling pursued by social actors who are always already affected by the terms and conditions of their own everyday lives (Massumi 1995), karaoke threatens/promises to infect, as it were, "*kata*-driven expression [as] a kind of hardware of patterned form" with the contingencies and materialities of everyday life. This privileging of telling everyday stories as/through karaoke carries important and ambiguous implications: as Fernandes has pointed out in her study of storytelling more broadly, "stories can exceed the framings and protocols that try to contain and direct them" (2017, 12), allowing the meaning and significance generated in karaoke performance to spill beyond the purported boundaries of the text and the frameworks that constrain meaning—and in ways that can (and in fact did, at the Kayōsai) provoke a disciplinary response. As I'll show later on this track with appeal to the very sorts of gatekeeping figures who featured in my discussion earlier (Tokuhisa, Mozu, Konishi), this sort of karaoke narration of the particularities of individual everyday lives at the Kayōsai generated a *tension,* one that put some participants at odds with the very *enka* gatekeepers who celebrated the karaoke "counterattack" against folk and rock around 1970 in the first place, interested as they often were in maintaining the (patterned) "Japanese" properties of *enka,* variously conceived. This tension also led the gatekeepers to appeal to various strategies to shore up and maintain the discursive integrity of *enka* that, as a storytelling regime of its own, now seemed to be under threat from the unpredictable, embodied, participatory nature of karaoke itself. What was revealed at the Kayōsai, in sum, was competing modes of musical storytelling, wherein *enka* were tapped by different actors and stakeholders—contest entrants on the one hand, judges and gatekeepers on the other—in order to tell stories that were fundamentally contested and never reducible to patterned reproductions or stable reflections of identity, "Japanese" or otherwise. In emphasizing these messy, contested appeals to *enka,* I aim to reveal some of the tensions and fissures at play in questions of how the music is *used,* and some of the things it may afford. At the end of this track I'll leave the competition hall behind to explore how karaoke potentiated different sorts of storytelling altogether, in Fukushima on the eve of its dark spring.

First Verse: The Contestants

Back inside the fifteen-hundred-seat Melparque Hall, the first performers have already taken the stage. The stage set and production format are remarkably similar to those commonly seen in televised concerts and performances that feature *enka* prominently, such as public broadcaster NHK's annual year-end musical blowout *Kōhaku Uta Gassen* [Red and White Song Competition], its weekly televised amateur singing contest *Nodo Jiman* [Proud of My Voice], and especially *Kayō Konsāto* [Tuesday Concert], a now defunct weekly *enka* showcase that aired across the nation each Tuesday evening between 1993 and 2016. Like these programs, the Kayōsai is presided over by a professional emcee (two, in fact, who took alternating shifts over the nine-hour marathon of music) charged with introducing each performer and often with relaying comments that situate the song to be performed within the wider context of the performer's life, dreams, or desires. Each performer sings the first verse of his or her selected song, while video cameras pan and zoom, projecting the performer's image onto a massive screen overhanging the stage. This camerawork, too, is nearly identical to that seen in the aforementioned television programs—with the combination of the professional-grade sound engineering, the professional emcee work, and the rapt, full-house audience, one would be forgiven for mistaking the Kayōsai for a taping of *Kayō Konsāto.* And indeed, at first glance, the contestants onstage seemed to be hard at work reproducing the musical "heart/soul of [the] Japanese" (Yano 2002, 7).

For Christine Yano, author of the authoritative study of *enka,* this "heart/soul" is expressed through modes of patterned cultural reproduction called *kata,* which I introduced briefly earlier. *Kata* affords a way of "giv[ing] force to [*enka*'s] particular version of nationhood" and is already part of "Japanese culture in general" (Yano 2002, 24–27). The link between *enka* musicking and (one vision of) "Japan" is reproduced on an ongoing basis, via engaging with the genre and putting it to a preordained use in the context of "Japanese" listeners' own lives:

For contemporary audiences, *enka* has become the emblem of a constructed past, one in which men followed a life-long path and women followed their hearts. In this past, men became noble through single-mindedness and sheer effort. ... These were men of duty and honor, of life-or-death commitment. In this past, too, women loved one only, and enduringly, until death and beyond. ... [These men and women] can pine for a Japanese self that can only be retrieved in the floating world of the spectacle, the stage, the dream. ... [E]*nka* has remained that internal place (or one of those places) where "Japaneseness" still exists. (Yano 2002, 183–185)

As contestants in a competition, each performer at the Kayōsai carefully reproduced the patterned expectations of *enka* performance—reasonably faithful reproduction of musical and compositional forms, striking poses, patterned physical movements (Yano 2002, 90–123). But as I'll describe later, each also brought her own life and experiences to the stage, and the event became a way to "talk back," to use the music and their own introductory, framing comments to tell some of the diverse stories of their everyday Japanese lives, as opposed to articulating a desire for transcendent "Japaneseness." Although each contestant adhered to the sorts of patterned expectations discussed earlier in singing their chosen song, in other words, the embodied, visceral experientialities of their own everyday lives tended to fuel performances that exceeded mimicry or patterned reproduction, and that were difficult to reduce to expressions of desire for ahistorical "Japanese" selfhood. The argument can be made, of course, that karaoke performance of *enka* actually limits the sorts of stories that can be told—that these stories can only ever unfurl within the confines of the limited elements of *kata* that comprise *enka* and its performance in the first place, and that everyday life is ultimately understood only in terms of the *enka* representations that are available. In other words, at the end of the day, there is a concern that stories of everyday life told via appeal to *enka* are ultimately hemmed in by *enka*'s patterned authority—that the story will always be inexorably closed-ended. While I acknowledge this complexity, I nonetheless want to keep the focus—as I do throughout this book—on the tactical, unpredictable ways in which the music is actually *used*, and what that use might be able to tell us about the desires of individual social actors and why they engage with *enka* in the first place. In other words, I want to emphasize actors' engagement with the music, not the purported singular authority of "the music itself" (Wade 2009, 32). Doing so, I hope, can point the discussion toward questions of how specific engagements with *enka* may (or may not) intersect with questions of what it means to live in Japan, to "be Japanese"—and what sorts of musical storytelling that may afford.

Pre-performance commentary often provided a window into the interplay between the contestants' chosen songs and the realities of their own lives, and how they used the music to navigate them. Sometimes, this commentary simply reflected the ways in which contestants took meaning and significance from the music. Entrant 53, for example, sang Fuse Akira's 1979 strings-heavy *ryūkōka* "*Quartier Latin no Yuki* [Snow in the Latin Quarter]" because it "reminded me of my younger days." Entrant 68, who sang Yamamoto Jōji's 2009 *enka* classic "*Sen-Ri no Michi Mo* [Even a Road of a Thousand *Ri*]," did so because it "speak[s] directly to my heart." Entrant 129, meanwhile, sang Misora Hibari's "*Owari Naki Tabi* [The Never-Ending Journey]"—a song from near the end of Misora's career and life in 1988, which is much closer to adult contemporary than *enka* per se—simply because "it moves me." These comments, of course, are generalized and vague; the specifics of *why* and *how* these contestants found their chosen works meaningful is knowable only to the contestants and can be revealed only in focused, contextualized discussion (something I'll pursue later, and especially on the next track). But as I'll continue to insist, this unknowability is precisely the point and begins to reveal what I'll call a remainder to *enka* (Dolar 2006), something that cannot be contained or accounted for in assessments of performance as patterned reproduction of form.

Other performers used their chosen music and their performances thereof to tell stories of their own everyday lives in more explicit fashion. Entrant 91, for instance, chose to sing the pop-tinged "*Akai Hana* [The Red Flower]," released in 1991 as the last single by Chiaki Naomi prior to her retirement from music. She prefaced her performance by stating that she wanted to sing this work "out of a sense of gratitude both for the memories that I've made in the past, and in thanks for the person that I've now become."

> Chasing after dreams of yesterday
> This night I play again in the din, alone
> I grow nostalgic for the person that I once was,
> And knock back a few.
> Who knew that time would pass so quickly
> As I was enjoying myself so noisily …

As was the case with the more general comments introduced earlier, the precise conditions of this performer's life—what sorts of "memories that [she's] made in the past," what sort of "person … [she's] now become"—and how these informed the significance that she found in the music remained mostly opaque here, in that she chose not to (or lacked the time to) share these particulars in greater detail. But again, the opacity is precisely the point. The significance that *enka* had for performers at the Kayōsai, the musical storytelling that it helped to afford, was rooted in conditions of everyday life that were individuated, embodied, and largely unknowable, and certainly not reducible to articulations of "Japaneseness" (notably, there was just one contestant—Entrant 30—who explicitly linked her performance to notions of "Japan" at all: she performed the 2009 Shimazu Aya work "Otsū," with lyrical content taken from a folk tale titled "Tsuru Nyōbo [Crane Wife]" and musical flourishes that might be readily linked to notions of rhetorical "Japaneseness," because she "liked the fact that it was taken from an old Japanese story"). For Entrant 91, "Akai Hana" afforded a way to bring her own lived experiences into a sharper focus and give narrative form to how she and her world are taking shape—itself a continuing process, not a static one.

Other stories told at the Kayōsai intersected with questions of furusato, the "old hometown." Enka are often composed to speak longingly and lovingly of "home," of lives lived (or longed for) in sometimes idealized, often rural locales. In both cultural production and scholarly analysis, citations of non-urban locality—inaka, "the countryside"—often tend to be associated with narratives of "authentic Japan": appeal to the margins as a site of vanishing, rustic authenticity, that is, becomes or is understood as part of an attempt to fold those margins into the center and tap them as the true locus of the national Volk, as a means of bolstering the center's authority and recalibrating claims to authentic national imagining (Stevens 2008, 27–28; Ivy 1995). But what was conspicuous at the Kayōsai was the way that furusato were referenced not as an ideologically weighted locus of "Japanese" national imagining but as a trope through which to tell stories of everyday life (this also anticipates the critical tactics deployed by rocker Nagabuchi Tsuyoshi in his own musical deployments of the inaka, and specifically of his "hometown" of Kagoshima—I'll discuss this in detail on the next track). Entrant 39, for example, sang "Hiei no Kaze [Winds at Mount Hiei]," a driving, march-inspired work released by Kitajima Saburō (b. 1936) as a single in 2009. Its lyrics read, in part:

One thousand days of austerities,
I walked ten thousand ri through mountain paths,
Through the winds of Hiei
Transcending heat and cold, rain and snow,
An undying light now illuminates
Ah ...
This flower growing in my selfless heart.

Mount Hiei straddles the border of Kyoto and Shiga Prefectures; the contestant's own home was in Shiga. Musically and lyrically, "Hiei no Kaze" invites imaginings of stoic, persevering "Japanese" manhood—as I showed on track 3, gender has an important role to play in conjuring and sustaining notions of National subjectivity. But Entrant 39 didn't seem concerned with such abstractions. Rather, his declared aim in singing "*Hiei no Kaze*" was to use it to tell part of the story of his own life—its challenges, its geographic specificities—as "naturally [*shizen-tai de*]," in his words, as possible.

The story that Entrant 39 was able to tell through his performance was of course partial and fragmented, and limited by the lyrical and musical content available to him in Kitajima's song. But the impact generated by harnessing the work to relay some of the story of his own everyday life was significant, and not lost on the judge charged with critiquing his performance. After the entrant's performance had concluded, the judge said, "You wore your life on your sleeve; yours was a powerful performance that reached your audience precisely because you make your life [at the foot of Mount Hiei]. This proximity between your life and the song made your performance overflow with emotion."

This is high praise for the way that Entrant 39 was able to harness the contingencies of his own life and generate a "powerful" storytelling through the music. In the judge's assessment, the power in the entrant's performance came not from masterful rearticulation of accepted patterns or form but from the way he was able to put the music to use in telling some of the story of his own life. Put differently, it was the entrant's own fleshly orientation in the world that rendered his performance meaningful and effective, not masterful appeals to or reproductions of patterned "Japaneseness." His impassioned negotiation with the work exceeded patterned prescriptions for *enka* reproduction: even as he reproduced Kitajima's song via karaoke performance, he also *rewrote* the song as a story of his own life. Put to use in musical storytelling, the song in the hands of Entrant 39 overflowed the discursive bounds of *enka* itself. But here the story gets tricky. Although the "power" of Entrant 39's performance won him the praise of his judge, the remainder that this generated—the ill-fitting, residual significance borne of embodied storytelling that could not be accounted for or constrained within the predictable reproduction of patterned musico-cultural form—also triggered disciplinary action, revealing the tension between two modes of musical storytelling and *enka*'s utility therein. As I'll show momentarily, this remainder could not be left to haunt the Kayōsai indefinitely—its messy, unpredictable ends had to be clipped to shore up the discursive integrity of *enka* itself.

Questions of locality and "home" were taken up by other contestants as well, including Entrant 41, an agricultural worker from rural Yamagata Prefecture, northeast of Tokyo. Entrant 41 chose to perform "*Sakata-Minato* [Sakata Port]," a conventional *enka* both written and performed (a relative rarity in *enka*) by Ōizumi Itsurō (b. 1942), with lyrics penned by Kinoshita Ryūtarō (1938–2008). Ōizumi is himself a native of Yamagata Prefecture; despite being a successful singer, he in fact understands his "real job" (*hongyō*) to be in agriculture (he owns and operates a cherry orchard there). In addition to conventional sonic markers of "rhetorical Japaneseness"—the "minor-sounding" *yonanuki* scale, which is frequently used in the form; heavy vibrato and other vocal ornamentation; occasional appeal to "traditional" instruments, or at least digitally generated representations thereof—the recording makes use of "sound effects" meant to be evocative of northeastern storms, particularly synthesized wind sounds. But although abstract sonic and lyrical markers of "Japan" certainly resounded through this *enka,* Entrant 41 seemed less interested in reproducing "Japanese" form than he was interested in tapping the work as a resource in his own embodied musical storytelling. He took to the stage with a simple yet profound introduction to his performance: "This song is about my life."

> The Kitamae boat relies on its white sails;
> Whether we go or not—all depends on the winds
> You see me off, here at Sakata Port
> Loaded with safflower, we head for Naniwa (Osaka)
> Our route takes us the long way—
> Round the coast to the west.

The lyrics of "*Sakata-Minato*" are set in another time, when agricultural products were loaded onto sailing ships for delivery to Osaka, Japan's third-largest city. But in his declaration that "[t]his song is about my life," we can get a sense of how Entrant 41 tapped this work to tell an important story of the contemporary material realities of agricultural life in Yamagata and beyond, where people (including both the composer and the entrant) still work long and hard raising agricultural products for sale to the urban centers. What the performance generated was not so much a transparent, "knowable" articulation or reproduction of patterned "Japanese" or regional "identity" as the telling of a story of geographically specific materialities of everyday life in Japan via the means that *enka* and its *kata* made available. It was a story that was made legible by the intertextual citation and assembly of different texts—Ōizumi's music, Kinoshita's lyrics, the realities of Entrant 41's own life, the *enka* form itself—and given meaning ("[t]his song is about my life") in the context of a specific music event.

As was the case with Entrant 39, the embodied closeness that characterized Entrant 41's musical storytelling was not lost on his judge. The judge critiquing this performer's work spoke to the ways that he bypassed mimicry altogether, literally *embodying* the contents of this specific *enka* on his own terms: "Your kind, gentle approach to the song really came across well to the audience. Your expression, too, was very relaxed and matched the tone of the work well. You really embodied [this] *enka* from the depths of your physical being (*karada no shin kara enka*)."

Entrant 41 himself stated that it was his ability to "superimpose" (*daburaseru*) this work over his own embodied experiences in the world, and vice versa, that fed this very close, impassioned performance. The judge agreed that the performer made the work his own, literally embodying it. This referencing of embodiment is significant, both in terms of the history of the emergence of karaoke as embodied musical engagement that I outlined earlier, and in terms of how these performers at the Kayōsai used the music and their performance thereof to tell stories—however partial and fragmented—of their own everyday lives. This musical storytelling generated the sort of remainder I'm describing here, a remainder that exceeds the predictable reproduction of patterned musico-cultural form. As the contestant and the judge both alluded to in different ways, this storytelling is after all a praxis that is rooted in the body. And as Massumi has pointed out, the body is embedded in the world and "enfolds [its] contexts … volitions and cognitions [in ways] that are nothing if not situated" (Massumi 1995, 91), engendering an affective orientation that informs both the significance that the practitioner may take from the musical text and the ways that she may tap that text in telling embodied stories of her own. But the very notion of embodiment—particularly in the case of a text as fraught and as weighty as *enka*—is intensely ambiguous and often obsessively policed: this ambiguity owes directly to competing claims on the authority to tell stories of how the body is oriented in the world (this is why, for example, bodily action and orientation—particularly among women—were so tightly controlled during Japan's fascist period, and indeed, why the polity of that moment was conceived of as *kokutai*, "national body," in the first place). I'll have more to say about this later.

Different contestants at the Kayōsai, in sum, made use of their chosen musical selections in different ways—but this tended to be irreducible to patterned performances of static identity, "Japanese" or otherwise. Rather, the contestants tended to use *enka* and *kayōkyoku*, and their own karaoke performances thereof, to frame and tell stories of their own lives and desires, sometimes in ways that were explicitly intended to have extra-musical, world-producing effects (some performers, including Entrant 67 and Entrant 118, framed their performances as literal interventions in the world and what they saw as its shortcomings, and aimed to send musical "messages" to rectify them). These tended to be performances that referenced individuated, embodied pasts and presents, and that embedded the storyteller in social and historical life in an open-ended manner, affording ways to comprehend and continue writing the storyteller's own story (cf. Entrant 91). As contestants in a karaoke competition, the entrants of course articulated those stories in ways that aligned with the performative expectations placed upon their performances—the donning of appropriate *enka* attire, the embodiment of certain performative rituals such as bowing before and after the performance, a reasonably faithful and skilled vocal reproduction of their chosen song. But this underscores the important point that these sorts of shared *kata,* rather than necessarily being an end in and of themselves, are in fact drawn upon as a means for rendering one's own story legible to others. In other words, they become an element enabling musical storytelling—not the story itself. The ways that the participants *used* their own performances resonated strongly with karaoke's "participatory" origins, allowing for the articulation of everyday realities in ways that, ironically, exceeded the discursive confines that were subsequently built around *enka* and *kayōkyoku* karaoke performance to lend it cohesiveness as "counterattack" against rock and folk. Telling musical stories of everyday life via appeal to *enka,* that is, necessarily caused these performances to overflow the boundaries placed upon them as putative rearticulations of fundamentally knowable, patterned cultural form (i.e., *kata*), generating a remainder borne of unpredictable, unknowable, embodied embeddedness in the world. This remainder, though, tended to elicit disciplinary responses on the part of the judges, who sought to defuse its messiness and unpredictability and shore up the discursive boundaries of *enka* by appealing to national language and Culture—key components of what I, following Sakai (1992), will momentarily call the "interior." Here we can already discern the outline of two different modes of musical storytelling—both world producing, to be sure, but one tended to be open-ended, while the other tended to be closed-circuited. This latter mode of musical storytelling—and the disciplining and taming of the "remainder" that it involved—was a task that fell to the judges.

Second Verse: The Judges

Despite *enka*'s well-established association with the national imaginary, most participants at the Kayōsai were generally disinterested in questions of "Japan," preferring instead to use the music to tell stories of their own everyday lives. But this doesn't mean that "Japan" had no role to play in the event—of course it did. *Enka*'s very discursive legibility, after all, is defined by its claim to be "Japan's music." As discussed earlier on this track, though, I want to de-emphasize a priori notions of "culture" and "identity" and think specifically about how "Japan" gets wrapped up in *enka* storytelling in the first place, when, and by whom. Attending to the historicity of the early 1970s—the moment of *enka*'s emergence—will help me do that. On track 2 of this book, I explained how the moment around 1970 saw "America's Japan" recast as "Japan's Japan," as the purported fulfillment of capitalism and the attendant end of history helped bolster a narrative that Japan had finally become exactly what it had been destined to be since the beginning of time. Contingent economic particularities were rationalized and stabilized through appeal to unchanging cultural values—the end of history, that is, had to be seen culturally, and premodern cultural endowment was turned to as a means of affirming the particularities of Japanese political economy in this moment (paradoxically, and significantly, "culture" and "tradition" also became resources to tap in steadying oneself against the turbulence wrought by the very developmental narrative that they authorized, as was seen in co-temporal phenomena like the Japan Railways Discover Japan Campaign [Ivy 1995]). In addition, stories of U.S.-Japan "friendship" and common destiny (discussed on track 1) continued to reverberate in the background, just as they had in the 1950s and 1960s, fueling ongoing anxieties over an autonomy that seemed perpetually out of reach in the geopolitical realm—but that could, perhaps, be more readily claimed in the cultural one (Bourdaghs 2012, 67). To the extent that the interplay between *enka* and "Japan" truly coalesced around 1970, when music industry and state stakeholders completed a commandeering of what had been a largely countercultural musical form and re-presented it as a "nostalgic representation of the nation's past" (Wajima 2014, 81), this commandeering took place in the context of the coagulation of a "Japanese" *interior* that was not new to this moment, but that was certainly taking on renewed resonance within it. *Enka*'s rise as "Japan's music" in the 1970s, in other words, was no coincidence—this was a moment in which the volume was being cranked up on telling stories of "Japan," for reasons both economic and political.

Now, when I write of "the interior," or of "interiority," I'm appealing to terminology from scholar Naoki Sakai, who has written extensively on the ethics and politics of language and translation. The "interior," or "interiority," suggests a shared discursive space (Sakai 1992, 4) within which sense making is achieved and sustained by virtue of mutually transparent (linguistic and "cultural") co-presence, one that is often more asserted than it is actual. The interior is the interior, that is, because it is a purportedly transparent space whose particularities are assumed/asserted to be universally comprehensible ("knowable," to revisit terminology I deployed earlier) and subscribed to by those deemed to be within it. This assumption is built upon the establishment and policing of strict barriers between "inside" and "outside," itself a key function of the modern nation-state. For Sakai (2009), "interiority [can be] determined as enclosure of the national language, national culture, and national subjectivity"—rather than constituting the nation itself, the interior is what gives the idea of the nation substance. The emergence of *enka* as "Japan's music" helped bolster the historically contingent calcification of a "Japanese" interior, even as it simultaneously fed off the circulating story of "Japan's Japan" (as both qualifier and antidote) for its discursive legibility.

To be clear, I want to think of both "Japan" and *enka* as "Japan's music" as interiors. Cogenerating and mutually reinforcing, these coalesced in the same moment, riffing off each other to conjure discursive realms of transparent common sense that helped to shore up each other's shaky foundations. Importantly, though, these interiors also require the eradication of (internal) heterogeneity to prevent their collapse. If left unchecked, the unpredictability and excess of individuated, embodied musical storytelling—what I earlier called the "remainder"—threatens to overrun the boundaries of the discursive space of *enka*: in other words, to undermine the integrity of *enka* itself. This heterogeneity, then, must be disciplined—not so much to uphold an Adornoian vision of shadowy ideological or nationalistic manipulation, but simply to ensure the viability and "appeal" of an important musical storytelling mechanism and its adjacent sense-making apparatuses (i.e., "Japan"), as well as to safeguard the authority of its gatekeepers. Practical strategies have occasionally been put in place to police the interiority of *enka* and lock it to "Japan": until very recently, for example, industry actors facilitated an *enka* "proficiency test" (*kentei*), conceived on the basis of the notion that "*enka* and *kayōkyoku* have [long] been widely adored as the music of the Japanese heart," and that the music, properly executed, could "revitalize Japan [*Nippon wo genki ni suru*]" itself. For a small fee (two thousand yen), one could purchase a verified, adjudicated place of belonging within the "Japanese heart"—as well as, probably at least as importantly, the authority to narrate its terms to others (NAK promotional materials 2010). At the Kayōsai, though, it was regulatory appeals to linguistic authenticity— verifications of the "proper" use of national/Japanese language—that became the key means by which adherence to and the reproduction of *enka*'s interior could be assessed. This adjudication was the job of the judges.

The judging panel of the Kayōsai consisted of eleven current and former prominent *enka* industry professionals. They were lyricists, record label executives, producers, and artist managers; between them, the group claimed *enka* greats like Toba Ichirō, Ishikawa Sayuri, Mori Masako, and Hikawa Kiyoshi under its collective managerial umbrella. The panel was presided over by Konishi Ryōtarō, who also featured in the NAK roundtable on karaoke that I discussed earlier. In addition to being a well-known music producer, critic, and former chief adjudicator for the Japan Record Awards, Konishi was a former managing director of the *Sports Nippon* newspaper and is broadly published on matters relating to *enka* (see, for example, Konishi 2001a, 2001b). Other judges included Kawamura Yasunao of Victor Entertainment; Sotomura Takao of Crown Records; and Yabe Kimihiro, formerly a producer with Japan Columbia and more recently the author of a book on music terminology marketed to karaoke fans. Kayōsai organizers did not make full biographical information available for all the judges, nor could this information be tracked down elsewhere in all cases. But a certain pattern could be detected among those judges for whom background details could be established. All were middle-aged (or older) men, and many were born and/or raised in areas outside the metropolitan power nexus of Tokyo. These were not individuals somehow born into the upper echelons of music industry power as elites; they started off as lyrical apprentices from the countryside (in one case) or local sales staff in rural branches of national production offices (in another), gradually honing and then perfecting their own grasp of an interior that would come to be known as "Japan's music." The judges bore an uncanny resemblance to what Tomiyama Ichirō (2000, 129; 2005) has called "leaders," nonelite or quasi-elite individuals who have found success in generating and perfecting their hold on an interior and the trappings associated with it. These "leaders" became the keepers and adjudicators of *enka* authenticity, and their critiques had the ultimate effect of corralling some of the remainders produced in the karaoke performances at the Kayōsai that day.

The performances were broken into three blocks of sixty, sixty, and thirty, beginning at 10:15 a.m. and concluding at 7:00 p.m., with thirty-minute breaks in between. Final standings were announced and awards distributed ahead of the event's end time of 7:50 p.m. The judges were tasked with providing brief critiques of each performer/performance following the conclusion of each block's performances, apparently with the aim of helping the performer sing "better." But there was much more involved in the judges' critiques than just musical instruction. They constituted mini-tutorials in how to better carry oneself within the discursive space of *enka* so as to better embody "Japan's music" and offered positive reinforcement where this was already being done to the judges' satisfaction. As I'll show, these sometimes moved beyond questions of musicality and performance to pontificate on how to better embody "Japanese" sensibilities and even to become a better resident of Japan. Sakai has argued that, in order for an interior to be stable in its sense making, "[t]he sociality [that is, the *unpredictability*] that is heterogeneous to the restricted economy of the interior must be controlled and eliminated" (Sakai 1992, 295). This is precisely the role that was played by the judges of the Kayōsai—again, not out of some sinister desire to manipulate or control, but rather because the judges were important gatekeepers of the discursive integrity of *enka* itself, and occupied the role of "leaders."

In some instances, the policing of these discursive boundaries meant reinforcing the gendered ideals that have been associated with "Japan's music" and indeed with "Japanese" subjectivity itself (recall here Kagawa Ryō's tactical scrambling of gender in his 1971 "*Kyōkun I* [Lesson I]," discussed on track 3). Entrant 32, for example, was praised for the "suitability" of her decision to sing "*Kami no Piano* [The Paper Piano]," a gentle *enka*/pops crossover ballad released by Nippon Crown recording artist Natsumi (b. 1980, also known as Kawano Natsumi) as a single in 2003. Following Entrant 32's performance, her judge gushed that "in terms of the aura that you bring to the stage, the song that you chose, and the way in which you sang it, I was put in mind of the so-called 'good wife, wise mother [*ryōsai kenbō*, itself a discursive construct that masquerades as tradition but that was in fact an integral part of national subject making after 1868],' so I think that this was a very good choice of song on your part." This is somewhat puzzling praise, given the fact that the lyrics of "*Kami no Piano*" reference how it is "[d]ifficult to get by / in a single-mother home," although the work nonetheless emphasizes the story of a mother's devotion to her child, itself an important element in the conjuring of modern stories of "Japan." In any event, this performer was praised not so much for her vocal prowess per se, but rather for the ways that she managed to evoke, through her embodiment of the work, the "aura … and the way in which you sang it," an aspect of the *enka* genre that is held (by this judge, at least) to be an important factor in the constitution of its "Japanese" form: its reinforcement of gendered notions of "Japaneseness."

In another example of the patrolling of gendered ideals, Entrant 122 was lauded for her handling of Ōtsuki Miyako's (b. 1946) 2009 *enka* release "*Hakanagawa* [Weary River]." The praise this entrant received not only stressed the importance of an idealized notion of (Japanese) "womanhood" to the interiority conjured and cited through *enka* but also acknowledged and effectively dismissed the heterogeneity brought to bear on the music by other performers that day: "Well, yours was the fifth rendition of '*Hakanagawa*' that we've heard today. Each of the [other four] entrants have performed their own interpretations of '*Hakanagawa*' (*sorezore no* '*Hakanagawa*'), but yours was, I think, best in terms of singing the *onna-gokoro* [the ideal 'woman's heart'] and getting that across."

As Yano has shown, discursive imaginings of "woman" and the ability to embody and express them are integral to imagining *enka* as "Japan's music" (Yano 2000, 122–141). Scholars dealing with other contexts have also shown how notions of "womanhood" have been integral to modern processes of conjuring stories about "Japan," both culturally and politically (see track 3). The persistent appeal to "Japanese womanhood" on the part of *enka* stakeholders— lyricists, critics and commentators, record label executives, judges at the Kayōsai—amounts to tapping circulating notions of gender in a way that lends authority and credence to *enka* as "Japan's music." Doing *enka* "authentically," then, also means embodying and reproducing idealized gendered forms in ways that help maintain the music's narrative integrity.

In other instances, the judges targeted the material properties of the performer's voice itself, and its relative ability (or inability) to reproduce some of the discursive imaginings associated with specific subsets of *enka*. Entrant 36, for example, sang "*Boshi Jongara* [Mother and Daughter *Jongara*]," a single released by Kozakura Maiko (b. 1948) in 2009. Set in the deep north of Aomori

Prefecture, this is a work that belongs to a subcategory of *enka* known as *Jongara-bushi* (songs of the Tsugaru region of Aomori). It tells the story of a mother-daughter musical duo—the mother on the shamisen, a stringed instrument often associated with Tsugaru (the shamisen of course plays a prominent role in the song's instrumentation, along with the shakuhachi flute, which frequently accompanies it), and the daughter on vocals—traveling the region in the face of blinding snow in search of their missing husband/father. Entrant 36 was from Kumamoto Prefecture, in Kyushu, about as far from Tsugaru as one can get in Japan. The criticism she faced, though, had to do with vocal particularities, not with notions of geographical legitimacy. "You had a strong vocal presence and gave a solid performance, but I think that your vocal qualities don't really fit well with a *Jongara-bushi*. These songs are what we [in the industry] often call Tsugaru-mono. A Tsugaru voice is a so-called *kan-no-koe;* that is, a high-pitched voice; that's the kind of voice that we want [in order to properly reproduce a work like this]. So from that standpoint, your vocal qualities are a bit off ..."

Kozakura Maiko, who recorded the work, is herself from Chigasaki (in the Tokyo area), but presumably re-creates the "Tsugaru voice" adequately. The issue here, in other words, is with the fleshly, vocal re-presentation of aspects of *enka*'s interior, not with locality or geographic "authenticity" per se. This emphasis on the voice reveals a desire on the part of the judge to yoke karaoke performance to circular reproduction of what Dolar (in a different context) calls the "law": in other words, "to pin down the voice to the letter, to limit its disruptive force, to dissipate its inherent ambiguity" (Dolar 2006, 49). The "law" here, of course, is nothing but the interiority of *enka* as "Japan's music."

But it was phonology and national language that emerged again and again at the Kayōsai as the main mechanisms through which the judges sought to neutralize the threat presented to the integrity of *enka,* a threat manifested in the unpredictable embodiments of everyday experience articulated in and through musical storytelling. The perceived connection between the "proper" use of the Japanese language and the maintenance of a smoothly unified interior, such as that associated with modern *enka,* had in fact already been articulated by the Kayōsai judges themselves: in a 2007 interview, for example, Yamaguchi Eikō—chief producer at EMI Music Japan in charge of *enka* diva Sakamoto Fuyumi, among other acts—spoke of there being "a real fragmentation of [Japanese] musical genres these days" but argued that *enka* could contribute to an overcoming of this fragmentation "with a simple melody and the use of *beautiful Japanese* [my italics]" (*Sports Hōchi,* September 25, 2007).

Yamaguchi, however, was merely adding to an already well-established narrative. Sakai asserts that Confucian scholar Ogyū Sorai (1666–1728) "introduced the very possibility of the realm of interiority" through introducing the concept of translation between Chinese and Japanese. The very concept of translatability between one linguistic interior and another helped introduce notions of propriety, correctness, and authenticity in reading via a positing of linguistic homogeneity and purity that could be revealed retroactively; this allowed "a new way of viewing the world and the possibility of imagining a new 'collectivity' [to be] introduced" (Sakai 1992, 221). The interior implied by Ogyū was refined by *kokugaku* ("national learning," the study of "Japan") nativist scholars and architects of a nascent Japanese nationalism (articulated in contradistinction to the Sinophone world) and further stabilized with the linguistic conjuring of "Japan" as a cohesive Imperial state in the context of modernity in the late nineteenth century: indeed, Imperial Japanese statecrafters asserted that the "independence, dissemination, and advancement of the nation's language is the first step to solidify the unity of the nation state" (Lee 2009, 53). The *genbun itchi* movement of this moment—the move to unify spoken and written Japanese, which helped lay the foundation for what would become *kokugo*, or "national language"—included, among other things, a push to unify and "correct" spoken/vocal language along the general lines of the Tokyo dialect, and specifically in line with that used by educated Tokyoites. This move to discipline the spoken/vocal language of Japanese individuals, for thinkers at the time, was "the only real way to pull closer" the written and spoken languages and ensure some degree of linguistic homogeneity for the emergent Imperial metropole (Lee 2009, 46–50).

Later, in 1949, the postwar government resurrected the 1934 Deliberative Council on National Language (Kokugo Shingikai), with the aims of "improving" national language and fostering learning of it. In fact, pop/folk singer-songwriter Nakajima Miyuki (b. 1952), highly regarded for her prowess as a lyricist, was invited to sit on this council in 1999, where she was tasked with engaging "problems of language usage centering on honorifics [*keigo*]"—likely a reaction to oft-heard conservative laments over declines in "proper" Japanese usage among youth (Super J Channel 1999). By the time of the twenty-sixth Kayōsai in 2010, in short, the interplay between language and its uses and a "Japanese" interiority—and, indeed, the ways that music can mediate this interplay—were well established. The idea of national language became one more circulating notion that *enka* stakeholders tapped to fortify the borders of the music's conjured interiority and bolster its claim to the title of constituting "Japan's music," or "the heart and soul of the Japanese." And significantly, despite their frequent appeal to non-Tokyo, *furusato* locality, the lyrics of the majority of *enka* works—including all those under discussion herein—are rendered in *hyōjungo*: so-called standard Japanese, *kokugo*, Tokyo dialect.

It is difficult to overstate just how central questions of proficiency in the articulation of national language were to how the amateur performers of the

Kayōsai were "judged." Indeed, the entire event was underscored by an incessant, almost obsessive fine-tuning of phonology—pronunciations, enunciations, breathing, spacing, and almost anything else that one might imagine to be associated with the correct use of (Japanese) language. The judges praised "proper pronunciation," declaring that it was the most authentic means by which to properly communicate the emotion wrapped up in a work. Entrant 62, for example, received particularly lavish praise for her handling of her chosen song, Kōzai Kaori's (b. 1963) "*Echizen Renka* [Fukui Love Song]," released in 1994. This praise was based, however, almost entirely upon her successful enunciation of language: "Your approach to the song is just [fantastic] … You handle the words with great care, and your voice carries really well, too. […] Your words are clear and unambiguous [*meiryō*]. This is exactly what is required to sing [properly]; it's very important." Entrant 68, whom I mentioned earlier, received similar praise for his proper handling of the lyrics of George Yamamoto's (2009) booming "*Sen-Ri no Michi Mo* [Even a Road of a Thousand *Ri*]": "You have an extremely sharp and concise way of enunciating your words. This is just a superb trait to have in order to sing [properly]."

It must be stressed here that in neither of these cases did the judge say that the entrant's manner of *singing* was exemplary—rather, the contestants were lauded for being able to negotiate well with the Japanese language itself, and this translated into the ability to sing "properly" and "unambiguously." Indeed, though the moment and contexts are much different, there are echoes here of the ways in which Eri Chiemi and Peggy Hayama were respectively lauded or ridiculed by writers at the *Stars and Stripes* for their ability—or lack thereof—to approximate and embody an American "white vocal norm" (Barg 2000) in the 1950s (see track 1).

Far more common than commendations for effective handling of words and language, however, were criticisms and cautions against their improper application. Earlier on this track I discussed how Entrant 39 wove the realities of his everyday life at the foot of Mount Hiei into his engagement with "*Hiei no Kaze* [Winds at Mount Hiei]" and how the judge immediately picked up on this and lauded him for his ability to bring "your life" to the work. But as soon as this potential for unpredictability in the form of individual life texts was acknowledged, it was immediately jailed again, through stabilizing appeals to language. The judge's comments, which I introduced in part earlier, continued in the following manner: "There was one thing that concerned me. When you are speaking [the judge caught himself here], er, rather, singing, you need to enunciate your words more clearly. If you would open your mouth a bit more and enunciate properly [*chanto*], the words would be communicated to your audience all the more …"

Here, the central tension that underpinned the Kayōsai becomes particularly clear. Whereas the karaoke performer sought to use *enka* to communicate (some of) the reality of his own life, generating a remainder that cannot be reduced to patterned form or to questions of "Japaneseness," the judge sought to redirect or repackage this unpredictability, encapsulating it in a cloak of proper language use and steering it back toward the interior. Cleansing the interiors of "Japan" and "Japan's music" of this heterogeneity and unpredictability, it seems, helps safeguard the discursive stability of both—and the musical storytelling engaged in by the judges was oriented toward these ends.

In a particularly powerful moment in the Kayōsai, Entrant 117 took to the stage to sing Mikami Shizu's mournful 2006 ballad "*Onna* [Woman]," in a performance that she dedicated to her recently deceased mother.

> Don't ever leave me, don't let me go
> Stay always at my side
> No, I don't mind at all
> Even should I endure the slings of scandal
> Woman ... I am woman
> And yours alone.

The story that this contestant aimed to tell was established in the way that she introduced her song to the audience. Rather than addressing the audience, or the judges, she addressed (via the emcee) her deceased mother directly: "O Mother, called up to heaven! You always listened so intently to my singing, a smile on your face. I am going to sing my heart out for you today, too [*kyou mo isshoukenmei utaimasu kara*], so please, hear my song."

An intertextual intermeshing of grief and Mikami's music afforded a performance that saw Entrant 117 sing with great passion, arm outstretched, as if beckoning into a different realm. But as far as her judge was concerned, the entrant's effectiveness (or lack thereof) in transmitting this passion to her audience and beyond did not come down to how she framed her performance, nor to the downcast sadness that was apparent in the way that she carried herself onstage, or even to the soaring, wavering voice that characterized her performance. Rather, it came down to her degree of proficiency in using that voice to "properly" convey the (Japanese) language of the lyrics. "And the words, the lyrics ... If you can be more precise in your pronunciation of the words, then I think that the contents of the song will really come across much better [*uta ga sugoku yoku naru to omoimasu*]."

Here, as in the example discussed earlier, notions of phonology and language are appealed to as a means of corralling the messy, heterogeneous remainders that were apparent in these unique and passionate performances. The judges' relentless obsession with enunciation and the reproduction of linguistic propriety here resonates with an appeal to linguistic interiority as a means of shoring up *enka*'s discursive integrity—by being rendered uniform and transparently accessible, the significance and meaning of the music is extirpated from the body of the performer as embedded in her own everyday life (and from the unknowable potentials that this implies) and resituated within the interior, as something accessible to all. *Enka* gatekeeper Mozu Shōhei, in the NAK roundtable discussed earlier, went so far as to insist that karaoke practitioners must embody lyrics in accordance with a purported "drama" or "mystery" that is somehow *inherent to the words themselves,* not to their utility in the world. To Mozu, the essential step to "moving" an audience is not telling stories of the everyday, but rather reproducing the "genius" of the lyrics properly and authentically. To do this well, Mozu suggested reading Japanese literature to enhance one's sensitivities to linguistic propriety and nuance.

What was perhaps the most revealing interaction between a Kayōsai performer and his judge, however, came very late in the day, in the performance of Julio Fujita (a pseudonym), a Brazilian of Japanese descent who had recently moved to Japan. Fujita was the 145th out of 150 entrants to perform, and like a handful of other contestants he chose a song that teetered on the very outer reaches of the musical spectrum that the organizers of the Kayōsai subsumed under the headings of *enka* and *kayōkyoku:* "*Itōshiki Kimi E* [To My Beloved You]," an acoustic work written and performed in 2004 by pop/folk singer-songwriter Moriyama Naotarō (b. 1976). As a non-Japanese resident of Japan from an often discriminated-against community (Tsuda 1999, 145–179), Fujita lived a different sort of everyday from that of most of the contestants and brought an altogether different sort of excess to his performance at the Kayōsai. His performance faced a disciplining that revealed an intent to guide him toward authentic musical expression, but also into the interior of "Japan" itself—and as a result, it revealed how these are inextricably intertwined for the gatekeepers of *enka,* and how they reflexively reinforce and constitute each other. In was an interaction, in other words, that revealed another facet of the politics of musical storytelling.

Moriyama Naotarō is known for his simple yet passionate piano-and-vocals compositions, and "*Itōshiki Kimi E*" is a simple, passionate song of love.

> I will hold you tighter
> Hold you tighter, and never let you go
> Please, just stay by my side;
> No questions now
> Please, give me more strength
> Strength that I can believe in until the end …

Fujita had declared an intent to sing a song of love and peace at the Kayōsai that day. "I would just be happy if this message reached the hearts of my family, indeed of all people," he proclaimed as he took the stage. It was a stage that Fujita had walked before (he'd performed in the Kayōsai nine years previously), and he was clearly aware of what was expected. He was draped in the proper *enka* regalia (in Fujita's case, a shimmering silver "gangster suit" that caught the spotlights in a way that outshone almost all the other entrants' stage costumes), and he diligently—though clearly self-consciously and in something less than surefooted manner—went through the common ritual of bowing to his audience both prior to and after his performance. In other words, Fujita fully immersed himself in the "culture" of *enka* performance, even though his selected work was not strictly of the genre. What seemed particularly significant about Fujita's reproduction of this "formal-izing behavior" (Sakai 1992, 169), though—and what ended up constituting the pivotal point determining how he was judged—was the fact that Fujita had just made the decision to relocate his life to Japan, taking up residence there barely a month before performing at the Kayōsai.

Fujita sang sweetly, and with great passion. The judge charged with review-ing his performance commended Fujita on the "sensitive" (*sensai*) way that he approached Moriyama's work—and then, as in the other examples reviewed earlier, promptly reconfigured this sensitivity in terms of questions of (Japa-nese) language proficiency. The connection between language and interiority was articulated explicitly: "Your singing is very sensitive, very detailed. These nuances, the subtleties of the language that even the Japanese do not catch—I think that you may have picked up on these precisely because you were raised in a foreign land. I understand that you are going to be living here in Japan from this spring, and given [your skills with these linguistic subtleties and nuances], I reckon that you are the best sort of person [*saikyō no hito*] to do so."

Fujita seemed particularly pleased with this compliment, barely containing a smile as he bowed deeply here. Indeed, he had every reason to be pleased, for he had just been declared the "best sort of person" to live in Japan; as a non-Japanese resident and member of an already marginalized community, this sort of enthusiastic acceptance—vital, in his eyes, if he is to secure the means of his own everyday survival in his new home—would probably be a rare occur-rence. But the judge continued: "Generally speaking, however, you have a ten-dency to be too passionate in your expression [*chikara no hairi sugiru keikou ga arimasu*]. After all, you know, here in Japan, we have *wabi* and *sabi* [aesthetic concepts that involve appreciation for subtlety and imperfection and that are often associated with notions of "Japaneseness"] and tend to prefer a 'moody' atmosphere, so now that you're going to be living in Japan, I would like to see you go and visit temples and take in the scenery in the countryside, and through doing so, to have you grasp the feeling of being Japanese [*Nihonjin no kanji wo tsukande itadaku*]."

In the NAK roundtable that I discussed earlier, Konishi Ryōtarō—head of the judging panel at the Kayōsai—discussed his priorities in judging amateur *enka* performances, and how these intersect with questions of ethnonationality. "Rather than *accomplished* singing, I'll always favor *good* singing," he said. "The Brazilians [who often enter the competition], they're so simple and straightforward [*sunao*]. The Japanese kids who are accomplished, they're always being tinkered with by so-called teachers, so their songs end up like manicured *bonsai* trees. They look good, but nothing of substance comes across." Konishi himself declared a preference for "straightforward," good (as opposed to accomplished) singing and described the complaints that he often faces for "too many Brazilians ending up with prizes"—implying that he often recommends bestowing them. In a way, Konishi's stance is at odds with the judge tasked with critiquing Fujita, whose comment is cited earlier. But what appears as a lauding of heterogeneous, embodied performativity in *enka* in fact serves merely to reinforce the dividing line between authentic, textured "Japanese" performance and simplistic, ultimately inauthentic (if enjoyable) foreign imitations of it.

As a Brazilian national of Japanese descent making a new life in Japan, Fujita straddled the implied demarcation line between "Brazilian" and "Japanese" in untenable ways. He was neither fully "Brazilian"/foreign/exterior nor fully "Japanese"/interior—or, perhaps better, he was incompletely both at the same time. This doubling generated a radical sort of remainder that simply could not be tolerated by the interiors of "Japan" or "Japan's music." His judge (who was not Konishi) resolved this crisis by interpellating him (Althusser 2001) as an *aspiring* member of the interiority that *enka* both cite and conjure, and in so doing robbed his performance of the potential of being "good," but simultaneously established it as not (yet) sufficiently "accomplished," either (Fujita did not win a prize that day). This was an interaction that ultimately promised Fujita access to the interior—but in the process also revealed the silhouette of his own other (the other within; the singer who was merely "good") and locked him outside of it, at least until the other within could be disciplined and the "feeling of being Japanese" adequately grasped, thereby reinforcing a category of persons who are *not* the "best sort of person" to live in Japan and who must face ongoing discrimination (Tomiyama 2005). In this, the interaction laid bare some of the important real-world, political implications of musical storytelling, and its deployment and channeling by different social actors.

It would be a grave error—worse, an instance of what Atkins (2010, 5) has called a "vulgarized version of Foucauldianism"—to paint the judges and gatekeepers of *enka* as manipulative, shadowy figures, working at the behest of a dominant social order to quash heterogeneity and reinforce (cultural) nationalism. That's not what I'm trying to argue here. Rather, as I've suggested throughout the preceding pages, the aim of these figures seems to be to "keep *enka* afloat" (Yano 2002, 178) as a discernable (and at least marginally profitable) musical form—and that means both policing and reinforcing its purported dis-cursive borders. In the NAK roundtable discussed earlier, Konishi, Takehisa, and Mozu decried the democratization of *enka* that karaoke, as an embodied, participatory form, necessarily implies. "Karaoke's becoming a hobby that's just about excretion," Konishi scoffed (perhaps not coincidentally, with dismis-sive reference to functions of the body). "If you can't [learn from, respect, and embody] the genius of the pros, then it's no different from taking a piss." Privi-leged access to the endlessly regenerated interior of *enka*—"Japan's music"—is what authorizes these figures to establish what Fernandes (2017, 23–28) calls "appropriate" tropes and story lines for molding and framing storytelling, the storytelling of "the pros," and this leads to the sorts of clashing, conflicted claims on that storytelling with those who would use the music to narrate, however partially, the embodied experience of their own everyday lives. But this story is as political as it is musical—as Fujita's story makes clear, precisely because of its proximity to one version of the National imaginary, this author-ity can also imply dictating the terms of, even granting access to, what Tomi-yama (2005) has called the "society of good people." The judges were earnest and engaged at the Kayōsai, never dismissive or scornful, and seemed to be sincerely trying to help, working to guide contestants like Fujita toward gaining admittance to the very interiors (musical and political, as if the two could ever be separated anyway) that they had worked so hard at cultivating and occupying over the course of their own careers. But indeed, therein lies the danger: the threat posed to the possibilities of embodied, heterogeneous musical storytelling—to one promise of karaoke politics—at the hands of those whom I, following Tomiyama, have already called "leaders." Different scholars and thinkers have conceived of "leaders" in different ways: they are, for example, (quasi-elite) per-sons "within the subjugated [who] join the subjugating class" (Ōsugi 2014), or the local teachers and officials "leading" the wartime Okinawan Lifestyle Reform Movement who set out, cheerfully and with the best of intentions, to kill the other within (Tomiyama 2000, 125–127); they are middle-class women under Empire who strategically pursued enhanced "power and influence" by "assuming public roles, often in alliance with the state" (Garon 1998, 134), including being "deputized" to further Imperial prerogatives (moral suasion, thrift, sacrifice) at the household and community levels, or the Korean rooming house managers in Osaka in the 1930s, who did all that they could to channel their newly arrived compatriots into harsh day-labor positions so as to "assist" them with their everyday survival (Kawashima 2009). The danger posed by the "leaders," in short, is the danger of extending a hand of help—only to find that it may serve a poison pill.

Thus far, I've shown how karaoke at the Kayōsai involved a storytelling borne of embodied experience in the world, one that produced a remainder that could never be confined to reproductions of patterned form, even as it required this form as the vessel enabling its articulability in the first place. To counteract the heterogeneity and unknowability that this storytelling implies and shore up the discursive integrity of *enka,* the judges enacted a disciplinary praxis that centered on questions of gender, the voice, and especially national language. Like the practitioners of sacred music discussed by Dolar—whose musicking always threatened to undermine religious authority as they pursued the God of joy—the contestants at the Kayōsai had to be disciplined, lest their own uses of the music scramble the signifier ("Japan," "Japan's music") and undermine *enka*'s interiority itself (Dolar 2006, 50–53). Their musical storytelling, in other words, was reorganized into stories of *enka* and of "Japan," reconfiguring the "participation" of karaoke away from everyday storytelling and back toward the embodiment and enunciation of ideal form and emplacement within the interior. These two markedly different modes of storytelling collided in Melparque Hall—but did not produce any sort of dialectic resolution. They remained, simply, at odds. But what happens when we leave the competition hall behind? On what remains of this track, I'll travel to Fukushima to talk with individual NAK members and *enka* aficionados there, to consider the ways in which the music and attendant notions of "Japan" circulate in the contexts of their own everyday lives.

Third Verse: Fukushima

The car zips through the streets of the northeastern city of Fukushima, then gradually starts to leave the bright lights of its small urban center behind as the world outside my window trades modestly sized office buildings for rural homes, and the many alleys and bars that dot the downtown core give way to darkened rice paddies and fruit fields. We are entering a mildly run-down, heavily agricultural section of town, north of the commercial district, and we eventually turn off Route 4—the main thoroughfare that runs through the interior of Tōhoku from Tokyo all the way up to Aomori—and bounce down a short gravel road, coming to a stop in a parking lot across from a dark, wooden house. "We're here!" says Mr. Satō (a pseudonym), head of the Fukushima Branch of the NAK and my guide for the evening, and we head for the entrance. For a man in his mid-seventies, he has a remarkable spring in his step.

We step through the front door and into a miniature karaoke studio that has somehow been wedged into this small countryside home. The studio is the equivalent of perhaps twelve tatami mats in size (around 214 square feet) and is adorned with an electric keyboard, a heavy microphone and steel stand (think Bruce Springsteen's stadium tours in the eighties), a well-worn television monitor, and other standard trappings of karaoke. The walls are plastered with posters—many signed—of Japan's *enka* royalty; reigning among these are images of Misora Hibari, the undisputed Queen of *Enka*. This is where NAK Fukushima holds its monthly meetings. The members whom I am to meet here tonight have put out oranges, watermelon, Japanese sweets, crackers, and tea in anticipation of my joining their session, and despite my invasion of their space, they seem genuinely happy to have me. One by one they trickle into the studio, speaking among themselves in a thick Fukushima dialect that for me would have been nearly impenetrable had it not been for my own years living in this town. Of the ten members of this branch, there are six in attendance this evening, five women and Mr. Satō. All are middle-aged or older, the demographic that scholars place at the center of the *enka* market (Yano 2002, 6–7). Several of the remaining male members were to attend as well, I am told, but are either still working (at 9:00 p.m.) or are sick in the hospital.

No one is exactly sure when NAK Fukushima was established; the best recollections of the group place the year at around 1990 (a date not without significance, as I'll explain later). The Fukushima Branch, like NAK's other 130 branches located across Japan and overseas, was established not through orchestrations carried out by NAK headquarters in Tokyo, but through a coming together of *enka* devotees in Fukushima who approached NAK with the hopes of setting up their own branch under its organizational umbrella. When at least ten such individuals have come together in a given area, the group may petition NAK for branch status. There are no particular benefits to this, aside from the solidification of a means by which to "facilitate communication with one's *uta-nakama* [comrades in song]" and "enjoy life with karaoke within a larger circle of solidarity [*rentai*] called NAK, each for his or her own purpose" (NAK promotional materials 2010). Indeed, such solidification of *nakama* interconnectivity seems to be the factor of most importance to NAK members— according to organizational literature, most members join the organization through the invite of friends or other interpersonal connections (the question of *nakama* and/as musicking will come up again on track 5). This was no different in Fukushima—but what would come to stand out particularly strongly during my visit there was how each of the members was struggling, in their own way, with the alienating terms and conditions of everyday life, and how the sense of "solidarity" afforded by participating in *enka* in these specific everyday contexts helped the members to survive them.

I had come to Fukushima hoping to explore why individuals belonging to the NAK branch there held such affection for *enka,* and to learn about the role that the music played in their lives. Following Hammersely and Atkinson, I pursued this goal by facilitating an informal chat among members of a single group who already knew each other well; I'd hoped that this tactic would have the advantage of being "less threatening for the interviewees ... thus [encouraging] them to be forthcoming" (Hammersely and Atkinson 2007, 111–112). Indeed, the discussion was lively and multifaceted. At a basic level, it clarified what this track has already established—that is, the fundamentally heterogeneous, often unknowable manner in which individual social actors approach *enka,* and the range of uses that the music might be put to. As the discussion got underway, some members shared how they found themselves moved by specific lyrical content and enjoyed "seeking that which we do not have [intensity and passion, for this respondent] through the music." Others lauded what they understood as the soothing or energizing functions of certain melodies or of the voices of specific performers: "I tend to go for the passionate, intense songs," said another. "The ones that really draw you in." And as was the case with many of the performers at the Kayōsai, some in Fukushima looked to the music as a means of articulating the terms and conditions of their own lives: "Songs that fit your own age, the circumstances of your own life. Those are the types of songs that I would tend to choose." In general, despite common appeal among the membership to a discursive form called "Japan's music"—which, as I've discussed earlier, demands a narrative cohesiveness, often centering on language or "culture," for its very legibility and viability—the discussion revealed the same unpredictable heterogeneity of application and approach to the music that was in evidence at the Kayōsai in Tokyo. In the words of one of the respondents, "The way that the song is interpreted ... is unique to each individual, I think."

But as the evening progressed, the messy heterogeneities of musicking that were apparent at the outset gradually began to synthesize into a single tune. The conditions of everyday life that enfolded these individuals in Fukushima circa 2010 proved a particularly important context informing the significance that they took from the music and the uses that they put it to.

Scott Aalgaard: There are so many "hobbies" available out there—why do you choose music? Why are these songs *important* to you?
                  [...]
Respondent 6:   Music is a relief [*sukkiri suru*].
        R2:   It's a stress release.
    R6, R4:   Yes, a stress release!
              [enthusiastic agreement with this]
        R6:   Well, we are housewives, and there are a lot of occupations represented here [*ironna shokugyou ga arimasu ne*]. We are exhausted and all the rest of it, but by going into that zone [*soko ni itte*] and singing, the stress and all of that—

SA: From work, and from being a housewife, and so on?

R6: Yes!

SA: Singing provides you with relief from all of that?

R6: That's right!

R3: I feel just the same way [ongoing murmured agreement with R6's comments].

R6: Also, there are lots of different occupations; sometimes you will get people in a group that share the same occupation. [Excitedly] People get trapped in their own little worlds [*doushitemo kataku naru*], you know. But if you bring all these people with different occupations into the world of song—people can talk and sing together there, and it provides a stress release. Yes, relief from stress; at least for me.

[...]

R4: I think that it's being able to be passionate about something, and through giving vent to your breath and your voice [that helps] …

For these individuals, *enka* seemed to serve something similar to what Wang (2012, 156), writing of different contexts and musics, has termed a "therapeutic function." But this is nothing that the music "does" of its own volition—indeed, as I've been stressing throughout this book, music doesn't "do" anything at all. DeNora has observed similar "therapeutic" uses of music among her own fieldwork communities and notes that "music's powers are constituted by [the user of music] herself; they derive from the ways she interacts with them. [...] The point is that music's power to 'soothe' derives not only from the musical 'stimulus' but from the ways in which [the user] appropriates that music, the things she brings to it, *the context within which it is set*" (DeNora 2000, 41–42). While I do not want to essentialize or homogenize the experiences of these practitioners on the bases of socioeconomic data (they would not recognize themselves in my work if I did so), the "context" in this case is none other than the everyday experience of ongoing precarity and socioeconomic unevenness in Fukushima (and other areas of Japan, particularly rural ones), and the senses of anxiety and alienation that help define that experience—I'll elaborate on this in a moment. Karaoke performances of *enka* are used here, in other words, as a "counterattack" of a different sort—the music, particularly in the collective, collaborative, and participatory form potentiated by membership in NAK Fukushima, affords the very sense of rootedness and connectedness that everyday life under capitalism tends to erode (Karatani 2014). As I'll discuss later, this rootedness and connectedness is narrated by the NAK membership under the conceptual heading of "Japan"—but the story that this "Japan" is tapped to tell is not the story that we might expect. To understand this, it's important to understand the conditions of everyday life that helped generate the desire for the "therapeutic function" in the first place.

In the wake of the triple crises of March 11, 2011—which hit Fukushima particularly and uniquely hard—the unevenness that has defined postwar Japanese economic development has received renewed attention and scrutiny. But this unevenness had, of course, been a key condition informing everyday life in Fukushima and other agricultural areas for decades prior to the earthquake (Harootunian 2019, 290–300). In one sense, rural, agricultural areas like Fukushima were left behind in Japan's postwar economic "recovery"—but in another, they were integral to it. Postwar land reform, for example, had the effect of both creating storage facilities for marginalized rural surplus populations and encouraging mass migration out of the countryside to the cities, ensuring a steady supply of inexpensive labor power for industry (Babb 2005, 193). Although Itoh notes that "during high economic growth [1955–1973] the Japanese economy actually moved toward an egalitarian economic order [and l]iving standards in rural [areas] became more and more equal to those of urban areas for the first time in Japanese history" (Itoh 2000, 44), this growth was relative (the rising tide, that is, did not lift all boats evenly), and the ideological promise of even development everywhere remained just that. Indeed, it was in the context of a persistently (i.e., reliably) depressed rural economy that the Tokyo Electric Power Company (TEPCO) was invited to build the Fukushima Dai'ichi Nuclear Power Station in the town of Ōkuma in 1971, a move resisted by some but welcomed by others because of its perceived economic benefits for the community. What appeared to be a moment of success in overcoming capitalism's untimeliness and unevenness and moving to "catch up" along a teleological Historical arc, in other words, became merely one more indication of a regional impoverishment that was required for National growth, and that would certainly inform the visceral realities of life in Fukushima in 2010, even before it was manifested so blatantly with the crises of 3.11.

Around 1990, Japan's urban-asset-based bubble economy began to deflate, heralding a long economic downturn and the onset of an everyday life defined by what Allison (2013) has aptly called "precarity." Although socioeconomic turbulence and unevenness between urban and rural areas had been firmly reentrenched following the end of high-speed economic growth and especially by the late 1980s, the post-bubble period has been particularly notorious for "increasingly difficult conditions at work and worsening conditions of life for working people, as well as [for] exacerbated socioeconomic unevenness" (Allison 2013, 20–21). It's been a moment, in short, in which more and more people across Japan have come to be haunted by the specter of the instability of their own existence. In the cities, men sought to ward this ghost off by raising the value of their own labor power through "spending extraordinary, stressful hours—perhaps one hundred or more per week—at work," much of it in the form of "what people called 'service' [that is, unpaid] overtime to the firm" (Gordon 2009, 304; recall here that many of the male members of NAK Fukushima were still at work when I visited at 9:00 p.m.). Meanwhile, more and more married women—including those who shared their time with me in Fukushima (all were employed, albeit precariously)— were compelled to enter the workforce and sell their own labor power however they could to offset the costs of housing, education, and so on amid a harsh reality of stagnant earnings by their spouses. In the meantime, the Japanese state under neoliberalism continued to shift the burden of its own budget crisis "onto the shoulders of weaker people through cuts in state expenditure for welfare and public education … [and increases to costs associated with] medical insurance" (Allison 2013, 22). Since the moment of NAK Fukushima's inception around 1990, in other words, everyday life in much of Japan had been haunted by a deepening sense of precarity, albeit one that was established well before the bubble burst.

Such was the historicity that informed everyday life in Fukushima in the summer of 2010. Like many across the country—especially in rural areas— people found themselves scrambling to survive the conditions of their own everyday lives and make ends meet, even at relatively advanced ages. At seventy-six, for example, Mr. Satō continued to farm full-time, not out of any romanticized fondness for the land, he said, but because his very existence— and that of his family—depended on it. In a particularly powerful moment, two of the female members of NAK Fukushima clearly articulated the challenges of everyday life there: "There's no such thing as retirement age for the self-employed!" said one, ruefully. "Yes, retirement's still a long way off," said another, sighing. Both respondents were well into their sixties. Everyday life, in sum, presented challenges to the membership of NAK Fukushima—and as will become clear later, these embodied experiences of precarity did much to inform how the members oriented themselves toward their karaoke performances of *enka,* and how they used their engagement with the music to tell stories of "Japan" itself and counteract the anxieties and alienation of the everyday.

As the discussion continued to unfold, it became increasingly clear that bolstering senses of rootedness and connectedness—precisely that which, as I pointed out earlier, everyday life under capitalism tends to erode—was a key factor giving substance to the "therapeutic function" of *enka.* This intersected with notions of *community* in explicit, important ways.

R2: I am … reminded that interpersonal connections are so very important, and I am grateful for being able to have those. I have been lucky enough to be allowed into this community here [*nakama ni irete itadakimashita*]; you just can't do anything by yourself. Lots has happened with this group of people, and that has led to the person that I am today; that's what I think …
[murmured agreement with R2]

SA: The music reminds you of this?
[further murmured agreement]

R2: Yes; it's gotta be *enka*. That's the whole starting point [*shuppatsu ten*]

SA [to group]: Do you all feel the same way?

All: Yes.

R4: Yes, you know, you are getting that support, even when it is unseen [*kage de sasaeteiru hito ga iru*]. Your community [*nakama*] is more important than anything.

A theory and praxis of *enka* that is specific to these individuals and their historical and geographical embeddedness in the world is beginning to emerge here. While "stress" has been raised in previous scholarship as an underlying factor in audience motivation for engaging *enka* (Yano 2002, 125), such discussions have tended to focus on the hectic nature of urban commutes, for example, or the challenges of fast-paced financial trading—a world that is alien to many *enka* listeners, especially those in the countryside. The "stress" announced by the membership of the Fukushima branch of the NAK was rather more fundamental: it was none other than the fundamental disconnect and unease identified by thinkers like Paolo Virno as being key facets of modern everyday life. Those in the precariat who are subjected to the relentless permeation of fear and anguish wrought by contemporary existence—made all the more pronounced in post-bubble Japan—are haunted by what Virno, writing of the broader, global political-economic context, calls the feeling of "not feeling at home" (Virno 2004, 30–32): "[T]he condition of 'not feeling at home' is permanent and irreversible. The absence of a substantial community and of any connected 'special places' makes it such that the life of the stranger, the not-feeling-at-home … are unavoidable and lasting experiences" (Virno 2004, 37).

Buffeted by their everyday encounters with the world, those tormented by the anguish of not feeling at home grasp at the chance to take shelter in what Virno calls the "common places" or the "general intellect," which "alone are what exist in terms of offering us a standard of orientation, and thus, some sort of refuge from the direction in which the world is going" (Virno 2004, 33–35). This "common place," for the membership of NAK Fukushima, took the form of "Japan" itself. Articulations of "Japan" by the members started out as rather banal rehashings of the supposedly mystical connectivities between music and ethnonational contingency that are promoted by *enka* stakeholders: "Well, because I'm Japanese, you know [*Nihonjin dakara ne*]," said one, early in the evening, "I can feel something in the lyrics [*kanjiru mono ga aru*]." But this quickly became more complex, and circled back to the discussions of connection and "community" referenced earlier.

SA: You mentioned earlier that you get a sense of "Japan" from the lyrics. What, exactly, does that mean? Do you all feel the same? Do you feel "Japan" in the lyrics of *enka*?

All: [General affirmation]

R3:   *Enka* is a genre that is defined by lyrics that speak of Japan's vistas, of culture [*fuudo*], of all sorts of human characteristics, you see.

SA: I see.

R4:   But even with the same song, there are instances in which someone might just be singing naturally, with regular feeling [*futsuu no kimochi de*], but someone else is listening to it in tears.

R2:   Yes, the circumstances of the lyrics.

R6:   Like if someone dies ...

R2:   Yes, that's right ...

R4:   So, depending on the lyrics—the circumstances of the lyrics—for example, if someone has lost their loved one ... We were doing a *meoto enka* once, and a student began to cry uncontrollably, unable to sing. Becoming aware of that situation, and showing compassion to the affected person—this can also be called the work of a "Japanese heart" [*Nihon no kokoro*], I think.

R3:   Yes, I agree.

Although the importance of "Japan" in the performance of *enka* is clearly foregrounded here, the members seemed mostly uninterested in "Japan" as a transcendent, homogenized narrative to be tapped in defining *enka*'s interiority and lending integrity to "Japan's music." Rather, they were interested in telling specific "Japanese" stories that helped facilitate the "interpersonal connections" and "community" that lay at the root of their desire to take part in *enka* musicking in the first place. *Enka* and karaoke performance thereof, that is, weren't a resource for articulating and shoring up an abstract interiority; rather, these were a fulcrum around which everyday stories of rootedness and connectivity could be told in ways that "help[ed members] live with the contradictions that are an unavoidable feature of existence" (Polletta 2006, 11). The "Japan" of *enka,* as such, was contingent and unstable; it was, as the members themselves pointed out, entirely dependent on "the circumstances of the lyrics." "Japan" as *concept*—the one appealed to by the Kayōsai judges to discipline heterogeneity and patrol the boundaries of *enka*'s discursive space, the one whose terms were laid out as a means by which to more authentically access "Japanese" interiority—was certainly circulating through these individuals' engagement with the music. But this concept was made to feed back into a story of "Japan" that was rather different from the sort of narrative that is often taken as the generating condition for scholarship on modern and contemporary *enka.* This "Japan," that is, became a medium for narrating day-to-day experiences and interpersonal relationships, removing it from transcendent conceptuality and positing it in the material midst of the here and now.

The theory and practice of *enka* that was revealed in my discussion with the membership of NAK Fukushima blended, in a way, the storytelling praxes that I introduced in the first and second sections of this track in that the members used the music to tell stories of their own everyday lives. Unlike the contestants at the Kayōsai, though, they framed these stories with explicit appeal to "Japan" as concept. In contrast to the Kayōsai judges, however, the membership of NAK Fukushima was mostly uninterested in patrolling or reinforcing the boundaries of a musical discourse that simultaneously referenced and conjured a "Japanese" interior, or with reproducing interiorized identity or patterned form. Rather, these individuals invoked a "Japan" that was inextricably intertwined with everyday life and that became a way of *narrating* that everyday life; it was contingent and open-ended (rather than closed and endlessly self-referential)—and as I'll suggest in a moment, its enunciation even presented the possibility of critique. What this suggested was an ethics of *enka,* and of karaoke performance thereof, that afforded a means of literally surviving the world. This ethics referenced "Japan" for its legibility—but not in the ways we might expect. "You see," said one of the respondents that evening, laughing self-consciously, "Japan is all that I know."

The "Japan" that was invoked during my discussion with the membership of NAK Fukushima was used, in other words, as a means to help these individuals tell the stories of their own everyday lives, to each other and to themselves—not because they were necessarily prone to nationalist sentiment, patriotic fervor, or nostalgic longing for the past (although these could conceivably be motivations for some), but because, as the members themselves pointed out, "Japan" is *familiar.* It's all that these individuals know, the key framework that the members have for organizing their own navigation of the world, and the only umbrella that they see available to keep the rain off their backs. "Japan" became a heading organizing the story of the love between a farmer and his wife in one member's telling; a means of articulating snowy, beautiful Tōhoku in another's. As I'll describe briefly later, it also provided a means of making sense of some of the material realities of everyday life in Fukushima itself, and of articulating the crises that can accompany it. And it resonated strongly with Virno's "common place," a steel vessel of sorts built to withstand the incessant blows of everyday life—a way of resolving the crisis of "not feeling at home," an anchor in turbulent seas. But although Virno describes the "common place" as abstract and banal, even dangerous (Virno 2004, 38), in the theory and praxis of *enka* pursued by NAK Fukushima, "Japan" as "common place" is in fact commandeered and spliced back into everyday life in a way that ascribes to it an embodied materiality, thus suggesting that it can be embodied—*performed,* as Wedeen (2008) has shown in other contexts—*differently,* in ways that certainly make use of the patterned particularities of *enka* but are not reducible to them. Thinking about when, why, and how "Japan" might be drawn into practices of musical storytelling through *enka* in the first place, that is, reveals an ambiguity that is important, and potentially productive.

The "Japan" of *enka,* then, is tricky. Its stories are told in disparate, contingent ways, by diverse social actors with heterogeneous aims and desires. On the one hand, we'll probably never shake free of the ghost of Althusser's (2001) interpellation—the possibility of "Japanese" practitioners (or non-Japanese practitioners, like Julio Fujita) answering the hail, recognizing themselves in the very stories that began to be told when *enka* were redirected away from "counterculture" around 1970 and toward a different status as a siren song offering musical affirmation of the "heart and soul of the Japanese." This is the enjoyment of what Žižek (1993) calls the Nation Thing. As Karatani points out, after all, the coupling of capital-state—the key framework underpinning and informing everyday life under capitalist modernity—requires Nation as a means of soothing the alienation that this very coupling generates, and it's not surprising that *enka* should have taken on this ideological baggage in the very moment of the purported fulfillment of capitalism, a development that had already been heralded two years earlier by students and others struggling against the effects of its calcification in 1968 (Oguma 2015). This is the "Japan" of "Culture," of the interior, and ultimately of the Kayōsai judges. But the "Japan" that was articulated by the membership of NAK Fukushima in their own musical storytelling was rather different. Precisely because of its embeddedness in and associability with the here and now of everyday life, this "Japan" presented the possibility of unpredictability and multiplicity, of being conjured in praxes of storytelling by historically and geographically specific individuals who bring different embodied experiences and desires to bear upon it and invest these within it. It is not "Japan" as interior, and yet, to those seeking shelter within it, it *is* "Japan"—it's a sort of "common place," potentially one of many bearing the same name; a way to organize knowledge and experience of the world and perhaps protect against its blows. None of this, of course, is to ascribe some sort of universally critical or resistive agency to these individuals, nor is it to ignore the fact that "Japan" is also the story told by the state—such stories can spiral (and have spiraled) into outright fascism, especially when a transcendent, ahistorical Nation is appealed to as an idealized, spiritual space from which to take shelter from the upheavals of modernity (Kawashima et al. 2014). But if it's true that the "nation" is first and foremost an imagined community (Anderson 1983), then the question of *how* it's imagined is of significant concern. Turning our ear toward these singers of the Homesick Blues, in short, points us away from a closed-ended, endlessly self-referential reflection and reproduction of "Japan" as patterned form and toward much trickier questions of the use of "Japan" as concept and its deployment in different music events and in unpredictable—sometimes even critical—praxes of storytelling. In the end, the form that "Japan" takes in this storytelling, and any ambiguous potential that this may have, utterly depends upon the lived conditions of everyday life, and the stories that the music—"Japan's music"—is conscripted to tell about it.

A final story from my visit to Fukushima will help me illustrate this point. When asked early in the evening to identify her favorite *enka* artist, the senior karaoke "teacher" in the group pointed to Kakyōin Shinobu (b. 1957), an *enka* artist from Sendai, just up the road from Fukushima City. Specifically, she cited the fact that Kakyōin's works incorporate *min'yō,* a mode of singing far more associable with "tradition" than modern *enka* is, and one that this particular respondent saw as a musical manifestation of the "heart of Japan" (her words). This was her chief reason for being drawn to Kakyōin's work. Strikingly, though, the respondent declared her favorite Kakyōin song to be the 2003 *enka* "*Bōkyō Shin-Sōma* [Longing for Home, Shin-Sōma]," a work that foregrounds the shamisen instrumentation and *minyō*-inspired vocal ornamentation of "Japan's music," and which portrays, with occasional appeal to hints of Fukushima dialect, the lonely existence of a laborer from Fukushima Prefecture who'd been forced to ride the rails to find work in the city. The lyrics find the laborer pining for home, reflecting on far-off Fukushima through a haze of *sake:*

> The flowers may be in bloom,
> But parting and spring rains bring loneliness
> I miss the distant Aizu sky
> Couldn't go home, even if I wanted to
> Not without something to show
> Ah, far off in the distance
> Is that the Sōma sky … ?

These are biting lyrics, whose contents resonate with other works—often set in Tōhoku—that describe the consequences of unevenness and the imperative to leave home and sell labor power in the cities in order to survive (Hosakawa Takashi's 1985 "*Bōkyō Jongara* [Longing for Home Jongara]," with lyrics that describe one such worker from Aomori "turn[ing] out the lights and scream[ing] at the Tokyo sky," is another well-known example). It's also a fascinating choice for a Fukushima respondent seeing the "heart of Japan" in the music. There's a hint of a tension here, as well, between National "culture" and the interior, on the one hand, and everyday life, on the other. To be sure, this tension can be resolved by displacing it onto patterned form and the hermeneutic enclosure of "Japan's music" in a way that eradicates the heterogeneities of storytelling—the move, perhaps, of the Kayōsai judges. But it can also be amplified in a way that accentuates an embodied experience of an uneven world, destabilizing received narratives and rendering "Japan" materially, not conceptually; opening it up to redefinition, and even critique (indeed, this rendering material also resonates with Tosaka Jun and the tactics deployed by Takada Wataru on the *Goaisatsu* LP [1971], discussed on track 2). In the context of our discussion in Fukushima, the tension remained just that—lurking, confounding, unresolved. But it did demand, to return to the opening pages of this track, that "Japan" be taken as an ending, not a starting point, to critical interrogations of *enka,* and that the emphasis be placed on the storytelling, not the story; on some of the ways in which "Japan" may (or may not) be conjured through those processes of musical storytelling, by whom, and why. The "communities of the us" that this implies are defined and interpreted in different ways. And it is this, of course, that lends the becoming-us that *enka* affords its danger—and its cool.

Reprise: March 11, 2011

Just eight months after visiting with the membership of NAK Fukushima, I stood in my apartment in Victoria, Canada, watching in horror as black tsunami waves washed over town after town in Japan's Northeast, taking lives and livelihoods with them. Thankfully, all members of NAK Fukushima survived. Many thousands of others did not. The immediate devastation was terrifying. But as the three reactors of the Fukushima Dai'ichi Nuclear Power Station melted down over the ensuing days and vast swaths of the prefecture became uninhabitable, new crises began to unfold that weren't yet apparent as I stared in disbelief at my television screen on March 11, 2011. These are crises that continue to resonate and unfold as I finish writing this book more than ten years later.

Manabe (2015) has shown how the crises of 3.11 and the events that followed helped to galvanize waves of protest, which were often articulated in or afforded by music. These protests often targeted the so-called nuclear village, the prime minister, or the state itself in ways that undermined authoritative signifiers of "Japan." But as I tried to show earlier, the pump was primed for a less oppositional and more destabilizing splintering of narratives of "Japan" well before the ground started to heave on that cold day in March. As I've discussed elsewhere (Aalgaard 2017), the state tried desperately to nationalize 3.11 and turn it into a story of "Japanese" suffering, repackaging a regional crisis into a national one in ways that help conceal the true nature of a purportedly egalitarian "national history" and camouflage the uneven development, rural-urban imbalances and inequalities, and sacrifice that fed the crises in the first place (Harootunian 2012). This repackaging was presented as *kizuna* ("Japanese" social bonds) and enunciated through cries of "*ganbarō Nippon*" ("let's give it our all, Japan"). But as my examination of the ways that "Japan" is actually understood and used by practitioners of "Japan's music" shows, this project was epistemologically flawed from the start. *Enka* are ostensibly the most "Japanese" of Japan's musics. But "Japan" for *enka* aficionados in Fukushima wasn't the transcendent, homogenizing conceptual space that those aiming to nationalize 3.11 hoped to evoke—in fact, the very enunciation of "Japan" tended to recall the fault lines that the crises helped to expose but that had been slowly gathering tension since long before the earthquake. Little wonder, then, that the early days of the crisis were marked by caller after caller phoning in to AM radio in Fukushima in the dead of night to voice their fury over the "Japanese" political economy that contributed such decidedly unnatural suffering to Japan's most horrific natural disaster since 1923. *Enka* might be the musical "heart and soul of Japan," that is, but the interior that they reference is not nearly as stable as it might seem.

In the roundtable that I introduced at the outset of this track, Konishi Ryōtarō argued that "karaoke isn't a theory of song; it's a theory of humanity. [...] In other words, 'songs' become intertwined with people's life philosophies [*ikikata*] in ways that are completely different from 'music.'" The implication here—whether Konishi, as *enka* gatekeeper, likes it or not—is that "song," as a singable, participatory, embodiable mode of engagement, becomes implicated in how we orient ourselves in the world in ways that "music" (Konishi seems to understand "music" as a more passive, stable sort of text here) never could. Tracing some of the implications of this, and the mechanisms of how it occurs, has been the aim of this track. Although "Japan" tends to be taken as the conceptual center of *enka*—the potentiating condition for much scholarly discussion thereof—the first section of this track showed that, for the most part, "Japan" was not something that contestants at the Kayōsai particularly prioritized or desired; the emphasis, rather, was on telling their own stories of everyday life through "Japan's music." (Indeed, although the genre and intent differ—karaoke singers are not explicitly trying to sidestep the trap of oppositional politics, for instance—there is something here of Takada Wataru's insistence on "singing the everyday" [track 2] as a means of negating the negation that a focus on "Japan" as locus of ahistorical desire might suggest.) For the judges and the gatekeepers, as I showed in the second section, "Japan" was much more important: it was a discursive and a disciplinary apparatus (Agamben 2009) that was appealed to in order to police the borders of "Japan's music" and shore up its viability as a modern musical genre, but that also helped to relentlessly conjure imaginings of that interior in the first place. And in Fukushima, these two perspectives merged, as individual members of the local NAK chapter did prioritize "Japan," but mostly as a means of conceptualizing and telling stories of everyday life, beckoning toward possibilities that are open-ended, perhaps even critical. This, of course, is a limited study, and there are different stories of *enka* engagement to be told in different geographical contexts and other historical moments. I leave that task to future researchers.

National performance is contingent, and ambiguous. What's important is to "understand the practical uses of the category 'nation,' the ways in which it can come to structure perception, to inform thought and experience, [and] to organize discourse and political action" (Brubaker 1996, 10). The key, that is, lies in how the story of the nation gets told in process, not in how it's reflected, or how its purportedly stable identities may be reproduced. If we start with "Japan," we will necessarily fail to see how "Japan" is in fact not a priori, but rather a posteriori. As others have rightly noted, and as I stressed at the outset, "Japan" is an integral component of *enka*—but its nature and utility are revealed in the storytelling, not in the story. My aim here has been to illuminate some of the mechanics and implications of this (musical) storytelling in highly situated contexts, and to open up ground for considering some of the complexities and ambiguities inherent in using "Japan's music" to sing one's own songs. The "Japan" of *enka* is contingent, and always in danger of collapse: it is precisely this contingency that allows "Japan" to be enunciated in heterogeneous, sometimes startling ways. This is true of other musics as well, as will become particularly clear on the next and final track, as I consider the musical storytelling pursued by one of Japan's most prominent rock stars—and his fans.

Winds out of the South

KAGOSHIMA, CRISIS, AND THE CRITICAL
POTENTIALS OF A "PROVINCIALIZED JAPAN"

THE Nippon Budōkan sits in Kitanomaru Park in Tokyo's Kudanshita district, on the northernmost tip of nearly four hundred acres of land situated within the system of moats that once encircled Edo Castle. It's embedded in a neighborhood dotted with sites and institutions linked into ongoing, contested conversations concerning what "Japan" is and has been all about—the Imperial Palace is next door; Yasukuni Shrine, which polishes Japan's fifteen-year war and Imperial misadventures to a blinding shine, is across the street; the National Shōwa Memorial Museum, which presents a much different perspective on some of the everyday experiences of that war, is just down the hill. These conversations arc through the Budōkan as well: built in 1964 as a martial arts venue for the first Tokyo Olympics (its name translates as "martial arts hall"), the Budōkan is the site of the annual National Memorial Service for the War Dead, presided over by the emperor and empress and the prime minister. It was also the site of the Beatles' first Japan concert in 1966, which became intensely controversial precisely because it was held there—voices on the right famously objected to the intrusion of a loud, foreign, and morally questionable musical presence in a place that was supposed to be defined by eternal "Japanese" values and tradition. With or without the help of the Fab Four, its cultural cachet in Japan today remains primarily that of a legendary live music venue, a site of mystique and artistic prestige: when you play the Budōkan, conventional wisdom states, you know you've really "made it." On this steamy summer night in 2018, I've come here for a concert by a musical storyteller who has made a career out of engaging critically with some of the shifting conditions of everyday life in modern Japan and embedding himself unflinchingly into some of the very conversations that arc through the Kudanshita neighborhood—Nagabuchi Tsuyoshi.

Nagabuchi is a towering cultural presence in modern and contemporary Japan, widely renowned for his uncompromising dedication to performance excellence, impassioned and engaged lyrical and musical mind, and blisteringly sharp social and political critiques. A singer-songwriter, actor on the big and small screens, calligrapher, sometimes author, and martial artist, Nagabuchi (in 2022) is now sixty-five and celebrating his forty-third year in music. Born in 1956 in Ishūin, on the outskirts of Kagoshima—capital city of the beautiful but relatively impoverished homonymous prefecture in far-southern Kyushu, a place heavily reliant on agriculture, tourism, and the nuclear power industry (I'll have more to say about the historicity of Kagoshima later)—Nagabuchi is the second child and only surviving son of a police officer and a homemaker. Strongly influenced by Kagawa Ryō (see track 3) and other key figures on Japan's critical "folk" scene of around 1970, Nagabuchi bought his first guitar in 1971 and put together his first band when he entered high school. After entering Kyushu Sangyō University in Fukuoka, he began playing profession-ally at Shōwa, an unimposing yet now legendary "live house" and café that sits beneath the bustling back alleys of Fukuoka's Tenjin-chō and that gave rise to other influential Japanese acts including Tulip, Kaientai, Kai Band, and Inoue Yōsui. In 1978, he had a successful showing in the Yamaha Popular Song Contest (POPCON, which ran from 1969 to 1986 and became a proving ground for other important artists including Sano Masaharu, Chage & Aska, and Nak-ajima Miyuki) as Nagabuchi Tsuyoshi and Salty Dog, and in 1979 the artist who would become known to history as Nagabuchi Tsuyoshi released his POPCON selection—"*Junrenka* [Roundabout Love]"—as his debut single (an earlier debut, under the pseudonym Nagabuchi Gō, sputtered). "*Junrenka*" launched Nagabuchi on a journey that would be marked by the heady successes of million-selling singles and albums and marred by controversy and scandal (he was arrested in 1995 for possession of a small amount of cannabis, for example, the possession and use of which remains a serious criminal offence in Japan) and that would be characterized by a performativity and musical textuality that shifted and evolved along with Japan's own changing historical moments. Over the course of a career that seems to produce no shortage of climactic, "topping" moments—the most recent being the massive all-night concert held at the foot of Mount Fuji in August 2015, with which I opened this book—Nagabuchi has established himself as one of contemporary Japan's most influential and suc-cessful musical figures: he's played the Budōkan nearly forty times since 1982, selling it out every time. Though not a "folk" singer—at least not anymore—he is the clearest heir to the critical musical storytelling that animated Japan's musical moment of around 1970 and that was exemplified in different ways by figures like Takada Wataru (see track 2) and Kagawa Ryō. And, as I'll describe later, he's one of contemporary Japan's most intriguing singers of the Homesick

Blues, owing his renown in no small part to an acidic musical storytelling that is inextricably embedded in experiences of everyday life and their intersectionality with questions of "Japan."

At the Budōkan, the grounds around the venue are buzzing hours before Nagabuchi's concert is scheduled to begin. Fans with guitars and harmonicas are everywhere, playing together in groups of twos and threes and attracting small crowds who circulate from act to act, singing along and sipping the canned beer and munching on the various snacks that vendors trundle out onto the grounds for occasions like these. What might be called "Nagabuchi fashion" is conspicuous—sunglasses, ripped jeans, bright colors, a few bandanas. The atmosphere is carnivalesque. Once the doors open, the party moves inside. Japanese flags, towels from previous tours, the equally sharp and garish uniforms worn by members of the artist's numerous unofficial "fan societies" (one of which, the Ougoukai, I'll introduce later on this track) and thousands of excited, keyed-up bodies—young and old, male and female, though the men perhaps outnumber the women six to four or so—help transform the often stoic, reserved Budōkan into a colorful, high-energy spectacle. And then, as the red digital clock high on the wall to stage left ticks toward showtime, sporadic chants begin breaking out here and there: on the floor, in the bleachers, high up in the stands. These are the so-called Tsuyoshi calls, which consist simply of a rhythmic chanting of the artist's first name: "*Tsuu-yoo-shi!! Tsuu-yoo-shi!!*" They rise and fall, seem to get going in one section and then falter when another tries to join in but is off by just a second or two. Gradually, though, they spool up in frequency and intensity and eventually click into a synchronous, unified rhythm, roaring through the venue and transforming thousands (sometimes tens of thousands) of voices into one. Having taken part in dozens of Nagabuchi concerts over a span of nearly thirty years, I've experienced the electricity that arcs through the audience when the calls finally find their groove. They simultaneously generate and articulate a powerful sonic and performative sense of community and collectivity—and they can be deceptive at first. The calls can seem like a full-throated articulation of a discomfiting sort of desire, especially considering how they're framed and amplified by the flags and by the artist's explicit and unrelenting focus on questions of solidarity, organic collectivity, and "Japan." But nothing in music (or politics) is ever quite so simple. What the calls *do* announce—aside from exuberance—is an invitation to confront questions of community and collectivity, and the ways that these can be navigated by engaging with music and taking part in music events. This, broadly speaking, is the thinking that I aim to do on this final track of *Homesick Blues*.

I strenuously avoid characterizing Japanese musical figures according to purported Euro-American standard-bearers. Not only does such a move deprive musical actors in Japan of their originality and creativity, reducing them to "consumers" of purported Western authenticity (Stevens 2008, 66), it also tends to wholly misunderstand the circulatory nature (Novak 2013) of music, and worse, papers over and reproduces any range of power imbalances and racial inequities that allow such supposed "models" to be perceived as "models" in the first place (think of the double erasure of Blackness that attends hypothetical invocations of the "Japanese Elvis," for instance). But in Nagabuchi's case, I must make an exception. There is remarkable overlap in musical style, cultural standing, and political significance between Nagabuchi and American rock icon Bruce Springsteen—remarkable, but not surprising, since Nagabuchi has made no secret of his esteem for the Boss (Nagabuchi Tsuyoshi Club vol. 11, 1992). Readers with even a passing familiarity with Springsteen's music and epic performances will already have a reasonably good idea of what Nagabuchi Tsuyoshi, and what a Nagabuchi show, is all about. But these men are attuned in ways that go beyond musicianship and performativity. Both are formidable rock stars and cultural icons, with dedicated, serious fan bases who put the artists' music to extensive use in the contexts of their own lives (Cavicchi 1998). Each has built a career out of telling musical stories of everyday life—indeed, it is this sharp attunement to the often harsh, frustrating particularities of day-to-day life in modern Japan that tends to draw listeners to Nagabuchi in the first place. And each pursues an art that is located squarely at the intersection of nationality and regionality (America/New Jersey for Springsteen; Japan/Kagoshima for Nagabuchi)—this is an intersectionality that I pay particular attention to later. Nagabuchi, that is, is not necessarily the "Japanese Springsteen." But if the reader is willing to envision these men as speaking the same musical and critical language, then she'll already have a reasonably good handle on Nagabuchi's art.

Cavicchi's study of Springsteen fans provides a helpful frame for the discussion that I want to pursue on this track. Through extensive interactions with fan communities, Cavicchi reveals how Springsteen fans find "meaning and direction" in the music, how it helps "to shape dreams and ideas, [and] serve as a place where people can find inspiration, knowledge, and guidance" (Cavicchi 1998, 108). But as is the case with music more broadly, this is not some mythical power that the music holds intrinsically and that is enacted on the bodies and minds of listeners like a potion or a spell. Rather, fans make music meaningful (Wade 2009, 12)—they put it to use—in the contexts of their own lives (Cavicchi 1998, 131–133). Riffing off of Springsteen's stories of everyday life, of love and heartbreak, of New Jersey and "America" and what it means to be "Born in the U.S.A," and of one another's belonging as members of the fan community, they spin up stories of themselves, "see[ing] their participation in the music as an act that ideally enables them to shape their sense of 'me,' to work out the complexities of who they are" (Cavicchi 1998, 149). Nagabuchi's stories of "Japan" (and, as I'll discuss later, of "Kagoshima") fill a similar role, providing important signposting around which fans can tell critical stories about what it means to "be Japanese," to be part of a community, to be linked into locality and nation. The stories may be written and told by Nagabuchi, but they're taken up by listeners and used as a means of telling stories of themselves to themselves, and are even reciprocal, becoming a way for artist and audience to affirm each other's belonging in the community in moments of live performance through call-and-response and so on. Such storytelling, as is the case more broadly in this book, "refers to a particular means of understanding the world. It is not simply a closed text which represents a factual or fictional occurrence but a *process* of organizing, interpreting, and enhancing experience" (Cavicchi 1998, 174). The ultimate aim—as is the case with Cavicchi's Springsteen fans, and as reflected sonically in the synchronous, in-time "clicking" of the "Tsuyoshi calls" that thunder through the Budōkan and other concert sites around Japan—is the generation of a feeling of "belonging together" (Cavicchi 1998, 158–183). More than *being* Japanese according to set terms and conditions, this is about *becoming* "Japanese" in ways that can be critical, destabilizing, and reimaginative.

Nagabuchi's career is long, his art complex and diverse. Considerations of length prevent me from mounting an exhaustive analysis of the artist and his work herein; indeed, an entire monograph could be written about Nagabuchi alone (a project for another occasion). For my present purposes, in a book called *Homesick Blues*, I've found it most helpful to focus on some of the ways that Nagabuchi navigates questions of "Japan" by traversing his hometown of Kagoshima and the implications that this has for his critical stance (Berger 2009)—and for the storytelling of fans who use his stories to articulate their own. Now, Nagabuchi's unrelenting focus on questions of "Japan" makes his project a tricky one. It's made trickier still by his explicit support for the SDF (as helpers, not fighters, especially after 3.11), his lyrical grappling with the ghosts of Japan's Imperial past, his frequent evocation and deployment of symbols like the Rising Sun flag, and so on. The go-to move in some popular discourse in Japan, and in the limited attention afforded him thus far in the academy (Gerow 2011), has been to characterize him as a "nationalist" in light of this stance and his lyrical citations. To be sure, as the flags at the Budōkan help attest, Nagabuchi and his fans flirt in disconcerting ways with markers of exclusionary nationalism. This flirtation, though, presents an open-ended question, not a closed one— it opens up ground for considering the ways that artist and audience engage more deeply and critically with some of the deeper, contested meaning embedded within them (indeed, this tends to resonate with what Kagawa Ryō, on track 3, called the quest for "Japan's one more time"). In other words, while there are certainly aspects of Nagabuchi's art that can and should give us pause—and not only in terms of "Japan"; some of his lyrical engagements with gender, for instance, can be troubling, particularly in older works—the shorthand linkage of the artist and his stance to exclusionary nationalism is rather limiting and obfuscates the complex critical storytelling that he (and, often, his fans) actually pursues. In the pages that follow, I want to untangle some of this critical story-telling—and I'll leave the Budōkan behind and head to Kagoshima to do so.

On this track I'm interested in two key questions. First, I want to explore how Nagabuchi Tsuyoshi makes use of Kagoshima in grappling with questions of "Japan," appealing to the former to challenge dominant stories of the latter and tell different ones. Second, I want to engage select fans of the artist and consider how they make use of Nagabuchi's music and his emphasis on Kagoshima in telling the stories of their own "Japanese" lives. Ideas of nation play an oversized role on this track—but as I've already suggested, this is trick-ier than it first appears. The "nation" itself is slippery, contested, and produc-tively approached in terms of how it is embedded and performed in everyday life (Wedeen 2008). Brubaker's reflections on nations and nationalisms, which I shared briefly on track 4, are again relevant here and worth revisiting: to "understand nationalism," he argues, "we have to understand the practical uses of the category 'nation,' the ways in which it can come to structure perception, to inform thought and experience, [and] to organize discourse and political action" (Brubaker 1996, 7). The nation—"Japan," for my purposes—is best understood as *contingent,* conjured in different ways by differently embedded social actors referencing the same signposting toponym. Exploring the ways that "Kagoshima" and "Japan" intersect in Nagabuchi's music and beyond will help reveal what I call a *provincialized Japan,* a "critical space" (Karatani and Asada 1991) informed by everyday life—its crises and possibilities—and a con-tingent place from which artist and fans scramble dominant national narra-tives and tell stories of some of the realities and possibilities of "Japan" differently. Although "provincialized Japan" is certainly about space and place—Kagoshima, in this case—and the qualitative experiences of Japanese everydayness that unfold there, it's even more about *time,* and Kagoshima's ability to disturb the singular, developmental, "normative" time (Harootunian 2012, 8, 20) underpinning the homogenized and homogenizing narratives of "Japan" that calcified around 1970. Provincialized Japan infects this storytell-ing regime with stories of backwardness and memories of underdevelopment that were never really memories at all, but rather what one fan introduced later calls "nonfiction" stories of everyday Japanese life.

"STANCE": Nagabuchi Tsuyoshi's Musical Storytelling

Nagabuchi hasn't always been a critical musical storyteller. Although critique did animate some of his early work—including "*Tsumetai Gaikokujin* [The

Cold-Hearted Foreigner]," from the 1983 album *HEAVY GAUGE*, which takes on Imperial Japan's infamous Unit 731 and its in vivo biological and chemical weapons testing and production—most of Nagabuchi's earlier recordings were characterized by soaring alto vocals and lyrics that tended to ruminate on questions of love, friendship, and heartbreak. But in the late 1980s, things started to change. From around this moment, Nagabuchi began grappling explicitly and extensively with questions of "home," collectivity, and "Japan." These weren't misty stories of longing for a romanticized "lost home" (such as are conspicuous in *enka*, for example), though—rather, they were piercing, acidic critiques that demanded to know what "Japan" had become, and where it was going.

It's no coincidence that Nagabuchi's critical zenith and the heights of his commercial success can be pinpointed to the end of the 1980s and the early 1990s—the very moment at which Japan's urban-centered bubble economy would run white-hot and eventually burn itself out. What some hailed as the heights of economic "success" alarmed Nagabuchi, spurring him to intense soul-searching over the nature of value and modern "Japanese" priorities, and critical interrogations of what it meant to "be Japanese" in the first place. His music around this moment features searing critiques of consumerism, capitalism, the geopolitics of the Cold War, and more, critiques that were largely afforded, not silenced, by the calcification of capitalism around 1970 (the aforementioned transition from "America's Japan" to "Japan's Japan") and its eventual amplification in the high-bubble economy around 1990. This is when he'd write works like the stadium rocker "*Naite Chinpira* [Cry, Gangster]" (1987), opening track to the album *LICENSE* and a scathing work whose lyrics quote liberally from Kaneko Shōji's critically acclaimed 1983 yakuza film *Ryūji* ("stab him and you end up in prison; get stabbed and you end up in hell," among other citations); it's likely that Nagabuchi was drawn to the romantic "myth … [of yakuza] fighting a rearguard action against the corrupt modern age" (Buruma 1985, 170). In 1990, he wrote the acerbic, blues-tinged "*O-uchi e Kaerō* [Head on Home]," which explicitly eviscerates postwar political economy ("Those forty-somethings born right after the war / went and made some shitty Japanese-style capitalism") and sings of a desire to go and literally "piss on" (*shonben hikkakete*) the National Diet buildings at Nagatachō before "whistl[ing] a tune and head[ing] on home." In 1991, Nagabuchi released the million-selling LP *JAPAN*—the artist tapped the rock-ballad title track of this album to open the aforementioned 2015 concert at the foot of Mount Fuji ("We're just like Persian Gulf seabirds, drenched in thick, black oil; out of breath, and yet, still trying to fly high into the heavens, because we want to find something beyond the wealth"). The first song on the B side of this LP, meanwhile—the sparse yet driving acoustic track "*Oyashirazu* [Wisdom Teeth]"—literally pleads with

"Japan, my homeland" to not "melt into America." "Money? Sure, I want money!" howls Nagabuchi in the work. "But no matter how much we make, no matter how much piles up, there are some things that I just won't give up." These years, in sum, were defining ones for Nagabuchi's musical storytelling, and he wrote prolifically during this moment—even the limited selection of songs I identify earlier could be unpacked far more extensively than I have room to do here. But like Springsteen, who despite having a lengthy and diverse career is probably best-known, fairly or unfairly, for his 1984 hit "Born in the U.S.A.," Nagabuchi's career will forever be linked to his 1988 rock anthem "*Tombo* [The Dragonfly]," later incorporated onto the 1989 LP *Shōwa*.

"*Tombo*" depicts a narrator (as with most of his works, based on Nagabuchi himself) who has left home—Kagoshima, implicitly, based on the direction of travel—and headed "north, ever north," to the "magnificent metropolis" (*hana no miyako*) of Tokyo, logistical and conceptual center of modern Japan (Yano 2002, 19–20) and arbiter of modern, "normative" Japanese time. Once in the capital, however, he finds the city disorienting and anxiety provoking: "With the sound of each footfall as I trudged along the asphalt," the song opens, "I prayed that I could continue to be myself." Surrounded by the sorts of "Tokyo assholes" (*Tōkyō no bakayarō*) that he himself had once "longed to death to become," the narrator wanders barefoot through the cold city, loving and hating it at the same time; he finds solace in drink imbibed in anger, whose effects worm their way into a "self" that seems doomed to be permanently cut in "half" (*hanpa-na ore*). It's a story that would've been familiar to many who made their way to Tokyo in Japan's modern moments, often from rural, marginalized sites like Kagoshima, seeking wealth and success but finding alienation instead (Oguma 2015). Indeed, the song resonated exceedingly well in its moment, as the exuberant, deafening screaming of the lyric eviscerating "Tokyo assholes" by a capacity crowd at Yokohama Arena in 1989, captured on the live recording of Nagabuchi's tour that year, helps make clear.

"*Tombo*" was also the theme song for Tokyo Broadcasting System (TBS)'s 1988 serialized television drama of the same name. Nagabuchi portrayed fictional, warm-hearted yakuza figure Ogawa Eiji in this program, his fifth prominent role in a television series. The song and the series marked an extension of the critical tactics that Nagabuchi began to develop with "*Naite Chinpira*," discussed earlier—indeed, he'd continue deploying this general yakuza persona for several years, until its "romantic outlaw" mystique began to fade (Kingston 2011, 214–215). But while "*Tombo*"—both song and show—is characterized by a seething, "anti-modern" despair, it also rejects the possibility of simply turning around and returning to a supposedly timeless, idyllic *furusato*, or "old home," an impulse that scholars have identified in other modes of storytelling (see, for example, Dodd 2004). Instead, the song busies itself lambasting "self-absorbed" (*shiran kao shita*) residents of the metropolis who just "stand around silently, doing nothing" and calls out the gritty, cold, and altogether discomfiting nature of Japan's capital; a harsh critique from a provincial interloper who evidently has no intention of backing away or going "home" ("but I love this city, even as I hated it, too," he sings in the song). Tokyo, it seems, is stuck with Nagabuchi as much as Nagabuchi is stuck with Tokyo. This unflinching occupation of Tokyo—and of Tokyo-centered notions of "Japan"—by critical voices from the margins is important, and I'll have more to say about it later.

Although "*Tombo*" was released as a single and found enhanced success as the theme song for TBS's primetime drama, it makes most sense when considered as a component track of the *Shōwa* LP. As I explained on track 2, the LP is an important medium for musical storytelling, and "*Tombo*" is preceded on the record by the lesser-known "*Itsuka no Shōnen* [The Sometime Boy]," a ballad that helps frame it. "*Itsuka no Shōnen*" reveals why turning away from Tokyo and taking shelter in an idyllic *furusato* is never an option for Nagabuchi—such a site simply doesn't exist. In this work, Kagoshima is an object of love, but it's also irredeemably marked by poverty, precarity, and pain. "To me, KAGOSHIMA [the city's name appears in Roman letters in the lyrics] was always in tears," "*Itsuka no Shōnen*" begins. It continues:

> It was a weak, unkind, hard-hearted city
> My old man and my ma, covered in mud, clinging jealously to what loose change we had
> And I'd be stuck in the middle, trembling.
>
> The icy winds whistled through our lives
> As the anxieties piled up, in a house that was more like a cage
> I couldn't stand watching the raindrops as they ran along the eaves
> Just wanted to get away, and spent all my time racking my brain to figure out how.

For Nagabuchi, there is no ahistorical, romantic purity in the "old home": unevenness and precarity in Kagoshima are ways of life. This everydayness is blatant and visceral, and to be sure, the material conditions of everyday life there are an important factor fueling Nagabuchi's desire to escape. But although Tokyo is found to be a site of coldness and alienation, there is no possibility of return to a pure, authentic and ahistorical "home" that exists out of time. Rejecting the possibility of running "home," though, is not the same as acquiescing to capital's terms and rejecting the possibility of critique itself—as I described earlier, "shitty Japanese-style capitalism" has been a constant target of Nagabuchi's critical wrath since at least the 1980s. Rather, refusing to run "home" and remaining in Tokyo can be helpfully understood as a way of forcing modern Japan to confront the specter of Kagoshima and the consequences of capitalism that play out there, disturbing capitalism's ideological claim to even development everywhere (Harootunian 2000a, 114–115).

At first glance, this seems to suggest an oppositional relationship between discrete sites that might be understood as "center" and "periphery." Doreen Massey (1994), however, has cautioned that this sort of analytical framework can be misleading and not entirely useful, since sites thus described—Tokyo and Kagoshima, respectively, for my purposes—are in fact always already linked through the social relations comprising the spatial entity of the modern nation-state. "*Itsuka no Shōnen*" and "*Tombo,*" that is, make sense *together,* not opposed, because they posit two geographical sites conjoined—albeit unevenly—by the social relations of capitalism. The crises and unevenness that Nagabuchi stealthily affixes to Tokyo-centric notions of "Japan" via this conjoinment of Kagoshima and the capital disturb the singular authority of the developmental narrative of postwar Japanese "modernity," a disruption that's amplified around the moment of the bubble, "when Japan was at the peak of its economic superpower status [and the] Japanese had their sense of national identity virtually constructed for them by *Nihonjinron* [theories of Japaneseness] writers seeking to explain the reasons for Japan's success" (Henshall 1999, 171). "*Itsuka no Shōnen*" is a different sort of "Japanese" story that challenges this modernization-theory narrative of "success," one that continues in "*Tombo*" (the next track on the LP) and ends in the sort of anxiety and alienation described in its lyrics—in other words, in precisely the same place that "*Itsuka no Shōnen*" started out. As I'll continue to discuss on this track via appeal to other works, Nagabuchi has often insisted on interrogating "Japan" through Kagoshima, embedding it amid the fluid social relations that link the capital and the countryside and dreaming of the possibility that challenging and recalibrating these social relations can lead to Japan's definition according to different terms. It's a tactic that muddies questions of both (developmental) time and place, centering unevenness in considerations of both, and that relies on confronting the material realities of everyday life in Kagoshima and dwelling upon them, not fleeing or trying to overcome them. Indeed, there's something here of Takada Wataru's making present of the materialities of everyday life as political intervention (see track 2)—but in Nagabuchi's case, the aim seems to be to destabilize the stories that "Japan" tells itself about itself and begin to tell them differently. This is the conjuring of "provincialized Japan."

Though the artist himself likely wouldn't put it in these terms, it might be conceptually helpful to consider Nagabuchi's project vis-à-vis Kagoshima in terms of the LP itself, as medium. Provincializing "Japan" involves centering Kagoshima's everydayness as a component track of Japan (not *JAPAN*) as an LP, so to speak—its grooves are inescapable, co-present, co-temporal (yet asynchronous) components making up Japan's modern story. Insisting on Kagoshima's co-presence with Tokyo demands that the album, as it were, be heard as a wider whole—Tokyo-centered narratives of "Japanese" development and backwardness, stories that demand disavowing and overcoming yawning temporal chasms in a quest to catch up with normative time, are disturbed and decentered, and troubled with different rhythms. Put differently—and here I really begin to stretch the metaphor—"Japan" is no longer permitted to make sense as a single; as with "*Tombo*" and "*Itsuka no Shōnen*," the full story can only really be grasped on the LP. On this "album," Kagoshima as site of disavowed unevenness, made to flow into "Japan," *haunts* Japan's story in ways that trouble its dominant developmental narrative and insists on displacing the normative temporality of modern Japan with a precarious, uneven, thoroughly "untimely" time of its own.

The incompleteness declared by the Kagoshima narrator of "*Tombo*" on his arrival to Tokyo—his "halfness" (*hanpa-na*)—is thus productively understood not as a double lack, or a belonging in *neither*, but rather as an ongoing straddling of and dispersal between *both*. The specter of Kagoshima is central to Nagabuchi's musical storytelling about "Japan"—but not as a peripheral site where a purported lost or alternative "national authenticity" still lurks, nor as an idyllic negation of everyday "Japanese" life where capitalist modernity can still be overcome. Rather, it's a key locus of Nagabuchi's critical musical storytelling *precisely because* it's untimely, mired in crisis and precarity—it puts the lie to the prevailing post-1970 narrative that disavowed the specter of unevenness, insisted on the mythology of even development everywhere, and promised the end of history itself (Fukuyama 1992). Kagoshima, that is, despite being inextricably entangled in "Japan" as a spatial entity, doesn't fit "Japan's" modern story—or, perhaps more precisely, fits it all too well. As such, it's a place from which the veracity of that story can be challenged, and different stories told.

Kagoshima

In a 2015 interview with the journal *Bungei* (The Literary Arts), Nagabuchi Tsuyoshi described some of the lived realities of his upbringing in Kagoshima, and how these would go on to impact his musical storytelling:

> Being on the outside [of Tokyo] looking in … this awareness is something that will stick with me my whole life, I think. I was twenty-five when my mother collapsed from illness, bleeding from the guts. "It hurts, it hurts," she'd say, bleeding bright red blood from her belly. By the time I hit my thirties, I found myself wanting to spray her blood all over the city of Tokyo. To me, the red of her blood was the red of the *Hinomaru*, of the

Rising Sun flag. I remember thinking that I wanted to stain [*someru*] everything with that red. Mine was the anger of a country bumpkin [*inaka-mono*], in other words ...

The father and mother who gave me life gave everything they had in the service of their region, of the prefecture, of the state itself. They didn't have any money; my father wasn't able to get ahead in his work because he didn't have much of an education. ... Just what was this thing that was putting my parents through so much pain? When I was looking for something to direct my angry glare towards from the standpoint of my *furusato*, of course the only things that fit the bill were Tokyo, and the state [i.e., "Japan"]. As I sang in my song "*Ouchi he Kaerō*" [discussed earlier], I was filled with this feeling that I just had to go and piss all over the National Diet buildings. I came up to Tokyo driven by the desire to take revenge on those things that had caused us so much pain. And that feeling has not changed in the slightest, right up to this very moment. (Nagabuchi 2015, 49)

Nagabuchi is reflecting here mainly on the conditions of his upbringing in Kagoshima. But these remarks also make clear that the experience of the everyday in Kagoshima can in no way be removed from "Japan" itself, reified, or placed in a relationship of simplified opposition with a national "center." Indeed, in the graphic imagery of his mother's blood, which stands in here for the red of the Japanese flag in a way that complicates a contentious symbol that tends to pop up in Nagabuchi's performance spaces, what appear to be two distinct sites in fact congeal in a relationship that is never discursively stable— oppositional—but made messy by the contingencies of everydayness. As the place at which Nagabuchi (and many of his fans) encounters these contingencies— literally and conceptually—Kagoshima becomes a text through which the nature of "Japan" itself is understood. In a way, Kagoshima constitutes a phantasm here, but not in the sense of constituting a ghostly image of ahistorical authenticity (Ivy 1995)—rather, it harbors the disavowed spirit of nonsynchronous synchronicity (Bloch 1977, 33), an untimely ghost haunting "Japan" that just won't die; an apparition not to be fled, but that can be summoned to spook the sense-making mechanisms of "Japan" itself. Kagoshima doesn't abide in solitude in Nagabuchi's work—as I explained earlier, it's usually situated, explicitly or implicitly, in a web of interconnectivity with "Japan" writ large, disturbing the latter's claims to uniformity (which have run the gamut from "Japan's Japan" around 1970 [Harootunian 1993] to "Japan as Number One" a decade or so later [Vogel 1979] to, more recently and in the wake of economic collapse, "Cool Japan") and serving as a signpost that can help direct the articulation of a practiced space still called "Japan" by social actors, but that nonetheless helps to introduce a productive critical tension between this practiced space of immediacy and the more abstract space of the state (Lefebvre 1991, 88). This tension, and the roots of Nagabuchi's own critical musical storytelling, can be clarified by considering the historicity of Kagoshima itself.

Nagabuchi was born into a Japan defined by the so-called 1955 system, which saw conservative political forces place a stranglehold on power (Dower 1993, 16) and on the authority to tell Japanese stories (Nozaki 2008, 2) that would last far beyond the artist's formative years. This year marked the consolidation of Liberal Democratic Party (LDP) rule and the beginning of the consolidation of "Japan's Japan" under the rubric of so-called high-speed economic growth. But if "Japan" was being steadily patched together according to a preordained narrative of unity under headings of capitalist modernization, development, and "culture" (Kawabata 1969) in this moment, the ways in which the story was playing out in places like Kagoshima were rather different (Haraguchi et al. 2011). Rather than a beginning, 1955 constituted an *end* of sorts for Kagoshima. This year saw the high-water mark for the prefecture's population, which would decline more or less constantly thereafter, part of the general gutting of rural areas in this moment and beyond that can be traced to the flow of people away from the countryside and toward the cities as sellers of labor power. Coming on the heels of massive destruction at and around the end of the Pacific War (93 percent of Kagoshima City was flattened by air raids, and the arrival of two typhoons in quick succession after the surrender wreaked even more havoc), and in the wake of plans drawn up in 1948 to boost prefectural income levels from half of the national average to at least 75 percent by 1953, the sudden onset of what was to be a prolonged population drain came as a shock and has been continually disheartening to prefectural policy makers desperate to effect some form of economic "recovery" (*fukkō*) even decades after the end of the war (depopulation was identified as a key issue facing the prefecture in a discussion I had with a senior Kagoshima official in 2014, for instance). It's instructive that the overcoming of so-called lateness in Kagoshima's Amami Islands and their transference to a Tokyo-centered, universal capitalist time following the chain's repatriation from American Occupation in 1953 constituted a cornerstone of prefectural recovery policy in this period (Haraguchi et al. 2011); it is precisely a foregrounding of this sort of nonsynchronous synchronicity—the "lateness" that prefectural officials sought to overcome—that serves as one key means by which Nagabuchi Tsuyoshi critiques the sense-making mechanisms of contemporary capitalism.

When Tokyo's tune shifted from economic "recovery" to economic "development" (*hatten*) in 1965—Ikeda's post-1960 income-doubling plan, discussed on track 2, was a key component of this policy shift—Kagoshima gamely tried to dance along and instituted its own plans for development. Kanemaru Saburō, who ascended to the governorship of Kagoshima in 1967 and stayed there for the next ten years, took "development" as the keyword of his administration, instigating an array of new projects under the rubric of the Shin-Ōsumi Development Plan. This plan saw the construction of expressways, the building of Kagoshima's new international airport, and so on. But it also called for the establishment of a heavy-chemicals plant on Shibushi Bay, and in light of both supply challenges wrought by the "oil shock" of 1973 and vigorous local opposition decrying the project on environmental grounds, it was ultimately scaled back considerably.

Regardless, however, Kanemaru's plan—and its second phase, which was instigated in 1971 and remained in effect through 1975—did have the effect of raising mean incomes during this period, ultimately to 73 percent of the national average. But the countering effect of accelerating depopulation, aging, and so on—increasingly problematic in this period—meant that spiking individual incomes had little positive effect on the overall economic situation in Kagoshima. Continuing its attempts to navigate the ceaseless crises of capitalism, the prefecture in 1978 enacted the awkwardly named Nukumori ni Michita Idai na Kagoshima Seizō (Constructing a Wondrous Kagoshima Steeped in Warmth) plan as a way of trying to stem the outflow of people from the prefecture by making life there more attractive. This plan, however, was concerned mostly with improvements to economic infrastructure and with flushing the countryside with cash, equating "warmth" with "money." In the name of "regional development," it led directly to the construction in 1984 of the Satsuma-Sendai Nuclear Power Station—the first nuclear plant to be successfully restarted on a full-time basis following the March 2011 meltdowns at Fukushima Dai'ichi and the subsequent shuttering of all plants in Japan. The plants and their positionality in a devil's bargain for economic survival in marginalized sites like Kagoshima (but not only Kagoshima) have been targets of sharp critique, especially after 3.11, and especially by voices cognizant of how they're actually embedded in uneven economic relations between their host communities and elsewhere. In 2012, for example, Nagabuchi himself would famously declare in concert at Kagoshima Arena that "what is generated by those nuclear power plants is not energy. What is generated there is *money*" (Yukawa 2012). Taken in the context of the plants' original construction and the rationale for that construction, this isn't just a criticism of the plants—it's a critique of capitalism itself.

The prefecture's well-intentioned plan had little real effect, and rural depopulation has continued unabated. Kagoshima City, the prefecture's main urban center, constitutes the only jurisdiction to have seen any growth over this period—its population increased 78 percent between 1955, when the drain began, and 1995. And while income has continued to edge up among those who remain in the prefecture, this rate of growth is still not on par with the national average. In 2019, for example, Kagoshima's average prefectural income was eighth lowest in the nation (for reference, Tokyo, Kanagawa, Aichi, and Osaka had incomes exceeding the national monthly average of 307,700 yen; Aomori was lowest at 239,000 yen; and Kagoshima's average was 257,300 yen [Ministry of Health, Labour, and Welfare 2020]), and in 2015 the rate of child poverty in Kagoshima was a staggering 20.6 percent, third worst in the country and surpassing the (equally alarming) national average of 13.8 percent by a considerable margin. Kagoshima's economic challenges, in short, remain dire to this day, and as is also the case in many other peripheral areas of Japan, local officials continue to try to counteract these challenges by playing a never-ending game of catch-up to a developmental, normative "Japanese" time that always seems just out of reach. None of this is new, of course—unevenness is as much at the core of Japan's postwar story as it propels capitalism everywhere. But centered tactically as part of musical storytelling that is committed to grappling with the nature of "Japan," this unevenness helps unsettle stubbornly prevalent Japanese stories of even development everywhere. This centering, along with a tactical refusal to play catch-up with normative, Tokyo-centric "Japanese" time, represents a key component of Nagabuchi's musical storytelling.

Other storytellers working in different moments help frame this approach. Through the construction and positing of Iihatov, for example—a quasifictional realm more or less meant to stand in for far-northeastern Iwate Prefecture—Iwate poet Miyazawa Kenji sought to establish a different framework for approaching questions of nation and locality, city and countryside, and the very logic of capitalist modernization and development itself. According to Long, "Miyazawa was able to use the idea of Iihatov to present an alternative to prominent strains of regional discourse, dominated as they were by talk of economic and political backwardness, and to thus expand the borders of what could and could not be said about the region" (Long 2012, 101). As a statement about a specific place that was made into a narrative field that already privileged a capital-centric, metropolitan discourse, this project carried with it the effect of disturbing Tokyo's claim on the right to be the sole teller of Japanese time: indeed, "critical to the message embodied in the strategy of Iihatov was that no line of sight had the right to claim absolute legitimacy over any other" (Long 2012, 129). The sort of provincializing perspective that attends Iihatov's (i.e., Iwate's) insistence upon speaking to/from its own realities makes Tokyo nothing more than one particular site among others, rendered susceptible to critique and robbed of its purported universality. In other words, by extracting Iihatov entirely from the sense-making mechanisms that privileged a Tokyo-centric, nationalized narrative of development and backwardness, allowing it to transcend both Tokyo and Iwate itself (enmeshed as that place was in Tokyo-centric narratives of understanding) and making it a place "uniquely its own" (Long 2012, 85), Miyazawa's work has helped to point the way toward a "methodology that does not try to tell the local time by setting it apart and below a universal time, but which instead views it as coexisting with other times in a differentiated present" (Long 2012, 33).

Nagabuchi does share with Miyazawa key elements of the latter's regionalizing project. Importantly, he is interested in finding ways to allow Kagoshima to speak for itself, without allowing it to devolve into a site of ahistorical longing for an imagined lost purity, or to be co-opted as an alternative source of authentic "national culture." And crucially, he insists that Kagoshima be allowed to tell a different time—what we might call Kagoshima-time (I'll expand on this later). But Nagabuchi goes about his critical project in markedly different ways. If Miyazawa's Iihatov *transcends* Tokyo-centric narrative and nationalized, commonsense time, essentially becoming one "Japanese" time among many, Nagabuchi ruthlessly *embeds* Kagoshima in the same, disturbing it. Amid the historical context of a Japan thought to have heralded the end of history and the end of critique by the early 1970s, that is (see "Liner Notes" and track 3), Nagabuchi's Kagoshima lurks as a discomfiting reminder of what Harootunian understands as "the specific encounter of time and place, historicality and contemporaneity, between capitalism's expansion and the conditions it generates or confronts" (Harootunian 2012, 18). These contradictions and unevennesses are infused into the graphic spectacles of Nagabuchi's mother's blood staining the metropolis, and of the artist's own urine soaking the Diet buildings at Nagatachō—and the effect is that Nagabuchi's narrative of Kagoshima does not run alongside other "line[s] of sight" (Long 2012, 129), but rather intrudes upon and violates the very commonsense narratives of capitalist development that have anchored "Japan" as concept since around 1970, and that continue, somehow, to supply the monotonous soundtrack to the never-ending quest to escape the very crises that they potentiate. It's a musical storytelling tactic that is impactful precisely because it constitutes a direct incursion on and undermining of prevailing discourse: as Fernandes has pointed out, "[p]eople's lived experiences ... may interject into the narrative in ways that disrupt the power of dominant discourses. Spaces of expression may open up within the text itself" (Fernandes 2017, 12). The different histories that this suggests are posited not through a privileging of Kagoshima as a site of supposed timeless purity, as if it were somehow untouched by the very ravages of capitalism that have given form to the crises of which the artist sings, but rather through attending to the ways in which Kagoshima and Japan are always already conjoined in the social relations of capitalism itself. It is here, in this inmixing of different lines of sight, that politics itself becomes possible (Long 2012, 61).

Nagabuchi's critical, provincializing traversal of the social relations that link Kagoshima and "Japan" plays out in different works in different ways. The ballad "LICENSE," for example—title track to the aforementioned 1987 album—opens with a nod to Kagoshima's celebrated marine vistas but immediately pivots toward a confrontation with the material realities of everyday life there:

> When I was a kid, I really loved the sea.
> The four of us, living in a barracks hut—we were very happy indeed.
> Naked gas spigots, coal-tar walls, half-broken shutters
> And my mother, her back to us in the evening light,
> Always in tears in that alleyway entrance.

The effect of this instantaneous change-up is jarring. The listener's attention is quickly ripped from Kagoshima's famed seascapes and thrust into the alleyways connecting the sparse living quarters provided to Kagoshima's public servants, as the very idea of countryside family happiness crumbles amid visions of poverty and parental despair. There are glimpses here of the harsh conditions of life in Kagoshima that propelled Nagabuchi's critical project, and that are embodied, again, in his parents: his mother "[a]lways in tears," his hardworking father (later in the work) "[f]illed with fury over a life lived only with the best of intentions." More cracked Kagoshima vistas appear—rusted train tracks upon which outdated steam locomotives run, textile factories belching smoke; manifestations of the uneven chronological regime that reigned in Kagoshima (and elsewhere) in support of centralized economic growth. But importantly, Nagabuchi doesn't leave Kagoshima-time and the bodies that it animates there. He brings them to Tokyo.

At the climax of "LICENSE," the song's geographic perspective shifts again, revealing Nagabuchi gazing upon an invisible Kagoshima sea from the veranda of an apartment in a "mildly filthy metropolis," or Tokyo. Of course, at 1,355 kilometers away (by car, keeping with a key theme of the work), Kagoshima cannot actually be seen from Tokyo—Nagabuchi carries it with him, and it continues to abide as a site through which his experiences in the capital are filtered and understood. "LICENSE" concludes, lyrically, with Nagabuchi's mother and father coming to the capital: the artist is "going to Haneda [Tokyo's main domestic airport] to pick them up tomorrow," making use of the driver's license that he's just obtained (the "license" of the song title, and of the album title itself). Now, on one hand, this might be taken simply as a happy family reunion. But recall that Nagabuchi's parents, though "loved to death" in the context of the storytelling that unfurls in the work, are far from posited as a symbol of purity or as embodiment of an idealized home—rather, they have been explicitly invested with the pain of Kagoshima's everyday and have become in this work fleshly manifestations thereof. By (lyrically) bringing the bearers of Kagoshima-time to Tokyo—locus of dominant "national" imagining and avowed object of Nagabuchi's critique—Nagabuchi seems insistent upon troubling the sense-making mechanisms of that center, infecting it with difference, and calling for a confrontation with its presence. And although the effect is probably coincidental, the initially sparse, later soaring instrumentation of "LICENSE" features just one constant throughout—carefully deployed strikes on wooden blocks, or perhaps rim clicks (a percussion technique that generates a clacking sound by striking a drumstick against the rim of a snare drum, rather than on the drawn skin of the drumhead itself), counting out an insistent four-four-time on-beat at roughly sixty beats per minute, and sounding for all the world like the ticking of a clock.

Nagabuchi's critique doesn't rely solely on questions of time—it unfurls in other ways as well, including via appeal to language. "*Kibai Yanse* [Fight It Out]," for example, a lumbering, minor-key shuffle from the aforementioned 1991 album *JAPAN,* is the only work composed by Nagabuchi to feature lyrics written entirely in Kagoshima dialect. While never quite not-Japanese, the lyrical content of this work is still dense to the point of being impenetrable to many beyond Kagoshima, or, at best, beyond Kyushu; the use of dialect here, in other words, is markedly different from benign dialect "signifiers" that are sometimes deployed in literature for the purposes of throwing the reader slightly off-balance but that never really jeopardize her ability to comprehend the story. Nagabuchi, that is, has no apparent interest in making "*Kibai Yanse*" understandable beyond Kagoshima; the work seems composed specifically to challenge what has become Tokyo-centered linguistic "common sense." This meant that for listeners across the country to follow the work—and it's important to remember that, for all his lyrical emphases on Kagoshima, Nagabuchi is a national figure, not a regional one—they had to slip out of their cloak of (linguistic) "Japaneseness" and engage with its lyrical storytelling on Nagabuchi's own, provincialized terms. Included as a track on an album titled *JAPAN,* "*Kibai Yanse*" seems designed to challenge the authority of *kokugo*—national language—that had rested at the center of Tokyo-centric nation-state building and time telling (Lee 2009; Anderson 1983, 26) since the Meiji period (1868–1912), an authority that is still appealed to in granting access to—and policing—notions of "authentic" national interiority (I discuss how gatekeepers of *enka* assume this role of policing language and/as "Japanese" interiority on track 4). And with lyrics that cry "[y]ou and I are the impure ones [*yogoremon*], after all / but still, even we have those things that we can't compromise / [...] If you really can't abide that shithead [*yatsu*] / then just knock him down," delivered in a Kagoshima dialect version of the guttural Ogawa Eiji growl that had come to define the grain of the artist's voice by 1991, Nagabuchi uses "*Kibai Yanse*" to develop what Pascale Casanova (2004) calls "strategies ... of differentiation," deploying his musical storytelling in ways that challenge not only "Japanese" linguistic norms but social ones as well.

But "*Kagoshima Chūō STATION*," from the 2007 album *Come on Stand Up!*, might constitute the best example of the provincializing, reimaginative critical musical storytelling that I'm describing here. Conceptually anchored by JR (Japan Railways) Kyushu's shiny, steel-and-glass Kagoshima Chūō terminal, which was until 2004 the smaller, rather decrepit Nishi-Kagoshima Station, the work's opening stanza explicitly sings of being "caught in a time slip." The song's droning refrain—"my home town, my home town," sung in English—and the harsh, Waits-esque vocals are set atop an instrumental track that features intermittent incursions by banjo and harmonica, an apparent reference to Nagabuchi's early days as a "folk" singer. Rhythmic shouting and metallic banging punctuate the work throughout its seven-minute duration; this may reference local festivals (a strategy that Nagabuchi, who references Kagoshima's Ohara Festival in his rousing "*SAKURAJIMA*," has used before)—or it might recall harsh physical labor and the struggles that the artist associates with his youth. And all of it, of course, is remixed using modern recording technology, in a song meant to speak to local realities in 2007. "*Kagoshima Chūō STATION*," in short, has the effect of evoking a time that is rather uncertain, and certainly not in step with linear, normative temporality. But the point is not to call for a return to the past, to urge reclamation of a site of purity that never existed in the first place, an antidote to capitalist modernity. Rather, the overall effect is to position Kagoshima rather unsteadily within the developmental temporal regime whose encroachment is announced by the arrival of the *shinkansen* (bullet train)—the place amounts to a watch that can't keep time, a warped gear in the clock. Malfunctional (irredeemably late) or not, though, Kagoshima's enhanced incorporation into the network of social relations that comprise "Japan" (Massey 1994)—given form here as train tracks—means that it's not simply a passive node in that network, but an active one as well; not just a destination, but a point of departure from which "Japan" might be thought differently.

Kagoshima Chūō Station—the station itself—opened in 2004, when the first section of the *shinkansen* line that would eventually link Kagoshima to Tokyo via terminals at Hakata (Fukuoka) and Osaka began operations (the line was completed in 2011). The link itself is not new—indeed, Nagabuchi sings in the work of his own departure for Tokyo from Nishi-Kagoshima Station decades earlier, deploying rhythmic onomatopoeia ("*gatagata chūchū*") to depict a lumbering, clumsy sort of rail travel that is far less sleek and stylish than contemporary *shinkansen* travel is. But the arrival of the *shinkansen* and the shiny new station, along with the attendant morphing of the downtown core (also described in the lyrics), seems to portend something different, something alarming—the impending loss of Kagoshima's ability to tell its own time. As Nagabuchi sings in this work, "the sad steam whistle of the trains" that once clattered into JR Kyushu's Nishi-Kagoshima Station seem much more suited to

Kagoshima—the artist can hear their sorrowful refrains "even now," but the suggestion is that others no longer can. It is this spiraling erosion of Kagoshima's (untimely) specificity that seems to ignite Nagabuchi's critical targeting of Kagoshima Chūō—but as with *"Kibai Yanse,"* the story that he tells here likely isn't meant to resonate in Kagoshima alone.

In the chorus of *"Kagoshima Chūō STATION,"* Nagabuchi bellows:

> Hey, wasn't my Kagoshima a backwater [*inaka*]?!

Inaka, like "backwater," is a mostly derogatory term, taken to imply untimeliness, backwardness, and a hopeless sort of *un-rhythmicality,* a being-out-of-step with the times. Importantly, *inaka* can never be an a priori condition: *inaka* and the purported backwardness that attends it can only be forged in conditions of modernity itself, through a contrast to a universalized, developmental, "normative time." Indeed, it's been escape from conditions of *inaka*-ness that has so preoccupied Kagoshima's bureaucrats in their attempts to "catch up" to national, "Japanese" time. Ivy (1995) argues that *inaka* is the locus of "vanishing"—it's a remainder of modernity that becomes a site at which the disaffected might try their hand at uncovering a "true" Japan that exists outside of history itself. But by virtue of positing the *inaka* as a remainder, a sandbar amid encroaching waters that is sure to vanish eventually, this perspective can paradoxically serve to validate capitalist modernity's own claims to universality, privileging a singular line of sight and way of telling time that flows from the metropole and that can be fled and overcome (Harootunian 2000b, 305–328) only through universalizing appeals to an imagined a priori, more "authentic" Japan that somehow exists *outside* of time altogether.

Nagabuchi's critique is rather different. Rather than fleeing modernity, or striving to overcome it, he challenges "shitty Japanese-style capitalism's" claims to common sense by foregrounding the crises and contradictions of Kagoshima's everyday and making them part of "Japan's" story. Kagoshima as *inaka* is explicitly not a place of ahistorical beauty and purity for Nagabuchi—his enduring love for the prefecture and the city notwithstanding, he has no interest in fleeing there, or sealing it off from "Japan" writ large. Indeed, as the artist's insistence on the train motif and lyrical depictions of his own shuttling back and forth between Kagoshima and Tokyo indicate, ensuring that Kagoshima is *not* isolated from Tokyo seems pivotal to his critical project—the sense-making mechanisms of Tokyo-centered national narratives can be disturbed only, it would seem, if they can be accessed, occupied, troubled, by the incursion of different bodies and other stories (recall here that, in the interview with the journal *Bungei* discussed earlier, Nagabuchi explicitly characterized the fury that has propelled so much of his critical work as "the anger of a country bumpkin," or *inaka-mono*). The railway is thus not merely, or even mainly, an object of anti-modernist suspicion and critique in this work—as a means of literally shuttling stories from place to place, it's also indispensable in facilitating Nagabuchi's broader critical project.

In the 1970s, advertising giant Dentsū joined forces with Japan Railways to engineer the so-called Discover Japan Campaign, a domestic rail travel initiative that encouraged sojourns to some of Japan's outlying (non-Tokyo) regions and that purportedly reflected "a generation's desire to escape to its origins" (Ivy 1995, 34). In her influential *Discourses of the Vanishing*, Ivy describes how the desire to travel and "find Japan" took as its premise an assumption that the traveler was not in Japan at all—or more specifically, was not in the correct/ authentic "Japan." The varied itineraries of the campaign faithfully delivered rail riders to a "Japan" that was a locus of (recuperable) loss, one with an essence that could be scooped up and brought back to bolster a better, more authentic national culture. The *inaka* in this formulation abides as a reservoir of restorative nostalgia (Boym 2001), a phantasm of purity that never really existed in the first place but which, as a spatialized time-out-of-time and transcendent repository of value, could be tapped as a "disciplinary apparatus ... for producing individuated Japanese subjects" (Ivy 1995, 41). "Japan" in this formulation becomes a closed question, rather than an open one, with very little room for critical interrogation or reimagination—it simply awaits "discovery" and (re) affirmation en route.

Rails thus imagined, though, only go one way. Even when the locomotives and carriages have reached their destinations and returned, their journey is oddly unidirectional, tracing a preordained closed loop: they only ever reach sites of purported authentic "national culture" on the margins as predeparture loci of desire and carry nothing more than amplified versions thereof in their luggage racks when they come "home." But in Nagabuchi's musical storytelling, Kagoshima isn't just an arrival point from the capital, nor is it simply a waypoint on circular itineraries such as those imagined by Dentsū and Japan Railways, which departed a not-yet-completed "Japan" but returned to fulfill it by virtue of bringing back the authentic Culture found along the way. It's also a departure point of its own, from which critical, discomfiting stories of what it means to "be Japanese" can embark and occupy points north, feeding back into and troubling the integrity of already completed narratives authored in the capital. Boym insists that "cultural memory," such as that signified by headers like "Japan," is never singular, or easily tamed: indeed, "everyday frameworks of collective or cultural memory offer us mere signposts for individual reminiscences that could suggest multiple narratives" (Boym 2001, 53). In the work of Nagabuchi Tsuyoshi, Kagoshima-time underwrites narratives that disturb homogenized, homogenizing stories of "Japan," forcing them to accommodate different possibilities and perspectives. In *"Kagoshima Chūō STATION"* in particular, Kagoshima is a "Japanese" departure point, to be sure, but one whose untimeliness authorizes narrative journeys that challenge self-fulfilling prophecies of History and returns signal interference that threatens to scramble Japanese normative temporality. If Nagabuchi could have his way, if Kagoshima-time could be shouted above the clack and din of arriving *shinkansen* and given its own Tokyo-bound seat, then the *inaka* that makes its way back northeast on the rails—as the artist himself did in 1978—would no longer announce "Japan's" own totalizing authenticity to itself. Rather, by foregrounding the crises, unevenness, and untimeliness of a provincialized Japan, it would announce the very impossibility thereof and demand that "Japan" be thought differently—though not discarded altogether.

In *"Kagoshima Chūō STATION,"* Nagabuchi is haunted by terrifying visions of the encroachment of Tokyo-centered capitalist modernity on Kagoshima. "That had better not," he growls, "be cash and rotting cadavers that I see bobbing on the surface of Kinkō Bay!!" But the resolution to this danger doesn't lie in sidestepping it and taking shelter in a romanticized local Culture: rather, the solution seems to ride on direct confrontation, on an insistence upon continuing the project that the artist started in "LICENSE," one that involves counting out Kagoshima's own uneven, crisis-ridden, thoroughly precarious time. "Go ride your Ferris wheel, and drink your Starbucks coffee [two new features of Kagoshima Chūō Station]," Nagabuchi sings at the end of the song in an uncharacteristically high and somehow mocking register. "And then"—now harsh, guttural, leather-throated Nagabuchi is back—"show them what a country bumpkin [*inaka-mono*] is made of!!"

As Nagabuchi's "Kagoshima songs" help attest, the historicity of Kagoshima is the ongoing history of precarity itself. Kagoshima as locus of everydayness and Nagabuchi's own experiences growing up there have helped afford the artist's critical stances on the world, which in turn manifest in his musical storytelling. Like Miyazawa's Iihatov, Nagabuchi's Kagoshima provides an important rhetorical means through which the artist can generate and articulate his critique, precisely because it is never isolated and is always connected to "Japan" itself. But these critiques, taking as they do the form of mass-produced, widely distributed musical texts, are never a merely personal project on the part of the artist. It's the nature of Nagabuchi's work as a best-selling musician that these texts should go out into the world and circulate among individual actors making their lives therein. Social actors with a stake in Kagoshima—be that stake physical, or, as I'll discuss later, conceptual—tap these circulating texts in ways that help them navigate and tell the stories of their own lives. On the latter half of this track, I explore some of the ways that fans of the artist make use of Nagabuchi's music and his focus on Kagoshima, and some of the different things this helps to afford. Engagement with Nagabuchi's music, his critiques, and his calls for what might be best termed a critical Japanese solidarity (Nikkan Sports 2015) help these social actors develop and articulate their own critical stances on "Japan" and on everyday life there, rendering them singers of the Homesick Blues as well.

The Ougoukai: Musical Storytelling among Fans

To this point, I've considered some of the ways that Nagabuchi Tsuyoshi uses music to tell stories of his own life, of Kagoshima, and of "Japan." Equally important, though, are the ways that social actors (i.e., fans) tap Nagabuchi's musical storytelling to spin up stories of their own. Spending time with a private, "unofficial" Nagabuchi Tsuyoshi fan organization called the Zenkoku Sakurajima Ougoukai (which translates rather awkwardly as the "National Sakurajima Cherry Blossom and Tsuyoshi Society"—I refer to it hereinafter simply as the Ougoukai) has helped me explore these questions. The Ougoukai was founded by a pair of Nagabuchi fans in Kyushu in 2011. It's built mostly around an online platform situated on Facebook and on the Japanese social media network LINE, although members also frequently gather for concerts, regional social events, and occasional charity work (the group facilitated fundraising for Tōhoku following the crises of 3.11, for example, and organized the distribution of supplies to Kumamoto following a major earthquake there in 2016). The organization's membership was originally comprised of just a few dozen people, but Ougoukai cofounder Yūji—whom I'll return to later—told me in 2014 that it then numbered around 400 nationwide. As of this writing and in the context of the ongoing SARS-CoV-2 pandemic, which has devastated live performance and opportunities for in-person gathering, it's decreased slightly to 325. In September 2014, I reached out to the Ougoukai via Facebook and connected with the group's executive, eventually meeting with Yūji— though only after, I'd later learn, much internal concern over the intentions of the Canadian interloper and debate over the degree to which I was to be accommodated. Later, through attending concerts and Ougoukai gatherings and via introductions extended to me by the group's executive, I developed connections with rank-and-file membership as well. My discussions with these individuals (I've assigned them pseudonyms herein, based mostly on characters in Nagabuchi Tsuyoshi songs) were highly revealing. They shared with me thoughtful, critical stances on the world afforded by their engagement with music and with one another, making them "philosophers" in their own right (Cavicchi 1998, 185). And although it's national in scale, the group's very name already reveals a conceptual positioning in Kagoshima, and thus a nod to the centrality of that site in Nagabuchi's musical storytelling—as I mentioned earlier, Sakurajima is the iconic volcanic island (actually a peninsula) that sits across Kinkō Bay from Kagoshima City, and that was the site of Nagabuchi's first all-night concert in 2004.

Nagabuchi's fan communities are diverse and can't be pigeonholed according to age, class, or even nationality. Still, as I'll discuss later, Ougoukai members tend to share considerable precarity in their everyday lives, and the intelligent, engaged critiques they develop—usually with reference to the ways in which Nagabuchi's music echoes, or is made to echo, in the context of those lives—reflect this. The principal desire uniting the group is the desire for *nakama*—camaraderie, belonging, organic collectivity, critical solidarity, "home" in its own right (I briefly explore the intersectionality between *nakama* and musicking on track 4 as well, in the contexts of *enka* fandom and musical storytelling). The group's "motto," in fact—displayed prominently on the backs of the T-shirts, jackets, and other "gear" the Ougoukai has created to lend itself a sense of cohesiveness—is *Hontō no nakama wa koko ni iru:* "This is where true camaraderie lives." It's a lyrical snippet from a Nagabuchi song titled "*Kamashitare!* [Go Get 'Em!]," from the aptly titled 2009 album *FRIENDS*. But it also dovetails with Nagabuchi's own aforementioned quest for solidarity, and with his critique of the alienating, anxiety-provoking effects of capitalist modernity and its penchant for undermining organic collectivity—"true camaraderie." Of course, the endpoint for the sort of quest for organic collectivity that precarity itself provokes can be—and has been—fascism itself (Žižek and Herscher 1997). But it doesn't have to be. In the same way that Nagabuchi confronts the crises of capitalism head-on, amplifying them in order to reveal the historicity of "Japan" and thus opening up ground for imagining its possibilities differently, the precarious lives of the Ougoukai members I spoke with tend to kindle desires that aren't about flight into an idealized past, but that rather involve a thoroughgoing grappling with the terms and conditions of the present in order to imagine and tell their own stories in various ways. And as it does for Nagabuchi himself, Kagoshima plays an important role here, both as a lived site where the material conditions of everydayness are revealed, and as a conceptual nexus for articulating political possibilities and imagining "Japanese" life differently.

In my very first meeting with him at Kagoshima's international airport café in 2014, Yūji made a comment that has stayed with me throughout this research. "We don't do this [engage in fandom, attend concerts, develop fan camaraderie] for Tsuyoshi-san's benefit, you know," he said. "We do it for ourselves." The uniforms, banners, flags, and memorabilia that the group deploys as a central part of its identity—both at concert sites, where the membership revels in its visibility and organizes cleanups of the areas surrounding the

Figure 5.1 Ougoukai members from across Japan, with flags and banners bearing the names of their home chapters, gather in Fumotoppara, Shizuoka Prefecture, for Nagabuchi Tsuyoshi's all-night concert at the foot of Mount Fuji on August 22, 2015. Photo courtesy of Tobita Masakuni.

venues, and in the members' own private homes—help show that fandom for the Ougoukai affords what Kelly has aptly called "vortices of self-fashioning" (2004, 7). But there's more to it than this. Engagement with Nagabuchi's music on the part of social actors embedded in the specific contexts of capitalist and geopolitical precarities helps the members survive the often-treacherous conditions of their everyday lives, and often affords a political stance upon the world that becomes articulable as a result of this engagement. Though each of the individuals introduced later taps Nagabuchi's musical storytelling differently, a common thread can nonetheless be identified herein in that each, in her own way, locates in Kagoshima the potential for *difference*—but, crucially, a potential that is never divorced from "Japan" itself. While Kagoshima must not be romanticized as a site of ahistorical purity or authenticity—such a move would run counter to Nagabuchi's project anyway—its positionality on the margins of "Japan's Japan" nonetheless renders Kagoshima an intriguing physical and conceptual site of critique, one at which precarity, and perceived alternatives to precarity, afford alternative visions of belonging that seem to seek neither to negate "Japan" nor to revivify absent phantoms of the past, but rather to *reimagine* it.

The concept of the *music event* is once again important here, as it has been in different ways throughout this book. It helps reveal how music and social actors are tied together in ways that can never be isolated from history, politics, and context, and affords an analytical paradigm shift "from what music depicts … to what it makes possible"—in other words, how it's *used* (DeNora 2003, 46).

What this framework calls for is attention to contextually specific circumstance, and the ways that music is deployed and takes on significance in lives lived therein—this can often be private, but its ramifications are anything but (Jackson 2013, 15). In what follows, I appeal to this analytical framework one last time to help me consider the deployment of Nagabuchi Tsuyoshi's music in the lives of individual social actors, and its implications for everyday "Japanese" life. As I'll show, the members of the Ougoukai tap Nagabuchi's music both to make sense of some of the terms and conditions of everyday life and to imagine them differently. Their contextually specific encounters with the music allow them to emerge as musical storytellers in their own right, as singers of the Homesick Blues, even though they may never play (or sing) a note.

Yūji

Yūji, the founding member of the Ougoukai introduced briefly earlier, lives not far from Kagoshima City, in a modest apartment building occupying a piece of land between the rocky outcroppings of coastline that look south over Kinkō Bay to one side, and the high plateaus that are home to Kagoshima's international airport on the other. He was the first representative of the group with whom I had contact, and after several informal chats I've returned to Kagoshima to delve more deeply into what Nagabuchi Tsuyoshi, his artistry, and the Ougoukai mean to him.

The terms of Yūji's life have not been easy. He was divorced at twenty-seven, and his former spouse disappeared with their children, only to suddenly return them when she discovered that she couldn't bear the stresses of child-rearing. Though trained as a chef—our discussion took place over an incredible feast of traditional Kagoshima cuisine that he'd prepared—lack of employment opportunities in Kagoshima and the need to provide for his small family saw him working at a confectionery assembly facility ("They didn't provide us with so much as a fan at that place, let alone AC," he recalls, describing particularly harsh conditions of work during Kagoshima's stifling summers), and in 2014 he was working as a "replacement driver" (daikō), shuttling cars on behalf of individuals who'd had too much to drink. Yūji's first real encounter with Nagabuchi's music was many years prior, when a friend with an extra ticket to the artist's 1995 *Itsuka no Shōnen* tour invited him to tag along—he recalled being "floored" by the experience and enraptured by Nagabuchi's critical musical storytelling. At the time of our chat, however, it had been only recently that he'd been able to indulge his love for Nagabuchi's music and persona through attending concerts, purchasing DVDs, and building relationships with fellow fans. "Until my kid was in high school, I just didn't have the wherewithal to get into [fandom]," he said. "Prior to that, it was work first, children first. I didn't have time for friends."

For Yūji, Nagabuchi's music has been an elixir deployed amid challenging and precarious conditions of everyday life. Engaging with it has been a way for him to build courage, to prop himself up when issues at work leave him feeling down and deflated (*hekotaeteru*). Asked directly if Nagabuchi's artistry had had a direct impact on how he lives his life, Yūji's answer was a resounding "yes." Nagabuchi isn't the only artist that Yūji listens to—he's also a fan of groups like the early visual-kei act SharanQ, and of pop-rock duo Dreams Come True. But the undergirding of his affinity for these acts is quite different from the importance that he places on Nagabuchi. "Those bands are happy, feel-good bands," he says. "For me, Nagabuchi's music isn't really about getting 'happy'; it's more about getting courage and strength when life gets me down." Yūji's comment here reflected something that I'd hear again and again from Nagabuchi's fans in the course of my research: conditions of precarity and struggle often constitute vital backdrops for many fans' appreciation for, and even reliance upon, Nagabuchi's music, and many reported that "getting courage and strength" was a key factor drawing them to it.

Although his "favorite" song changes according to his own lived circumstances, Yūji identified Nagabuchi's ballad "*Karasu* [Crows]," from the 1990 album *JEEP*, as a work that holds particular, consistent significance for him. It's a revealing choice. "*Karasu*" is a bitter, biting work about the nearly, but not yet totally, futile effort to forestall being swept along in the money-centered terms of capitalist survival ("Our destination isn't preordained to be the darkness," Nagabuchi sings in the chorus, "but oh, when I see the sunset, it does make me cry"). These are conditions that defined the apex of the bubble economy around 1990— Nagabuchi's critical heyday, as mentioned earlier—but that remain resonant well into the so-called lost decades, and, as the conditions of Yūji's life help show, not just in the metropolises of Tokyo and Osaka. "*Karasu*" satirizes the choices that "we" (*oretachi*) make in modern, urbanized Japan, "making our murders" in the cities just as crows do (crows are widely reviled in Japan as both consumers and strewers of trash), and eviscerates a "we" that is subservient to "money, always money" (*zeni da, zeni*) and the resultant prioritizing of economic prerogatives over community and collectivity. The life of the crow in this work is a lonely one, irredeemably urbanized, fundamentally alienated both from others and from its natural habitat. Though not a resident of the big city—Tokyo, implicitly, in this work; as I've already described, the capital is a frequent target of Nagabuchi's wrath—the significance that Yūji finds in "*Karasu*" seems linked to his ability to tap the work as a means of framing and narrating some of his own experiences navigating capitalist modernity. He becomes a musical storyteller in his own right, that is, by telling his story with appeal to Nagabuchi's voice.

The story that Yūji wanted to tell cited his own experiences with underemployment in relatively impoverished Kagoshima, harsh working conditions where employment was available, and so on. But he also expressed alarm over the subjugation/sacrifice of Kagoshima's renowned natural beauty in the name of playing a game of economic catch-up to normative Japanese time (recall here Kanemaru's development plan, discussed earlier; Yūji specifically objected to ongoing heavy construction in Kagoshima Bay and what he saw as environmental "exploitation" in our discussion). This, however, doesn't amount to placing "Kagoshima" and "Japan" (or "Tokyo") in opposition. Rather, Kagoshima is a Japanese site where specific consequences of national economic policy unfurl. To be sure, Yūji attaches great significance to the fact that Nagabuchi hails from Kagoshima: "If he didn't," says Yūji, "I likely wouldn't have gotten this passionate about the music." But he also rejects the idea that Nagabuchi could ever be solely "our [i.e., Kagoshima's] hero," seeing the artist as a national figure from Kagoshima who is attempting to spur change in Japan more broadly. "If Abe Shinzō [prime minister at the time of our conversation] would just listen to Nagabuchi's music," he said, sighing, "then things would be different." Indeed, it's precisely as the purported boundaries between "local" and "national" are blurred—as Kagoshima emerges in Nagabuchi's musical storytelling in ways that challenge Tokyo-centered claims to the sole right to tell Japanese time—that the storytelling of contextually embedded fans like Yūji becomes *political,* even though he doesn't describe it (or Nagabuchi's musical storytelling, for that matter) in those terms.

Yūji is deeply invested in the concept of *nakama* (camaraderie), the principle upon which the Ougoukai itself is founded. His modest apartment is filled with pictures, concert towels, and other mementos of connections established with like-minded fans from across Kyushu and around Japan. "If this group [the Ougoukai] disappeared," he says, "I'd be really lonesome. All this stuff—it provides a connection with other members across the country. If I lost that, I'd lose the feeling of being plugged in [*tsunagari*]." This feeling of "being plugged in" is afforded by a shared love of the music, but also through shared appreciation for Nagabuchi's sharp critiques of capitalism and/as alienation in works like "*Karasu*" (this work was a favorite of other fans as well). For Yūji and others, that is, Nagabuchi's musical storytelling both reveals the conditions that threaten to undermine *nakama*—and affords different means for bolstering it. As the privileging of the Japanese flag by the Ougoukai helps demonstrate—these are often creatively desecrated (Welch 2000) to bear the name of the local chapter—this critical solidarity orbits around the discourses of (provincialized) "Japan" that Nagabuchi centers in his art. There is, of course, a danger in de-emphasizing the individual in the interest of collective understandings of belonging (Tansman 2009, 254–267), just as there's a danger in flirting with markers of exclusionary nationalism. But Yūji helps point in a different direction—toward a critical solidarity (*nakama*) that is destabilizing and reimaginative even as it continues to be known as "Japan."

Iwashi and Masako

Nagabuchi fandom tends to run in families; it's common to find parents with children in tow in attendance at concerts, for example. Iwashi and Masako are one such parent-child unit. Although Masako lives on her own in Kagoshima City, away from the family home in Satsuma-Sendai, they maintain a close bond through their shared love of the music, attending local concerts and traveling together to shows held as far away as Fumotoppara, in Shizuoka Prefecture, site of Nagabuchi's 2015 Mount Fuji concert. After meeting and chatting with Iwashi and Masako informally several times in both Kagoshima and at Fumotoppara, I had the chance to sit down with them at a coffee shop in Kagoshima in autumn 2015 to delve more deeply into how they deploy Nagabuchi's music to understand and navigate their own lives and circumstances.

Iwashi works in livestock, raising some of Japan's most prized cattle for consumption as extravagantly priced beef nationwide. As a lifelong Nagabuchi fan who happens to bear a striking physical resemblance to the artist, Iwashi also moonlights as a *monomane* (tribute) performer, mounting live performances that are crafted to resemble Nagabuchi's own as closely as possible. Iwashi is his stage name, shortened from Nagabuchi Iwashi, which in turn developed from "*Nagabuchi to iwashitai*," or "I want [to be so good that I'm able] to make people call me 'Nagabuchi.'" Nagabuchi's art and persona thus take on a level of embeddedness in Iwashi's life that is probably unparalleled among the other individuals I spoke with. For Iwashi, Nagabuchi and his music are nothing short of what he called "*mokuhyō*" (purpose, objective), on both a personal and professional level.

With her father so committed to Nagabuchi's music, it's unsurprising that Masako grew up steeped in it, too. Today she simply calls it "*nakute ha naranai mono*" (something that I couldn't do without). A shy young woman then in her late teens, Masako defies the stereotypical image often associated with Nagabuchi fans: male, somewhere around forty, vaguely "frightening" due to the prevalence of dyed hair, piercings, sunglasses, or other accessories of Nagabuchi fandom (these are often regarded in Japan with some degree of distaste, especially away from the larger centers). She recalls growing up with Nagabuchi's music playing constantly at home, in the car, and so on. "I went to my first concert when I was in grade six; I think I've been six or seven times since then," she says. "I can remember how his music would always be playing in the car when my dad would come and pick me up from kindergarten; for a long time I thought that 'music' was just 'Nagabuchi Tsuyoshi.'" Asked to identify her favorite Nagabuchi songs, she responds with what might be expected of a more youthful outlook: "'*Natsumatsuri* [Summer Festivals]'" and '*Junrenka*' [two older, "folk"-tinged works that forefront the artist's acoustic fingerpicking skills]. The guitar work is just so *cool!*" But it doesn't take her long to pick up a thread that runs consistently through other fans' engagement with the music—that of its deployment as an elixir amid the stresses of everyday life. "I turn the music on when I'm just mentally exhausted," she says, "and it picks me up." Specifically, she identifies Nagabuchi's 1990 "*Nishi-Shinjuku no Oyaji no Uta* [Song for the Old Man from West Shinjuku]," a fan favorite, as her go-to work—its refrain of "*yaru nara ima shika nee*" (if you're gonna do it, you've gotta do it now), she says, is the phrase that helps to pull her through.

Iwashi also discussed how he uses Nagabuchi's music to put himself into energized mental, emotional, and physical states—particularly ahead of *mono-mane* performances—and how incorporating specific lyrical snippets (such as "*mada mada misuteta monja nai ze*" [I'm not worthless yet!], from the 1985 arena anthem and fan favorite "*Ashita he Mukatte* [Head for Tomorrow]") into the stories he tells himself about himself helps to restore a feeling of confidence. Such deployment of Nagabuchi's music as an elixir in individual circumstance is by now a familiar refrain; indeed, DeNora (2000, 93–96) has noted similar uses of music among aerobics practitioners. What was perhaps more remarkable was the speed and ease with which both Iwashi and Masako shifted registers from the personal to the political (as if the two could ever be meaningfully separated anyway). Songs they identified as go-to favorites were particularly biting in their critique. The aforementioned "JAPAN," the hard-rocking "*Ashita wo Kudasee* [Gimme a Tomorrow]" from the 2012 album *Stay Alive*, with lyrics that demand fair remuneration for work, sufficient sleep, and other "luxuries" and that grieve being exposed to the "black rain that falls under the American umbrella," and "*Fuji-no-Kuni* [The Fuji Nation]"—written as alarm over Abe's so-called war bills was coming to a head ("There is no nation that can stand on a foundation of violence," the lyrics insist)—were all singled out for special mention, and all targeted national prerogatives. History, as always, is important here. Our discussion took place in the highly politicized moment of 2015, and both father and daughter voiced distress over the "reinterpretation" of Japan's security relationship with the United States (so-called collective self-defense) that lay behind Abe's "war bills." This reinterpretation was understood by both as constituting an erosion of, as opposed to the official state line claiming an enhancement for, Japan's peace and security: "Whatever happens, I don't want to see Japan go to war [*sensō dake ha shite hoshikunai*]," Iwashi said. Both Iwashi and Masako, in short, articulated political stances that were deeply intertwined with the music they love.

"There are things wrong with this country," Iwashi said quietly, early on in our discussion. "Japan as a political entity needs to be criticized." Importantly, both Iwashi and Masako relied upon citations of individual Nagabuchi songs and snippets of lyrics to express this criticism. In addition to the works identified earlier, they cited songs like the 2004 single "*Shizuka-naru Afugan* [Quiet in Afghanistan]," which eviscerates the American-led war in Afghanistan and Japan's support for it and was effectively banned from Japanese radio for its lyrical characterization of Osama bin Laden as an "American-grown terrorist," and the aforementioned "*Oyashirazu* [Wisdom Teeth]," which exhorts Japan not to become a lackey for U.S. priorities, to frame and articulate their specific dismay over the potential for war and their desire for enduring peace. Nagabuchi's critical interventions, that is, became key means by which critical sentiment on the part of both Iwashi and Masako could be articulated, allowing them to tell critical stories of "Japan" to each other and to themselves. One crucial key to being able to enunciate that critique seemed to lie in the ways in which Nagabuchi and his artistry link Kagoshima and "Japan."

Asked if Nagabuchi Tsuyoshi was a Kagoshima singer or a "Japan" singer, both father and daughter answered instantly that he was the latter. At the same time, however, both declared that the fact that the artist hailed from Kagoshima held special significance for them: Iwashi, for example, lauded the artist as "the pride of Kagoshima," while Masako described how she once hated the fact that she was from a "backward, countryside [*inaka*]" place like Kagoshima but eventually came to possess a deep pride in her home precisely because "it could give rise to someone like Nagabuchi Tsuyoshi." Kagoshima, then, is of great importance to both. But importantly, it is the *qualitative* nature of that shared home and history, not the mere fact thereof, that seems to open key pathways for critiquing "Japan as a political entity." Although Nagabuchi's critical story-telling makes sense to Iwashi and Masako on a number of levels, particularly important here is their association with a place that is entangled in Japanese economic and energy prerogatives, and the ways that this entanglement challenges some of the stories that Japan tells itself about itself, setting the stage for broader critical interrogation.

Iwashi and Masako hail from Satsuma-Sendai, home to the Satsuma-Sendai Nuclear Power Station. Iwashi, working as he does in livestock farming in the very shadow of this facility, is particularly leery of its presence. Nagabuchi, for his part, is vociferously opposed to nuclear power, a key cornerstone of Japanese economic and energy policy, in no small part due to its prominence as a dangerous means of economic "survival" in Kagoshima Prefecture. As I have argued elsewhere (Aalgaard 2017), Nagabuchi's evisceration of nuclear power is part and parcel of a longer critique of the developmental "fixed terms" of a Japan in which capitalism trumps human relations, profit-seeking trumps concern for the natural environment, and so on. This critique, in turn, is built in part out of a confrontation with the ways that places like Kagoshima both reveal and continue to be mired in histories of crisis and unevenness. Though Iwashi's own circumstances are relatively lucrative—Kagoshima and Miyazaki beef are in high demand as luxury items across much of Japan—the fact remains that he and Masako remain surrounded by relative poverty in Satsuma-Sendai; he describes his home region as *sabireteru* (literally "rusted out," indicating decayed, decrepit, falling apart and behind), in addition to being constantly subjected to the threat of catastrophe as a nuclear sacrifice zone. This reality, flying in the face of the promises that hosting nuclear plants would help rural, marginalized areas like Kagoshima and Fukushima "catch up" to normative Japanese time, further reveals the fallacy of "shitty Japanese capitalism"—the key object of Nagabuchi's critique—and its promises of even development everywhere. Iwashi's (and Masako's) ability to comprehend and adopt Nagabuchi's critical musical storytelling writ large, that is, seems anchored in the specific conditions and anxieties of their own life in Kagoshima, and their own embeddedness in Kagoshima-time.

As much as it is about the pursuit of pleasure, then, a key effect of Iwashi's and Masako's fandom lies in discovering ways to package and express latent critical sentiment—in other words, to develop a storytelling praxis of their own. The musical storytelling of Nagabuchi as Kagoshima compatriot—anchored as it is in a grounded critique of conditions of everyday life in Kagoshima that is familiar to both—helps them define and articulate the "things wrong with this country." Nagabuchi's grounded critique of familiar conditions of everyday life in Kagoshima and how these conditions are linked into broader, national priorities (nuclear power, capitalism) helps clear a path for a broader critical interrogation of Japan itself. There is something here of Yano's assertion that music can have the effect of generating the "nation" by bringing the margins to the center (Yano 2002, 19), but the effect is the inverse of what this sort of assessment suggests. What results from this is not the reanimation of a national phantasm, but rather the emergence of a spirit of a different, more productive sort, one that seeks to undermine the storytelling regime of "Japan's Japan," replacing it with something new. Iwashi and Masako, of course, are residents of Kagoshima, and the material realities of their lives there inform how that site becomes a key conduit in the development of their own critical musical storytelling. But is the centrality of Kagoshima only applicable to those who actually live there? What happens when we leave the geographical bounds of Kagoshima behind?

Eiji

After repeated trips to Kagoshima to converse with fans of Nagabuchi Tsuyoshi, it was a novelty to find myself on the other side of the tracks one October day, on a *shinkansen* barreling northeastward rather than southwest. I was traveling from my base of research in Kyoto to Kakegawa, in Shizuoka

Prefecture, to meet with Eiji, an executive member of the Ougoukai with whom I'd cultivated an online relationship and with whom I'd chatted in person at live events over a period of several months. And it was precisely because this key member of the Ougoukai resided far from Kyushu that I hoped to hear his thoughts on Nagabuchi and his artistry.

Eiji's life, like that of others visited herein, has not been easy. Previously employed by a motorcycle parts factory in Shizuoka (the region is home to many of the small-to-medium parts manufacturers that make up the backbone of Japan's automotive industry), Eiji now works for a delivery service, literally running his way through each day to provide for himself and his new family. If things are difficult for Eiji now, they've been much worse. Abandoned by a former spouse Eiji was left to raise his young son alone, and faced crushing despair and gut-wrenching choices: with connections in Japan's criminal underworld, he even came close to joining a yakuza crew. What kept his head above water, Eiji says, was his son, and his engagement with the music of Nagabuchi Tsuyoshi. Eiji explained that the music hits him "directly," without artifice (a sentiment echoed by nearly all those I spoke with), and attributed this to what he calls a "nonfiction life" on the part of the artist: Nagabuchi has seen not only the highest of the highs, Eiji insists, but also, like himself, the lowest of the lows. Like others, he describes deploying Nagabuchi's music as a literal elixir: it helps him not only to persevere, but also, in his words, to "find balance": "When we grow up and enter the adult world, there are far fewer opportunities for us to be scolded, taken to task for the choices we make," he says. "Tuning in to songs like 'Myself' [a soaring, medium-tempo fan favorite that urges the listener to press on with life on his own terms and that assures him that he's "never alone in weeping over loneliness"] helps me think about whether I'm making the right choice in a given situation or not."

Like the other members of the Ougoukai, for Eiji "Japan" constitutes a key signpost around which he orients his everyday life and critique; it also lies near the center of his engagement with Nagabuchi's music. Like Yūji, Eiji considers "Japan" to be definable by *nakama* itself—it's a community of like-minded (or, more specifically, like-hearted) social actors anchored in tangible interpersonal relations, and the organic collectivity that results therefrom (Kelly's "community of mutual concern" [2004, 7] likely comes closer to capturing Eiji's imagination of "Japan" than does Anderson's [1983] idea of the "imagined community"). This *nakama* can be realized, for him, by tracing connections. Eiji is proactive in tracing the linkages that he insists constitute "Japan"—he enjoys traveling the archipelago creating and maintaining interpersonal bonds, and in the aftermath of 3.11 drove hundreds of kilometers from Shizuoka to Fukushima for the purpose of establishing actually existing connections with compatriots there. This literal tracing of the outlines of "Japan" as it could be echoes the tactics deployed by (anti-)"folk" legend Kagawa Ryō (see track 3)—and like Kagawa's *tabi,* Eiji's travels present critical connotations.

Due precisely to the ways that he envisions and traces it, Eiji's "Japan" is never complete, never unifiable simply through stories of "ethnicity" (*minzoku*) or "culture." The reach and extent of "Japan"-as-*nakama* depends entirely upon the degree of engagement and mutual concern expressed by its constituent membership—and on this point, Eiji finds much of the country lacking. Recalling 3.11 and its aftermath, he said, "As a fellow Japanese [*onaji Nihonjin to shite*], I just couldn't forgive those people in Tokyo and Shizuoka calling for everyone to close their windows after the meltdowns at Fukushima, without so much as a thought for the people who were actually there. What about them?" Eiji was articulating a frustration with what he understood as a detached sort of coolness or disconnect—a reluctance to engage in the "community of mutual concern" that "Japan" as *nakama* should, to him, rightly be—that served to exacerbate the isolation of individuals in times of crisis, and that was incompatible with his vision of "Japan." In his formulation, this aloofness was/is at least partially geographic in nature; to him, people in Tokyo and Shizuoka were particularly guilty of it. This led Eiji to reach beyond his geographical home for an antidote.

"I don't belong in Shizuoka," Eiji told me. "People roll their eyes at me all the time [*shiroi me de mirareru*]; they judge me on how I look and they think I look scary [Eiji wears dark sunglasses and is a fan of the "regent," a pompadour-like hairstyle sometimes associated with Japan's gangland]. My friends always ask me, 'What are you getting so worked up about [*nani atsuku narundayo*]?' when I get involved with different things [here he is referencing the critical engagement with questions of "Japan" and struggles for critical solidarity that he sees Nagabuchi involved in and that inform his own stances on the world]. I really feel drawn to the passion [*atsusa*] in Kyushu—culturally, I feel a lot closer to Kyushu than I do to Shizuoka." Whether or not such cultural attributes are empirically demonstrable in Kyushu is, of course, open to debate—but the question is also rather beside the point. What's key here is the fact that Eiji detects and attributes such difference in and to Kyushu—and his vehicle for doing so is the persona and music of Nagabuchi Tsuyoshi. These become pathways via which Eiji can imagine and tell the story of his own idealized "Japan," one that is built upon human interconnectivity and *nakama.* These pathways lead through Kagoshima, if slightly differently than they do for others addressed herein.

For Eiji to access what he understands as "Japan," then, he needs to bypass a cultural gap between his own self and his immediate surroundings. This can only be accomplished by routing his journeys—conceptually—through (an idealized) Kagoshima itself. "With 'LICENSE' and '*Itsuka no Shōnen*' [both addressed earlier], Nagabuchi sings about specific ways of life in Kagoshima—and I get these vast visual scenes that I can base myself in when thinking about Japan, how it is, how it should be." Though conceptual rather than physical, then, Kagoshima becomes a generative site at which "Japan" can be pondered and re-posited according to new terms—provincialized, in the terminology I'm using herein. Eiji's esteem for Nagabuchi leads him to Kagoshima, where the artist's works and the physical site are literally conflated, and Eiji is reenergized to trace "Japan" anew. Inspired by Nagabuchi's artistic stance and ongoing quest for critical solidarity, Eiji takes his vision of the "community of mutual concern" on the road, forging and tracing the *nakama* connectivities that, to him, make up "Japan." As he travels the archipelago, Eiji is conceptually grounded by an idealized Kagoshima, which always informs his engagement and passion as he literally carves out the contours of a "Japan" as an engaged, compassionate, and critical community of concern that is explicitly not the "Japan" announced by structures of power within the state. "I love Japan," he told me. "Japan is all that I know. But I hate the state [*kokka*]."

In 2020, Eiji took over as chair of the Ougoukai. In the midst of the COVID-19 pandemic, he saw an enhanced role for the organization in effecting the *nakama* that for him constitutes "Japan" itself, precisely when actual interpersonal connectivity, in light of public health mandates, needed to be so limited. "This is a group of really passionate folks connected by their love of Nagabuchi Tsuyoshi," he said, "so I want to make this an association that prioritizes connections between people at the level of the heart." He continued: "The Ougoukai is a place where folks can connect on the basis of human warmth and the heart, and where members can learn from each other, and grow; it's a place for learning about society, if you will. Our group has stricter regulations than others, and my hope is that each of the members will respect those regulations and open their hearts, set goals for themselves, grow. Dignified, with a high bar. That's the sort of group I'd like the Ougoukai to be."

These words of the new chairman reveal a dedication to *nakama*—collectivity—that goes beyond simple shared enjoyment of music, even as it's potentiated by it. The "self-fashioning" suggested here is about more than becoming a fan or finding identity in song—it's about the organized coming together of social actors who, united in their love for Japan's preeminent critical musical storyteller, can tell their own world-producing stories of what it means (to them) to "become Japanese." As Polletta points out, "storytelling sustains groups [like the Ougoukai] as they fight for reform, helping them build new collective identities [that can] provide a counterpoint to the myths promoted by the powerful" (Polletta 2006, 3). For Eiji and others, it's a storytelling practice that traverses and cites Kagoshima—in different ways—for its legibility.

Masao

Satsuma-Hayato is a small, sleepy town situated forty-five minutes or so by rail from Kagoshima City. Surrounded by lush green hills and dotted with volcanic hot springs, this area was once populated by the Hayato, or "falcon men," a culturally distinct people who lived in southern Kyushu until around the eighth century. The Hayato had a history of resisting centralized rule, and on subsequent reflection the town would seem a fitting site at which to discuss the music of Nagabuchi Tsuyoshi and how it's deployed by Masao, whom I met for the first time at a Nagabuchi concert at Kagoshima Arena some months earlier, and who met me at Hayato Station one early autumn day in 2015 for a chat.

"I've always liked this place," he says, stirring his coffee at a small café just outside the station. "It's quiet and I love the nature, but it's not inconvenient." Originally from Tanegashima, a tiny island to the south of Kyushu known primarily as the site of launch facilities for Japan's space program (JAXA) but with few opportunities for residents to make a living aside from farming, Masao works at a hotel in nearby Kirishima, and until recently had lived in that city as well. But "[o]ne day a Nagabuchi fan-club newsletter showed up in the mail that mentioned Hayato and how much Tsuyoshi-san himself liked it," says Masao. "So, I decided to move here." This casual comment, made in passing at the outset of our conversation, helped demonstrate just how important the artist and his music are to Masao, how central to his processes of "self-fashioning." It also foreshadowed the stories Masao would tell about the centrality of Nagabuchi's music in navigating, understanding, and indeed surviving the terms of his own existence, and articulating his own critical stance on the world.

Masao, in his thirties at the time of our discussion, has faced massive challenges in his life. Socially withdrawn as a youth and reluctant to go to school (a condition now widely recognized in Japan as *hikikomori*), Masao recalls being tormented by thoughts of suicide as early as fourth grade. He spent his elementary school days mostly alone, his nights in tears. This was also the time at which he began to be exposed to Nagabuchi's music. Masao recalls catching glimpses of the aforementioned 1988 TBS drama *Tombo* on television—but being forbidden to actually watch it due to the violence that it portrayed. His parents, however, would watch the program regularly, and Masao would listen from his room—and specifically to its theme song, "*Tombo*," which I introduced earlier. As I noted earlier, the late 1980s marked the height of Nagabuchi's commercial success, and other songs by the artist would find their way to Masao via televised music shows as well: he recalls being particularly affected by "*Rokunamonjanee* [Ain't No Good]" (1987), a driving rock song that sings of being a social outsider, and by the anguished ballad "STAY DREAM" (1986), whose explosive, unadorned opening lyric—"*shinjimaitai* [I just want to die]"—hit Masao hard. "Music saved me," he told me in Hayato. "There's no doubt that the fact that I'm alive today is thanks to those songs [*machigainaku ikiteita no ha sono uta no okage da*]." He recalls going to the beach on Tanegashima and howling the biting lyrics of Nagabuchi songs—so many of which speak of isolation and loneliness, even as they sing of a desire to face down society and persevere on one's own terms—at the top of his lungs, "externalizing," in his words, much of the pain that had entrapped him. "It was through externalizing my own seclusion in voice," he says, "that I was able to become strong [*tojikomotteta no wo kuchi ni dashite tsuyoku nareta*]."

But engaging with Nagabuchi's artistry didn't just afford a way for Masao to survive a tormented childhood (though this is remarkable in and of itself). It also opened paths for him to understand his surroundings and develop a critical stance on everyday life. The prominence of Kagoshima in Nagabuchi's work played an important role here. "At first, I didn't know that Tsuyoshi-san was from Kagoshima," he says. "It was my teachers that told me. After that, I respected him all the more." Asked if he saw Nagabuchi as a Kagoshima singer or a "Japan" singer, Masao was somewhat taken aback. "I've never really thought about it," he says. "I guess that he's a Kagoshima singer, singing at the Japan level." For Masao, like others, Nagabuchi seems to occupy two places at once—like the provincial interloper (the *inaka-mono*) narrating "*Tombo*," he occupies a place of *co-presence* that allows him to engage critically and productively with "Japan" from the perspective of Kagoshima. In Masao's view, Nagabuchi never falls into insularity, nor does he permit himself to be drawn into what Masao sees as toxic state mechanisms and prerogatives simply by virtue of association with the national pronoun. Indeed, for Masao, it is precisely in bringing a Kagoshima line of sight to "Japan," insisting that Kagoshima be allowed to tell its own time, that allows for the critique of abstract, dominant imaginings (Lefebvre 1991, 39) of "Japan," and that allows for the destabilization of dominant "Japanese" stories and their recalibration according to different, "provincialized" terms.

In a way that resonated with my discussion with Iwashi and Masako, earlier, Masao told me how tapping Nagabuchi's musical storytelling helped him articulate a political stance of his own. He describes having come to engage critically with the issue of nuclear power in Japan, for example, through listening to musical stories that tackle that issue head-on, and through observing various relief efforts pursued by Nagabuchi after the meltdowns at Fukushima Dai'ichi (including inviting children from Fukushima to "summer camps" that the artist arranged in and around Hayato). "If it wasn't Tsuyoshi-san talking, I may not have been able to come to terms with the dangers of the nuclear power plants," he says. But in a way that resonates with some of Nagabuchi's most critical works, Masao's critique is geopolitical in scope, as well. The revision of Japan's security treaties with the United States (AMPO), the American military presence on Okinawa, the state and the LDP—all are the target of Masao's fiery critical energies, and nurturing such critique, he insists, is something that he learned from Nagabuchi Tsuyoshi.

Kyōkan, or "empathy," is (in his words) what music is all about to Masao. Like Iwashi and Masako, a sense of empathetic camaraderie and shared "home" with Nagabuchi rendered Masao susceptible to the artist's critical voice—and grappling with it allowed him to find his own. "We can't let these things just become someone else's problem [*hitogoto*]," he insists. "The point is for us not to keep that anger to ourselves, but to *share it around.*" This ethics of "shar[ing] it around" suggests a storytelling praxis par excellence, one built out of an engagement with Nagabuchi's own critical musical storytelling and engagement with "Japan," and that presents political, world-producing potentials. This empathetic, critical storytelling, in short, can provide a means through which to reimagine "Japan" itself, as love of the immediacy of home and locality (what he called *kyōdoai*) and love of "Japan" become intermixed in an incisive political practice, one that—like others discussed in this book—constitutes a sort of politics done differently: "We *are* Japanese. It's precisely because we love Japan that we want to figure out issues relating to the future, to the kids, ourselves, and not just get carried along by whatever the politicians decide to do," he says. "We *are* Japanese! Let's get it done ourselves [*uchira de yarō ze*]!"

Asked if the political awareness that he insisted had been awakened in him by Nagabuchi's music could prod him to action, Misao quietly told me the story of Mageshima, a tiny, uninhabited island in the Ōsumi chain that had hosted a Japanese airfield in the closing days of the Pacific War, and that had been rumored for years to be a candidate site for American and Japanese military flight training. Mageshima is right next door to Tanegashima, just a couple of miles off the coast, and Tanegashima—Masao's home—is where the consequences of Mageshima's militarization can be expected to play out. "People on the island don't *need* the money," Masao says. "It's subsistence farming there, and there's nothing that anyone really wants for; the culture is really welcoming, and if somebody asked to use their land for military purposes they'd probably say sure, come on in. This is exactly when we need to remember that their problem, like Okinawa's, is everybody's problem, and get out there in protest and stick up for them. I'd have to. I wouldn't have a choice [*ikanaito ikenai deshō ne*]." He continued. "There's lots of shitty grown-ups [*kitanai otona,* echoing one of Nagabuchi's favorite phrases] around these parts," he says, referring to policy makers at the prefectural and town levels who would welcome such state incursions for their perceived financial benefit (and who have also been responsible for the construction of the nuclear power station at Satsuma-Sendai and other bids for economic "survival"). "Wave a bit of money at them and no one knows what they'll do."

In December 2019, Mageshima was in fact purchased by the Japanese state, for sixteen billion yen. In 2020 I reached out to Masao for his take on this development, and to see if his earlier insistence on ground-level "protest" still held. Predictably, given the cooling of Japan's political environment in the interim and the failure (like AMPO in 1960 and 1970) of 2015 "protest" to effect meaningful change, Masao had pivoted away from embodied, performative action. But his commitment to the critical possibilities of storytelling—inspired, in an ongoing way, by Nagabuchi's own musical storytelling—seemed to remain strong.

"With the militarization of Mageshima, there'll certainly be noise pollution issues, environmental issues, and humanitarian issues that arise not just there, but on Tanegashima, too," Masao told me. "I'm pretty pessimistic about a lot of that." But in his assessment, these were consequences of a more fundamental issue whose roots lay elsewhere. He continued: "My parents and elder brother still live there in my hometown; [when thinking about this issue] the everyday lives [*seikatsu*] of the people there are more important than anything." He went on to describe people on the island who, in his words, are "out for the money" as militarization expands—feigning opposition on environmental grounds, for example, but actually (in his assessment) setting the stage to demand financial reparations from the state. In Masao's view, it seems, this diverse scrambling to secure the means of survival—of shoring up "everyday li[fe]" according to developmental, monetized narratives, in a hopelessly marginal and out-of-time place—is at the root of the problem, and the factor making his hometown (where the SDF is already conducting remote-island exercises) "unrecognizable."

According to Masao, the state knows what it's doing here. Its trundling out of tired stories of "modernization" and "economic development," its promise to help islanders overcome what I've been calling Kagoshima-time, is strategic and intentional. "The Mageshima issue is a result of the government needling the Achilles' heel of depopulation [and its economic effects]," he says. "But if we think about the future of the people of the island, we can't just focus in on the dangers and simply 'oppose.'" Here, it seems, Masao wanted to think about how the stories that the state told about the islands—stories of development, of catch-up to normative Japanese time—could be robbed of some of their potency. He pointed to the arrival of surfers and escapees from the cities who are choosing to come to the island to take up farming and fishing as developments that might bolster the population and expand the possible range of stories that can be told about its survival while also defusing some of the sway that state-centered "developmental" stories hold over local politicians. It's not a perfect solution, of course—nor is it a call to establish the islands as an anti-modern site of tranquility that can somehow exist out of history. But it is a small step toward being able to dislodge the stories that (some) people on

Tanegashima have told themselves about what it means to survive in modern Japan—and setting the stage for telling new ones. Being critically aware of structures of unevenness and their local consequences, it seems—an awareness that has been at the core of Nagabuchi's critical artistry for decades, and that has prodded Masao into his own critical reflections—trumps performative "protest," at least for Masao. The rest, he says, is up to the islanders themselves: "The choices they make," Masao says anxiously, "will be the choices they make."

Fade-Out

In late 2020, I asked Eiji, chair of the Ougoukai, whether Japan still needed Nagabuchi Tsuyoshi and his music. His answer was a resounding "yes." Asked why, he said, "Because Nagabuchi's music is nonfiction."

> [Nagabuchi] always takes the things that Japanese people want to scream about … and expresses them through music. Those Japanese who listen to his songs, it's like their hearts just get run through with this overpowering message, almost like he's singing the story of their own heart at that moment on their behalf. […] If you close your eyes and listen to Nagabuchi's songs, you can *see* it—there's a vista that just floats up before your eyes on those lyrics. He expresses it in a way that's more real than the feeling of everyday life itself.

What Eiji is pointing to is a musical storytelling that can capture and express what he called the "feelings of the moment (delight, anger, sorrow, pleasure)." But a "nonfiction" tapping of the affective foundations of everyday life means taking up its material conditions and amplifying them, in ways that resonate with listeners' own stories and desires. Nagabuchi's musical stories frequently becomes listeners' own; they resonate in their lived everyday, affording listeners the means to make sense of their own lives and their own hearts—and to dream of difference. As I've been describing in the preceding pages, although the storytelling is "Japanese," it frequently cites everyday life in Kagoshima to be legible. Part of this is telling the disavowed, uneven time that many of his fans across the country still live—Kagoshima-time. Destabilizing the stories that "Japan" tells itself about itself by amplifying Kagoshima-time resonates with listeners in "nonfiction" ways and helps conjure visions of possibility that are "more real than the feeling of everyday life itself" as well. These might be understood as the critical potentials of "provincialized Japan."

Nagabuchi maintains a fierce, unwavering love for Kagoshima. He returns frequently for short trips and continues to engage with the area in other ways, as well. But at the very moment he boarded that train at Nishi-Kagoshima Station, headed "north, ever north," Kagoshima also became a site of *memory* for the artist—and all the more so in the decades that he's been a resident of Tokyo. Memory, though, is never merely a faculty of "putting away," of consigning the past to a somehow isolated storehouse—rather, the past perseveres, always looming over the present. "[A]ll that we have felt, thought, and willed from our earliest infancy is there," Bergson writes, "leaning over the present which is about to join it, pressing against the portals of consciousness that would fain leave it outside" (Bergson 2011, 7). Nagabuchi's own past—his experiences of lived everydayness growing up in Kagoshima—continues to loom over his present and infect his "Japanese" art with critique. Memory here thus serves a purpose that is quite distantly removed from restorative reanimations of national-cultural phantasms. Indeed, the focus of such memory is not the past at all, but rather the present, and the portals that it opens lead not to a spatialized time-as-destination that exists outside of History, but rather to pathways through which understandings of the present might be critically rewired. These are the potentials of what Boym has called "reflective nostalgia": such nostalgia opens possibilities, as opposed to closing them, by "linger[ing] on ruins, the patina of time and history, in the dreams of another place and another time" (Boym 2001, 41).

The members of the Ougoukai whom I introduced earlier also center Kagoshima in ways that serve both to clarify the crises and contradictions of everyday "Japanese" life and to gesture toward different possibilities for it. Kagoshima, that is, is important to these fans as a space (material or conceptual) that helps them develop and articulate their own critical stances upon the world—even if, like Eiji, they've never lived there. As is the case with Nagabuchi himself, the point is never to simply submerse oneself in a misty, romanticized Kagoshima, but rather to use the site in ways that allow for different stories of what it means to "be Japanese" to be told—to insist that Kagoshima be allowed to challenge Tokyo-centric Japanese time with its own. The actual mechanics of this, as I've shown, is slightly different for each member of the Ougoukai. But each uses the music in open-ended, "reflective" ways—not closed ones.

This isn't necessarily true of all Nagabuchi listeners, though. The endpoint of Nagabuchi's critical project—and the locus of desires of the members of the Ougoukai—is critical Japanese solidarity, organic collectivity, *nakama*. As I pointed out at the beginning of this track, this is a very tricky path to walk. Sakai cautions that "generalized organicity … is more often than not superimposed upon the putative spatio-temporal unity of [the] nation-state" (Sakai 2004, 229–257). To be sure, there is a subset of Nagabuchi listeners who celebrate what they consider to be the "nationalist" undertones of his work. Simply insisting that Nagabuchi's citations of "Japan" are mostly part and parcel of a broader critical project aimed at forcing a confrontation with questions of what it means to "be Japanese"—much like Springsteen's oft-misunderstood "Born in the U.S.A." is in the United States—doesn't help much here; as Takada Wataru pointed out on track 2, once a song or a performance is out in the world, listeners will take it up and do with it what they will, finding significance that is often unintended and putting it to uses of which the artist may not approve. And indeed, finding supporters waving Imperial Japanese army and navy ensigns at events like the artist's all-night concert at the foot of Mount Fuji certainly doesn't help encourage a more expansive reading of his work. Musical storytelling—in Nagabuchi's orbit and beyond it—is a fraught, ambiguous undertaking indeed.

I hope, though, to have been able to present Nagabuchi's critique in a slightly clearer light. Nagabuchi is, among other things, a sharp critic of fascism, particularly amid the rise of state-sanctioned populism in Japan and around the world. "It smells [like fascism] something awful," he said in a fan club interview in 2017. "If we don't get a signal out from a different direction, we're just going to run right into it." But perhaps to critique fascism effectively, one needs to reach right into its jaws to reclaim some of the terms by which it's made to work—in a sense, to negate the negation. And if fascism is itself a temporal critique, one that seeks to re-occupy temporal islands of purity free of contradiction, islands that never existed in the first place, then hijacking fascism means, in part, diverting the "restored" time that it seeks to tell and relishing in the very unevenness and contradictions that it aims to overcome. For Nagabuchi Tsuyoshi, to sing the Homesick Blues is not to pine after an idyllic "home" that exists beyond the reach of capitalist modernity. Rather, it's to traverse the contradictions and crises of Kagoshima in order to put pressure on commonsensical notions of "Japan" and generate the possibility of thinking about it differently, critically. As I hope to have demonstrated on this track, this is what telling Kagoshima-time—for Nagabuchi and for his fans—is really all about.

Back, finally, to the Budōkan, where the "Tsuyoshi calls" are thundering through the packed venue just seconds before Nagabuchi and his band are slated to take the stage. After many stops and starts, the call has finally found its groove, and the fourteen-thousand-person-capacity crowd is in a synchronized, ecstatic frenzy. But even as the crowd counts down the seconds to opening time with its deafening, four-second or so call cycles—"*Tsuu-yoo-shi!*" … "*Tsuu-yoo-shi!*"—this time-telling remains out of sync with the broader, state-centered, homogenizing "Japanese" story of the neighborhood of which the Budōkan is a part, and even with the Budōkan itself. In a way, the Nagabuchi *nakama* packing the Budōkan is marking out a time all its own. This exuberant, collective untimeliness, it seems to me, reveals the promise that the world *can* be thought and lived differently—it reveals the world-producing potentials of musical storytelling itself. The longevity of Nagabuchi Tsuyoshi's critical stories of Kagoshima and "provincialized Japan," told across decades by an artist who remains at the top of Japan's rock world and put to use in everyday life by fans young and old in navigating their own crises of the everyday, reflects more than the musical and poetic prowess of the artist himself. It reveals an ongoing desire on the part of artist and fans alike to confront the crises of everyday life head-on, to keep on telling critical, reimaginative stories of what it means to live in Japan, to "be Japanese"—a desire, that is, to keep on singing the Homesick Blues.

Overture

As I finish writing this book in the summer of 2022, the United States—where I am based—is reeling amid a discordant symphony of ongoing crises, of various type and origin. The SARS-CoV-2 pandemic, which erupted in March 2020, has killed more than a million people in this country alone, and many millions more beyond its borders. Meanwhile, the aftereffects of a violent attack on the seat of U.S. government in the wake of Donald Trump's 2020 election loss continue to reverberate, with eyes cast nervously to what the future of "politics" may portend for America and for those who call America home. Storytelling, of course, intersects with both these crises. In the case of the former, certain pundits, political talking heads, and others persist in unhelpful, even harmful veins of storytelling, often along partisan lines, insisting that the vaccines and other measures developed to stem the pandemic's spread somehow represent an infringement upon American liberties and freedoms (here, one story intersects with another). This is storytelling that's helped beget illness and death. In the case of the latter, delusional storytelling by a former president and his enablers concerning a purportedly fraudulent election—storytelling that, as repeated recounts, audits, and court challenges made clear, has no basis in fact—engendered a disturbing, violent reality as thousands of his supporters descended upon the U.S. Capitol on January 6, 2021, resulting in injury, bloodshed, and loss of life. Granted, these are limited, extreme examples. But they do much to demonstrate the material implications of even the most "imaginative, affective" (Jackson 2013, 21–22) storytelling. Storytelling, as Jackson and others argue, is never outside the world—it's in it; it generates it.

I started this book by insisting that *storytelling matters.* The crises of the early 2020s in the United States certainly demonstrate that, as does the rise of nationalism, populism, and outright fascism the world over—all of which, too, intersects with restorative, fearful storytelling about the nature of the *Volk,* for instance, or ways to resolve the crises of life under capitalism (a fuller exploration of this will have to wait for another day). The "world-producing" potentials of storytelling insisted upon by Jackson, Polletta, Fernandes, and others, that is, find sickly and sickening form in the upheavals of the third decade of the twenty-first century in the United States and beyond. Storytelling, in other words, really does matter. That much is clear.

But it's not all doom and gloom. The very fact that these particularly horrifying modes of storytelling have generated tangible, material results in the world leaves open the possibility that other modes can as well. The musical storytellers I've introduced in these pages have used music in different ways to conjure, articulate, and share stories of everyday social, (geo)political, and economic life that can challenge and decenter dominant stories of what it means to live in Japan and "be Japanese," usually in reflective, reimaginative ways. From Princess Princess's contextually embedded flipping of the script on powerful stories of U.S.-Japan "friendship" to Takada Wataru's scrambling of normative notions of Japanese economic development and the fulfillment of capitalism around 1970, from Kagawa Ryō's "unpatriotic" undermining of gendered notions of Japanese subjectivity to the creative ways in which some *enka* aficionados deploy "Japan's music" in ways critical of Japan itself, to the ways that Nagabuchi Tsuyoshi and his fans use music to spotlight and confront the unevenness and crises of capitalism and dream of a new/better Japan, each of the musical storytellers I've introduced in these pages has pursued tactics by which they not so much *negate,* but destabilize and *scramble* some of the terms and conditions of everyday life in modern Japan, and tell its stories differently. And as the experiences of some members of the Ougoukai, in particular—the "unofficial" Nagabuchi Tsuyoshi fan club that I explored on track 5—make especially clear, the sorts of musical storytelling I described in this book do intersect with how bodies and minds are oriented in the world. Musical storytelling matters, that is, because it's one means by which the world can be produced at the level of everyday life, even if the production of a new world simply means the destabilization of the old one. And as I've shown, this is often—though not always—a sharply critical, reimaginative enterprise.

None of this, I want to reiterate, is reducible to "protest." As I described at the beginning of this book, organized, oppositional "protest" in Japan had largely faded away by the mid-1970s. But as I've insisted throughout, that doesn't mean that critical political engagement met the same fate. The Homesick Blues, that is, aren't exactly protest songs—but they still afford means of imagining, *generating,* the world differently. Micah White—cofounder of the Occupy movement that took much of the world by storm in 2011—has argued that "protest" is broken, that holders of power are simply no longer beholden to oppositional voices in the ways that they may have been in earlier moments

(White 2016). If this is true, then it behooves us to think about other means by which normative terms and conditions of everyday life can be challenged productively. As a world-producing, contextually specific, and often shared process, musical storytelling provides one of those means. To return to Takada Wataru—who memorably called anti-war protest "wishy-washy [and] not enough" on track 2 of this book—this doesn't mean simply opposing existing structures and phenomena in endless cycles of negation. It means bringing critical attention to the terms and conditions of everyday life, scrambling them, rejecting their sense-making authority outright, imagining them anew—a process that he called "singing the everyday." This confrontation with everyday life was, in one way or another, at the core of nearly all the musical storytelling that I explored in *Homesick Blues*.

Takada and the others whose voices animated this book, of course, pursue(d) these tactics in the contexts of modern and contemporary Japan. But none of the thinking that these figures do—and that I've tried to introduce herein—is necessarily limited in relevance to the place that goes by that name (the transnational appeal of Nagabuchi Tsuyoshi—probably the most acerbic musical storyteller I introduced in this book—helps prove this point). To the extent that capitalist modernity and its attendant crises and unevenness, the U.S.-led military industrial complex, and even the nation-state form itself are shared conditions informing everyday life across so much of the globe, the interventions mounted by these musical storytellers can be tapped, repurposed and redeployed, and learned from by social actors in other places, too, as they work to develop tactics aimed at generating different possibilities for living in the world. I hope, then, that this book will resonate within Japan Studies—but even more importantly, that it resonates beyond it, as well.

Where, then, does this leave my own story, the one I've tried to tell in this book? What I'm laying out for readers in these final lines of *Homesick Blues* isn't really an ending—a "conclusion"—at all, but rather another starting point. That's why I've called these last few pages an overture, and not (for instance) a coda. I often tell students in my popular music seminars that "[i]f you come away from this experience just thinking 'wow, Japanese music is cool,' then I will have failed to do my job." Something similar applies to *Homesick Blues*. I hope that you, dear reader, have been inspired—even entertained—by some of the musical storytellers that I've introduced in these pages, and that you may even have taken the time to search out some of the songs and performances that I've cited herein for yourself. But I also hope that these Japanese singers and social actors have prompted you to think about your own world, how you navigate it and critique it, what "world-producing" potentials may exist for telling its stories differently—in other words, how you might sing your own renditions of the Homesick Blues. Nagabuchi Tsuyoshi has a provocative take on the potentials of not only musical storytelling, but cultural production and the production of knowledge writ large. "Expression is a destructive impulse," he says. "Become a body that destroys, even as it creates" (Kurihara 2017). This is an ambiguous exhortation, one that even resonates in uncomfortable ways with the aforementioned crises of the early 2020s. But it's also a declaration that expression, creativity, cultural production, and storytelling can undermine the normative ways in which the world is understood—and become means of generating new ones. To that end, it seems worth our while to keep the world-producing potentials of storytelling—musical or otherwise—in mind as we attempt to navigate a fractured, polarized, burning world in the first half of the twenty-first century and try (I hope) to step back from the precipice of even more crisis and catastrophe. Now, as I warned at the outset, none of this is necessarily an emancipatory exercise—as evidenced on track 1 of this book, powerful bodies and institutions are perfectly capable of telling world-producing stories, too. But at its best, singing the Homesick Blues—even if we're a little off-key—promises to reveal different histories, to articulate new futures, and to constitute one means by which we can tell our own stories anew.

In 2018, Japanese hip-hop artist SKY-HI released "The Story of J," an intriguing piece of musical storytelling that transforms "J(apan)" and other geopolitical actors, including the United States ("Mary," in the song), into characters in a cheesy, tongue-in-cheek romance. The song recalls the story of U.S.-Japan "friendship" that opened this book, and its fleshly, sexualized implications—although the gendered roles here, intriguingly, are reversed. It narrates a condensed version of modern Japanese history through Mary and J's encounters, following the ups and downs in their "relationship" across a historical arc that commences in the Meiji period (1868–1912), traverses the Pacific War and its aftermath, and stretches through the 2000s, when the couple encounters a sort of third wheel in "Cody," who represents North Korea. Eventually, the story reaches a moment—implicitly in the wake of the 2018 Singapore Summit between Donald Trump and North Korea's Kim Jong-un—when the (post–)Cold War regional order centered on the relationship between Mary and J seems to be on the verge of collapse: J chances upon Mary finishing up a date at a café with Cody, and the newly happy couple leaves J to foot the bill. In its final seconds, as J leaves the café alone, "The Story of J" throws the subsequent directions of Japanese history open to question—"Is the future dark? Or is it bright?"—as SKY-HI pivots to address his listeners directly in a way that resonates with the stakes of musical storytelling that I'm trying to articulate here. "Figuring out the next part of this story," he raps in the last lines of the song, "is up to you."

REFERENCES

Aalgaard, Scott W. 2017. "Summertime Blues: Musical Critique in the Aftermaths of Japan's Dark Spring." In *Fukushima and the Arts: Negotiating Nuclear Disaster,* edited by Barbara Geilhorn and Kristina Weickgennant, chap. 2. New York: Routledge.

———. 2019. "Crickets in the Weeds: Yū Miri, Critical Sonority, and the Crises of the Everyday." *Japan Forum* 33, no. 2:278–300.

Ackmann, Martha. 2020. *These Fevered Days: Ten Pivotal Moments in the Making of Emily Dickinson.* New York: W. W. Norton.

Agamben, Giorgio. 2009. *What Is an Apparatus? and Other Essays.* Stanford, CA: Stanford University Press.

Allen, Bruce. 2013. "First There Were Stories: Michiko Ishimure's Narratives of Resistance and Reconciliation." In *East Asian Criticisms: A Critical Reader,* edited by Simon C. Estok and Won-Chung Kim, chap. 3. New York: Palgrave Macmillan.

Allison, Anne. 2013. *Precarious Japan.* Durham, NC: Duke University Press.

All-Night Fuji. 1988. Late night variety and entertainment program broadcast live on the Fuji TV network between 1983 and 1991. June 1988. Specific broadcast date unknown.

Althusser, Louis. 2001. *Lenin and Philosophy and Other Essays.* New York: Monthly Review Press.

Anderson, Benedict. 1983. *Imagined Communities: Reflections on the Origins and Spread of Nationalism.* London: Verso.

Angst, Linda Isako. 2003. "The Rape of a Schoolgirl: Discourses of Power and Women's Lives in Okinawa." In *Islands of Discontent: Okinawan Responses to Japanese and American Power,* edited by Laura Elizabeth Hein and Mark Selden, 135–157. Lanham, MD: Rowman and Littlefield.

Atkins, E. Taylor. 2001. *Blue Nippon: Authenticating Jazz in Japan.* Durham, NC: Duke University Press.

———. 2010. *Primitive Selves: Koreana in the Japanese Colonial Gaze, 1910–1945.* Berkeley: University of California Press.

Babb, James. 2005. "Making Farmers Conservative: Japanese Farmers, Land Reform and Socialism." *Social Science Japan Journal* 8, no. 2:175–195.

Barg, Lisa. 2000. "Black Voices / White Sounds: Race and Representation in Virgil Thomson's Four Saints in Three Acts." *American Music* 18, no. 2:121–161.

Barthes, Roland. 1978. *Image-Music-Text.* Translated by Stephen Heath. Paris: Farrar, Straus and Giroux.

Berger, Harris M. 2009. *Stance: Ideas about Emotion, Style, and Meaning for the Study of Expressive Culture.* Middletown, CT: Wesleyan University Press.

Bergson, Henri. 2011. *Creative Evolution.* New York: Henry Holt and Company.

Bloch, Ernst. 1977. "Nonsynchronism and the Obligation to Its Dialectics." Translated by Mark Ritter. *New German Critique* 11:22–38.

Bourdaghs, Michael K. 2012. *Sayonara Amerika, Sayonara Nippon: A Geopolitical Prehistory of J-Pop.* New York: Columbia University Press.

boyd, danah. 2007. "The Role of Networked Publics in Teenage Social Life." In *Youth, Identity, and Digital Media,* edited by David Buckingham, 119–142. Cambridge, MA: MIT Press.

Boym, Svetlana. 2001. *The Future of Nostalgia.* New York: Basic Books.

Brown, Kevin. 2015. *Karaoke Idols: Popular Music and the Performance of Identity.* Bristol, UK: Intellect.

Brubaker, Rogers. 1996. *Nationalism Reframed: Nationhood and the National Question in the New Europe.* Cambridge: Cambridge University Press.

Buruma, Ian. 1985. *Behind the Mask: On Sexual Demons, Sacred Mothers, Transvestites, Gangsters and Other Japanese Cultural Heroes.* New York: Meridian.

Butler, Judith. 1990. *Gender Trouble: Feminism and the Subversion of Identity.* New York: Routledge.

———. 2004. *Undoing Gender.* New York: Routledge.

Casanova, Pascale. 2004. *The World Republic of Letters.* Translated by M. B. Debevoise. Cambridge, MA: Harvard University Press.

Cavicchi, Daniel. 1998. *Tramps Like Us: Music and Meaning among Springsteen Fans.* New York: Oxford University Press.

Cherry, Kittredge. 1987. *Womansword: What Japanese Words Say about Women.* Tokyo: Kodansha International.

Chiavacci, David, and Julia Obinger, eds. 2018. *Social Movements and Political Activism in Contemporary Japan: Re-emerging from Invisibility.* Abingdon, Oxon: Routledge.

Condry, Ian. 2006. *Hip-Hop Japan: Rap and the Paths of Cultural Globalization.* Durham, NC: Duke University Press.

Connor, Steven. 2000. *Dumbstruck: A Cultural History of Ventriloquism.* Oxford: Oxford University Press.

Cumings, Bruce. 2020. "Seeing like an Area Specialist." In *Reconsidering American Power: Pax Americana and the Social Sciences,* edited by John D. Kelly, Kurt Jacobsen, and Marston H. Morgan, 84–135. New York: Oxford University Press.

de Becker, J. E. 1909. *Annotated Civil Code of Japan, First Edition.* London: Butterworth.

de Certeau, Michel. 1984. *The Practice of Everyday Life.* Translated by Steven Rendall. Berkeley: University of California Press.

Defense Visual Information Distribution Service. 2019. *Friendship Through Music: One Couple Bridges International Gap through Music.* https://www.dvidshub.net /news/307432/friendship-through-music-one-couple-bridges-international-gap-through-music. Accessed February 10, 2023.

———. 2023. *III MEF Band, JGSDF Brigade Band Perform 25th "Friendship Through Music"* *Concert.* https://www.dvidshub.net/image/7614835/iii-mef-band-jgsdf-15th-brigade -band-perform-25th-friendship-through-music-concert. Accessed February 10, 2023.

Deleuze, Gilles, and Felix Guattari. 1986. *Kafka: Toward a Minor Literature.* Translated by Dana Polan. Minneapolis: University of Minnesota Press.

———. 1998. *A Thousand Plateaus.* Translated by Brian Massumi. London: Athlone Press.

Dell, Katharine J., and Will Kynes. 2014. *Reading Ecclesiastes Intertextually.* London: Bloomsbury Publishing.

DeNora, Tia. 2000. *Music in Everyday Life.* Cambridge: Cambridge University Press.

———. 2003. *After Adorno: Rethinking Music Sociology.* Cambridge: Cambridge University Press.

Derrida, Jacques. 1976. *Of Grammatology,* corrected ed. Translated by Gayatri Chakravorty Spivak. Baltimore, MD: Johns Hopkins University Press.

Dodd, Stephen. 2004. *Writing Home: Representations of the Native Place in Modern Japanese Literature.* Cambridge, MA: Harvard University Asia Center.

Dolar, Mladen. 2006. *A Voice and Nothing More.* Cambridge, MA: MIT Press.

Dorsey, James. 2013. "Breaking Records: Media, Censorship, and the Folk Song Movement of Japan's 1960s." In *Asian Popular Culture: New, Popular, and Hybrid Media,* edited by John A. Lent and Lorna Fitzsimmons, chap. 5. Lanham, MD: Lexington Books.

Dower, John W. 1986. *War without Mercy: Race and Power in the Pacific War.* New York: Pantheon Books.

———. 1993. "Peace and Democracy in Two Systems: External Policy and Internal Conflict." In *Postwar Japan as History,* edited by Andrew Gordon, chap. 1. Berkeley: University of California Press.

———. 2017. *The Violent America Century: War and Terror since World War II.* Chicago: Haymarket Books.

Eagleton, Terry. 2007. *How to Read a Poem.* Malden, MA: Blackwell Publishing.

———. 2008. *Literary Theory: An Introduction,* anniversary ed. Minneapolis: University of Minnesota Press.

Eckert, Penny. 2003. "Sociolinguistics and Authenticity: An Elephant in the Room." *Journal of Sociolinguistics* 7, no. 3:392–431.

Elmore, Cindy. 2010. "Stars and Stripes: A Unique American Newspaper's Historical Struggle against Military Interference and Control." *Media History* 16, no. 3:301–317.

———. 2011. "When the Department of Defense Writes the Rules: A History of Changes to Policy Instructions Governing the *Stars and Stripes* Newspaper." *Journal of Communication Inquiry* 35, no. 1:70–85.

Endo, Katsuhiko. 2012. "A Unique Tradition of Materialism in Japan." *Positions* 20, no. 4:1009–1039.

Fernandes, Sujatha. 2017. *Curated Stories: The Uses and Misuses of Storytelling.* New York: Oxford University Press.

Fernandez, P., I. Marti, and T. Farchi. 2017. "Mundane and Everyday Politics for and from the Neighborhood." *Organization Studies* 38, no. 2:201–223.

Fox, Aaron A. 2004. *Real Country: Music and Language in Working-Class Culture.* Durham, NC: Duke University Press.

Frankel, Max. 1971. "'Japan Inc.' And 'Nixon Shocks.'" *New York Times,* November 25, 1971.

French, Thomas. 2014. *National Police Reserve: The Origin of Japan's Self-Defense Forces.* Leiden: Global Oriental.

Fujimoto, Kunihiko, et al., eds. 2007. *Takada Wataru dokuhon* [The Takada Wataru reader]. Tokyo: Ongaku Shuppansha.

Fukuyama, Francis. 1992. *The End of History and the Last Man.* New York: Free Press.

Galbraith, Patrick W. 2018. "AKB Business: Idols and Affective Economics in Contemporary Japan." In *Introducing Japanese Popular Culture,* edited by Alisa Freedman and Toby Slade, 158–167. London: Routledge.

Garon, Sheldon. 1998. *Molding Japanese Minds: The State in Everyday Life.* Princeton, NJ: Princeton University Press.

Geertz, Clifford. 1973. *The Interpretation of Cultures: Selected Essays.* New York: Basic Books.

General Headquarters Far East Command, Public Information Office. 1952. *Text of Remarks Prepared for Delivery by Ambassador Dean Rusk, Special Representative of the President, at a Luncheon Meeting of the America-Japan Society in Tokyo at 1 P.M. Friday, February 1.* Archived online at https://www-archivesdirect-amdigital-co-uk. Accessed May 27, 2021.

Gerow, Aaron. 2011. "War and Nationalism in Yamato: Trauma and Forgetting the Postwar." *Asia-Pacific Journal: Japan Focus* 9, no. 24-1.

Gordon, Andrew. 2009. *A Modern History of Japan.* New York: Oxford University Press.

Gottlieb, Nanette. 2005. *Language and Society in Japan.* Cambridge: Cambridge University Press.

Hammersley, Martyn, and Paul Atkinson. 2007. *Ethnography.* New York: Routledge.

Haraguchi, Izumi, et al. 2011. *Kagoshima-ken no rekishi* [The history of Kagoshima Prefecture]. Tokyo: Yamakawa Shuppan.

Harootunian, Harry. 1993. "America's Japan / Japan's Japan." In *Japan in the World,* edited by Masao Miyoshi and Harry Harootunian, 196–221. Durham, NC: Duke University Press.

———. 2000a. *History's Disquiet: Modernity, Cultural Practice, and the Question of Everyday Life.* New York: Columbia University Press.

———. 2000b. *Overcome by Modernity: History, Culture, and Community in Interwar Japan.* Princeton, NJ: Princeton University Press.

———. 2006. "Japan's Long Postwar: The Trick of Memory and the Ruse of History." In *Japan after Japan: Social and Cultural Life from the Recessionary 1990s to the Present,* edited by Tomiko Yoda and Harry D. Harootunian, 98–121. Durham, NC: Duke University Press.

———. 2012. "'Memories of Underdevelopment' after Area Studies." *Positions: East Asian Cultures Critique* 20, no. 1:7–35.

———. 2019. *Uneven Moments: Reflections on Japan's Modern History.* New York: Columbia University Press.

Havens, Thomas. 1987. *Fire across the Sea: The Vietnam War and Japan, 1965–1975.* Princeton, NJ: Princeton University Press.

Hayama, Peggy, and Minobu Shiozawa. 2014. "*Yakeato ni hibiku merodī wo minna de kuchizusanda ano hi* [That day when we all sang a melody that echoed through the burned-out ruins]." *Chūō Kōron* 129, no. 9:156–165.

Henshall, Kenneth G. 1999. *Dimensions of Japanese Society: Gender, Margins and Main-stream*. New York: St. Martin's Press.

Hikihara, Tadeo, and John M. Kuzell, eds. 1993. *Journey to the Real: Selected Poems of Takashi Arima*. New York: Weatherhill.

Hiroshima FM. 2012. *Shokutaku ongaku* [Tabletop music]. Broadcast March 2, 2012. Transcript archived online at http://hfm.jp/blog/shokutaku/m/e/_201216_19832tdk5_5_198431st13.php. Accessed April 16, 2021.

Hoaglund, Linda, dir. 2010. *ANPO: Art X War*. New York: New Day Films. DVD.

Holloway, Susan D. 2010. *Women and Family in Contemporary Japan*. Cambridge: Cambridge University Press.

Hughes, Langston, Arnold Rampersad, David E. Roessel, and Bemis/Flaherty Collection of Gay Poetry. 1994. *The Collected Poems of Langston Hughes*. 1st ed. New York: Knopf.

Huh, Jang Wook. 2017. "Beyond Afro-Orientalism: Langston Hughes, Koreans, and the Poetics of Overlapping Dispossessions." *Comparative Literature* 69, no. 2:201–221.

Igarashi, Yoshikuni. 2000. *Bodies of Memory: Narratives of War in Postwar Japanese Culture, 1945–1970*. Princeton, NJ: Princeton University Press.

———. 2021. *Japan, 1972: Visions of Masculinity in an Age of Mass Consumerism*. New York: Columbia University Press.

Inoue, Mayumo. 2017. "The Inter-state 'Frames of War': On 'Japan-US Friendship' and Okinawa in the Transpacific." *American Quarterly* 69, no. 3:491–499.

Itakura, Hiroko. 2008. "Attitudes towards Masculine Japanese Speech in Multilingual Professional Contexts of Hong Kong: Gender, Identity, and Native-Speaker Status." *Journal of Multilingual and Multicultural Development* 29, no. 6:467–482.

Itoh, Makoto. 2000. *The Japanese Economy Reconsidered*. New York: St. Martin's Press.

Ivy, Marilyn. 1995. *Discourses of the Vanishing: Modernity, Phantasm, Japan*. Chicago: University of Chicago Press.

———. 2009. "Fascism, Yet?" In *The Culture of Japanese Fascism*, edited by Alan Tansman, vii–xi. Durham, NC: Duke University Press.

Jackson, Michael. 2013. *The Politics of Storytelling: Variations on a Theme by Hannah Arendt*, 2nd ed. Copenhagen: Museum Tusculanum Press.

Jackson, Travis A. 2012. *Blowin' the Blues Away: Performance and Meaning on the New York Jazz Scene*. Berkeley: University of California Press.

Kadota, Ryusho. 2017. *Kiseki no uta: Sensō to bōkyo to Pegī Hayama* [The miraculous song: War, longing for home, and Peggy Hayama]. Tokyo: Shōgakukan.

Kagawa, Ryō. 1972. "*Onna ni tsuite* [Regarding women]." In *Takada Wataru, Kagawa Ryo, Yoshida Takurō sakuhinshū* [The collected works of Takada Wataru, Kagawa Ryō, and Yoshida Takurō]. Tokyo: Kyōgakusha.

Kanagawa shinbunsha. 1990. "*Yokohama—Oka to umi no matsuri Shisei 100 shūnen, kaikō 130 shūnen kinen jigyō kōshiki kiroku* [Yokohama: A festival of hills and sea: A public record of the special events marking 100 years since city incorporation, and 130 years from the opening of the port]." Special to the Yokohama City Finance Bureau 100th Anniversary of Municipal Government Special Event Planning Section, March 1990, 170–171.

Kapur, Nick. 2018. *Japan at the Crossroads: Conflict and Compromise after Anpo*. Cambridge, MA: Harvard University Press.

Karatani, Kojin. 2014. *The Structure of World History: From Modes of Production to Modes of Exchange*. Translated by Michael K. Bourdaghs. Durham, NC: Duke University Press.

Karatani, Kojin, and Asada Akira, eds. 1991. *Hihyō kūkan* [Critical space] 1.

Kawabata, Yasunari. 1969. *Japan the Beautiful and Myself*. Tokyo: Kodansha International.

Kawashima, Ken C. 2009. *The Proletarian Gamble: Korean Workers in Interwar Japan*. Durham, NC: Duke University Press.

Kawashima, Ken C., Fabian Schafer, and Robert Stolz, eds. 2014. *Tosaka Jun: A Critical Reader*. Honolulu: University of Hawai'i Press.

Kawato, Yuko. 2015. *Protests against U.S. Military Base Policy in Asia: Persuasion and Its Limits*. Stanford, CA: Stanford University Press.

Kelly, William W., ed. 2004. *Fanning the Flames: Fans and Consumer Culture in Contemporary Japan*. Albany: SUNY Press.

King, Angela. 2004. "The Prisoner of Gender: Foucault and the Disciplining of the Female Body." *Journal of International Women's Studies* 5, no. 2:29–39.

King, Thomas. 2003. *The Truth about Stories: A Native Narrative*. Minneapolis: University of Minnesota Press.

Kingston, Jeff. 2011. *Contemporary Japan: History, Politics, and Social Change since the 1980s*. Oxford: Wiley-Blackwell.

Kleeman, Faye. 2003. *Under an Imperial Sun: Japanese Colonial Literature of Taiwan and the South*. Honolulu: University of Hawai'i Press.

Konishi, Ryōtarō. 2001a. *Misora Hibari Namida no kawa wo koete* [Misora Hibari: Beyond the river of tears]. Tokyo: Kōbunsha.

———. 2001b. *Onnatachi no ryūkōka* [Women's popular songs]. Tokyo: Sankei Shinbun News Service.

Kono, Kimberly T. 2012. "Imperializing Motherhood: The Education of a 'Manchu Girl' in Colonial Manchuria." In *Reading Colonial Japan: Text, Context, and Critique*, edited by Michele Mason and Helen J. S. Lee, 228–261. Stanford, CA: Stanford University Press.

Koshiro, Yukiko. 1994. "The U.S. Occupation of Japan as a Mutual Racial Experience." *Journal of American-East Asian Relations* 3, no. 4:299–323.

Kurihara, Yasushi. 2017. "Live Report: One Night Premium Live at Nippon Budōkan." August 22. Published online at https://tsuyoshinagabuchi.com/live/one-night-premium -live/.

Latour, Bruno. 1993. *We Have Never Been Modern*. Translated by Catherine Porter. Cambridge, MA: Harvard University Press.

———. 2005. *Reassembling the Social: An Introduction to Actor-Network Theory*. Oxford: Oxford University Press.

Lee, Yeounsuk. 2009. *The Ideology of Kokugo: Nationalizing Language in Modern Japan*. Honolulu: University of Hawai'i Press.

Lefebvre, Henri. 1991. *The Production of Space*. Translated by Donald Nicholson Smith. Malden, MA: Blackwell.

Lichten, Jack. 2012. "Japan's Vietnam War: 1960s Politics, Korea, and the US in the Films of Ōshima Nagisa." *AGLOS: Journal of Area-Based Global Studies*, 1–24.

Long, Hoyt. 2012. *On Uneven Ground: Miyazawa Kenji and the Making of Place in Modern Japan*. Stanford, CA: Stanford University Press.

Malm, William P. 1986. "A Century of Proletarian Music in Japan." *Journal of Musicological Research* 6:185–206.

Manabe, Noriko. 2015. *The Revolution Will Not Be Televised: Protest Music after Fukushima*. New York: Oxford University Press.

Marotti, William. 2013. *Money, Trains, and Guillotines: Art and Revolution in 1960s Japan*. Durham, NC: Duke University Press.

Mason, Michele, and Helen Lee, eds. 2012. *Reading Colonial Japan: Text, Context, and Critique*. Stanford, CA: Stanford University Press.

Massey, Doreen. 1994. *Space, Place, and Gender*. Cambridge: Polity Press.

Massumi, Brian. 1995. "The Autonomy of Affect." *Cultural Critique* 31:83–109.

Matsuda, Takashi. 2007. *Soft Power and Its Perils: U.S. Cultural Policy in Early Postwar Japan and Permanent Dependency*. Washington, DC: Woodrow Wilson Center Press.

Matsumoto, Takashi. 2019. *"Kotoba wo kaze ni nosete sekai he* [Putting words on the wind and sending them out into the world]." Interview by *Keio Student Press*. February 3. https://www.jukushin.com/archives/35871/.

Matsuyama, Chiharu. 2000. Interview with Kinki Kids and Yoshida Takurō. *Love-Love Aishiteru* [Love-Love I Love You]. Fuji TV, July 29, 2000.

McCormack, Gavan, and Satoko Oka Norimatsu. 2012. *Resistant Islands: Okinawa Confronts Japan and the United States*. Lanham, MD: Rowman and Littlefield.

McKay, George. 2015. *The Pop Festival: History, Music, Media, Culture*. New York: Bloomsbury.

Mes, Tom. 2002. "Hayao Miyazaki." Interview published online in *Midnight Eye: Visions of Japanese Cinema*, January 7. https://www.midnighteye.com/interviews/hayao-miyazaki/.

Midford, Paul. 2011. *Rethinking Japanese Public Opinion and Security: From Pacifism to Realism?* Stanford, CA: Stanford University Press.

Migge, Bettina, and Isabelle Léglise. 2007. "Language and Colonialism (Applied Linguistics in the Context of Creole Communities)." In *Language and Communication: Diversity and Change: Handbook of Applied Linguistics,* edited by Marlis Hellinger and Anne Pauwels, 297–338. Berlin: Mouton de Gruyter.

Ministry of Foreign Affairs of Japan. 1996. "The SACO Final Report." December 2. https://www.mofa.go.jp/region/n-america/us/security/96saco1.html.

Ministry of Health, Labour, and Welfare. 2020. *Reiwa Gan'nen chingin kōzō kihon tōkei chōsa* [2019 Basic survey on wage structure]. Amended September 18, 2020. https://www.mhlw.go.jp/toukei/itiran/roudou/chingin/kouzou/z2019/.

Mishima, Yukio. 1961. *"Yūkoku* [Patriotism]." *Shōsetsu Chūō Kōron* 2, no. 1. Also available in English translation as Yukio Mishima, 1966, *Patriotism*. Translated by Geoffrey W. Sargent. New York: New Directions Publishing Corporation.

Mitsui, Tōru. 2013. "Music and Protest in Japan: The Rise of Underground Folk Song in 1968." In *Music and Protest in 1968*, edited by Beate Kutsche and Barley Norton, 81–96. New York: Cambridge University Press.

Mitsui, Tōru, and Shūhei Hosokawa. 1998. *Karaoke around the World: Global Technology, Local Singing*. London: Routledge.

Mizohata, Sachie. 2016. "Nippon Kaigi: Empire, Contradiction, and Japan's Future." *Asia Pacific Journal: Japan Focus* 14, no. 21.

Muramoto, Takeshi. 2003. *"Rirekisho wo okuttano wa boku gurai janai, myūjishan de* [I think that I was about the only musician to send in a résumé]." *Unyū Tenka* 34:10–18.

Murphy, Alex. 2022. "What the Ear Sees: Media, Performance, and the Politics of the Voice in Japan, 1918–1942." PhD diss., University of Chicago.

Muto, Ichiyo. 2016. "Retaking Japan: The Abe Administration's Campaign to Overturn the Postwar Constitution." Translated by John Junkerman. *Asia Pacific Journal: Japan Focus* 14, no. 13-3.

Nagabuchi, Tsuyoshi. 2015. *"Nagabuchi Tsuyoshi: Minshū no ikari to inori no uta* [Nagabuchi Tsuyoshi: Songs of the fury and prayer of the people]." Special issue, *Bungei*. Tokyo: Kawade Shobo Shinsha.

Nagabuchi Tsuyoshi Club. 1992. "Tsuyoshi Nagabuchi in Detroit with Bruce Springsteen." *Nagabuchi Tsuyoshi Club Special Press for Members*, vol. 11.

Nagahara, Hiromu. 2017. *Tokyo Boogie-Woogie: Japan's Pop Era and Its Discontents.* Cambridge, MA: Harvard University Press, 2.

Nagaike, Kazumi. 2012. "Johnny's Idols as Icons: Female Desires to Fantasize and Consume Male Idol Images." In *Idols and Celebrity in Japanese Media Culture,* edited by Patrick W. Galbraith and Jason G. Karlin, 97–112. New York: Palgrave Macmillan.

Nagira, Ken'ichi. 1999. *Nihon fōku shiteki daizen* [Japanese folk: My own collection]. Tokyo: Chikuma Shobō.

Naregal, Veena. 1999. "Colonial Bilingualism and Hierarchies of Language and Power: Making of a Vernacular Sphere in Western India." *Economic and Political Weekly* 34, no. 49:3446–3456.

National Bureau of Asian Research. 2021. "Timeline of Operation Tomodachi." Accessed June 30, 2021. https://www.nbr.org/publication/timeline-of-operation-tomodachi/.

Nihon Amachua Kayō Renmei [Japan Amateur Popular Song Federation] (NAK). 2002. *NAK 20 shūnen kinen zadan-kai: uta to sono jidai wo katarō* [NAK 20th anniversary special roundtable: Speaking of songs and their times]. Tokyo: NAK Publication for Members.

———. 2010. *Enka kentei: Nippon yo, matasete gomen! Enka kentei, hajimaru* [Hey Japan, sorry to keep you waiting! The *enka* proficiency test starts now]. Promotional documentation provided to the author by NAK staff on May 29, 2010. Tokyo: NAK Publication for Members.

Nikkan Sports. 2015. *Inochi wo kakete nani ga dekiru no ka / Nagabuchi Fuji ni tatsu* [What can be accomplished when you bet your very life? Nagabuchi stands at Fuji]. Nikkan Sports, August 4, 2015. https://www.nikkansports.com/entertainment/news/1517198.html.

Novak, David. 2013. *Japanoise: Music at the Edge of Circulation.* Durham, NC: Duke University Press.

Nozaki, Yoshiko. 2008. *War Memory, Nationalism and Education in Postwar Japan, 1945–2007.* New York: Routledge.

Nye, Joseph S. 2004. *Soft Power: The Means to Success in World Politics.* New York: Public Affairs.

———. 2009. "Get Smart: Combining Hard and Soft Power." *Foreign Affairs* 88, no. 4: 160–163.

Office of the Director of National Intelligence. 1952. *Daily Intelligence Briefing: JAPAN (Secret).* February 27. Archived online at https://www-archivesdirect-amdigital-co-uk. Accessed May 27, 2021.

Oguma, Eiji. 2015. "Japan's 1968: A Collective Reaction to Rapid Economic Growth in an Age of Turmoil." Translated by Nick Kapur. *Asia Pacific Journal: Japan Focus* 13, no. 12-1.

Ohara, Yumiko, Scott Saft, and Graham Crookes. 2001. "Toward a Feminist Critical Pedagogy in a Beginning Japanese-as-a-Foreign-Language Class." *Japanese Language and Literature* 35, no. 2:105–133.

Okamoto, Shigeko. 2006. "Variability in Japanese (Discourse)." *Encyclopedia of Language and Linguistics* 13:319–326.

Okui, Kaori. 1998. *Bakatare* [Idiot]. Tokyo: HOME-SHA.

Ōsugi, Sakae. 2014. *"Minzokukokka-shugi no kyogi"* [The falsehood of nationalist statism]. In *Ōsugi Sakae zenshū* [The complete works of Ōsugi Sakae]. Vol. 4, edited by the Ōsugi Sakae Zenshū Editorial Committee. Tokyo: Palu Publishing.

Ota, Fumio. 2008. "Ethics of Training for the Samurai Warrior." In *Ethics Education in the Military,* edited by Nigel de Lee and Paul Robinson, 147–158. London: Routledge.

Poetry Foundation. n.d. "Shuntaro Tanikawa." https://www.poetryfoundation.org/poets/shuntaro-tanikawa. Accessed May 21, 2022.

Polletta, Francesca. 2006. *It Was like a Fever Storytelling in Protest and Politics.* Chicago: University of Chicago Press.

Rabson, Steve. 1998. *Righteous Cause or Tragic Folly: Changing Views of War in Japanese Poetry.* Ann Arbor: University of Michigan Center for Japanese Studies.

Roberson, James. 2011. "'Doin' Our Thing': Identity and Colonial Modernity in Okinawan Rock Music." *Popular Music and Society* 34, no. 5:593–620.

Roy, Arundhati. 2003. *War Talk.* Cambridge: South End Press.

Sakai, Naoki. 1992. *Voices of the Past.* Ithaca, NY: Cornell University Press.

———. 2004. "Two Negations: Fear of Being Excluded and the Logic of Self-Esteem." *Novel: A Forum on Fiction* 37, no. 3:229–257.

———. 2006. "'You Asians': On the Historical Role of the West and Asia Binary." In *Japan after Japan: Social and Cultural Life from the Recessionary 1990s to the Present,* edited by Tomiko Yoda and Harry D. Harootunian, 168–194. Durham, NC: Duke University Press.

———. 2009. "Translation and the Schematism of Bordering." Conference paper given at *Translating Society: A Commentators Conference,* October 29–31, 2009, University of Konstanz.

Sakamoto, Michitaka. 2007. *"Hikokumin no seishin—fōku shingā Kagawa Ryō* [The spirit of an anti-patriot: Folk singer Kagawa Ryō]. *Hokuriku Chūnichi shinbun,* January 10, 2007.

Sankei Sports. 2015. *"Nagabuchi Tsuyoshi, Anpo hōan de netsuben 'Oira no taishō ni "Chotto chigaunjanai" to iitai'* [Tsuyoshi Nagabuchi speaks passionately on the proposed security treaty legislation: 'I'd like to say to our leader, "hey, you're a bit off-base here"'].*" Sankei Sports Geinō,* July 19, 2015. https://www.sanspo.com/article/20150719-GCCCXKKDL5NJZPA42JHDNL3RMI.

Sankei West. 2014. *"Kyōdai popopro keisatsu mudan tachi'iri* [Police enter the campus of Kyoto University without authorization]." *Sankei West,* November 8, 2014. https://www.sankei.com/west/news/141108/wst1411080056-n1.html.

Sasaki, Tomoyuki. 2015. *Japan's Postwar Military and Civil Society: Contesting a Better Life.* London: Bloomsbury.

Satō, Fumika. 2012. "A Camouflaged Military: Japan's Self-Defense Forces and Globalized Gender Mainstreaming." *Asia-Pacific Journal* 10, no. 36-3.

Satō, Gō. 2019. *"Piito Shiigaa wo tazuneta juuhassai no Takada Wataru ni honnin kara watasareta saizenretsu no chiketto* [On reaching out to Pete Seeger, 18-year-old Takada Wataru receives a front row-center ticket from the artist himself]." *Tap the Pop* online Japanese music journal. Accessed July 18, 2020. http://www.tapthepop .net/extra/36491.

Satō, Yukie. 2013. "Interview with Gopchang-Jeongol." Interview by *Gekkan Gurutogi, Korean Beat,* May 2013. http://www.koreanbeat.co.jp/new09/gurutogi/inter1305.php.

Schmidt, Michael. 2018. "The Louis Armstrong Story, Reissues, and the LP Record: Anchors of Significance." *Journal of Social History* 52, no. 2:304–331.

Shibuichi, Daiki. 2017. "The Article 9 Association, Leftist Elites, and the Movement to Save Article 9 of Japan's Postwar Constitution." *East Asia* 34:147–161.

Shibusawa, Naoko. 2006. *America's Geisha Ally: Reimagining the Japanese Enemy.* Cambridge, MA: Harvard University Press.

Silverberg, Miriam. 2006. *Erotic Grotesque Nonsense: The Mass Culture of Japanese Modern Times.* Berkeley: University of California Press.

Singh, Bhubhindar. 2015. "The Development of Japanese Security Policy: A Long-Term Defensive Strategy." *Asia Policy* 19:49–64.

Small, Christopher. 1998. *Musicking: The Meanings of Performing and Listening.* Middletown, CT: Wesleyan University Press.

Soeda, Azembō. 2009. *A Life Adrift: Soeda Azembo, Popular Song, and Modern Mass Culture in Japan.* Translated by Michael Lewis. Oxon: Routledge.

Sone Yūji. 2010. "Beyond Performance: Yukio Mishima's Theatre of Death." *Performance Research* 15, no. 1:32–40.

Sports Hōchi. 2007. *"Gyōkai Project X EMI Producer Yamaguchi Eikō-shi* [Music Biz Project X: EMI producer Yamaguchi Eikō]." *Sports Hōchi shinbun,* September 25, 2007.

Sports Nippon. 2015. *"Puri-Piro egao shien Sendai ni raibu hausu 3.11 kokera otoshi kōen* [Princess Princess bring smiles and support: A live house for Sendai, opening concert on 3.11]." *Sponichi Annex,* August 28, 2015. Archived online at https://www .sponichi.co.jp/entertainment/news/2015/08/28/kiji/K20150828011020220.html. Accessed May 28, 2001.

Stevens, Carolyn. 1999. "Rocking the Bomb: A Case Study in the Politicization of Popular Culture." *Japanese Studies* 19, no. 1:49–67.

———. 2008. *Japanese Popular Music: Culture, Authenticity, and Power.* New York: Routledge.

Stimeling, Travis D. 2011. "'Phases and Stages, Circles and Cycles': Willie Nelson and the Concept Album." *Popular Music* 30, no. 3:389–408.

Stirr, Anna Marie. 2017. *Singing across Divides: Music and Intimate Politics in Nepal.* New York: Oxford University Press.

Stone, Ruth. 1982. *Let the Inside Be Sweet: The Interpretation of Music Event among the Kpelle of Liberia.* Bloomington, IN: Trickster Press.

Super J Channel. 1999. Episode featuring Nakajima Miyuki's work with the Deliberative Council on National Language. TV Asahi, February 19, 1999.

Takada, Ren. 2015. *"Densetsu no fooku shingaa Takada Wataru ga musuko Ren ni hikitsuida seikatsusha no uta* [The songs of everyday people passed down by legendary folk singer Takada Wataru to his son Ren]." Interview by Kaneko Atsutake, *CINRA,*

April 14, 2015. https://www.cinra.net/interview/201504-takadaren?path=%2Finterview%2F201504-takadaren&page=4.

Takada, Wataru. 2004. Untitled televised interview with Chikushi Tetsuya. *Chikushi Tetsuya no News23*. Tokyo Broadcasting System, July 3, 2004.

———. 2008. *Bābon sutorīto burūsu* [Bourbon Street blues]. Tokyo: Chikuma Shobō.

Takada, Wataru, and Takada Ren. 2015. *Mai furendo Takada Wataru seishun nikki, 1966–1969* [My friend: Takada Wataru's diary of youth, 1966–1969]. Tokyo: Kawade Shobō Shinsha.

Tamanoi, Mariko Asano. 1998. *Under the Shadow of Nationalism: Politics and Poetics of Rural Japanese Women*. Honolulu: University of Hawai'i Press.

Tansman, Alan, ed. 2009. *The Aesthetics of Japanese Fascism*. Berkeley: University of California Press.

Time. 1961. "The Press: 100% Un-American." February 24, 1961.

Todd, Mabell Loomis, ed. 1896. *Poems by Emily Dickinson*. Boston: Roberts Brothers.

Tomiyama, Ichirō. 2000. "'Spy': Mobilization and Identity in Wartime Okinawa." *Senri Ethnological Studies* 51:121–132.

———. 2005. "On Becoming 'a Japanese': The Community of Oblivion and Memories of the Battlefield." *Asia Pacific Journal: Japan Focus* 3, no. 10.

Treat, John Whittier, ed. 1996. *Contemporary Japan and Popular Culture*. Honolulu: University of Hawai'i Press.

Tsuda, Takeyuki. 1999. "Transnational Migration and the Nationalization of Ethnic Identity among Japanese Brazilian Return Migrants." *Ethos* 27:145–179.

Ueno, Ryō. 1967. *Chotto kawatta jinsei ron* [A slightly odd philosophy of life]. Tokyo: San-Ichi Shobō.

———. 1985. *Nihon no Pū Yokochō: Shiteki-na, amari nimo shiteki-na jidō bungakushi* [Japan's Pooh Alley: A personal, exceedingly personal history of children's literature]. Tokyo: Mitsumura Tosho.

Urayama, Yoshiko. 2016. *"Fooku buumu kara 40 nen, Kagawa Ryō ha ima mo koko ni iru* [Forty years from the folk boom, Kagawa Ryō is still here]." *Chicago Shinpō*, October 21, 2016, 21–22.

U.S. Foreign Office, Tokyo. 1952. *Your Telegram No. 179: Anti-Colonial Day Demonstrations in Japan. Priority Confidential*. February 25, 1952. Archived online at https://www.archivesdirect.amdigital.co.uk. Accessed May 27, 2021.

U.S. General Accounting Office. 1986. Report to the Chairman, Readiness Subcommittee, Armed Services Committee, House of Representatives. *STARS & STRIPES: Appropriated, Funds Should Be Reduced*. May 1986.

Virno, Paolo. 2004. Translated by Isabella Bertoletti, James Cascaito, and Andrea Casson. *A Grammar of the Multitude: For an Analysis of Contemporary Forms of Life*. Los Angeles: Semiotexte.

Vogel, Ezra F. 1979. *Japan as Number One: Lessons for America*. New York: Harper.

Wade, Bonnie C. 2009. *Thinking Musically: Experiencing Music, Expressing Culture*. New York: Oxford University Press.

———. 2014. *Composing Japanese Musical Modernity*. Chicago: University of Chicago Press.

Wajima, Yūsuke. 2014. "The Birth of Enka." In *Made in Japan: Studies in Popular Music*, edited by Tōru Mitsui, 71–83. New York: Routledge.

Walker, Brett L. 2010. *Toxic Archipelago: A History of Industrial Disease in Japan*. Seattle: University of Washington Press.

Wang, Yiman. 2012. "Affective Politics and the Legend of Yamaguchi Yoshiko / Li Xianglan." In *Sino-Japanese Transculturation,* edited by Richard King, Cody Poulton, and Katsuhiko Endo, 143–166. Plymouth: Lexington Books.

Washburn, Dennis C. 2007. *Translating Mt. Fuji: Modern Japanese Fiction and the Ethics of Identity.* New York: Columbia University Press.

Watanabe, Anne. 2020. Cover of *"Kyōkun I* [Lesson I]," by Kagawa Ryō. April 14, 2020, video, 2:27. Accessed January 11, 2021. https://www.youtube.com/watch?v=8Oo_DaRTJWM.

Wedeen, Lisa. 2008. *Peripheral Visions: Publics, Power, and Performance in Yemen.* Chicago: University of Chicago Press.

Welch, Michael. 2000. *Flag Burning: Moral Panic and the Criminalization of Protest.* New York: Aldine de Gruyter.

White, Micah. 2016. *The End of Protest: A New Playbook for Revolution.* Toronto: Knopf Canada.

Wilson, Jean. 1993. "Enka: The Music People Love or Hate." *Japan Quarterly* 40, no. 2:283–292.

Yamaguchi, Jiro. 1992. "The Gulf War and the Transformation of Japanese Constitutional Politics." *Journal of Japanese Studies* 18, no. 1:155–172.

Yamanokuchi, Baku. 1964. *Maguro ni iwashi: Yamanokuchi Baku shishū* [Sardines for tuna: Yamanokuchi Baku poetry collection]. Tokyo: Hara Shobō.

Yano, Christine R. 1996. "The Floating World of Karaoke in Japan." *Popular Music and Society* 20, no. 2:1–17.

———. 2000. "Dream Girl: Imaging the 'Girl Next Door' within the Heart/Soul of Japan." *U.S.-Japan Women's Journal English Supplement* 19:122–141.

———. 2002. *Tears of Longing: Nostalgia and the Nation in Japanese Popular Song.* Cambridge, MA: Harvard University Press.

Yasar, Kerim. 2018. *Electrified Voices: How the Telegraph, Phonograph, and Radio Shaped Modern Japan, 1868–1945.* New York: Columbia University Press.

Yomiuri shinbun. 1988a. *"Manatsu no yoru no ongakusai: Nōsu dokku, Nichi-Bei yūkō he kaihō* [A midsummer night's musical festival: North Dock to be opened for U.S.-Japan friendship]." *Yomiuri shinbun,* April 26, 1988, 22.

———. 1988b. *"Tomahōku yori rokku?! Hassen-nin fībā* [Rock instead of tomahawks?! 8,000 people get the fever]." *Yomiuri shinbun,* September 1, 1988, 14.

Yoshida, Reiji, and Mizuho Aoki. 2015. "Diet Enacts Security Laws, Marking Japan's Departure from Pacifism." *Japan Times,* September 19, 2015.

Young, Louise. 1998. *Japan's Total Empire: Manchuria and the Culture of Wartime Imperialism.* Berkeley: University of California Press.

Yukawa, Reiko (@yukawareiko). 2012. *"Nagabuchi Tsuyoshi san ga senjitsu okonawareta Kagoshima Shimin Bunka Hall no konsāto no sutēji de katatta kotoba desu* [This is what Tsuyoshi Nagabuchi had to say onstage during his concert held at the Kagoshima Shimin Bunka Hall the other day]." Twitter, July 2, 2012, 2:33 a.m., https://twitter.com/yukawareiko/status/219680068333608960.

Žižek, Slavoj. 1993. *Tarrying with the Negative: Kant, Hegel, and the Critique of Ideology.* Durham, NC: Duke University Press.

Žižek, Slavoj, and Andrew Herscher. 1997. "Everything Provokes Fascism/Plečnik Avec Laibach." *Assemblage* 33:59–75.

DISCOGRAPHY

Akasaka Komachi. *"Hōkago Jugyō* [After-School Class]." TDK Records, March 21, 1984, vinyl single.

Animals, The. "House of the Rising Sun." Track 1 on *The Animals.* ABKCO Records, September 1964, LP album.

Baez, Joan. *"Le Déserteur."* Track 6 on *Tournée Européenne.* Epic Records, 1980, LP album.

Byrds, The. "Turn! Turn! Turn!" Track 1 on *Turn! Turn! Turn!* Columbia Records, December 6, 1965, LP album.

Carter Family, The. "Will the Circle Be Unbroken." Track B3 on *Keep on the Sunny Side.* Columbia Nashville Legacy, 1964, LP album.

Chiaki, Naomi. *"Akai Hana* [The Red Flower]." Teichiku Records, October 23, 1991, CD single.

Eri, Chiemi. "Tennessee Waltz." King Records, January 23, 1952, vinyl single.

Folk Crusaders. *"Kanashikute Yarikirenai* [I'm So Sad That I Can't Go On]." Capital Records, March 21, 1968, vinyl single.

Fuse, Akira. *"Karuchie Rasoartan no Yuki* [Snow in the Latin Quarter]." King Records, December 21, 1971, vinyl single.

Happy End. *Kazemachi Roman* [Romance in the City of Wind]. URC Records, November 20, 1971, LP album.

Hatakeyama, Midori. *"Kyōkun* [Lessons]." RCA Victor, November 1972, vinyl single.

Hayama, Peggy. "Domino." King Records, 1952, vinyl single.

———. *"Nangoku Tosa wo Ato ni Shite* [Leaving Behind Tosa, That Southern Land]." King Records, April 1959, vinyl single.

Hidaka, Mitsuhiro, a.k.a SKY-HI. "The Story of J." Track 6 on *FREE TOKYO.* Avex Trax, August 21, 2018, CD album.

Iwai, Hiroshi. *Boku no Shirushi: Warabeuta* [A Sign of My Existence: Nursery Rhymes]. URC Records, 1970, LP album.

Kagawa, Ryō. *"Akai Tsuchi no Shita de* [Under the Red Earth]." Track 10 on *Kyōkun* [Lessons]. URC Records, 1971, LP album.

———. *"D no Tsuki* [Waxing Moon]." Track 2 on *Mirai* [The Future]. TWINS Records, 2016, CD album.

———. *"Kyōkun I* [Lesson I]." Track 1 on *Kyōkun* [Lessons]. URC Records, 1971, LP album.

———. *Minami-yuki Haiuei* [Southbound Highway]. Teichiku/Black Records, 1976, LP album.

———. "*Mune ni Afureru Kono Omoi* [This Feeling That Floods My Heart]." Track 2 on *2/tu*. Japan Records, 1993, CD album.

———. "*Sensō Shimashō* [Let Us Go to War]." Track 5 on *Kyōkun* [Lessons]. URC Records, 1971, LP album.

———. "*Shiawasesō na Hitotachi* [Happy-Looking People]." Track 6 on *Mirai* [The Future]. TWINS Records, 2016, CD album.

———. "*Sono Asa* [That Morning]." Track 6 on *Kyōkun* [Lessons]. URC Records, 1971, LP album.

Kagawa, Ryō, with Sugino Nobu. "*Kyōkun I* [Lesson I]." Track 6 on *USED*. TWINS Records, October 2002, CD album.

———. "*Kyōkun I* [Lesson I]." Track 7 on *USED END*. Greenwood Records, 2007, CD album.

Kagawa, Ryō, with Te-Chili. "*Kyōkun I* [Lesson I]." Track 2 on *Rock*. UK.Project, November 21, 1996, CD album.

Kagawa, Ryō, with Tokyo Kid Brothers. *Jū-gatsu ha Tasogare no Kuni* [The October Country]. Greenwood Records, 1975, LP album.

Kakyōin, Shinobu. "*Bōkyō Shin-Sōma* [Longing for Home, Shin-Sōma]." Victor Entertainment, October 22, 2003, CD single.

Kasagi, Shizuko. "*Tōkyō Bugiugi* [Tokyo Boogie-Woogie]." Japan Columbia, January 1948, vinyl single.

Kōzai, Kaori. "*Echizen Renka* [Fukui Love Song]." Universal Music, December 19, 1994, CD maxi single.

Kozakura, Maiko. "*Boshi Jongara* [Mother and Daughter *Jongara*]." Teichiku Entertainment, July 22, 2009, CD maxi single.

Kitajima, Saburō. "*Hiei no Kaze* [Winds at Mount Hiei]." Japan Crown, June 5, 2009, CD single.

Maki, Mike. "*Bara ga Saita* [The Rose Bloomed]." Philips Records, 1966, vinyl single.

Mikami, Shizu. "*Onna* [Woman]." Tokuma Japan Communications, September 6, 2006, CD single.

Misora, Hibari. "*Owari Naki Tabi* [The Never-Ending Journey]." Track 14 on *Fushichō* [Phoenix]. Japan Columbia, April 11, 1988, CD album.

Moriyama, Naotarō. "*Itoshi Kimi E* [To My Beloved You]." Track 3 on *Arata-naru Kōshinryō wo Motomete* [In Search of New Ingredients]. Universal Music Japan, May 26, 2004, CD album.

Nagabuchi, Tsuyoshi. "*Ashita wo Kudasee* [Gimme a Tomorrow]." Track 6 on *Stay Alive*. Nayuta Wave Records, May 16, 2012, CD album.

———. "CLOSE YOUR EYES." Track 2, disc 2, on *YAMATO*. For Life Music Entertainment, October 19, 2005, double-length CD album.

———. "*Fuji-no-Kuni* [The Fuji Nation]." Universal Music, June 22, 2015, CD maxi single.

———. "*Hitotsu* [One]." Universal Music, February 1, 2012, CD maxi single.

———. "*Itsuka no Shōnen* [The Sometime Boy]." Track 3 on *Shōwa*. EMI Music Japan, March 25, 1989, LP/CD album.

———. "JAPAN." Track 1 on *JAPAN*. EMI Music Japan, December 14, 1991, LP/CD album.

———. "*Junrenka* [Roundabout Love]." Toshiba EMI, October 5, 1978, vinyl single.

———. "*Kagoshima Chūō* STATION." Track 1 on *Come on Stand Up*. For Life Music Entertainment, May 16, 2007, CD album.

———. "*Kamashitare!* [Go Get 'Em!]." Track 12 on *FRIENDS*. Nayuta Wave Records, August 12, 2009, CD album.

———. "*Kamome* [Seagulls]." Track 5 on *STAY ALIVE*. Nayuta Wave Records, May 16, 2012, CD album.

———. "*Karasu* [Crows]." Track 6 on *JEEP*. EMI Music Japan, August 25, 1990, CD album.

———. "*Kazoku* [Family]." Track 9 on *Kazoku*. Toshiba EMI, January 1, 1996, CD album.

———. "*Kibai-yanse* [Fight It Out]." Track 9 on *JAPAN*. EMI Music Japan, December 14, 1991, CD album.

———. "LICENSE." Track 8 on *LICENSE*. EMI Music Japan, August 5, 1987, CD album.

———. "Myself." Track 12 on *JEEP*. EMI Music Japan, August 25, 1990, CD album.

———. "*Naite Chinpira* [Cry, Gangster]." Track 1 on *LICENSE*. EMI Music Japan, August 5, 1987, CD album.

———. "*Natsu-matsuri* [Summer Festival]." Track 1 on *BEST COLLECTION—Itsuka no Shōnen*. EMI Music Japan, December 1, 1994, CD album.

———. "*Nishi-Shinjuku no Oyaji no Uta* [Song for the Old Man from West Shinjuku]." Track 10 on *JEEP*. EMI Music Japan, August 25, 1990, CD album.

———. "*O-uchi e Kaerō* [Head on Home]." Track 7 on *JEEP*. EMI Music Japan, August 25, 1990, CD album.

———. "*Oyashirazu* [Wisdom Teeth]." Track 7 on *JAPAN*. EMI Music Japan, December 14, 1991, CD album.

———. "*Rokunamonjanee* [Ain't No Good]." Track 4 on *LICENSE*. EMI Music Japan, August 5, 1987, CD album.

———. "SAKURAJIMA." Track 9 on *Keep on Fighting*. For Life Music Entertainment, May 14, 2003, CD album.

———. "*Shizuka-naru Afugan* [Quiet in Afghanistan]." For Life Music Entertainment, May 9, 2002, CD single.

———. "STAY DREAM." Track 11 on *STAY DREAM*. Toshiba EMI, October 22, 1986, CD album.

———. "*Tombo* [The Dragonfly]." Track 4 on *Shōwa*. EMI Music Japan, March 25, 1989, LP/CD album.

———. "*Tsumetai Gaikokujin* [The Cold-Hearted Foreigner]." Track 4 on *HEAVY GAUGE*. Toshiba EMI, June 21, 1983, LP album.

Natsumi. "*Kami no Piano* [The Paper Piano]." Japan Crown, May 21, 2004, CD maxi single.

Nelson, Willie. *Yesterday's Wine*. RCA Records, August 1971, LP album.

Nishikata, Hiroyuki. "*Otoko Nara ~ Heisei Bushi* [If You Are a Man: The Heisei Ditty]." King Records, January 26, 2011, CD maxi single.

Nishioka, Suirō, and Kusabue Keizō. "*Otoko Nara* [If You Are a Man]." King Records, May 1937, vinyl single.

Ōizumi, Itsurō. "*Sakata-Minato* [Sakata Port]." Teichiku Entertainment, April 23, 2008, CD maxi single.

Okabayashi, Nobuyasu. "*Kusokurae-bushi* [The Eat Shit Ballad]." URC Records, August 1, 1969, vinyl single.

———. "*San'ya Burūsu* [San'ya Blues]." URC Records, September 25, 1968, vinyl single.

Okabayashi, Nobuyasu, and Takaishi Tomoya. "*Tomo-yo* [O Friend]." Victor Records, September 5, 1968, vinyl single.

Ōtsuki, Miyako. "*Hakana Kawa* [Weary River]." King Records, July 23, 2009, CD single.

Peter, Paul and Mary. "*Le Déserteur.*" Track C1 on *In Concert*. Warner Bros. Records, 1964, double-length LP album.

Princess Princess. "19 GROWING UP ~Ode to My Buddy~." CBS Sony, February 1988, vinyl single.

———. "Diamonds." CBS Sony, April 21, 1989, CD single.

———. *DOLLS IN ACTION*. Sony Records, December 7, 1991, LP album.

———. "GO AWAY BOY." CBS Sony, May 21, 1988, CD single.

———. *LOVERS*. CBS Sony, November 17, 1989, LP album.

———. "M." Track 10 on *Let's Get Crazy*. CBS Sony, November 21, 1988, LP album.

———. "*Sekai de Ichiban Atsui Natsu* [The Hottest Summer in the World]." CBS Sony, July 16, 1987, EP single.

———. "SHE." Track 7 on *Here We Are*. CBS Sony, February 26, 1988, LP album.

Seeger, Pete. "Guantanamera." CBS Records, 1963, vinyl single.

Seeger, Pete, and Malvina Reynolds. "Andorra." Track B5 on *The Bitter and the Sweet*. Columbia Records, 1962, LP album.

Shimazu, Aya. "*Otsū*." Teichiku Entertainment, January 21, 2009, CD maxi single.

Springsteen, Bruce. "Born in the U.S.A." Track 1 on *Born in the U.S.A.* Columbia Records, June 4, 1984, LP album.

Takada, Wataru. "*Akirame-bushi* [The Give-Up Ditty]." Track 6 on *Takada Wataru / Itsutsu no Akai Fūsen* [Takada Wataru and the Five Red Balloons]. URC Records, February 1969, LP album.

———. "*Asahirō* [The House of the Rising Sun]." Track 7 on *Kisha ga Inaka wo Tōru Sono Toki* [At That Moment When the Train Passes through the Countryside]. URC Records, October 1969, LP album.

———. *Goaisatsu* [Greetings]. King Records, June 1, 1971, LP album.

———. "*Jieitai ni Hairō* [Let's Join the SDF]." Track 3 on *Takada Wataru / Itsutsu no Akai Fūsen* [Takada Wataru and the Five Red Balloons]. URC Records, February 1969, LP album.

———. "*Tōkyō Fooku Gerira no Shokun-tachi wo Kataru* [Speaking of the Young Men of the Tokyo Folk Guerrilla]." URC Records, December 1969, vinyl single.

Takaishi, Tomoya. "*Hō Chi Min no Barādo* [The Ballad of Ho Chi Minh]." URC Records, October 1969, vinyl single.

Takakura, Ken. "*Otoko Nara* [If You Are a Man]." King Records, 1966, vinyl single.

Takamine, Hideko. "*Ginza Kankan Musume* [The Ginza Can-Can Girl]." Victor, April 1949, vinyl single.

Yamamoto, Jōji. "*Sen-Ri no Michi Mo* [Even a Road of a Thousand *Ri*]." Teichiku Records, October 21, 2009, CD single.

Yashiro, Aki. "*Ai wo Shinjitai* [I Want to Believe in Love]." Track 10 on *Ai wo Shinjitai*. Japan Columbia, September 1, 1991, CD album.

INDEX

Page numbers in bold refer to figures.

122–126; Nagabuchi and, 189; role in U.S.-Japan friendship and, 30–31

"Geshukuya [The Boardinghouse]" (song), 111

"Ginza Kankan Musume" (song), 35

girls rock, 18. *See also* Princess Princess

gnkosaiBAND, 141

Goaisatsu [Greetings] (Takada), 18; components of, 93–104; everyday politics of, 69, 79; polyvocality of, 85–93; potentials of the LP and, 81–85; recording of, 74. *See also* Takada, Wataru

goaisatsu, as term, 97

Gojira [Godzilla] (film), 90

Goodman, Benny, 40

Gopchang-Jeongol, 107

Great East Japan Earthquake (2011), 22, 62

"Guantanamera" (song), 83

"Guide to Tokyo Night Life" (publication), 39

Gulf Wars, 67

Hachimitsu Pie, 85, 115

hansen fooku, 108, 141. *See also* anti-folk; folk music (*fooku*); Kansai Folk movement

Hanshin-Awaji (Kobe) Earthquake (1995), 81

Han'ya, 2

Happy End, 74, 85, 96, 115, 116

Harootunian, H. D., 14

Haruichiban concert series, 81

Hatakeyama, Midori, 107

Hattori, Ryōichi, 35

Hayama, Peggy, 18, 26, 28, 37–44

HEAVY GAUGE (Nagabuchi), 190–191

heckling, 4–5

Hibari, Misora, 27

"Hiei no Kaze [Winds at Mount Hiei]" (song), 154–155

High Treason Incident (1910), 76

Hiroshima nuclear bombing, 90

History, as mode of storytelling, 6, 72–73, 97–99

"Homesick Blues" (song by Kagawa), 19–20

Homesick Blues, as concept, 10–12

homesickness, as concept, 10

House Party (Linkletter), 29

Hughes, Langston, 87, 89

Humbert Humbert, 103, 107, 133

identity: musical storytelling and, 6–7, 10–11, 106–107; Nagabuchi's fans and, 188–189, 207–224; performative gender and, 129, 149–150; politics and, 4, 82; Springsteen and, 188. *See also* belonging

idol manufacturing, 54. *See also* doll trope; Princess Princess

Iihatov, 199–200, 206

Ikeda, Hayato, 45, 81, 149, 197

imagined community, 12

Imperial Palace, Tokyo, 185

Imperial Precepts to Soldiers and Sailors (1882), 124–125

inaka, 154, 204–205, 206, 215, 221

internal negation, 15

intersectionality, 8, 57, 66, 100, 187, 188, 208

Iraq War, 65, 67

Ishikawa, Sayuri, 147

Ishimure, Michiko, 5–6

"Itsuka no Shōnen [The Sometime Boy]" (song), 193, 194, 195, 218–219

Itsuki, Hiroyuki, 80, 144, 147

Itsutsu no Akai Fūsen, 72, 96, 112

Iwai, Hiroshi, 85, 110–111, 119

Iwakuni district, 36

Iwashi, 213–216

Jackson, Michael, 7, 11, 136

JAPAN (album by Nagabuchi), 191

"JAPAN" (song by Nagabuchi), 1–2, 191, 214

Japan Amateur Popular Song Festival. *See* NAK (Nihon Amachua Kayōsai)

Japanese identity. *See* identity

Japanese Iraq Reconstruction Group, 67

Japanese rock, 73–74

Japanism, as term, 98

Japan Record Awards, 147

Japan Revolutionary Communist League, 122

jazz, 28, 38, 44, 45

JEEP (Nagabuchi), 211

"Jieitai ni Hairō [Let's Join the SDF]" (song), 65, 66, 67, 68, 71–72, 81, 82, 105

"Jitensha ni Notte [Riding a Bike]" (song), 86, 96

liberal paternalism, 36, 42–44. *See also* neoliberalism

LICENSE (Nagabuchi), 191

"LICENSE" (song), 201, 218–219

"Life's Trades" (Dickinson), 85–86

Linkletter, Art, 29

Long, Hoyt, 199

love songs, 141–142

Lucky Dragon No. 5 incident (1954), 90–92

MacColl, Ewan, 120–121

Madame Bola's News (TBS), 66

"*Maguro ni Iwashi* [Sardines for Tuna]" (song), 90, 91–92

Maico, 2

Manchu Girl (Koizumi), 125–126

Martí, José, 83

Martin, Tony, 38

Masaaki, Hata, 110

Masako, 213–216

Masao, 220–224

masculinity, 122–131

Mason, Michele, 6

Matsumoto, Takashi, 96–97

Matsuyama, Chiharu, 133

Meiji Civil Code (1896), 124–125

Meiji Club, 36

Meiji Period (1868–1912), 75, 78, 79, 125, 126, 202, 231

Melparque Hall, 143, 146, 149, 151

Metronome (publication), 40

Mihashi, Kazuo, 75

Mikado, Haruki, 135

military forces. *See* SDF (Self-Defense Forces); U.S. Occupation of Japan (1945–1952)

Minami, Masato, 71

Misawa Air Base, 50

Mishima, Yukio, 82, 126

misogyny, 124

Misora, Hibari, 29, 147

Mississippi John Hurt, 86

Miyazaki, Hayao, 6

Miyazawa, Kenji, 199–200

Moonriders, 115

Morio, Agata, 115

Mozu, Shōhei, 147

Mr. Saitō of Heaven Building (Yamanokuchi), 90

Murakami, Ritsu, 115

Murata, Taku, 71

musical storytelling, overview, 5–17. *See also* Kagawa, Ryō; Nagabuchi, Tsuyoshi; political engagement and storytelling; storytelling; Takada, Wataru

music event, defined, 9

musicking, as term, 6. *See also* musical storytelling, overview

Nagabuchi, Tsuyoshi: background of, 186; career endpoint of, 224–227; *Come on Stand Up!,* 203; *FRIENDS,* 208; Kagoshima and, 19, 154, 186, 188, 189–190, 193–207; *LICENSE* (album), 191; musical events by, 1–4, 106, 185–187; musical storytelling by, 9, 190–195; *Stay Alive,* 214. *See also* Ougoukai; *names of specific songs*

Nagabuchi fashion, 187

Nagasaki nuclear bombing, 90

"*Naite Chinpira* [Cry, Gangster]" (song), 191

NAK (Nihon Amachua Kayōsai), 143–144, 160, 167–168, 170–186. *See also* Fukushima NAK; karaoke

Nakagawa, Gorō, 85

Nakajima, Miyuki, 186

Nakajima, Tamotsu, 85

nakama, 208, 212, 217, 225

Nakatsugawa Folk Jamboree, 81, 111, 112

"*Nangoku Tosa wo Ato ni Shite* [Leaving Behind Tosa, That Southern Land]" (song), 44

Narita International Airport, 82

nation, as category, 122, 180, 188–190

National Bureau of Asian Research, 22

National Diet, 76, 105, 106, 191

National Memorial Service for the War Dead, 185

National Police Reserve, 65, 105

National Safety Force, 65

National Shōwa Memorial Museum, 185

National Workers Music Association, 110

NCO Wives' Club, Tachikawa, 39

"*Neage* [Price Increases]" (song), 87

Nelson, Willie, 96, 97

concert of, 102–103; legacy of, 103–104; *NEWS23* interview of, 64–65, 67; on release of music, 2; war critique by, 65–69. See also *Goaisatsu* [Greetings] (Takada); *names of specific songs*
Takadawataruteki (film), 64–65
Takaishi, Tomoya, 85, 110, 120–121
Takakura, Ken, 29
Tanikawa, Shuntarō, 85
TDK Records, 54, 55
Te-Chili, 131, 141
techne, 11
"*Tegami*" (song), 89
"Tennessee Waltz" (song), 29, 32
Thomson, Virgil, 33
3.11 Earthquake (2011), 22, 62
Tokuhisa, Kōji, 147
"Tokyo Boogie-Woogie" (song), 35
Tokyo Electric Power Company, 22
Tokyo Folk Guerrilla, 82
"*Tōkyō Fooku Gerira no Shokun-tachi wo Kataru* [Speaking of the Young Men of the Tokyo Folk Guerrilla]" (song), 82–83
Tokyo Olympics (1964), 96, 185
Tokyo Takarazuka Theater, 29
"*Tombo* [The Dragonfly]" (song), 192–193, 194, 195
Tombo (television show), 220, 221
Tōru, Mitsui, 66
Tosaka, Jun, 18, 97–98, 100, 104
Treaty of Amity and Commerce, 56
Treaty of Mutual Cooperation and Security. See AMPO Treaty
Treaty of San Francisco, 47
Trump, Donald, 228, 231
"*Tsumetai Gaikokujin* [The Cold-Hearted Foreigner]" (song), 190–191
"*Tsuru Nyōbo* [Crane Wife]" (folk tale), 154
"Turn! Turn! Turn!" (song), 83

Ueno, Ryō, 117–120, 122, 135
Underground Record Club (URC), 72, 78, 96, 110, 112, 148
United Red Army, 14, 122
USARJ (U.S. Army Japan), 57, 58, 59

U.S. Capitol riot (2021), 228
U.S. General Accounting Office, 26
U.S.-Japan Security Treaty, 13, 47, 49, 90. See also security alliance of U.S.-Japan
U.S. Occupation of Japan (1945–1952), 13, 17, 25–28. See also friendship of U.S.-Japan
USS *Ronald Reagan,* 22

Vian, Boris, 89, 101
Vietnam War, 14, 27, 36, 44
Virno, Paolo, 177

Wajima, Yusuke, 145
Watanabe, Anne, 142
Watanabe, Hamako, 29
White, Micah, 229
World War I, 77

Yamaha Popular Song Contest (POPCON), 186
Yamanokuchi, Baku, 90, 93
Yanagiya, Mikimatsu, 28
Yano, Christine, 150, 151–152, 162
Yasar, Kerim, 94
Yashiro, Aki, 147
Yasukuni Shrine, Tokyo, 123, 185
Yesterday's Wine (Nelson), 96, 97
Yokohama military installation, 5, 18, 24–25
yonanuki, 156
Yoshida, Takurō, 133
Yoshimoto Kōgyō, 28
Yoshino, Hiroshi, 86
Young, Louise, 6
Yūji, 207, 208, 210–212
Yukimura, Izumi, 29
Yūkō Day, 50, 51
Yūkoku (Mishima), 126
Yūnyūdō, 2
"*Yūyake* [The Sunset]" (song), 86

ZELDA, 55
Zenkoku Sakurajima Ougoukai. See Ougoukai

ABOUT THE AUTHOR

Scott W. Aalgaard teaches in the College of East Asian Studies at Wesleyan University in Middletown, Connecticut. Originally from Vancouver Island, Canada, he's a lifelong music fan and a longtime resident of Japan, having lived and worked in Hokkaido, Osaka, Kyoto, Fukushima, Yokohama, and Tokyo, where he was a staff member for a time with a music industry production office. In addition to popular music, Aalgaard's research and teaching focus on modern and contemporary Japanese literature, history, political economy, fascism, and area studies methodologies. He earned his PhD in East Asian Languages and Civilizations from the University of Chicago in 2017.

MUSIC AND PERFORMING ARTS
OF ASIA AND THE PACIFIC